AUTOBIOGRAPHY

OF

REV. JAMES B. FINLEY

OR,

PIONEER LIFE IN THE WEST

EDITED BY

W. P. STRICKLAND D. D.

CINCINNATI:

CRANSTON AND CURTS.

NEW YORK:

HUNT AND EATON.

PREFACE.

Don't run; I shall not be long-winded. Just hold on a moment, as I have but few words to say. I always did despise long introductions to sermons, and scarcely ever listen to one with any degree of patience. I have an equal dislike to a long introduction to a book, and, hence, *verbum sat.*

The following pages contain a brief, unvarnished narrative of the incidents of my life; and as, in the providence of God, I was permitted to grow up with the west, it may not be uninteresting to the people of the west, to be made more fully acquainted with my somewhat eventful history.

For upward of forty years I have been constantly engaged in preaching the Gospel of Jesus Christ in the woods, cities, and villages of the west; and nearly all that time, with few exceptions, such as I have noted, my name has been on the effective list of traveling preachers.

My time, with what talents I had, has all been consecrated to the Church of my choice, and now, after the lapse of almost half a century in the service of the Church, I would not recall what I have done and suffered for Christ's sake. The only regret that I have is, that I did not accomplish more.

While the work was going through the press, I was engaged in the enterprise of building a new church, the one occupied by my charge being too small. Part of my time has been employed in raising funds for this object, and I am pledged to see this infant Church through its difficulties.

The proceeds of this work, after paying the expenses of its publication, are to be appropriated to a benevolent object; and I trust it may meet with favor among the thousands of Christian friends with whom in life I have had pleasant communion, and with whom I hope to spend a happy eternity in the communings of a better world.

J. B. Finley.

Cincinnati, Ohio, May, 1853.

CONTENTS.

CHAPTER I.

CHAPTER II.

CHAPTER III.

CHAPTER IV.

CHAPTER X.

CHAPTER XI.

CHAPTER XII.

CHAPTER XIII.

CHAPTER XIV.

CHAPTER XIX.

CHAPTER XX.

CHAPTER XXI.

CHAPTER XXII.

CHAPTER XXIII.

CHAPTER XXIV.

CHAPTER XXV.

CHAPTER XXVI.

CHAPTER XXVII.

CHAPTER XXVIII.

AUTOBIOGRAPHY

OF

REV. JAMES B. FINLEY,

AUTOBIOGRAPHY

OF

REV. JAMES B. FINLEY.

CHAPTER I.

PARENTAGE AND EARLY LIFE.

MY ancestors were Europeans. My paternal grandfather was of the old stock of Pennsylvanians from Scotland. He being one of the younger sons, his elder brother who, according to the laws of primogeniture, inherited the Finley manor, sent him to the El Dorado of the western world, in quest of his fortune. Having made Pennsylvania his home, he was in due time married to Miss Mary Patterson, a lady from Germany. My maternal grandfather—Mr. James Bradley—was a native of Wales. My grandmother was from England; she was a lady of rare endowments, thoroughly educated, being well-read in the ancient languages. During the period of revolutionary strife and suffering she made herself acquainted with medical science, and opened a hospital for the sick and wounded soldiers, administering to their necessities with her own benevolent hand.

My father—Robert W. Finley—was born in Bucks county, Pennsylvania; and, after having received all the advantages of literary training from the schools of his neighborhood and the instructions of his patriot mother, he was sent to Princeton College, New Jersey, and placed under the care of the venerable and talented Dr. Witherspoon, President of that institution. After having passed through his collegiate course, he spent several years in studying theology, and was occasionally employed as a teacher of languages. Being prepared, as far as a theological training could prepare him, for the work of the ministry, he was licensed, by the Presbytery, to preach the Gospel.

At that time there were great and pressing calls for ministerial labor in the new settlements of the Carolinas and Georgia; and, obeying the command of his Master, to "go into all the world, and preach the Gospel to every creature," he volunteered his services as a missionary to that then distant field.

The country was in an unsettled state; the gloomy clouds of war hung bodingly over the American horizon; and although our patriot fathers had cast off their allegiance to the British crown, had struck the decisive blow, and erected a broad, strong platform of national independence, yet the days of trial and conflict had not passed. The Red Sea had been crossed, the Rubicon had been passed, and their enemies overthrown like the enemies of ancient Israel; yet, before they could gain entire and undisputed possession of the fair inheritance they claimed, every foe had to be vanquished.

The times in which men live develop a corresponding character. A missionary of that day, imbued with the heroic spirit of the times, would not be likely to stop to count the cost of a perilous enterprise where the advancement of the kingdom of his Lord was concerned, but, buckling on his armor, would courageously go forth at once to "glorious war." There being no missionary bank in any of the American Churches at that day, on whose resources the missionary could draw the needed supplies, young Finley bade adieu to home and friends, and, in the name of his Master, trusting in God for help and direction, hastened to his distant field of labor.

No sooner did he arrive, than he entered upon his work of visiting the towns, villages, and settlements in North and South Carolina, and Georgia, preaching the Gospel, and planting Churches in destitute places. Here he labored for three consecutive years; at the end of which time he married Miss Rebecca Bradley, whose father—Mr. James Bradley, as above noticed—believing he could better the condition of his family by removing to a new country, sold out his possessions on the Delaware river, and removed to North Carolina. The marriage was celebrated in the year 1780, and on the following year, in the month of July, I was born.

The horrors of a civil war raged with great fury; neighbor was massacred by his neighbor. The Tory party, urged on by the British, resorted to every conceivable means of oppression and violence to drive all the Whigs from the country, or keep up a war of extermination. In this relentless persecution every feeling of humanity was outraged; and the barbarity of the savages contending for their native hunting grounds against the invasions of the pale face, falls below the savagism of Tory warfare. All of my mother's brothers were killed in this most deadly strife. Captain James Bradley fell in Gates's defeat, fighting by the side of that heroic stranger, Baron De Kalb, who, filled with generous emotions, left his father-land, to join in our struggles, and water the tree of liberty with his heroic blood. My uncle, Mr. Francis Bradley, was murdered by four Tories near his own house. He was assailed by them, and, knowing their purpose, he resolved to sell his life at the dearest rate. A fierce and deadly encounter ensued; but, being overpowered by numbers, he was conquered, and the cowardly ruffians shot him with his own rifle.

Mr. John Bradley was taken prisoner, and died on board a prison-ship. My father and his congregation were very odious to the Tory party, and they were watched and waylaid on every occasion; so that their lives were in jeopardy every hour. Even the sanctuary and the family altar afforded no security, but were ruthlessly invaded by these more than savage white men. One of the elders of my father's Church, while engaged in solemn prayer around the domestic altar, was shot down in the midst of his family by one of his Tory neighbors. The Tory on passing was arrested by the voice of prayer, and stealthily slipping to the window, which, like Daniel's, was open, he took a cool and deliberate aim at the heart of the worshiper, and his spirit fled to join the worshipers above. On that same morning my father was shot at as he stepped out of the door, the ball passing through the clothes on his breast. Those who killed Mr. Francis Bradley were followed, and three of them killed; the other making his escape. After the war, the fugitive being found by my uncle Price, was summarily punished.

A Tory major, who lived in the neighborhood, on a certain occasion collected together at one house, by stratagem, all the wives of the Whigs, and hung them up by the neck till almost dead. This species of torture was resorted to for the purpose of extorting from them the place of their husbands' concealment. Their love and courage proved entirely too strong for this trial, and not in one single instance was the slightest disclosure made. They despised alike the Tory and his threats. Some time after the war, this same valorous major returned to the same neighborhood where he had committed the dastardly act, and the sons of those mothers whom he had so shamefully abused took him out one night to a swamp, and gave him twenty lashes on his back for every woman he had hung; they then tarred and feathered him, ducked him in the swamp, and told him if he did not leave the country in one month, they would draw every drop of Tory blood out of his body.

My grandparents were subjected to the severest trials; not only suffering the loss of their children, but their property; and their condition as well as that of all others similarly situated, would have been vastly worse, had it not been for the untiring vigilance and indomitable courage of the heroic Marion.

Like ancient Israel, who, while rebuilding the temple in troublous times, had to bear about them the weapons of war, so the ministers of the Gospel at that day were obliged to carry carnal as well as spiritual weapons. My father was obliged, from the necessity of the case, to take up arms in the defense of his country and family. Often while a little boy have I stood by my mother's knee and heard her tell the bloody conflicts of those days; and her tongue grew eloquent as she described the thrilling adventures of the courageous Marion. She frequently entertained us with the war-songs of those times. I recollect a verse of one of those songs, and will give it to the reader, as a specimen of the epic poetry of the times. The song was composed on the battle of King's Mountain, and ran thus:

"Proud Ferguson, he placed himself,
All with his ragged race,* man;
He most defied the living God,
To take him from that place, man;
But brave Campbell did him there surround,
And beat him on his chosen ground,
And gave him there a deadly wound.
With pell and mell the Tories fell;
It's hard to tell how bad a smell
They left upon the place, man."

* Tories.

During the eventful struggle of the Revolution, the fires of patriotism glowed as intensely in the hearts of the females as the males. Often have I listened, with indescribable emotions, to the patriotic songs sung by the melodious and soul-inspiring voices of the patriot mothers and daughters of that day.

One has said, let me write the songs of a country, and I care not who makes its laws. This remark is full of meaning. No one can tell the wonders achieved by the power of the patriotic songs of a country. It matters not how homely they are. If they breathe the spirit of the times, they touch the heart and rouse it to action. The "Hail Columbia" of America, "Hail to the chief" of Scotland, "Britannia rules the wave" of England, the "Marseilles Hymn" of France, the "Erin go Bragh" of Ireland, have accomplished more in infusing patriotism and a military spirit into the minds of the people than all other agencies combined.

We well understand the power of *holy* song in rousing the dormant soul and raising the thoughts to heaven. That inimitable poet Charles Wesley understood the power and influence of song, who, when asked by a dissolute company for a song, and being allowed to sing one of his own composing, commenced,

"Listed into the cause of sin,
Why should a good be evil?
Music, alas! too long has been
Press'd to obey the devil.
Drunken, or light, or lewd, the lay
Tends to the soul's undoing;
Widens, and strews with flowers the way
Down to eternal ruin."

So, gentle reader, you see I took my birth in the storm of war, and my nursery tales and songs were all of war. Often while my precious mother would sing to me the mournful dirge of death, have I seen the tears steal down her calm and quiet face, and, while my heart would beat with unutterable emotions, I have felt the spirit of revenge rise and kindle my whole nature into a storm.

My parents and relatives were all Presbyterians, except my grandmother Bradley, who was a Whitefield Methodist, and had been converted to God in her early life by the ministry of that distinguished and eloquent man of God, Rev. George Whitefield. She was a zealous and happy Christian. Her experience was bright and clear on the subject of experimental religion, and differed from the most of professors, as also from the experience of her ministers. This often brought on a controversy between her and her ministers and Christian friends. She expressed, in clear and direct terms, her belief in the witness of the Spirit, and always bore testimony to the fact that she knew God had power on earth to forgive sins, because she felt in her own heart the pardoning love of God. Such a profession was regarded by both preachers and people as presumptuous, if not, indeed, a species of fanaticism. The doctrine then taught was, that forgiveness of sins could not be known till death or after death, and that it was necessary for us to commit some sin to prevent self-exaltation and vain confidence. It was urged as impossible for man to know his sins forgiven, because the decrees of God concerning election were secret, and could not be revealed or made known till death, or after the soul passed into the spirit-world. From all this she warmly dissented, affirming that she knew the time and place of her conversion, and that she had the witness of the divine Spirit bearing witness with her spirit that she was a child of God.

At the close of the Revolutionary war, the new world, as it was then called, or, in other words, the land of Boone—Kentucky—excited the attention of my father and others, who were personally acquainted with Colonel

Boone; and, taking with him two of his brothers and as many others of the neighbors as desired to accompany him, he started out on a tour of exploration. It was in the spring of 1784 that they entered upon this expedition; and, after traversing the length and breadth of the land, they returned in the summer, with the most glowing accounts of this terrestrial paradise, this new Canaan, "flowing with milk and honey." No sooner had this intelligence been received, than many families resolved to emigrate. My grandparents, being too old to encounter the perils and fatigues of the wilderness, were not inclined to go: whereupon my father yielded to their wishes, abandoned his purpose of going to Kentucky, and removed with his parents to Virginia, and settled between the north and south branches of the Potomac. Here my father had two congregations, to whom he ministered the word of life.

Not satisfied with his location, and still yearning after Kentucky, in the course of two years he crossed the Mountains, and came to George's creek, near to where the town of Geneva now stands. In this place he gathered a congregation, and preached with great success and popularity.

At the time my father resided in the Redstone country there was a great excitement in the Presbyterian Church about Psalmody. The introduction of Watts's hymns was considered a monstrous departure from the faith of the Church, and, in some instances, divided Churches and families. My father used them alternately, and thus brought on him and the Rev. Joseph Smith much persecution. But the work of the Lord revived, and his power was greatly manifested in the awakening of sinners. I recollect at a sacrament held in Mr. Griffin's barn, on the Sabbath day, that forty persons cried aloud for mercy, and many of them fell to the floor. This was considered the greatest meeting ever known in the country for the noise; but many of them professed to obtain religion. Some time after this a sacramental meeting was held at Laurel Hill Meeting-house, in the vicinity of Uniontown, as now called. On Saturday afternoon, my father asked a Methodist minister to conclude the public services by an exhortation. This was much lauded by some of the old folks, and inquiries were made as to who he was. One Mr. Cree, who knew him, said that he was a Methodist. Then said one of the ruling men, "Finley has shown his cloven foot." The next morning Rev. Carey Allen was to preach, and he saw an advertisement stuck up on the stand, which he took down, and read, as follows: "I do hereby publish the bans of marriage between Robert W. Finley and the Methodist preacher. Any person having any lawful objection let him now declare it, or forever after hold his peace." Mr. Allen instantly exclaimed, with a loud voice, "I forbid the bans; and the reason is, they are too near akin." This made many leave the congregation; but the Lord continued to pour out his Spirit, and many professed to find peace in believing.

My father labored in this field for two years; but he was not yet satisfied; Kentucky was the land of promise; and, accordingly, in the fall of 1788, when Pomona was pouring her richest treasures into the lap of the husbandman, he, in company with several others, cut loose from their moorings at the mouth of George's creek, to emigrate to the rich cane-brakes of Kentucky. I shall never forget the deeply-thrilling and interesting scene which occurred at parting. Ministers and people were collected together, and after an exhortation and the singing of a hymn, they all fell upon their knees, and engaged in ardent supplication to God, that the emigrants might be protected amid the perils of the wilderness. I felt as though we were taking leave of the world. After mingling together our tears and prayers, the boats were oosed, and we floated out into the waters of the beautiful Ohio. It was a hazardous undertaking; but such was the insatiable desire to inherit those rich lands, and enjoy the advantages of the wide-spreading cane-brakes, that many were the adventurers; and although many lost theii lives, and others all they possessed, yet it did not for a moment deter others from the perilous undertaking. The rush to California at the present time shows what is the extent of hardships men, with the bare possibility of bettering their condition, will cheerfully undergo.

The Indians, jealous of the white man, and fearful of losing their immense and profitable hunting-grounds, from the great tide of emigration which was constantly pouring in upon them, were wrought up to the highest pitch of fury, and determined to guard, as far as possible, both passes to it; namely, the Ohio river and the Old Crab Orchard road, or Boone's old trace, leading from the southern portion of Kentucky to North Carolina. They attacked all boats they had any probability of being able to take, using all the strategy of which they were masters to decoy them to the shore. Many boats were taken and many lives were lost through the deceit and treachery of the Indians and white spies employed by them.

The day on which the emigrants started was pleasant, and all nature seemed to smile upon the pioneer band. They had made every preparation they deemed necessary to defend themselves from the attack of their wily foes. The boat which led the way as a pilot was well manned and armed, on which sentinels, relieved by turns, kept watch day and night. Then followed two other boats at a convenient distance. While floating down the river we frequently saw Indians on the banks, watching for an opportunity to make an attack.

Just below the mouth of the Great Scioto, where th

town of Portsmouth now stands, a long and desperate effort was made to get some of the boats to land by a white man, who feigned to be in great distress; but the fate of William Orr and his family was too fresh in the minds of the adventurers to be thus decoyed. A few months previous to the time of which I am writing, this gentleman and his whole family were murdered, being lured to shore by a similar stratagem. But a few weeks before we passed, the Indians attacked three boats, two of which were taken, and all the passengers destroyed. The other barely escaped, having lost all the men on board, except the Rev. Mr. Tucker, a Methodist missionary, who was sent by the bishop to Kentucky. Mr. Tucker was wounded in several places, but he fought manfully. The Indians got into a canoe and paddled for the boat, determined to board it; but the women loaded the rifles of their deceased husbands, and handed them to Mr. Tucker, who took such deadly aim, every shot making the number in the canoe less, that they abandoned all hope of reaching the boat, and returned to the shore.

After the conflict this noble man fell from sheer exhaustion, and the women were obliged to take the oars, and manage the boat as best they could. They were enabled to effect a landing at Limestone, now Maysville; and a few days after their protector died of his wounds, and they followed him weeping to his grave. Peace to his dust, till it shall be bidden to rise! Though no stone marks the spot where this young hero-missionary lies, away from his home and kindred, among strangers in a strange land, his dust is sacred, till the resurrection morn, when it shall come forth reanimate to inherit immortality.

But to resume our narrative. Being too well posted in Indian strategy to be decoyed, we pursued our journey unmolested. Nothing remarkable occurred, save the death of my much-loved grandmother. The day before we landed at Limestone she took her mystic flight to a better world. This was the first time I was privileged to see a Christian die. Her faith was strong in the God of her salvation; and while surrounded by her weeping friends, whom she affectionately addressed, and bidding them all a last farewell, she repeated the following verse, and then sweetly fell asleep in Jesus:

"O, who can tell a Savior's worth,
Or speak of grace's power,
Or benefits of the new birth,
In a departing hour?
Come nigh, kind death;
Untie life's thread;
I shall to God ascend;
In joys I shall then with him dwell—
Joys that shall never end."

The recollections of this kind mother in Israel are still fresh in my memory. When a child she would frequently take me into her closet, and there, while engaged in her private devotions, like Hannah of old, she would lay her hands on my head, and dedicate me to God. Her remains were committed to the dust in Maysville, and the Rev. Carey Allen, of blessed memory, preached her funeral sermon. The impressions made on my youthful mind by the prayers and invocations of my sainted grandmother were never erased; and when the natural inclinations of my depraved heart would have led me into infidelity, her godly life and triumphant death would come to my recollection with irresistible power, and confirm me in the truth of Christianity.

In company with my father, and in his boat, there were two missionaries—the Revs. Carey Allen and Robert Marshall—and also Mr. James Walsh and Mr. Richard M'Nemar, both of whom afterward became ministers in the Presbyterian Church. As soon as my father could make the necessary arrangements, he removed his family to the town of Washington, Mason county, Ky., and remained there during the winter. It was in this place that I saw for the first time that great adventurer, Simon Kenton. He was truly the master-spirit of the times in that region of country. He was looked up to by all as the great defender of the inhabitants, always on the *qui vive,* and ready to fly at a moment's warning to the place of danger, for the protection of the scattered families in the wilderness. Providence seems to have raised up this man for a special purpose; and his eventful life, and the many wonderful and almost miraculous deliverances, in which he was preserved amidst the greatest perils and dangers, are confirmatory of the fact, that he was a child of Providence.

The Indians made great depredations during the winter, and stole almost all the horses, so that the farmers were scarcely able to carry on their business. In this posture of affairs, Colonel Kenton, with a party of men, started from Kentucky and went to Oldtown, now Chilicothe, for the purpose of recovering them. Having succeeded, by way of reprisal, in taking as many as they could manage, they returned, and being pursued, when near the Ohio river, they were overtaken, and the men and horses were captured. Colonel Kenton was taken a prisoner to Lower Sandusky, where he was tried by a council and condemned to be burnt at the stake. Simon Girty, a brave and daring white man, who had, on account of the cruel treatment he had received from General Lewis, at Point Pleasant, Virginia, foresworn his race and been adopted by the Wyandott nation, was, at that time, at Lower Sandusky. Years before Kenton and Girty had been bosom companions at Fort Pitt, and had served together subsequently in the commencement of Dunmore's expedition. Girty had just returned from an unsuccessful expedition in Pennsylvania against the whites, and was enraged by disappointment. Hearing that a prisoner was in the camp, condemned and already blackened for execution, he hastened to his presence; and, not recognizing Kenton, he commenced abusing him in the most shameful and indignant manner, eventually knocking him down. He knew that the prisoner was from Kentucky, and the object of his cruel treatment was to frighten him into a disclosure of all he wished to know about the enemy. He inquired of him in relation to the number of men there were in Kentucky. This the prisoner could not answer, but ran over the names and rank of such officers as he could recollect. Girty then asked:

"Do you know William Stewart?"

"Perfectly well," replied the prisoner; "he is an old and intimate acquaintance."

"Ah! what is your name, then?"

"Simon Butler;" for that was the name by which he was previously known.

As soon as Girty heard the name, he became strongly agitated; and springing from his seat, he threw his arms around Kenton's neck, and embraced him with much emotion. Then turning to the assembled warriors, who remained astonished spectators of this extraordinary scene, he addressed them in a short speech, which the deep earnestness of his tone, and the energy of his gesture, rendered eloquent. He informed them that the prisoner, whom they had just condemned to the stake, was his ancient comrade and bosom friend; that they had traveled the same war-path, slept upon the same blanket, and dwelt in the same wigwam. He entreated them to have compassion on his feelings; to spare him the agony of witnessing the torture of an old friend, by the hands of his adopted brothers; and not to refuse so trifling a favor as the life of a white man, to the earnest intercession of one who had proved, by three years' faithful service, that he was sincerely and zealously devoted to the cause of the Indians.

The speech was listened to in unbroken silence. As soon as he had finished, several chiefs expressed their approbation by a deep guttural interjection, while others were equally as forward in making known their objections to the proposal. They urged that his fate had already been determined in a large and solemn council, and that they would be acting like squaws to change their minds every hour. They insisted upon the flagrant misdemeanors of Kenton—that he had not only stolen their horses, but had flashed his gun at one of their young men; that it was vain to suppose that so bad a man could ever become an Indian at heart, like their brother Girty; that the Kentuckians were all alike—very bad people—and ought to be killed as fast as they were taken; and finally, they observed that many of their people had come from a distance, solely to assist at the torture of the prisoner, and pathetically painted the disappointment and chagrin with which they would hear that all their trouble had been for nothing.

Girty listened with obvious impatience to the young warriors who had so ably argued against a reprieve; and starting to his feet, as soon as the others had concluded, he urged his former request with great earnestness. He briefly, but strongly, recapitulated his own services, and the many and weighty instances of attachment he had given. He asked if *he* could be suspected of partiality to the whites? When had he ever before interceded for any of that hated race? Had he not brought seven scalps home with him from the last expedition? and had he not submitted seven white prisoners that very evening to their discretion? Had he expressed a wish that a single one of the captives should be saved? *This* was his first and should be his last request; for if they refused to *him*, what was never refused to the intercession of one of their natural chiefs, he would look upon himself as disgraced in their eyes, and considered as unworthy of confidence Which of their own natural warriors had been more zealous than himself? From what expedition had he ever shrunk?—what white man had ever seen his back? Whose tomahawk had been bloodier than his? He would say no more. He asked it as a first and last favor, as an evidence that they approved of his zeal and fidelity, that the life of his bosom friend might be spared. Fresh speakers arose upon each side, and the debate was carried on for an hour and a half with great heat and energy.

During the whole of this time, Kenton's feelings may readily be imagined. He could not understand a syllable of what was said. He saw that Girty spoke with deep earnestness, and that the eyes of the assembly were often turned upon himself with various expressions. He felt satisfied that his friend was pleading for his life, and that he was violently opposed by a large part of the council. At length the war-club was produced, and the final vote taken. Kenton watched its progress with thrilling emotion—which yielded to the most rapturous delight, as he perceived that those who struck the floor of the council-house, were decidedly inferior in number to those who passed it in silence. Having thus succeeded in his benevolent purpose, Girty lost no time in attending to the comfort of his friend. He led him into his own wigwam, and from his own store gave him a pair of moccasins and leggins, a breech-cloth, a hat, a coat, a handkerchief for his neck, and another for his head.

In the course of a few weeks, and after passing through some further difficulties, in which the renegado again stood by him faithfully, Kenton was sent to Detroit, from which place he effected his escape and returned to Kentucky. Girty remained with the Indians, retaining his old influence, and continuing his old career; and four years after the occurrences last detailed, in 1782, we find him a prominent figure in one of the blackest tragedies that has ever disgraced the annals of mankind. It is generally believed, by the old settlers and their immediate descendants, that the influence of Girty at this period, over the confederate tribes of the whole north-west, was almost supreme. He had, it is true, no delegated authority, and, of course, was powerless as regarded the final determination of any important measure; but his voice was permitted in council among the chiefs, and his inflaming harangues were always listened to with delight by the young warriors. Among the sachems and other headmen, he was what may well be styled a "power behind the throne;" and as it is well known that this unseen power is often "greater than the throne itself," it may reasonably be presumed that Girty's influence was, in reality, all which it is supposed to have been. The horrible event alluded to above, was the *burning of Crawford*, at Sandusky.

Simon Girty lived the inveterate enemy of his race, and, in carrying out his fearful oath, grew more and more desperate in cruelty to the whites, till he was finally abandoned of God and man. He died a most melancholy death, and went down as the traitor to an unhonored grave.

Simon Kenton was the friend and benefactor of his race, and lived respected and beloved by all who knew him. In the latter part of his life he embraced religion; and it may not be improper here to relate the circumstances connected with his conversion. In the fall of 1819 General Kenton and my father met at a camp meeting on the waters of Mad river, after a separation of many years. Their early acquaintance in Kentucky rendered this interview interesting to both of them. The meeting had been in progress for several days without any great excitement till Sabbath evening, when it pleased God to pour out his

Spirit in a remarkable manner. Many were awakened, and among the number were several of the General's relatives. It was not long till their awakening was followed by conversion. The old hero was a witness to these scenes. He had faced danger and death in every form with an unquailed eye and an unfaltering courage, but the tears and sobs of penitence, and the outbursts of rapturous joy from

"Souls renewed,
And sins forgiven,"

proved too strong for the hardy veteran. His heart was touched, and the tear was seen to kindle the eye and start down the furrow of his manly cheek. Say not the man of courage can not weep.

On Monday morning he asked my father to retire with him to the woods. To this he readily assented, and, as they were passing along in silence and the song of the worshipers had died upon their ears, addressing my father, he said, "Mr. Finley, I am going to communicate to you some things which I want you to promise me you will never divulge." My father replied, "If it will not affect any but ourselves, then I promise to keep it forever." By this time they were far from the encampment in the depths of the forest. They were alone; no eye could see them, and no ear could hear them, but the eye and ear of the great Omnipresent. Sitting down on a log, the General commenced to tell the story of his heart and disclose its wretchedness; what a great sinner he had been, and how merciful was God in preserving him amid all the conflicts and dangers of the wilderness. While he thus unburdened his heart and told the anguish of his sin-wounded spirit, his lip quivered and the tears of penitence fell from his weeping eyes. They both fell to the earth and, prostrate, cried aloud to God for mercy and salvation. The penitent was pointed to Jesus as the almighty Savior; and after a long and agonizing struggle the gate of eternal life was entered, and

"Hymns of joy proclaimed through heaven
The triumphs of a soul forgiven."

Then from the old veteran, who immediately sprang to his feet, there went up a shout toward heaven which made the woods resound with its gladness. Leaving my father he started for the camp, like the man healed at the Beautiful Gate, leaping, and praising God, so that the faster and farther he went, the louder did he shout glory to God. His appearance startled the whole encampment; and when my father arrived he found an immense crowd gathered around him, to whom he was declaring the goodness of God and his power to save. Approaching him, my father said, "General, I thought we were to keep this matter a secret!" He instantly replied, "O, it is too glorious for that. If I had all the world here I would tell of the goodness and mercy of God!"

At this time he joined the Methodist Episcopal Church, lived a consistent, happy Christian, and died in the open sunshine of a Savior's love. If there is any one of all the pioneers of this valley, to whom the country owes the largest debt of gratitude, that one is General Simon Kenton. His body sleeps on the waters of Mad river, about six miles north of Zanesfield, and

"When that winding stream shall cease to flow,
And those surrounding hills exist no more,
His sleeping dust reanimate shall rise,
Bursting to life at the last trumpet's sound;
Shall bear a part in nature's grand assize,
When sun, and time, and stars no more are found."

But to the narrative. Nothing transpired during the winter, save occasional visits from the Indians, who stole several horses and sometimes succeeded in taking a few prisoners, one or two of whom were killed. Notwithstanding the return of spring was dreaded, fearing it would be an occasion for great depredations on the part of the Indians, it passed without any hostile invasion.

I will here give an account of the manner of administering justice in certain cases in those times. Almost all new countries become places of refuge for criminals who flee from justice. Many of this description had fled from the older states, and had taken up their abode in Kentucky. To provide against this, the Legislature of the state passed what was termed the vagrant act. It operated on this wise. When any person was found without employment or any visible means of obtaining a livelihood, he was taken up, and after having been advertised ten days, was sold to the highest bidder for a short time, say two or three months. All that was earned above the necessary costs was given to him at the end of service. A good-looking and well-dressed man was found in the town of Washington who had no employment. He was taken up, and, on examination, found to be a gambler, who was corrupting the morals of the youth. The magistrate informed him, if he did not leave the place in a short time he would put the law in force against him. This warning was entirely disregarded, and accordingly the gentleman was taken up and sold to a blacksmith, who chained him to the anvil-block and made him blow and strike all day, and at night he was put in the county prison. Thus he was obliged to do the honest though hard work of blowing and striking till his term expired, when he left for parts unknown, with a very bad opinion of the law.

If such a law were put in force in our towns and cities, the innumerable hordes of gamblers and loafers that infest them would soon become as scarce as musketoes in mid-winter.

When the fall of the year came, we found ourselves scarce of provisions for the coming winter; yet we were not destitute of the never-failing staples of the back woodsman; namely, hominy, buffalo, venison, and bear-meat; and any man can live well on these, and come out fat and hearty in the spring.

In the spring of 1789 my father purchased some land in the vicinity of Stockton's station, near where the town of Flemingsburg now stands, and we removed into the woods, three-quarters of a mile from the station. This was the frontier house of the settlement, there being none between it and the Ohio river. The house was built of round logs from the forest trees: the first story made of the largest we were able to put up; the second story of smaller ones, which jutted over two or three feet, to prevent any one from climbing to the top of the house. The chimneys were built on the inside. The door was made of puncheon slabs, six inches thick, and was barred on the inside by strong iron staples driven into the logs on both sides, into which were placed strong bars. In the upper part of the house there were port-holes, out of which we could shoot as occasion might require; and, as no windows were allowed, they also answered for the purposes of light and ventilation. The house for our colored people was built in the same way, and immediately adjoining the one in which the family lived. My father treated his slaves with great tenderness—more like children than servants. He never punished one of them, to my recollection. They were all taught to read, and we all joined together in praise and prayer to God. I have often thought that slavery existed in my father's family only in form, and that it was in the power of every master to enjoy all the benefits resulting from servitude, without the evils too often, alas! connected with it.

Our houses being thus strongly constructed, and all of us armed with a gun and plenty of ammunition, we were always prepared for war. While some were engaged in working, others acted as sentinels. About the middle of April the Indians paid a visit to our new home. They came in the night, while my father was engaged in family prayer, and rapped, with a wiping stick, three times on the door. The dogs barked most furiously, and the time for prayer having ended, the time of watching having come, every one of us seized our guns, and hastened to our posts. The night was so dark, it was impossible for us to discover any one. After some time all things became quiet without, and some laid themselves down to sleep, while others kept watch till welcome day dispelled our fears. With great caution the door was unbarred and opened, and, on examination, the tracks of three Indians were found as they passed over the newly-cleared field. Believing it was the purpose of the Indians to steal horses, and ours being in the woods, my father took his rifle and went to hunt them. As he proceeded cautiously on his way, he came to a ridge, on ascending which he perceived a smoke rising up from the other side. Stealthily advancing, he saw the camp of the Indians, one of whom was sitting up, and the other two were lying down. He crept back slowly, and, taking another direction, he soon found the horses, and returned home. As soon as he returned, he sent to the station to give the alarm. It was considered best not to go out in quest of the Indians that night, but that all should keep on the look-out, and thus be prepared for them should they make an attack. That night they took six horses, and started for the Ohio river, which was distant about seventy miles. Captain Cassady immediately started in pursuit, and on the second day overtook them; but, fearful of the consequences, they left the horses, and fled with such celerity that they were not overtaken.

During the summer they stole several horses and killed a few persons, but made no formidable attack on any house or station. We were visited again by the Indians the following spring. It was the time of sugar making. It was in the night, and we were boiling sugar water. The distance of our camp from the house was about forty rods. All at once we were startled by what we supposed to be the hooting of several owls, and shortly after we heard a low whistle from a charger. The obvious design which we gathered from these movements, was that they intended to surround us. My mother, who was with us, being accustomed to Indian strategy and warfare, was not in the least intimidated; beside she had passed through too many dark and bloody scenes to be faint-hearted. Approaching the colored man, she said, "Indians! Stand behind that tree; let the fire burn till you think we have reached home; then throw a bucketful of water on the fire, slip out in the dark, and run home as soon as you can." The faithful servant obeyed all these directions; and the Indians, being thwarted in their purposes, reconnoitered the houses. My father being absent from home, mother assumed the command, and, directing all to their posts, told us to stand firm, and not fire a gun till we were sure of our mark. The dogs set up a howl, as if they were frantic, till about midnight, when all became quiet. The Indians passed on to another settlement, where they took a prisoner and several horses, and then started for the river.

The ever-vigilant Captain Cassady, with his minute-men, were soon on the trail, and urged the pursuit so hotly, that on the second day they came on them so suddenly, that they fled, leaving their prisoner, and receiving the fire of the whole party. They made their escape with their wounded, and the company returned.

An event occurred about this time, of a most melancholy character, and which threw a gloom over the whole community. A young man, who was employed as a spy, and was, of course, dressed like an Indian, in coming into the station, saw a young lad with his gun coming toward him. He ran behind a tree, and made a noise like an Indian, for the purpose of frightening the boy. The boy, on seeing this, and supposing him to be a veritable Indian, also took to a tree. When the spy looked out from his retreat, to see the boy run, the boy, who was on the watch, instantly fired, and the unfortunate spy fell dead on the spot. A similar occurrence came very near happening with myself. One of our neighbors, named Jack Williams, had been out to watch a deer-lick. Seeing me coming on a cow-path, for the purpose of alarming me, he jumped behind a tree and gave an Indian whoop, supposing I would run. I drew up my gun, and would have shot him if he had not cried out for quarters, in honest old Anglo Saxon. He was much alarmed, and was doubtless satisfied that it was entirely too hazardous to repeat the trick.

We all lived in constant danger, and exposed to death; and although there were spies constantly ranging between the settlements and the Ohio river, from Limestone to Big Sandy, yet the Indians would come in undiscovered, and kill our friends, and steal the horses. We had to depend, for our daily living, on the hunters, and what we could kill ourselves of the wild game. This gave me an early love for the chase, which grew with my growth and strengthened with my strength, till I had almost, at the age of sixteen, become an Indian in my habits and feelings. The country was infested with wolves, and they were remarkably daring and impudent. They would attack grown cattle, and kill colts and two-years old cows. While hunting the cows one morning in the woods, in company with a lad a little older than myself, we heard a cow bellowing at a piteous rate; and, supposing it was Indians trying to decoy us, we crept up with the tread of a sat, and, from the top of the ridge, looked over and saw five wolves hanging on to a large cow, while she was struggling to free herself, and aiming for home. As she came toward us, we took the best position we could, and waited their arrival. We fired by concert, killing two, and wounding a third. The wolves instantly loosed their hold, ran a few paces, and set up a terrible howl. Fearing a fresh supply of this ferocious animal, we ran home, and returning with help, to see what was done, we found two, and tracked the other by its blood some distance.

Such were the dangers and hardships to which we were constantly exposed, that my father sold out his possessions, and removed to Bourbon county, and settled on what was then called the Cane Ridge. This was in the spring of 1790.

The land purchased by my father was a part of an unbroken cane-brake extending for twenty miles toward what was called the Little Mountain. We had to cut out roads before we could haul the logs to build our cabins. The cane was so thick and tall, that it was almost impossible for a horse or cow to pass through it. We first cut the cane, and gathered it into piles to be burned. This was performed by a cane-hoe. The next thing was to plow, which was done by first cutting the cane roots with a coulter fastened to a stock of wood, which was called the blue boar. This turned no furrow; and hence it was necessary to follow it with the bar shear, which turned over the sod.

My father had two congregations, one at this place and the other at Concord, both of which were prosperous. Many were gathered into the Church and devoted to religion.

Here my father opened a high school, in which was taught the languages as well as the higher branches of an English education. It was the first school of the kind in the state; and ten or twelve young men were educated here who afterward became Presbyterian preachers. Judges Trimble and Mills here learned their first grammar lesson. This institution flourished for a number of years. The subject of education was of great importance in the early settlement of the country; but its importance increases in proportion to its growth and advancement The mind of man on his entrance into our disordered world, is destitute of knowledge of every kind, but is capable of vast acquirements and prodigious expansion; and on this his happiness and usefulness depend. But it must be acquired by education; and whatever opens the door to facilitate this object, will be productive of the greatest good, both to the individual and the community at large. The expansion of the mind makes the man, therefore, this gem of the greatest value ought to be sought after with interest by the whole mass of mankind; and, instead of pursuing, with so much avidity, the things which belong to the body, and are only calculated to gratify the animal passions and appetites, and alone to promote that kind of happiness which is the lowest of which man is capable, the whole world, and every man and woman in it, ought to regard the improvement of the mind as the most valuable acquisition within their grasp, both for here and hereafter. It was the purpose of God, in the very constitution of the human mind, that he should be wise; and that in this consists alone his true greatness and unending, consummate felicity. On this depends the happiness of social intercourse, the enjoyments of all civil and religious privileges, the advancement in the arts and sciences, and the commerce of the world. Indeed, it raises man from the common level of a beast and brutish enjoyments, to the exalted dignity of a rational being. Is it not for a want of a proper conception of the great worth of the improvement of the mind, that it is so much neglected, and so little sought after? Ignorance, like a deep and dark cloud, has hung over the mind of man, and has obscured the brilliant rays of this hallowed intellectual sun; and but few in the world, comparatively, have felt its warming rays, or seen the glory of its brightness; and yet it is within the reach of all, in a greater or less degree.

Every good man, every lover of his country, every bad man ought to use his influence to encourage and sustain, with his property and by the education of his children, every effort to banish the cursed monster ignorance from our happy country. A man may boast of his patriotism, and his exceeding great love of our free and happy institutions, but if he neglects to lend his aid to the work of education, he does most emphatically contradict, by his conduct, his profession, and, like all other such men, may justly be branded with the disgraceful appellation of hypocrite. Will men make this boast loud and vociferous: look at their children at home; and, when not yoked up, like their oxen, to work, they are running at large, and not the least attention paid to the improvement of their minds. If they can have the benefit of a public school for three months in the winter, it is very well; for, at this time of year, they have no use for them, and it costs them nothing to send them to school. Now, my friend, let me ask you a question: Which would you rather see: your son go out into the world with the attainments of a good, sound, English education, and be able to associate with the wise, and good, and great; or set him down on a farm a novice, and, in point of intelligence, but a very little above the horse he plows with? If you prefer the last, I pity both you and your children. If you have any thing to give your children, do, for their sakes and for the sake of society, put some of it into their heads; for you would feel much better to see your son or daughter poor, but wise, than to see him a rich fool, the butt and ridicule of society. And let me ask the parents, what kind of a man do you think he would be, who would marry your daughter, if a rich fool; or how mean must the man be, that would marry a fool for her riches? Make them intelligent, for men of intelligence will seek such for their companions through life.

The facilities for education are now opening in almost every part of the country, and this invaluable fortune for your children can now be had on easy terms. Embrace it; do not curse your offspring with being the dupes and servants of their better-educated fellow-citizens. An ignorant man must always remain a Liliput in intellect, and a Tom-Thumb-being in society, comparatively speaking. A few years since, when the subject of instruction was enjoined on our people from the pulpit, the excuse then was, "We have no institution of our own; none convenient." Now we have gotten up several, and the hard times is now the grand excuse; so there seems to be a lack of disposition. Reflect soberly on this mighty question, and decide on the side of duty, and not of dollars and cents; for it does appear to me, that if a poor man could be justified for theft on any principle whatever, it would be to steal to educate his children.

CHAPTER II.

CHARACTER OF THE BACKWOODSMAN.

I DEEM it proper, before proceeding further with my narrative, to give the reader an account of some of the early settlers of the western country, denominated backwoodsmen. On this subject I hope my readers will pardon me, should they think I indulge in a too highly-wrought eulogy of their character. I am well aware that those who are not acquainted with the scenes and circumstances of those early days, will be disposed to regard a description of the deeds of daring and the heroism displayed by the hardy pioneer, as the product of an exuberant fancy instead of plain, unvarnished matter of fact.

To relieve the mind of the reader on this point, I will here state that nothing shall be chronicled by me which is not a veritable history of my life and times. "Truth needs not the foreign aid of ornament;" and the facts which I am prepared to communicate are many of them more wonderful and interesting than fiction. I have no doubt that had these pioneers lived in other ages, they would have ranked with the deified heroes of antiquity.

The stream of immigration which continued to pour in from the older states into all parts of the western country, roused all the native jealousy of the Indians, and they concentrated all their powers to keep the white man from seizing their rich hunting-grounds and robbing them of the homes and graves of their fathers. Every Indian swore his child upon the altar of eternal hatred to the white man. So constant, persevering, and daring were the attacks of the Indians upon the frontier settlements, that all the force which could be raised was not sufficient to repel their invasions.

It was found to be absolutely necessary to change the policy from that of a defensive to an offensive war. Accordingly, General Washington raised an army for the purpose of carrying the war into the enemy's country. The command of this army was given to General Harmar. The history of this ill-fated campaign I shall not stop here to relate; suffice it to say, that it only served to whet the appetite of the Indians and give them a keener relish for deeds of revenge and cruelty. Soon after followed the defeat of St. Clair, which added fuel to the flames; and the Indians, flushed with success and full of hope of being able finally to drive the white man from their hunting-grounds, made the conflict desperate indeed. It was a day of gloom and darkness to the white population, and it seemed doubtful which would gain the mastery. Hundreds of the early settlers and their families were butchered by the Indians. Many who retired for the night were surprised and murdered, and the glare of their burning habitations, shooting up amid the darkness, told the surrounding settlements of the work of death.

To prevent this state of things, and as the only way to be secure from the surprise of the savages, the choicest men of the country were selected as spies. Men of the greatest integrity, courage, and activity, and who were well skilled in all the modes of savage warfare, were chosen, and among the number I will mention the names of William Bennet, Mercer Beason, Duncan M'Arthur, Nathaniel Beasley, and Samuel Davis. These men were dressed like Indians. They were to guard the passes of the Ohio from Maysville to Big Sandy. While some of these were passing up the river between these two points others were coming down, so that it was almost impossible for the Indians, in any considerable numbers, to cross over from the Ohio side without discovery. When they did cross the river, the settlements were apprised of the fact and put on their guard. These sentinels often encountered great hardship and dangers. The ordeals through which they passed were abundantly sufficient to test the courage of the stoutest heart.

On one occasion M'Arthur and Davis stopped at the mouth of the Scioto river, where Portsmouth now stands, and went across the bottom to watch a deer-lick, well known, near the foot of the hill. It was a foggy morning, and an object could not be discerned distinctly fifty yards off. M'Arthur stopped and Davis crawled up to the lick with the stealth of a cat. When he straightened himself up to look into the lick, instantly he heard the sharp crack of a rifle, the ball of which whistled by his head. The fog, together with the smoke of the gun, prevented the Indian from seeing whether he had effected his object. Without moving out of his place, Davis raised his gun and the moment the Indian stepped out of the smoke of his rifle he fired, and the savage fell dead in his tracks. M'Arthur knowing that the firing was in too quick succession to be made by one person, ran up to the spot; but no sooner had he reached it than they heard the yell and rush of many Indians. They instantly started for the river, and being covered, in their retreat, by the dense fog, they reached their canoe and darted out into the stream.

Some time during the next season, M'Arthur went to watch the same lick. He had not been seated long in his blind till two Indians made their appearance and were coming directly toward him. As the best and safest course he chose the boldest, and with a firm nerve and steady aim he fired. Whiz went the ball, and down fell one of the Indians. The other, instead of running, stood still. Several other Indians, hearing the report of the gun, came running to the lick, whereupon M'Arthur sprang from his hiding-place and bounded away. As he ran they fired upon him, and one of the balls striking his powder-horn, drove the splinters into his side. Not seeing him fall, they started in hot pursuit. Being exceedingly fleet-footed, he distanced them so far that they slackened their pace. He aimed his course for the river, and finding his faithful companion waiting for him they pushed out into the stream. Scarcely had they reached the middle of the stream ere they were saluted with the yell of the savages on the bank. Fearing they might be fired upon, they redoubled their energy, and the swift canoe sped over the surface like a bird. They soon were out of the gunshot of the enemy, and reached in safety the other shore.

As a further illustration of a backwoods life, I will here give the reader an account of some deeds of noble daring which occurred in Ohio:

As early as the year 1790 the block-house and stockade above the mouth of the Hockhocking river was a frontier post for the hardy pioneers of the North-western territory. There nature was in her undisturbed livery of dark and thick forests, interspersed with green and flowing prairies. Then the forest had not heard the sound of the woodman's ax, nor the plow of the husbandman opened the bosom of the earth. Then the beautiful prairies waved their golden bloom to the God of nature; and among the most luxuriant of these were those which lay along the Hockhocking valley, and especially that portion of it on which the town of Lancaster now stands. This place, for its beauty, its richness of soil, and picturesque scenery, was selected as a location for an Indian village. This afforded a suitable place for the gambols of the Indian sportsman, as well as a central spot for concentrating the Indian warriors.

Here the tribes of the west and north met to counsel, and from this spot led forth the war-path in different directions. Upon one of those occasions, when the war spirit moved mightily among those sons of nature, and the tomahawk leaped in its scabbard, and the spirits of their friends, who had died in the field of battle, visited the warrior in his night visions and called loudly for revenge, it was ascertained at the garrison above the mouth of the Hockhocking river, that the Indians were gathering in great numbers for the purpose of striking a blow on some post of the frontiers. To meet this crisis, two of the most skilled and indefatigable spies were dispatched to watch their movements and report. White and M'Cleland, two spirits that never quailed at danger, and as unconquerable as the Lybian lion, in the month of October, and on one of those balmy days of Indian summer, took leave of their fellows and moved on through the thick plum and hazel bushes with the noiseless tread of the panther, armed with their unerring and trusty rifles. They continued their march, skirting the prairies, till they reached that most remarkable prominence, now known by the name of Mount Pleasant, the western termination of which is a perpendicular cliff of rocks of some hundreds feet high, and whose summit, from a western view, towers to the clouds and overlooks the vast plain below. When this point was gained, our hardy spies held a position from which they could see every movement of the Indians below in the valley. Every day added a new accession of warriors to the company. They witnessed their exercises of horse-racing, running foot-races, jumping, throwing the tomahawk, and dancing—the old sachems looking on with their Indian indifference, the squaws engaged in their usual drudgery, and the children in their playful gambols. The arrival of a new war-party was greeted with terrible shouts, which, striking the mural face of Mount Pleasant, were driven back in the various indentations of the surrounding hills, producing reverberations and echoes as if ten thousand fiends were gathered at a universal levee. Such yells would have struck terror to the hearts of those unaccustomed to Indian revelry. To our spies this was but martial music—strains which waked their watchfulness, and newly strung their veteran courage. From their early youth they had been always on the frontier, and were well practiced in all the subtilty, craft, and cunning of Indian warfare, as well as the ferocity and bloodthirsty nature of these savage warriors. They were, therefore, not likely to be insnared by their cunning, nor without a desperate conflict to fall victims to their scalping-knives or tomahawks. On several occasions, small parties left the prairie and ascended the mount from the eastern side. On these occasions the spies would hide in the deep fissures of the rocks on the west, and again leave their hiding-places when their uninvited and unwelcome visitors had disappeared.

For food they depended on jerked venison and corn bread, with which their knapsacks were well stored. They dare not kindle a fire, and the report of one of their rifles would bring upon them the entire force of the Indians. For drink they depended on some rain-water which still stood in the hollows of some of the rocks; but in a short time this store was exhausted, and M'Cleland and White must abandon their enterprise or find a new supply. To accomplish this most hazardous enterprise, M'Cleland, being the oldest, resolved to make the attempt; and with his trusty rifle in his hand and their two canteens strung across his shoulders, he cautiously descended, by a circuitous route, to the prairie, skirting the hills on the north, and under covert of the hazel thickets he reached the river, and turning a bold point of a hill, he found a beautiful spring within a few feet of the river, now known by the name of the Cold Spring, on the farm of D. Talmadge, Esq. He filled his canteens and returned in safety to his watchful companion. It was now determined to have a fresh supply of water every day, and this duty was performed alternately.

On one of these occasions, after White had filled his canteens, he sat a few moments watching the limpid element as it came gurgling out of the bosom of the earth, when the light sound of footsteps caught his practiced ear, and upon turning round he saw two squaws within a few feet of him. Upon turning the jut of the hill, the eldest squaw gave one of those far-reaching whoops peculiar to Indians. White at once comprehended his perilous situation. If the alarm should reach the camps or town, he and his companion must inevitably perish. Self-preservation compelled him to inflict a noiseless death on the squaws, and in such a manner as, if possible, to leave no trace behind. Ever rapid in thought and prompt in action, he sprang upon his victims with the rapidity and power of the lion, and grasping the throat of each sprang into the river. He thrust the head of the eldest under the water. While making strong efforts to submerge the younger, who, however, powerfully resisted him, and during the short struggle with this young athletic, to his astonishment she addressed him in his own language, though in almost inarticulate sounds. Releasing his hold she informed him that she had been a prisoner for ten years, and was taken from below Wheeling, and that the Indians had killed all the family, and that her brother and herself were taken prisoners, but he succeeded, on the second night, in making his escape. During this narrative White had drowned the elder squaw, and had let hei float off with the current, where it would not probably be found out soon. He now directed the girl to follow him, and witn his usual speed and energy pushed foı the mount. They had scarcely gone half way when they heard the alarm cry some quarter of a mile down the stream. It was supposed some party of Indians, returning from hunting, struck the river just as the body of the squaw floated past. White and the girl succeeded in reaching the mount, where M'Cleland had been no indifferent spectator to the sudden commotion among the Indians. The prairie parties of warriors were seen immediately to strike off in every direction, and White and the girl had scarcely arrived before a party of some twenty warriors had reached the eastern acclivity of the mount, and were cautiously and carefully keeping under cover. Soon the spies saw their swarthy foes as they glided from tree to tree and rock to rock, till their position was surrounded, except on the west perpendicular side, and all hope of escape was cut off. In this perilous condition, nothing was left but to sell their lives as dear as possible, and this they resolved to do, and advised the girl to escape to the Indians and tell them she had been taken prisoner. She said, "No! death to me, in the presence of my own people, is a thousand times sweeter than captivity and slavery. Furnish me with a gun, and I will show you I can fight as well as die. This place I leave not. Here my bones shall lie bleaching with yours, and should either of you escape you will carry the tidings of my death to my few relations." Remonstrance proved fruitless. The two spies quickly matured their plan of defense, and vigorously commenced the attack from the front, where, from the very narrow backbone of the mount, the savages had to advance in single file, and without any covert. Beyond this neck the warriors availed themselves of the rocks and trees in advancing, but in passing from one to the other they must be exposed for a short time, and a moment's exposure of their swarthy forms was enough for the unerring rifles of the spies. The Indians being entirely ignorant of how many were in ambuscade, made them the more cautious how they advanced.

After bravely maintaining the fight in front and keeping the enemy in check, they discovered a new danger threatening them. The arch foe now made evident preparations to attack them on the flank, which could be most successfully done by reaching an isolated rock lying in one of the ravines on the southern hill-side. This rock once gained by the Indians, they could bring the spies under point-blank shot of the rifle without the possibility of escape. Our brave spies saw the hopelessness of their situation, which nothing could avert but a brave companion and an unerring shot. These they had not; but the brave never despair. With this impending fate resting upon them, they continued calm and calculating, and as unwearied as the strongest desire of life and the resistance of a numerous foe could produce. Soon M'Cleland saw a tall and swarthy figure preparing to spring from a covert so near to the fatal rock that a bound or two would reach it, and all hope of life then was gone. He felt that all depended on one single advantageous shot; and although but an inch or two of the warrior's body was exposed, and that at the distance of eighty or a hundred yards, he resolved to risk all, coolly raised his rifle to his face, and shading the sight with his hand, he drew a bead so sure that he felt conscious it would do the deed. He touched the trigger with his finger; the hammer came down, but in place of striking fire, it broke his flint into many pieces; and although he felt that the Indian must reach the rock before he could adjust another flint, he proceeded to the task with the utmost composure. Casting his eye toward the fearful point, suddenly he saw the warrior stretching every muscle for the leap; and with the agility of the panther he made the spring, but instead of reaching the rock, he gave a most hideous yell, and his dark body fell and rolled down the steep into the valley below. He had evidently received a death shot from some unknown hand. A hundred voices re-echoed, from below, the terrible shout. It was evident that they had lost a favorite warrior, as well as being disappointed, for a time, of the most important movement. A very few minutes proved that the advantage gained would be of short duration; for already the spies caught a glimpse of a tall, swarthy warrior cautiously advancing to the covert so recently occupied by his fellow-companion. Now, too, the attack in front was renewed with increased fury, so as to require the incessant fire of both spies to prevent the Indians from gaining the eminence; and in a short time M'Cleland saw a warrior making preparations to leap to the fatal rock. The leap was made, and the Indian turning a somerset, his corpse rolled down the hill toward his former companion. Again an unknown agent had interposed in their behalf. This second sacrifice cast dismay into the ranks of the assailants, and just as the sun was disappearing behind the western hills the foe withdrew for a short distance, to devise some new mode of attack. This respite came most seasonable to our spies, who had kept their ground and bravely maintained the unequal fight from nearly the middle of the day.

Now for the first time was the girl missing; and the spies thought that through terror she had escaped to her former captors, or that she had been killed during the fight; but they were not long left to conjecture. The girl was seen emerging from behind a rock and coming to them with a rifle in her hand. During the heat of the fight she saw a warrior fall who had advanced some distance before the rest, and while some of them changed their position she resolved at once, live or die, to possess herself of his gun and ammunition; and crouching down beneath the underbrush, she crawled to the place and succeeded in er enterprise. Her keen and watchful eye had early noiced the fatal rock, and hers was the mysterious hand by which the two warriors fell; the last being the most intrepid and bloodthirsty of the Shawnee tribe, and the leader of the company which killed her mother and sisters, and took her and her brother prisoners.

Now, in the west, arose dark clouds, which soon overspread the whole heavens, and the elements were rent with the peals of thunder. Darkness, deep and gloomy, shrouded the whole heavens: this darkness greatly embarrassed the spies in their contemplated night escape, supposing that they might readily lose their way, and accidentally fall on their enemy; but a short consultation decided the plan; it was agreed that the girl should go foremost, from her intimate knowledge of the localities, and another advantage might be gained in case they should fall in with any of the parties or outposts. From her knowledge of their language, she might deceive the sentinels, as the sequel proved; for scarcely had they descended a hundred yards, when a low whist from the girl warned them of their danger. The spies sunk silently to the ground, where, by previous engagement, they were to remain till the signal was given, by the girl, to move on. Her absence, for the space of a quarter of an hour, began to excite the most serious apprehensions. Again she appeared, and told them she had succeeded in removing two sentinels to a short distance, who were directly in their route. The descent was noiselessly resumed, and the spies followed their intrepid leader for a half mile in the most profound silence, when the barking of a dog at a short distance apprised them of new danger. The almost simultaneous click of the spies' rifles was heard by the girl, who stated that they were now in the midst of the Indian camps, and their lives now depended on the most profound silence, and implicitly following her footsteps. A moment afterward, the girl was accosted by a squaw, from an opening in her wigwam: she replied in the Indian language, and, without stopping, still pressed forward. In a short time she stopped, and assured the spies that the village was now cleared, and that they had passed the greatest danger. She knew that every leading pass was guarded safely by the Indians, and at once resolved to adopt the bold adventure of passing through the center of the village, as the least hazardous, and the sequel proved the correctness of her judgment. They now steered a course for the Ohio river, and, after three days' travel, arrived safe at the block-house. Their escape and adventure prevented the Indians from their contemplated attack; and the rescued girl proved to be the sister of the intrepid Corneal Washburn, celebrated in the history of Indian warfare, and as the renowned spy of Captain Simon Kenton's bloody Kentuckians.*

Robert M'Cleland was afterward, in 1794, a spy in Wayne's army; and few men were ever his equal in activity, courage, and enduring perseverance; and, as we are giving specimens of the backwoodsmen, we will follow M'Cleland in the history of his life, as it was known and narrated by others. Colonel John M'Donald, in his Sketches of the West, and who was also a spy in Wayne's army, and personally acquainted with M'Cleland, gives the following account of him:

General Wayne, to secure his army from the possibility of being ambuscaded, employed a number of the best woodsmen the frontier afforded to act as spies or rangers. Captain Ephraim Kibby, one of the first settlers of Columbia, above Cincinnati, commanded the principal part of the spies. A very effective division of the rangers was

---

*I am indebted to General Sanderson, of Lancaster, for this interesting narrative

commanded by Captain William Wells, who had been taken prisoner by the Indians when a youth. He grew to manhood with them, and was well acquainted with al their wiles and stratagems. About eighteen months previous to this campaign, he left them and returned to civilized life; he was well acquainted with several of their languages, and could converse fluently. Attached to his command were a few choice spirits. Henry Miller and his brother Christopher had been both taken prisoners when quite young, adopted into an Indian family, and reared up with them; and Henry lived with them till he was twenty-four years of age. About this time, although adopted into all their customs and manners, he thought of making his escape, and returning home. This he communicated to his brother Christopher, and tried to persuade him to accompany him; but all his arguments were ineffectual. Christopher was very young when made a captive; he was now a good hunter, an expert woodsman, and, in the full sense, a free and independent Indian. Henry set off alone, and arrived safe in Kentucky. Captain Wells was well acquainted with him during their captivity, and knew that he possessed that firm intrepidity which would render him a valuable companion in time of need. To these were added Messrs. Hickman, Thorp, and M'Cleland. Colonel M'Donald says he was one of the most athletic and active men on foot that has appeared on this globe. On the grand parade at Fort Greenville, where there was a very little declivity, to show his activity he leaped over a road-wagon with the cover stretched over it. The wagon and bows were eight feet high from the ground. Captain Wells and his four companions were privileged gentlemen in camp, and only called on to do duty on certain special occasions, and when on duty went well mounted. The headquarters of the army being at Fort Greenville, in the month of June General Wayne dispatched Captain Wells, M'Cleland, and Miller, with orders to bring into camp an Indian prisoner, in order that he might interrogate him as to the future intentions of the Indians. They proceeded with cautious steps through the Indian country, crossed the St. Mary's, and thence proceeded to the Auglaize river, without meeting any straggling Indian. In passing up the Auglaize they discovered a smoke, and, dismounting, tied their horses, and proceeded cautiously to reconnoiter the enemy. They found three Indians camped on a high, open piece of ground, clear of brush or underwood. They found it would be difficult to approach within gunshot, without being discovered. At a proper distance from their camp, they saw the top of a tree which had been blown down, and full of leaves. Believing this would answer their purpose, and screen them from observation, they returned, went round, and crept on their hands and knees with the noiseless movement of the panther. The Indians were engaged roasting their venison, talking and laughing, not dreaming that death was stealing a march upon them. Having arrived at the fallen tree, their mode of attack was soon settled. They determined to kill two of the enemy, and take the third prisoner. M'Cleland, who was almost as swift on foot as a deer, was to catch the Indian, while to Miller and Wells was confided the duty of shooting the other two; one was to shoot the one on the right, and the other the one on the left; and at the sharp crack of their rifles, two fell; for their aim was at the heart. Before the smoke of the powder had risen six feet, M'Cleland was running at full stretch, with tomahawk in hand, for the Indian. The Indian bounded off at the top of his speed, down the river. But, continuing in that direction, he discovered that M'Cleland would head him, and he turned his course. The river here had a bluff bank, about twenty feet high. When he came to the bank, he sprang down into the river, the bottom of which was soft mud, and he sunk up to his middle. At this moment, M'Cleland came to the top, and sprang on him without hesitation. As they were wallowing in the mire, the Indian drew his knife; M'Cleland raised his tomahawk, and told him to throw down his knife, or he would instantly kill him. This he did, and surrendered without further resistance. By this time, Wells and his comrade came to the bank, and discovered that they were both sticking in the mud. As the prisoner was now secure, they went round and helped drag the prisoner out of the mud, and tied him. He was very sulky, and refused to speak either English or Indian. One went for the horses, while the other two washed the prisoner. When washed, he turned out to be a white man, but still refused to speak, or give any account of himself. After they had scalped the dead, they set out, with the prisoner, to head-quarters. While on their return, Henry Miller began to admit the idea that it was possible the prisoner might be his brother, whom he had left with the Indians some years previous. Under this impression, he rode along side of him, and called him by his Indian name. At the sound of his name he started, and eagerly inquired how he came to know his name. The mystery was solved; the prisoner was indeed Christopher Miller, his brother. A mysterious Providence appeared to have placed Christopher Miller in a position by which his life was preserved. Had he been standing on the right or left, he would have been killed. When they arrived at camp, the prisoner was placed in the guard-house. General Wayne frequently interrogated him; he continued sulky. Captain Wells and Henry Miller were constantly with him, and at length prevailed on him to relinquish his thoughts of returning to savage life, and to join with his brother and white friends. He finally assented to their proposition, was released, and well mounted, and became one of Wells's party.

As soon as Captain Wells and company had rested themselves and horses, they were anxious for another adventure with the red men. Time without action becomes very irksome to such stirring spirits. Early in July they again left Greenville. Their company was now increased by the addition of Christopher Miller. Their orders were to bring in prisoners They pushed through the country, all mounted, dressed, and painted in the best Indian style. Near the Auglaize, they met a single Indian, and called on him to surrender. This Indian, notwithstanding there were six to one, refused to obey: he leveled his rifle, and, as the whites approached, he fired, but missed his mark, and took to his heels. The undergrowth of brush was so thick, that he gained on them. M'Cleland and Christopher Miller dismounted, and M'Cleland soon overtook him. The Indian, finding himself overtaken, turned, and made a blow at M'Cleland with his rifle; and as M'Cleland's intention was not to kill, he kept him at bay, till Miller came up; then they closed in on him, and made him prisoner. They then returned to headquarters, at Fort Greenville. Their prisoner was a powerful Pottawatamie chief, whose prowess and courage were scarcely equaled. As Christopher Miller had acted his part on this occasion to the satisfaction of his comrades he had, as he merited, their entire confidence.

As it is not the intention to narrate all the acts of these spies attached to Wayne's army, although it would be a most interesting narrative to western readers, we have selected a few of the adventures performed by Captain Wells and his intrepid companions, and especially of Robert M'Cleland. History, in no age of the world, furnishes so many instances of repeated acts of bravery, as were performed by the frontier men, especially of western

Pennsylvania, Virginia, and Kentucky; yet these acts of desperation were so frequently repeated by numbers, that they were scarcely noticed at the time as being any other than the common occurrences of the day. There can be no doubt that during General Wayne's campaign, Wells and his comrades brought in not less than twenty prisoners, and killed more than an equal number. Desperate as they were in combat, that bravery was only a part of their merit, as the following circumstance will show:

On one of their tours through the Indian country, as they came to the bank of the river St. Mary's, they discovered a family of Indians coming up the river, in a canoe. They dismounted, and concealed themselves near the bank of the river, while Wells went upon the bank, in open view, and called to the Indians to come over; and, as he was dressed like them, and could speak their language as well as themselves, and they not expecting an enemy in that part of the country, without any suspicion of danger, came over. The moment the canoe struck the shore, Wells heard his comrades cock their rifles, as they prepared to shoot down the whole company. But who should be in the canoe but Wells's Indian father and mother—with whom he had lived—and their children! He called on his comrades, who were ready to pour the deadly fire, to desist. He then informed them who these Indians were, and solemnly declared that if any one did injure one of them, he would put a ball through his head. He said to his men, that that family had fed him when hungry, clothed him when naked, and kindly nursed him when sick, and, in every respect, were as kind and affectionate to him as they were to their own children. This short, pathetic speech found its way to the sympathetic hearts of his leather hunting-shirt comrades, although they would have made but a shabby appearance, on being introduced to a fashionable tea party, or into a splendid ball-room, among polished grandees, or into a ceremonious levee, to pass through unmeaning becks, bows, and courtesies. The present was a scene of nature and gratitude. They all at once entered into their leader's feelings. There never was a truly-brave man who could hold back his tear of sympathy at the joy, grief, or sorrow of his fellow-man. It is the timid coward who is cruel when he has the advantage. These hardy soldiers approved of the motives of their captain, threw down their guns and tomahawks, went to the canoe, and shook hands with the trembling Indians in the most friendly manner. Captain Wells assured his Indian friends they had nothing to fear from them, and advised them, as General Wayne was coming with an overwhelming army, to make peace, and his Indian father to take his family, and get out of all danger. They then bid them farewell, and they departed in haste. This act does honor to the hearts of these desperadoes in fight, and shows largely that real gratitude of heart which alone belongs to truly-brave men.

Early in the month of August, when the main army had arrived at the place where Fort Defiance was built, General Wayne wishing to know the intentions and situation of the enemy, dispatched Captain Wells and his company to bring in another prisoner. The army now lay within forty-five miles of the British fort at the mouth of the Maumee river, and they would not have to travel far till they would find Indians. As the object was to take a prisoner, it was necessary for them to keep out of the way of large parties. They went cautiously down the Maumee till within two miles of the British fort, where stood an Indian village. All being dressed and painted as Indians, they rode into the village as if they had come from the fort, occasionally stopping and talking with the Indians in their own language. No suspicion was excited, the Indians believing they were from a distance, and had come to take part in the expected battle.

After they had passed the village some distance, they met an Indian man and woman on horseback, who were returning from a hunting expedition. This man and woman were made captives without resistance. They then set off for headquarters. As they were proceeding up the Maumee after dark, they came near a large encampment of Indians, who were merrily amusing themselves around their camp fires. Their prisoners were ordered to be silent under pain of instant death. They went round their camp with their prisoners till they got half a mile above them, where they halted to consult on their future operations. After consultation they concluded to tie and gag their prisoners, ride back to the Indian camp and give them a rally, in which each should kill his Indian. This they did—rode boldly into the Indian camp and halted, with their rifles lying on the pommel of their saddles. They inquired when they had heard of General Wayne and the movements of his army? how soon and where the battle would be fought? The Indians who were standing around them were very communicative, and without suspicion. At length an Indian, who was sitting some distance from them, said in an undertone of voice, and in another tongue, to some who were near him, that he suspected that these strangers had some mischief in their heads. Wells overheard what was said, and gave the preconcerted signal, and each fired his rifle into an Indian not six feet distant. At this instant the Indians arose with their rifles in their hands, and as soon as Wells and his party fired they wheeled and put spurs to their horses, laying with their breasts on the horses necks, so as to lessen the mark for the Indians to fire at. They had not got out of sight of the camp fire till the Indians shot at them. As M'Cleland lay close on his horse's neck he was shot, the ball passing under his shoulder-blade and coming out at the top of his shoulder Captain Wells was shot through the arm on which he carried his rifle, and it fell. The rest of the party or their horses received no injury.

There was in this terrific encounter a display of confidence and self-possession almost unparalleled. They had escaped in so many desperate combats that they seemed to be entirely insensible to danger. As they had no rivals in the army, they aimed to outdo all their former exploits.

To ride into an enemy's camp and enter into conversation with them, without betraying the least appearance of trepidation or confusion, shows how well their hearts were steeled. Their actions of real life even rival the fictions of the Grecian poet. Homer sends forth his invincible hero, protected by the invulnerable panoply of Jupiter, to make a night attack upon the enemy. Diomede makes the successful attack upon sleeping foes. Not so with our western heroes. They boldly went into the midst of the enemy while their camp fires were burning bright and they were on the watch, and openly commenced the work of death. After having performed this chivalrous act, they rode at full speed to where their prisoners were tied, mounted them on horses, and set off for Fort Defiance.

Wells and M'Cleland were severely wounded, and to Fort Defiance, a distance of thirty-five miles, they had to ride before they could rest or have the aid of a surgeon. One of the party was dispatched at full speed for a guard and surgeon. As soon as the tidings of the wounds and perilous condition of the spies reached the fort, without a moment's delay a dispatch of the swiftest dragoons and a surgeon were off to meet them. Suffice it to say, that they arrived safely in camp, and the wounded recovered in a short time; and as the battle was fought and a brilliant victory won a few days after, these brave and daring spirits were not engaged in further hostilities. The war with the Indians was closed with a lasting treaty of peace in 1795.

It will be natural for the reader to wish to know what became of those brave men—of Thorp, Hickman, and the two Millers. Concerning these history is silent; but like many other valorous backwoodsmen, if living, may reside in some poor cabin in the far west, unknown and unhonored. The brave Captain Wells fell, during the last war with England, on the 15th of August, 1812, near Fort Dearborn, at the mouth of the Chicago river. He was slain in an unequal combat, where sixty-four whites were attacked by upward of four hundred Indians. He fell, lamented by his whole country, and never fell a bolder or more intrepid spirit. Nothing more is heard of the intrepid M'Cleland till 1812. This hardy, brave, and active backwoodsman had returned to St. Louis from an expedition across the Rocky Mountains. He had been to the Pacific Ocean, at the mouth of the Columbia river. Such a tour through uncultivated, unpeopled oceans of prairie, and such labor through the tempestuous bursts of storm, sleet, and snow that whirled in almost continual tornadoes around the hights of frightful rocks which compose these dreary mountains, where winter eternally reigns; such a tour, I repeat, was equal to the daring genius of a man like M'Cleland.

Washington Irving, in his Astoria, gives the following description of M'Cleland. He says he was a remarkable man. He had been a partisan under General Wayne in his Indian wars, where he distinguished himself by his fiery spirit and reckless daring, and marvelous stories were told of his exploits. His appearance answered to his character. His frame was meager but muscular; showing strength, activity, and iron firmness. His eyes were dark, deep set, and piercing. He was restless, fearless, but of impetuous and, sometimes, ungovernable temper He was invited by Mr. Hunt, the partner of Jacob Astor, to join the party for the mouth of the Columbia river This he did, about four hundred and fifty miles up the Missouri river, and for the special purpose of taking revenge on a party of Indians that had robbed him and his partner—Crooks—some time before. This robbery, by the Sioux, was instigated by Emanuel Lisa, the leading partner and agent of the Missouri Fur Company. This intelligence so roused the fiery temper of M'Cleland, that he swore if he met with Lisa in the Indian country he would shoot him on the spot—a mode of redress perfectly in unison with the character of the man and the code of honor prevalent beyond the frontier.

I will close the history of this extraordinary man by giving one more specimen of his character. In returning, after sufferings almost indescribable, in passing across to the mouth of the Columbia river, his fare was no better. In company with Mr. Stewart and five others, they were robbed of all their horses by the Blackfeet Indians, in the fall of 1812, and had to combat all the perils of the journey on foot. On a certain occasion, to avoid coming in contact with the perfidious savages, it was thought safest by all but M'Cleland, to cross some stupendous mountains than go round. At this M'Cleland demurred; and notwithstanding the remonstrances of his comrades, he turned a deaf ear and left them, and took his own way. Some days after, when they passed the top of the mountain, they saw M'Cleland at a distance in advance traversing the plain, and whether he saw them or not he showed no disposition to rejoin them. On the eleventh night after they parted, they met with signs of that wayward and solitary being, M'Cleland, who was still keeping ahead of them through those solitary mountains. He had en camped, the night before, on a small stream, where they found the embers of the fire by which he slept, and the remains of a miserable wolf on which he supped. The next day at evening, almost starved to death and with no prospect of food, they stopped to encamp, when they saw a smoke at a distance, which they hailed with joy, hoping it was some Indian's camp, where they might obtain something to prevent them from starving. They dispatched one of their company to reconnoiter. They waited till a late hour for his return. On the next morning they set out early. They had not traveled far till they saw their comrade, whom they hastened to meet, in hope he had obtained something for them to eat; but of this he had none. The smoke had arisen from the fire of M'Cleland, which had broken out while he was trying to catch some small fish. When the party reached the place they found the poor fellow lying on a parcel of withered grass, wasted to a perfect skeleton, and so feeble he could scarcely raise his head to speak. The presence of his old companions seemed to revive him; but they had no food to give him, for they were almost starved themselves. They urged him to arise and accompany them, but he shook his head. It was all in vain, for there was no prospect of relief, and he might as well die where he was. After much persuasion they got him on his feet, and while some shared the burden of carrying his rifle, he was cheered and urged forward. After one or two days' travel they succeeded in killing an old rundown buffalo bull, which preserved the whole party from starving. Suffice it to say, that the party sustained themselves through the winter, and the next spring arrived safely at St. Louis. From this M'Cleland returned to the wilderness, and there is no certain account of where or how he died

Thus, reader, we have conducted you along with the history of one of those intrepid and fearless spirits who were the pioneers of the vast west, and he is a good specimen of all the rest. It will take many volumes to record the daring deeds and the indescribable sufferings of those who penetrated the vast wilderness which now has risen to a mighty empire. Their dauntless and daring spirits have passed off unknown, unhonored, and unregarded; a new race has followed after, who are now reveling in all the luxuries of the richest and most fertile spot on the globe.

An anecdote is told of one of those adventurous trappers, who had been trapping and trading for some years in the mountain passes, and came with his furs to St. Louis. He sold all his peltry and buffalo-robes, and had received three checks on the bank. He went into the bank to draw his money. His dress and appearance were those of a backwoods trapper, and the bank room being filled with the gentry, they looked upon his greasy buckskin hunting-shirt and leggins as though they feared he would touch them and spoil or soil their delicate clothing; and after looking all round the room and its inmates, he threw down his first check; this was cashed. He then threw down his second, and then his third. The gentlemen began by this time to look at one another, and the cashier said, "Where are you from, sir?" The trapper replied, "Just from the moon, sir." "How did you get down, sir?" "Why, I just greased my hunting-shirt, sir, and slid down on a rainbow."

Here, gentle reader, permit me to record my testimony with others, and say to you and to generations unborn, that there never lived a nobler race of men on the green earth, than those pioneers of the great valley of the Mississippi, from Finley and Boone down to General William Henry Harrison, who had the honor and glory of closing the long and bloody British and Indian war, which had lasted for more than fifty years; and no man, of any taste or genius, can read the accounts of the settlement of this vast wilderness, and the daring deeds of valor displayed by the first adventurers, without feeling the highest degree of admiration at their patriotism and unflinching perseverance. While every young and true-hearted American will feel himself identified with them, and have a filial regard for their memory, while he beholds them, like a Boone, a Kenton, a Finley, and a Stewart, treading the lonely desert, and braving the horrors of savage rage and fury, amid the distress of famine and war, he admires their courage, and is interested with the thrilling accounts and their narrow escapes from death, as well as their perseverance and toil in turning this most delightful and richest of all countries into the fruitful field and smiling garden, and opening the way for millions of our race to enjoy the inestimable blessings of religion and liberty. No class of men ever acted more nobly, or conferred a greater temporal blessing on posterity; nor did ever any make greater sacrifices; danger, poverty, and death were their constant companions. It is said by a wise man, that ingratitude is a sin of greater magnitude than witchcraft; and thousands now live at their ease, and roll in their wealth, who can not feel toward those brave men as I do. They stood, with gun and tomahawk in hand, between our mothers and their children and the incensed and revengeful rage of the red man. They were our guardians from savage barbarity; their names were precious then, and still are to those for whom they ventured their lives and their all. In those days of blood and carnage all were warriors. Our mothers, like the women of Amazonia, were trained to war, and could handle the rifle with great dexterity, and the children were trained up to be soldiers from childhood. A boy ten years old was counted able to carry arms, and fight; and at sixteen would enter the regular service. One of this age was enlisted as a soldier in the last war; his captain asked him, "John, can you ride and carry a gun?" "I can try, sir." "Can you shoot, John?" "I can try, sir." "Can you fight Indians, John?" "I can try, sir," said the lad. At one time, when on a scouting party with his captain, they were chased by a body of Indians, and crossing a prairie one pressed them hard. The captain said, "John, can you light off when we get to those woods and shoot that Indian?" He sprang from his horse, drew his rifle to his face, and fired; down fell the Indian. After they arrived at camp the captain called him up and said, "John, when I enlisted you, I was afraid that you would not stand fire, but would run." John said, "I am not one of that breed, sir."

CHAPTER III.

LIFE IN THE BACKWOODS.

The first settlers could not have sustained themselves, had it not been for the wild game that was in the country. This was their principal subsistence; and this they took at the peril of their lives, and often many of them came near starving to death. Wild meat, without bread or salt, was often their food for weeks together. If they obtained bread, the meal was pounded in a mortar, or ground on a hand-mill. Hominy was a good substitute for bread, or parched corn pounded and sifted, then mixed with a little sugar and eaten dry; or mixed with water was a good beverage. On this coarse fare the people were remarkably healthy and cheerful. No complaints were heard of dyspepsia: I never heard of this fashionable complaint till I was more than thirty years old; and if the emigrants had come to these backwoods with dyspepsia, they would not have been troubled long with it; for a few months' living on buffalo, venison, and good, fat bear-meat, with the oil of the raccoon and opossum mixed up with plenty of hominy, would soon have effected a cure.

Their children were fat and hearty, not having been fed with plum-pudding, sweetmeats, and pound-cake. A more hardy race of men and women grew up in this wilderness than has ever been produced since; with more common sense and enterprise than is common to those who sleep on beds of down, and feast on jellies and preserves; and although they had not the same advantages of obtaining learning that the present generation have, yet they had this advantage—they were sooner thrown upon the world, became acquainted with men and things, and entirely dependent on their own resources for a living. A boy at the age of sixteen was counted a man in labor and hunting, and was ready to go to war; and now, one of that age hardly knows the road to mill or market.

Their attire was in perfect keeping with their fare. The men's apparel was mostly made of the deer's skin. This, well dressed, was made into hunting-shirts, pantaloons, coats, waistcoats, leggins, and moccasins. The women sometimes wore petticoats made of this most common and useful article; and it supplied, almost universally, the place of shoes and boots. If a man was blessed with a linsey hunting-shirt, and the ladies with linsey dresses, and the children with the same, it was counted of the first order, even if the linsey was made of the wool of the buffalo. On some occasions, the men could purchase a calico shirt; this was thought to be extra; for which they paid one dollar and fifty cents or two dollars in skins or furs. And if a woman had one calico dress to go abroad in, she was considered a finely-dressed lady. Deer's hair or oak leaves was generally put into the moccasin, and worn in place of stockings or socks. The household furniture consisted of stools, and bedsteads made with forks driven into the ground and poles laid on these, with the bark of the trees, and on this beds made of oak leaves, or cattail stripped off and dried in the sun. They rocked their children in a sugar trough or pack-saddle. The cooking utensils consisted of a pot, Dutch oven, skillet, frying pan, wooden trays and trenchers, and boards made smooth and clean. The table was made of a broad slab. And with these fixtures, there never was a heartier, happier, more hospitable or cheerful people. Their interests were one, and their dependence on each other was indispensable, and all things were common. Thus united, they lived as one family. They generally married early in life—the men from eighteen to twenty-one, and the girls from sixteen to twenty. The difficulties of commencing the world were not so great; and, as both parties were contented to begin with nothing, there was no looking out for fortunes, or the expectation of living without labor. Their affections were personal and sincere, which constituted a chief part of their domestic happiness, and endeared them to home. The sparkling log-fire in the backwoods cabin, the gambols of half a dozen cheerful, healthy children, and the smiles of the happy wife and mother, made an earthly paradise. Nothing could excite more hilarity than a backwoods wedding. Most generally, all the neighborhood, for miles around, were invited; and if it was in the winter, there would be a log-heap or two somewhere near the cabin. Around these fires the men assembled with their rifles; the women in the cabin; and if there was a fiddler in the neighborhood, he must be present at an hour stated. The parson, if one could be had, if not, the Justice of the Peace, called the assembly together, then the couple to be married. After the ceremony was over, and all had wished the happy pair much joy, then, if it could be had, the bottle passed round; the men then went some to shooting at a mark, some to throwing the tomahawk, others to hopping and jumping, throwing the rail or shoulder-stone, others to running foot-races; the women were employed in cooking. When dinner was ready, the guests all partook of the very best venison, bear-meat, roast turkeys, etc. This being over, the dance commences, and, if there is no room in the cabin, the company repair to or near one of the log-fires; there they dance till night, and then they mostly return home; yet many of the young people stay, and perhaps dance all night on a rough puncheon floor, till the moccasins are worn through. The next day is the infair: the same scenes are again enacted, when the newly-married pair single off to a cabin built for themselves, without twenty dollars' worth of property to begin the world with, and live more happily than those who roll in wealth and fortune.

I recollect, when a boy, to have seen a pair of those backwoods folks come to my father's to get married. The groom and bride had a bell on each of their horses' necks, and a horse-collar made of corn-husks on each horse, to pay the marriage fee. The groomsman had a bottle of whisky in his hunting-shirt bosom. When they had entered the house, the groom asked if the parson was at home. My father replied that he was the parson. Then said the groom, "May it please you, Mary M'Lain and I have come to get married. Will you do it for us?" "Yes," replied my father. "Well, then," said the groom, "we are in a hurry." So the knot was tied, and the groomsman pulled out his bottle of whisky to treat the company. He then went out, and took the collars off the horses of the bride and groom, and brought them in as the marriage fee; and soon after they started for home, in Indian file, with the bells on their horses open, to keep the younger colts which had followed them together.

The manner in which the cabins were built, I have described elsewhere. The chimneys were built on the inside of the house, by throwing on an extra log, three feet and a half from the wall, on which to build the chimney, from this it was carried up with sticks and clay, to the roof of the house, and some two feet above it. The whole width of the house was occupied for a fireplace, and wood ten or twelve feet long could be laid on; when burned in two in the middle, the ends could be pushed up, so as to keep a good fire through a long winter's night. When there was but one bed in the cabin, it was no sign that you would not have a good night's rest; for, after supper was over, and the feats of the day about hunting were all talked over, the skins were brought forth—bear, buffalo, or deer—and spread down before a sparkling fire, and a blanket or buffalo robe to cover with; and you could sleep sweetly as the visions of the night roll over the senses, till the morning dawn announced the approach of day. There were no windows, and but one opening for a door; this was generally narrow, and the shutter made of two slabs, or a tree split in two, then hewed off to the thickness say of six or eight inches, then set up endwise, and made with a bevel to lap over. The fastenings consisted of three large bars, fastened to staples in the walls. The floor, if not of the earth, was of hewn slabs, and covered with clapboards. These cabins, if there was some care taken in putting down the logs close together, and they were scutched down, would make the sweetest and healthiest habitations that man can live in. They are much healthier than either stone or brick houses; and I have no doubt but that there is a greater amount of health and happiness enjoyed by the inmates of the former than the latter.

All the mills that the early settlers had, was the hominy block or a hand-mill. The water-mills or horse-mills were so far off, that it was like going on a pilgrimage to get a grist; and besides the toll was so enormously high—one half being required for grinding the other half—that they preferred doing their own milling.

Almost every man and boy were hunters, and some of the women of those times were expert in the chase. The game which was considered the most profitable and useful was the buffalo, the elk, the bear, and the deer. The smaller game consisted of raccoon, turkey, opossum, and ground-hog. The panther was sometimes used for food, and considered by some as good. The flesh of the wolf and wild-cat was only used when nothing else could be obtained.

The buffalo is of the kine species, with a large hump on its shoulders, generally of a dun color, with short, thick horns. The male buffalo is distinguished from the female by having a short mane. They go usually in large droves or herds, feeding on cane in the winter. They frequent salt-licks; and in going to and from these places they beat large roads.

Buffaloes were abundant in Kentucky, and were used by the first settlers as their most common food. They have a very shaggy or woolly skin. The wool was often spun and woven into cloth by the women; and sometimes it was mixed with raccoon fur and knit into stockings, which were very warm and serviceable. The fashionable clothes cut out of the finest French and English broadcloths, and made in such a style as to provoke the idea that they were designed to invite instead of protect us from the chilling blasts of winter, would bear no comparison with the warm and comfortable clothing which was worn at that day.

After the wool was taken off, the hide answered a valuable purpose. Being cut into strips and twisted, it made strong tugs, which were used for plowing. It was also made into plow-lines, bed-cords, etc. When dressed it was made into shoe-packs, or a kind of half shoe and half moccasin. The way of hunting the buffalo was in the following manner: A company was formed, well supplied with dogs and guns. Being mounted on horses, they started for the woods. When a herd was found, one of the company would creep up softly and fire into their midst; then the whole company would rush in upon them with their dogs, which would throw them into confusion. After all had discharged their pieces the dogs would attack

THE BUFFALO.

THE BEAR.

them; and while they were engaged in fighting with the dogs, the hunters would have time to reload and pursue the chase. After the conflict was over they would return and collect the spoil. To enable the horses to carry them, they would take out the entrails and split them in two, and then throw them over the pack-saddles and carry them home.

The elk is of the deer or moose species. It resembles the deer very much in form, but it is much larger. It has large branching horns, which sometimes grow to an enormous size. To look at the forest of horns which they carry on their heads, one would think it impossible for them ever to make their way through the woods. I have seen these antlers so large, that when set up on their points a man six feet high could pass under them without stooping. The flesh of the elk is coarse and dark, like that of the buffalo, but has a good taste; is nutritious and easily digested. This animal, like the buffalo, is gregarious in its habits. They go in large droves, and can be easily taken if the leader is first killed by the hunter. The leader is, generally, some old doe. If the hunter is successful in finding her out and shooting her, the whole drove is thrown into confusion and easily captured; but if he be mistaken, on the first alarm they bound away with the velocity almost of lightning, and run three or four miles in a straight line without stopping. They are very sagacious. If an old buck is wounded he will fight most desperately, and woe betide the man who comes within the swing of his horns. The skin of the elk serves many useful and valuable purposes.

The bear seems to be *sui generis*, bearing no particular resemblance to any other animal in this country. They are generally black, and when fat their skins are well covered with a loose fur. The flesh of the bear is the most delicious, as well as the most nutritious, of any food.

When they are fattened on beech-nuts, the oil of this animal is the most penetrating of any in the world. The bear seems to be an awkward, clumsy, inactive animal; but this is far from being the case, as any one has reason to know who has been chased by them. They can climb the highest trees with great facility. When lean they can run with great rapidity and fight with tremendous fury, especially when wounded or bereaved of their cubs. They will become immensely fat on good mast, so much so that it is sometimes difficult for them to move very quickly. When rendered thus unwieldy, they will, by a peculiar instinct, seek some cave in a rock or hollow tree, where they will hibernate; and about the latter part of March, waking from their winter's sleep, they will come forth to greet the opening spring.

Should they wake at any time during the winter, they will not leave their place, but suck their fore-paws till they fall asleep again. After dissection, the alimentary canal has been found to contain from one to two gallons of oil. This oil is pure and unmixed. Various conjectures have been given to account for the existence of this oil; but the most plausible is, that it is taken up by the absorbent vessels and thrown into the canal for the purpose of supplying the wants of nature in the absence of food. If they have young ones they will remain longer in and about their winter quarters. When they come out they seek for some green vegetables, especially for the nettle-weed, which they take as a medicine for its purgative properties. She bears have from one to three cubs. At first they are quite small, not much larger than a kitten. They are destitute of hair, and blind till about the tenth day. Of all the young animals I have ever seen they are the most uncomely. Notwithstanding their ungainly appearance, the mother is tenderly attached to her cubs, and will protect them to the last.

Bears seldom go in droves or herds, except in the month of August, at which time they are considered by the hunters as the most ravenous. The cubs usually stay with their dams about a year, when they start out to seek a living for themselves. These animals display a wonderful instinct. They seem not only to be competent judges of the best kind of mast, but they know exactly where to find it. They will go as directly from one part of the country to the other, in quest of food, as though they understood thoroughly its geography. They act with wonderful concert; and if one bear finds a place where mast is good and plenty, all in the woods will be apprised of it in some way or other. They all seem to start at once, and no two of them together; but they all take the same course and arrive at the same place. They prefer the beech-nut to any other food; next to this the chestnut and chestnut oak; then the acorn. If all these nuts happen to be plentiful in one year, the hunter knows precisely where to go to find the game, as all kind of game prefer the beech-nut. Should there be no beech mast, then he must go to the chestnut, and if these fail, to the white and black oak woods. These things form part of the hunter's study.

These animals become very poor in the summer and live on lesser animals, if they can take them, or upon the wild honey which they take from the yellow-jacket or humblebee. They will turn over large logs in quest of this food. The sting of the bees does not deter them, especially if hungry. They will get all the honey, and then hasten to a bear-wallow or a branch of water, and throwing themselves into the same, will thus get rid of their assailants. At this season of the year they attack the swine, and have been known to carry off large hogs. Sometimes they are defeated when they get into a drove of hogs. Instead of running they will attack them, and frequently bruin has to run for a tree to save his life Once my comrade in the woods heard a wonderful noise among a gang of hogs, and they came running from al. quarters, attracted by the grunting and squealing. He crept up softly to see what was the cause of all this commotion, and found that they had treed a bear, who had stolen a pig from the gang. He shot at the bear and wounded him. Bruin, letting go all holds, fell to the ground, whereupon a hot contest ensued, in which the swine were victorious, tearing their enemy to pieces without mercy. They were also very troublesome in our cornfields about roasting-ear time—entering them in the night and destroying the corn. They sometimes attacked persons and killed them. The hunter, or backwoodsman, for all backwoodsmen were hunters, made his summer bacon out of bear-meat. He would take out the fat and salt it—if he had salt—and then hang it up to smoke. The fat was rendered into oil, which was put away in deer skins, neatly and cleanly dressed, for the purpose. This oil served many valuable purposes to the hunter, supplying the place of butter and hog's lard. He could fry his venison and turkey in it; and if he had neither of these, it was admirable sop for his corn-dodger; and when mixed with his jerk and parched corn, was regarded as one of the greatest delicacies of a hunter's larder.

The bear is hunted with dogs, and if they are well trained but few will escape. They are remarkably afraid of the dogs; and as they will attack them no where else than at their hind legs, which are very tender, they tree as soon as possible, and generally remain till the hunter can come up and shoot them. Sometimes, however, they will let go and fall fifty or sixty feet without doing themselves the slightest injury. Often, when fat, they go to a hole in a tree and must be sought for. A well-trained hunter can tell by the marks of the claws in the bark of the tree, whether the bear is holed or not. A tree or sapling is fallen and lodged against the one in which is the bear. If a tree should be near, the hunter takes a long, slim pole, attaches some spunk or rotten wood to it, climbs up as far as the hole, and, igniting the end, sets fire to the hole, which is filled with rotten wood. He then descends and gets his gun, and awaits the appearance of bruin, who, being unable to stand the fire, rushes out in great rage and meets his fate.

If he has made his den in the rocks, greater caution is necessary; for if he should only be wounded, the hunter must be prepared for a swift retreat or a single combat with spear or tomahawk. These animals, in the fall, before the time of mast, climb up trees, pull in the limbs, and gather the fruit, which is called lopping. Often the hunter steals up and kills them; but if they should happen to see him before he fires they let all go and fall down.

Some fifty-six years ago, one of the first emigrants to Kentucky went out to cut a broomstick and saw a bear lopping. He concluded he could kill it with his ax, and crawling up noiselessly to the root of the tree, he no sooner arrived there than down came bruin at his feet. Mr. M. immediately made a blow with his ax, but it was dexterously warded off by the bear and wrested out of his hands. The bear then seized him by the left arm and disabled it. It then made an effort to seize him by the face, but the intrepid hunter caught the nose of the bear in his teeth and held him fast. In the struggle he was thrown down, but not disheartened; he thrust his thumb into the eyes of the bear and gouged them both out of their sockets. Bruin screamed most piteously, and soon help came, when it was killed and the hunter relieved from his perilous position. Some years after, some of Mr M.'s friends coming out to the west asked him,

"How do you and the bears make it?" His reply was, "They can't stand Kentucky play. Biting and gouging are too hard for them."

The deer is the most beautiful wild animal that roams in American forests. They change their color three times a year, and every winter they cast their horns. The color they assume in the spring is red, in the fall it is blue, and in the winter it is gray. Their skins are the most valuable when in the red or blue. In the gray they are worth but little. The meat of this animal is the sweetest and most easily digested of all animal food. Who does not like venison? Besides, they are decidedly the cleanest of all animals, living entirely upon vegetables. No vegetable poison affects them, and they live all winter upon laurel. There is something exceedingly strange in their animal economy. They have no gall, and, therefore, do not need this agent to digest their food. They herd more in the winter than in summer. The does have seldom more than two fawns, whose skins are covered with white and red spots. They are careful to keep from their enemies, which are many, and among which man is not the least. The fawns have no scent by which they can be tracked by the wolf or the dog; and as the dam leaves them when very young, this constitutes a great preservative. When they are hungry they bleat like a lamb, and the low wail falling upon the keen and sensitive ear of the mother, she hastens to supply her young with food, which being accomplished she leaves them again.

About June they begin to follow the doe, and soon learn to run from their pursuers. The dam is often decoyed and shot by the crafty hunter, whose fawn-like bleating brings her immediately into his presence. The death-dealing ball pierces the mother's heart, and the fawn is left to perish without her care. In giving this sound of distress, it often happens that other animals seeking prey

THE DEER.

are attracted by it, and, coming together, a terrible conflict ensues. The hungry panther and bear, or the bear and wolf, meet in deadly conflict, and one or the other falls a prey to the hunter who witnesses the scene.

Once, in company with my comrade, we were traveling in the woods, and having a load of meat on our backs we sat down to rest ourselves. While we were resting, I said to my companion, "John, these logs—having been newly turned over—look as though a bear might be in the vicinity. Suppose I bleat him up." "Do," said he. I then made a noise like a fawn in distress, and soon we heard the brush cracking. "Here he comes," said I, and, sure enough, old bruin made his appearance. Coming within two rods of where we were standing, he rose upon his hind feet, and placing his fore feet on a log looked all around for his prey. A ball from one of our rifles soon dispatched him.

I have often brought wolves within gunshot in like manner.

But we are not done with the history of the deer. The skin was manufactured into almost all kinds of clothing, such as hunting-shirts, waistcoats, pantaloons, leggins, petticoats, moccasins, sieves, wallets, and, sometimes, shirts. It was perhaps to the backwoods families the most useful of all animals. The dressing of deer skins did not require a long process. As soon as the skin was off the deer's back, while yet warm and green, was the best time to begin the graining process, which was as follows: The brains of the animal were dried on a board before the fire, then they were put into a cloth and washed out in warm water, which made a kind of suds, into which the skin was put, and after being well rubbed was taken out and wrung as dry as possible. Then it was pulled and worked over a board, made for the purpose, till it was dry. It was then taken again through the same process, with the exception that the brain water was stronger, and worked till it became soft, when it was hung up and smoked with rotten hickory wood for a short time, and was then ready for use. The ladies had but little time to devote to making clothes for the gentlemen, and but little was required, as the fashions were then as simple as the material out of which the clothes were made. They generally cut out the garment with a butcher-knife and used an awl in the place of a needle, and the sinews of the deer instead of thread. With this article the moccasins are always made when they are made neatly, though sometimes they were made with a whang cut from the skin. A hunting-shirt made of this article will wear a long time. The hunting-shirt is a very comfortable garment in cold weather, and when worn awhile and well saturated with deer's tallow or bear's oil, will turn the rain like a goose's back; and for the brush and green-brier there is nothing so good.

The deer is taken by what is called still-hunting. Great skill is necessary in being able to find out and accommodate one's self to the habits of this animal. A skillful hunter can generally tell by the weather and the direction of the wind, where to go to find deer. As they are very watchful, it takes a noiseless step and a good look-out to steal a march upon them. As they often go to licks, hunters make blinds near by in which they conceal themselves. A great many are killed at night, being decoyed by the light of a fire. For this purpose a fire is built in the bow of a canoe, which is left to float down the stream. The hunter can steer it directly toward them. The deer on the shore, becoming fascinated by the light, will gaze upon it till the canoe comes directly against them. This is generally considered an unfair way of hunting, and it is not used by the regular hunter.

The panther, though much dreaded, is a fearful animal, and unless wounded will run at the first appearance of

THE WOLF.

THE RACCOON.

man or dog, and will tree as quick as a cat. When sud denly surprised, however, it is dangerous. It is carnivorous, and makes prey of the lesser animals of the forest When hungry it is exceedingly ferocious and ravenous, and will attack a man. Their proper mode of attack is made by leaping from a tree upon their victim. They select a tree near to a deer-lick or path, and watch till they see the prey. When sufficiently near, with fearful precision they spring from their hiding-place upon the back of their victim, and fastening their long claws and teeth in the body, they hold them till they are exhausted with pain and fatigue and yield to death. They watch their prey, and will fight for it to the last. Their flesh is good to eat, and their skins, when well tanned, make good razor-strops and tolerably good shoes.

The wolf is the most sneaking and thievish of all animals, and of the least use. He is seldom seen in the day-time, but prowls about and howls all night. He lives a prey on the world, is remarkably cowardly, and will never attack unless he has greatly the advantage, or is forced to fight. The wolf, like all useless animals and obnoxious things, is very prolific, and were it not for their almost constant state of starvation, would soon fill the world. They have a kind of instinctive dialect. When they have been disappointed in seeking their prey, they will set up the most terrific and hideous howling. One of them can make such a chorus of howls as to make you think there are a dozen. Their skin is worth but little, except, it is said, it is good for drum-heads; and their flesh is never eaten, except by those who may be in a starving condition.

The raccoon is a valuable animal, both as an article of food and for the fur. Its color is grayish. Its skin, including, of course, the fur, in early times, was in good demand, and the backwoodsmen used it as a kind of circulating medium in the absence of coin and bank notes, and it was universally current, always being considered a lawful tender. Four coon-skins were considered a dollar, and such were vastly more valuable than an Owl Creek or Red Dog bank note, which often proved, to the possessor, to be of no more value than a rag. The coon is domesticated with little labor, but he is quite mischievous as well as cunning and shy. Coons live on mast, and sometimes on flesh. They are great lovers of poultry, and understand well the art of robbing a hen-roost. They are fond also, like the Frenchman, of frogs, which they catch with great dexterity, and which they prepare for their meals with all the nicety of an epicurean. They are fond also of corn, and will enter the field and help themselves bountifully. Many were the sports, in an early day, connected with coon-hunting. They are a nocturnal animal, and hence they are hunted in the night. Dogs, well trained to the business, will find them and tree them. When this is accomplished, the next thing is to cut down the tree or send up some one to shake them off. Many are the anecdotes that are told of coon-hunters. A laughable one is related of a clerical friend of mine during his younger days. He was out with a party one night coon-hunting, and the dogs having treed an old coon, it was determined, by the party, that our friend should climb the tree and shake him off, so that the dogs might catch him. Accordingly he ascended, and stealing softly from branch to branch, in search of the coon, he finally espied him snugly ensconsed on one of the topmost branches, a somewhat interested spectator of the scene which was transacting below. Proceeding cautiously, he reached the limb below that on which was the coon. Raising himself up for the purpose of reaching the limb which he intended to shake, the one on which he stood was heard to crack and began to give way. He was now thirty feet from the ground. Aware of his perilous condition, he cried out to his companions below, "I'm falling." Seeing his danger and that nothing scarcely less than a miracle could save him from death, they besought him to pray. "Pray," said he; "I haven't time; I can't pray." "But you must pray. If you fall, you will be killed." He then commenced repeating the only prayer he knew: "Now I lay me down to sleep;" but he could proceed no further, as the cracking of the limb indicated its speedy severance from the trunk, and he cried out at the top of his voice, "Hold the dogs; I'm coming." And sure enough, down he came with a crash; and the dogs, thinking it to be the coon, were with difficulty restrained from attacking the coon-hunter, who was considerably stunned by the fall.

A negro obtained permission from his master to start out coon-hunting one night, and on seeing his master in the morning, who was anxious to know about his success, related the following: "Well, massa, you know I treed de coon, and I climbs up to shake him off de limb. When I got by him, I begins to shake, and presently I hearn something drap, and what does you think it was, massa?" "Why, the coon to be sure." "No it wan't, massa; it was dis here nigga." It appears that, instead of shaking off the coon, he shook himself off.

Coons are sometimes caught in traps and dead-falls. A hunter will sometimes make a great many, and go round twice a week to examine them, and in this way will take from ten to twenty at a time. Another plan is adopted late in the fall, which is to make fire-hunts; which is done by setting fire to the leaves in a circle including an area of several miles. As this fire advances toward the center, it drives the coons up the trees, and the deer and other game are brought together into what is called a pound, where they are shot.

The opossum is an ugly and deceitful animal. If you strike him, he will roll over, and appear as if dead, and as soon as you leave him he starts up and hastens to his den. His tail is entirely bare, and serves many good purposes to the animal. He is not easily shaken off a tree, like the coon, but clings to it with the greatest tenacity, winding his tail around the limb, and defying all efforts to shake him down. A hard-shell Baptist preacher once introduced this animal into his discourse, to illustrate the doctrine of final perseverance. The female opossum has a kind of sack, in which she carries her young. The flesh of this animal is like that of the young pig; the oil is abundant, and answers well to burn in lamps, or grease harness. The flesh of the opossum and new corn mush was considered a most delicate dish among backwoods families. Their skins, when dressed, are as white as the skin of the chamois, and make fine gloves for backwoods ladies.

A hunter's life is one of constant excitement. He is always on the look-out, and filled with constant expectation. His narratives always possess a thrilling interest, and are listened to with the greatest attention. His wants are but few, and he is not disturbed with cankering care about the future. His employment does not lead him to covetousness, and he is always characterized by a generous hospitality. His hut or cabin is always a sure asylum for the hungry and destitute. Who ever crossed its threshold, and was turned away unfed and uncared for? The poor and the stranger will feel much better in the log-cabin, partaking of its hospitalities by a cheerful fire, than when surrounded by the cold constraint of a nabob's table. With these sons and daughters of nature will be found the genuine hospitalities of nature's noblemen.

I will close this chapter with a few remarks on the dress of those days. The backwoodsman usually wore a hunting-shirt and trowsers made of buckskin, and moccasins of the same material. His cap was made of coonskin, and sometimes ornamented with a fox's tail. The ladies dressed in linsey-woolsey, and sometimes buckskin. A gradual improvement, however, took place in the manners and customs of the people.

About the period in which the British forces at Yorktown surrendered, the colonists were in a complete state of transition. Commerce began to revive. Many small prizes were taken by the American cruisers, brought in, condemned, and sold. Many merchant vessels, richly laden, sailing under the protection of the French flag, reached in safety their ports of destination; and the merchandise thus brought in soon found its way into the interior, and was exchanged for skins, furs, ginseng, black and Seneca snake roots, sarsaparilla, etc. In search of those roots the mountains were traversed, and employment given to vast numbers of persons.

The effects from thence resulting soon manifested themselves in the improved dress of the females, as well as in the furniture of each household, and in many other particulars. Singing and common reading schools began to be encouraged, and males and females vied with each other in the culture of their intellects, conversational powers, and address. There were several ancient families in Oldtown and its vicinity, who, in early life, had been well educated, whose wealth enabled them to procure the richest articles of dress and furniture to be had in the cities. By them the ancient customs and fashions of the English were kept up, till modified or changed by the introduction of French customs and manners.

Prior to the commencement of the transition indicated, the dress of females, as at present, greatly differed. Among the laboring classes, the usual summer dress consisted of a tow or linen chemise, short gown, and petticoat, which extended down a little below the calf of the leg, without stockings or shoes. The hair was either tied in a hard knot on the nape of the neck, or plaited and confined on the top of the head; and their toilet was completed either with or without a coarse neckerchief. The dress on gala days of those who moved in the higher circles of society also varied. Their shoes differed from those worn by ladies of the present day in this: they had high heels. Those heels were made of wood, beautifully tapered, neatly covered with leather, and varied in hight from one to two inches. The under clothing was confined by stays, tightly laced. The outer covering was composed of the richest brocade, or other silks and satins, and stomacher, neckerchief, gloves, rings, and ruffles in profusion. The hair was combed forward, and a cushion, suited to the form of the head, varying from three to six inches in hight, was placed upon the top of the head, over which the hair was neatly spread, and fastened behind with a comb and ribbons, by which a rich, towering plume of feathers was also fastened. A lady in full dress, entering a drawing-room, would appear to be as tall as a May-pole, if not as cadaverous as a death's head. The bonnet was of enormous size, and usually measured from three to three and a half feet in circumference. Hence, against the form of dressing here indicated, the rule in the Methodist Discipline was framed: "Give no tickets to any who wear high heads, enormous bonnets, ruffles, or rings." The rule has become a dead letter among preachers and people.

CHAPTER IV.

NARRATIVE CONTINUED.

In the summer of 1794 General Wayne crossed the mountains with an army, for the purpose of quelling the Indians. After a successful battle, in which "Mad Anthony," as the Indians termed him, became a terror to all the tribes, he was enabled to effect a treaty with them at Greenville. This gave the country rest and quiet from the horrors of Indian war, and brought about a new era in the history of the west.

Immigration poured into Kentucky like a flood, and vast multitudes engaged in land speculation. Whole tracts of country were sold by these speculators with or without title, and thousands were stripped of their all. Dispossession was carried on to so great a length that many became utterly dissatisfied, having bought their farms two or three times over, and they began to look elsewhere for a habitation.

The North-western territory was beginning to open to western enterprise, and my father and his congregation resolved to seek a new home. Many of them had paid every farthing they had for land; had encountered all the dangers of an Indian warfare in settling it, and had spent the vigor of their strength in clearing and bringing it under cultivation; and just when they found themselves beginning to live comfortably, some other claimant would come and dispossess them of their homes. In vain did they seek redress of those from whom they purchased; for more frequently than otherwise did it happen that he was some land harpie himself. So odious did those men become, who engaged in land speculation, that they were looked upon generally as a class of villains; and whenever the poor farmer went to search for them they were gone, and they had hopelessly to return, and in a penniless condition seek a new home.

In view of this state of things, my father addressed the following letter to General Massie, for a copy of which I am indebted to his son, N. Massie, Esq., of Chilicothe:

"BOURBON COUNTY, KY., *December* 12, 1794.

"SIR,—After compliments to you, I take the liberty of addressing you for information. I understand you have a large quantity of land on the Scioto and Paint creek for sale. I would be pleased to know its qualities, and what advantages two large societies could have. A number have thought of purchasing fifteen or twenty miles square for the settlement of two congregations, and have been informed that you could supply us. Sir, I request the favor of you, by Mr. Rogers, the bearer, to furnish me with the situation, quality, and the quantity you could sell, and what would be your price per hundred acres, and what your terms of payment, by taking such a quantity of land as would be sufficient to settle two congregations, or say three hundred families. But it is probable the present circumstances of the country would require some time to make a settlement in it with prudence. You will please let me know at what time this winter it would meet your convenience to go with us and show us these lands. A number of us would love to see the advantages which the country will afford for such a settlement. Your compliance will much oblige your humble servant,

"ROBT. W. FINLEY.

"MR. NATHANIEL MASSIE, ESQ."

The next spring was fixed on by the parties to visit the country and explore the land.

Accordingly, while General Wayne was treating with the Indians, at Greenville, a company of forty persons met at Manchester, on the Ohio river, with the intention of exploring the Scioto country. General Massie was the principal in this expedition. My father and several of his congregation formed a part of the company. After proceeding cautiously for a number of days, in a northerly direction, they reached Paint creek near the falls. This stream is a tributary of the Scioto, and, with the Scioto, waters one of the finest agricultural countries in the world. Here they discovered fresh traces of Indians, the signs being such as to indicate that they could not be far off. They had not proceeded far till they heard the bells on their horses. Some of the company were what was called new hands, and previous to this had been very anxious to smell Indian powder. One of the old men remarked, on witnessing their anxiety, "If you get a sight of the Indians you will run, or I am mistaken." A council was called of the most experienced in Indian warfare, and the result of their deliberations was, that it was too late to retreat with safety and without great danger. They resolved, as the best possible course, to attack the enemy by surprise. It was agreed that General Massie, Fallenash, and my father should take the command and lead on the men, and Captain Petty was to bring up the rear.

The Indians were encamped on the bank of Paint creek precisely where the turnpike now crosses it, at what was called Reeves's old crossing. Out of the forty in company only about twenty engaged in battle. Those who were so anxious to smell Indian powder retreated, and Captain Patte reported them as having taken refuge between old logs and other defenses, trembling with fear. The remainder advanced cautiously till within fifty yards, when they fired and rushed into the Indians' camp. Astounded by this attack, the Indians fled down the bank and across the stream, many of them leaving their guns Several were killed and wounded. One of the company—Mr. Robinson—was shot, and died in a few minutes. The Indians were Shawnees, and would not go to the treaty. They had a prisoner with them, who, in the fight, made his escape, and finally succeeded in reaching his home. His name was Armstrong. As soon as the company could bury the dead and gather up the horses and plunder of the Indians, they directed their course to Manchester; but night overtook them on Scioto Brush creek, and as they expected to be followed by the Indians, they stopped and made the necessary preparations for defense. The next morning, an hour before daylight, the Indians made their appearance, and opened upon them a vigorous fire, which was promptly and vigorously returned. Those who would not fight took shelter from the balls of the enemy in a large sink-hole in the bounds of the encampment. After a hot contest, which lasted an hour, the Indians were repulsed and fled. One of the party of the whites was wounded in the battle, but not mortally. As soon as preparations could be made for departure they left, and the next day reached Manchester, and thus ended the expedition for that time.

In the spring of 1796, about the last of April, another company met at Manchester for the purpose of proceeding to the Scioto Valley and raising a crop of corn, and making other preparations for removing in the fall or winter, and so make a permanent settlement. Some of this company proceeded by land, and others by water. Those who took the land route took their horses well ladened, and those who went by water carried the farming utensils and the necessary breadstuffs. There was no road, not even a path or a way blazed through the deep forest. In all the route there was no inhabitant. All was a perfect and continuous wilderness to Wheeling, Virginia.

Near where the town of West Union now stands, there was one cabin built by Mr. Oiler, but no one lived in it. The pioneers, however, entered upon their journey, and found their way without much difficulty, arriving safe at the place of their destination, which was a beautiful prairie, below where Chilicothe now stands, called the Station prairie. Their companions, after a laborious voyage up the Scioto, arrived safely and joined the overland party. Theirs were the first crafts of the white man that stemmed the rapids of the Scioto. Here in this prairie the plow of the white man first turned up the virgin soil. The prairie being plowed, the corn was planted, and all that the husbandman had to do, was to brush down the weeds with a wooden harrow. With such simple cultivation a large crop was produced. Mr. Kilgore raised on one acre one hundred and twenty-five bushels of corn without any fence to inclose his field.

During this summer General Massie laid out the town of Chilicothe, and Mr. John M'Coy raised the first log-cabin. This pioneer habitation was followed by several others during the fall and winter. The place where Chilicothe now stands was a hickory flat, and so plentiful were the nuts that they might have been raked up in almost any quantity.

This fall Mr. Zane, by a contract with the Government, marked out a trace, through the wilderness, from Wheeling to Maysville. This was done by merely blazing the trees and bushes; and with this guide the traveling commenced. Soon great companies passed over Zane's trace, and settlements were made at the Muskingum river, where the town of Zanesville now stands, and also on Wills creek. There were several points toward which the attention of the emigrant was directed; such, for instance, as the Muskingum, Hock-Hocking, and Scioto Valleys, with their tributaries. The population in these valleys in creased with a rapidity unknown to any country before so great, that, in a period of fifty years, from a population of three thousand, Ohio has increased to two millions. The blazed road of the white man and the war-path of the Indian have been cleared out and paved with stone, over which roll post-coaches at the rate of ten miles an hour; or have been laid with iron tracks, over which the locomotive with its numerous cars attached is propelled at the rate of forty miles an hour. Beside this, canals, extending across the state, have united the waters of the lakes of the north with the rivers of the south. Splendid steamers, resembling floating palaces, which make the earth tremble with the thunder of their steam and the roar of their machinery, covered with passengers, and freighted with the commerce of the world, have taken the place of the canoe, the broadhorn, and the keel-boat, as coaches, canal boats, and railroad cars have taken the place of the pack-horse, the ox-cart, and the covered wagon. Instead of the log-cabin with its rude furniture, we have stately palaces with the most elegant and costly furniture; the tables of which groan with the luxuries of every clime. Instead of villages with trees, stumps, and bear-wallows in the streets, we have magnificent cities with streets extending for miles, all paved, and brilliantly illuminated with gas, the burners of which are almost as numerous as the fire-flies which illuminated our meadows in olden times. Instead of the tedious process of the mail department, by which it took a letter several weeks to reach the seat of government, now the lightning, which had been caught by our Franklin, domesticated, and taught to speak by our Morse, will carry not only our words, but our very thoughts over plains, rivers, valleys, and mountains—outstripping the horses and chariots of fire—almost instantly from one extreme of the continent to the other, annihilating space, and distancing time itself.

Such a change never entered the most fervent imagination of our backwoodsmen; and he who would have intimated the possibility of such a thing, would have been set down as a lunatic. All we hoped for or expected, was to have some rich farms in these luxuriant bottoms, and always plenty of deers and bear on our hills. Even this was not likely to be realized, for immigration poured in upon us like the locusts of Egypt, and threatened to devour every thing. Keel-boats commenced running up the Scioto river, and we were constantly advised, by the boatman's horn, of their arrival and departure.

William Craig was the first man who drove a wagon and team to Chilicothe, over Zane's trace. It was a most tedious and difficult undertaking; for he had to cut his way through for a distance of seventy miles. Patience and perseverance, however, had its reward, and he with his family finally succeeded in reaching the encampment.

It would be impossible for me to describe the beauty of these rich bottoms. The soil itself for richness was not exceeded by any in the world. The lofty sugar-tree, spreading its beautiful branches; the graceful elm, waving its tall head, the monarch of the forest; the black and white walnut; the giant oak, the tall hickory; the cherry and hackberry; the spicewood, with its fragrance; the papaw, with its luscious fruit; the wild plum; the rich clusters of grapes, which, hanging from the massy vines, festooned the forest; and, beneath all, the wild rye, green as a wheat-field, mixed with the prairie and buffalo clover—all formed a garden of nature most enchanting to behold. The clear and beautiful rivulet creeping through the grass, and softly rippling over pebbly bottoms, the gentle zephyrs freighted with nature's incense, pure and sweet, regaled our senses, and filled us with delight. All nature had a voice which spoke most impressively to the soul, and while all the senses were pervaded with an unutterable delight, the solemn stillness seemed to say, *God reigns here.* The song of the lark and nightingale, the melancholy wail of the dove or whistle of the whippowil, the low hum of the bee, the chirping of the grasshopper, the bark of the squirrel, the drumming of the pheasant, the bleat of the fawn, the growl of the bear, the hoot of the owl, the howl of the wolf, the scream of the panther, and the yell of the Indian, were all that broke the silence in this deep and beautiful forest.

Although I had parted with my Kentucky home and her favorite cane-brakes, my much-loved school-mates and playfellows, with great reluctance, yet when I was introduced to the delightful scenes in Ohio, my tears were all dried up, and the beautiful cane-brakes were cheerfully resigned for the rich and more beautiful meadows enameled with flowers of every hue. I shall never forget the first night I took up my lodgings in the valley of Paint creek. It was near the falls. A large flock of wild geese, on their passage, had stopped for the night, and were sporting in the foaming waters just below the falls. They seemed to have met by concert, to hold a soiree or feast of rejoicing at the approach of spring. It was a calm and quiet day. The sun was throwing his last gentle rays among the branches of the towering elms which lined the banks of this beautiful stream, and the heavens were tinged with his mellow beams, just as we arrived at our destination, and unloading our horses, we unstopped their bells, and turned them out to feed on the grass and wild rye of the bottom. Soon the shades of night gathered around us. With spunk and steel we soon struck up a cheerful fire, and taking the corn-bread and bacon from our sacks, with the cool water of the rivulet which glided by us, we slaked our thirst and had a good repast. After talking over the adventures of the day we rolled ourselves up in blankets and went into a refreshing slumber which lasted undisturbed till the gray beams of morning admonished us of the hour to rise. Resuming our journey, we proceeded down main Paint creek, and in the afternoon of the same day reached our destination.

With all the richness of the country, the beauty of its birds and flowers, the softness of the climate, and the fragrance of the atmosphere, redolent as Eden, still it was earth, and the effects of sin had reached this charming abode. The new settlements were regularly visited with autumnal fevers. They were of the bilious type, and, sometimes, the symptoms resembled those of yellow fever. Bilious intermittents, or fever and ague, prevailed to a great extent. These were supposed to have been caused by the effluvia arising from the decomposition of the luxuriant vegetation which grew so abundantly every-where. These fevers were attended with great mortality, and the sufferings occasioned by them were immense. Often there was not one member of the family able to help the others; and instances occurred in which the dead lay unburied for days, because no one could report. The extensive prevalence of sickness, however, did not deter immigration. A desire to possess the rich lands overcame all fear of sickness, and the living tide rolled on heedless of death. In the summer of 1798 the bloody flux raged as an epidemic with great violence, and for a while threatened to depopulate the whole town of Chilicothe and its vicinity. Medical skill was exerted to its utmost, but all to no purpose, as but very few who were attacked recovered. From eight to ten were buried per day. At length a French trader, by the name of Drouillard, came and administered to the sick with great success, giving relief in a few hours, and, in almost every case, effecting a permanent cure.

During this summer an event occurred in Chilicothe

very unfavorable to the peace and safety of the country Mr. Stoops, preparatory to opening a house of entertainment, called together his neighbors for the purpose of raising his house a story higher. In the evening an Indian, of the Wyandott nation, somewhat intoxicated, came into town and behaved himself very rudely at the raising He was reprimanded by Mr. Thomas Thompson, who was a very athletic man. The Indian drew his knife, and, concealing the blade of it in his arm sleeve, waited his opportunity to attack Thompson. A person who observed him advised him to leave for the camp; for if Thompson should find out that he had drawn his knife he would kill him. The Indian mounted his horse, but refused to leave the place. Some one informed Thompson of his danger, and he immediately seized a handspike, and, striking the Indian on the head, felled him to the earth. That night the Indian died of his wounds and was carried to the Indian encampment. As soon as the Indians learned the cause of his death they immediately demanded Thompson, that they might punish him according to their law, which was life for life; and informed the town that if he was not given up they would fall on the place and murder, in revenge, men, women, and children, which they could easily have done, as they were much more numerous than the whites. Some of the inhabitants were for complying, but the majority were opposed to it. After some considerable consultation it was agreed to try another method, which was to buy the life of the murderer by making presents to the relations of the murdered, and promising to punish the murderer according to our law. This plan succeeded, and Thompson was placed under guard of four men, there being no jail there at that time. After some two months he was permitted to make his escape, and one of the guards went with him. The half-brother of the deceased determining to avenge the death of his brother, took with him another Indian, and waylaying Zane's trace, they found two young men traveling alone, whom they killed and robbed of their horses and effects; and thus two innocent men paid the debt of a murderer, who, under the influence of whisky, committed the crime. Such were some of the evils and dangers brought on the community by strong drink.

The first public house, or hotel, kept in Chilicothe, was by a man by the name of Benjamin Urmstedt. The first store was kept by Mr. John M'Dougal. The first Presbyterian minister was the Rev. Robert W. Finley, and the first Methodist ministers were the Rev. Messrs. Harr and Tiffin. The first physician was Dr. Samuel M'Adow. The first Legislature met on the bank of the Scioto river, near the mouth of Mulberry-street, under a large sycamore-tree. This was entirely democratic, as the people represented themselves. The principal matter which occupied the attention of this Legislature, was the enactment of a law for the suppression of drunkenness. It was the custom of the traders to give and sell whisky to the Indians, and the consequence was, that many of them became intoxicated; and as a drunken Indian is a dangerous creature, the peace of society was disturbed and the women and children were in a constant state of alarm, day and night. After mature deliberation and free discussion, it was enacted that all traders who sold spirits to the Indians, or in any way furnished them with intoxicating liquors, should be required to keep all the Indians made drunk by them in their own storehouse till they were sober, on penalty, for the first offense, of being reprimanded by two persons appointed for that purpose, and on the second offense, their kegs or barrels of whisky, or strong drink, were to be taken into the street and tomahawked till all the contents were run out. This law was set at naught by one of the traders, a Mr. M., but it was promptly executed to the letter the next day after the sentence. This vigorous maintenance of the law, on the part of the citizens, made the traders more cautious, and gave more safety and comfort to the inhabitants.

I will give an instance of another somewhat novel punishment adopted in those times. A certain man stole some clothes from Mr. Crawford, and started out on the trace toward Zanesville. He was followed and overtaken with the clothes, which he had in his possession. A court was organized, and he had a fair trial by a jury of his own selection, who found him guilty, and sentenced him to ten lashes upon his bare back, or, if he preferred it, to mount a pack-saddle on his pony, and his wife—who was a *particeps criminis*—was to take it by the halter and lead it to every door in town, and cry aloud, "This is Brannon, who stole the big coat, handkerchief, and shirt." He chose the latter, which was executed fully.

In the fall of 1796 my father set all his slaves free. He had been for years convinced that it was wrong to hold his fellow-men in bondage, and thus deprive them of their natural rights; and he was particularly impressed with the belief that there could be no civil regulation authorizing the possession of human beings as goods and chattels, that would justify a minister of the Gospel in living upon the sweat, and blood, and tears of his fellow-beings, as dear to Christ as himself, bought with the same precious blood, and destined to the same eternity of existence. Nor could he bear the idea, for a moment, of involving his children in the evils of slavery. Not, however, till the present period, of which I am writing, had arrived, had he the opportunity of carrying out the doctrines of practical emancipation. My grandfather having died and willed all his slaves to my mother and her children, making my father the sole executor of the estate, he immediately went to Paris, Ky., and executed a deed of emanci nation to all the slaves, from the oldest to the youngest, amounting, in all, to fourteen. This being accomplished, he gave them all the offer of removing with him to the new country—as Ohio was then called—with provision for support for one year after their arrival; with but two exceptions of those who desired to remain in Kentucky, this offer was accepted.

Preparations being made for their removal, about the first of December in the year above named, twelve of the emancipated negroes were mounted on pack-horses, and started for Ohio. My father placed me in charge of the company, though I was but sixteen years of age. We carried with us clothes, bed-clothes, provisions, and cooking utensils. We were accompanied with parts of three families, with a great drove of hogs, cows, and sheep. After we crossed the Ohio river it became excessively cold; and, having no road but a path through the woods, we were not able to travel more than eight or ten miles per day. Some days we were under the necessity of lying by, it was so intensely cold. The colored people are, at best, a helpless race, and unable to stand the cold; and it was with difficulty that some of them were kept from freezing. After sixteen days of toil and hardship, we reached our place of destination on the bank of the Scioto below Chilicothe. Here we built our winter camps, making them as warm as we could. Our bread was made of pounded hominy and corn meal, and we lived on this together with what we could find in the woods. Fortunately for us, game was plenty, and we caught opossums by the score. The colored people lived well on this food, and were as sleek and black as the raven. In the spring my father and the rest of the family moved out, and, as soon as we could erect a cabin, all hands went to work to put in a crop of corn.

It was necessary to fence in the prairie, and every one

had to inclose with a fence as much ground as he had planted. The work of fencing fell to my lot. Myself and another lad built a camp, in which we lodged at night and cooked our provisions. We frequently killed turkeys and wild ducks, with which we supplied our larder, and with our johnny-cake, baked on a board before the fire, we had a good supply for a vigorous appetite.

After our corn was gathered and laid by, the immigrants came pouring into the country. From that time to the beginning of March I traveled over the trace from Chilicothe to Manchester sixteen times. On one of these visits my brother John accompanied me, father having sent us by that route to Kentucky for seed-wheat. We took three horses with us, and after having procured the seed, we started back. On our homeward journey we found considerable difficulty in loading our horses with the bags. We could take them off when we stopped for the night, without any difficulty, but how to replace them when we wished to start in the morning, was not so easy a matter. Necessity, however, which is the mother of inventions, taught us a way by which the difficulty was obviated. It was this: when we wished to stop we would seek the largest logs, and unload upon them, by which means we had less difficulty in placing the bags on the backs of the horses. Thus we tugged our way through the wilderness, without seeing the face of a human being till we reached Paint creek. This wheat, I believe, was the first sown on the waters of the Scioto.

This year our horses ran away, and my father sent me in company with an Indian, whom he had employed for that purpose, to go and hunt them. We had not gone four miles from the settlement, before the Indian was bitten by a rattlesnake on the ankle, between his leggin and moccasin. It was one of the large, yellow kind, full of poison. As soon as the Indian killed his enemy, he took his knife, went a few paces, and dug up a root, the stalk of which resembled very much the stalk of flax, about nine inches long. The root was yellow and very slender, being no thicker than a knitting-needle. This root he chewed and swallowed. He then put more in his mouth, and after chewing it, put it upon the wound. Soon after he became deathly sick, and vomited. He repeated the dose three times, with the same result, and then putting some fresh root on the bite, we traveled on. The place where he was bitten after awhile became swollen, but it did not extend far, and soon subsided. This root is undoubtedly the most effectual cure for poison in the world—a specific antidote.

I frequently hunted with John Cushon, an Indian of the Tuscarora tribe, and had good living and much fine sport. I became so passionately fond of the gun and the woods, and Indian life, that my parents feared I would go off with the Indians and become connected with them. They were as fondly attached to me as I to them; and notwithstanding I had heard so much of their treachery and savage barbarity, I felt that I could repose the most implicit confidence in them. The mode of living and manner of life, which consisted in hunting the buffalo, bear, and deer in the wild woods and glens, free from care and the restraints of civilization, made Indian life to me most desirable; and so powerfully had these things taken hold of my youthful mind, that the advice and entreaties of my beloved parents could scarcely restrain me from following it. My filial affection, however, overcame the love of the chase, and I was persuaded to resume the study of medicine, which I had commenced in Kentucky. Let it not be supposed that, though I was a backwoods boy, I had not tasted of the sweets of classical literature. In my father's academy I enjoyed the advantages of a thorough drilling in Latin and Greek, and even now I can repeat whole books of the Æneid of Virgil and the Iliac of Homer. I could scan Latin or Greek verse with as much fluency as I can now sing a Methodist hymn; and I could find the square root of a given number with as much precision as in my youthful days I could drive a center with my rifle. And yet, strange to say, my English education was neglected. The first grammar placed in my hands was a Latin grammar, and I have no recollection of having studied the English grammar while a youth. Though I know it is said that the ancient languages are more readily acquired in youth, and boys when very young are taught the languages, yet I doubt the propriety of this early devotion to heathen classics at the expense of Christian English literature. I am not sorry that I was educated in classical literature, but I am sorry that I was not first well grounded in my vernacular.

In my father's academy, it being the first institution of learning in which the classics were taught in the western country, were many students who came from a distance; and among the number were the Howes, Robinsons, and M'Nemar, Dunlevy, Welsh, Steele, and Thompson, all of whom became Presbyterian preachers. Judges Trimble and Mills were educated here, and several students who afterward became doctors of medicine. Here my brother John and myself studied the Greek and Latin languages, and mathematics.

For the study of medicine I had, I confess, but little inclination. My heart was away in the woods, and an Indian, my dog and gun had more charms for me than anatomy, surgery, and physiology. I think it perfect folly to give a boy any trade or profession for which he has no inclination. However, as I did not wish to disoblige my parents, and did not wish to be a mere novice in any thing, I bent down to my studies, with a full determination to understand the theory of medicine, though

I never intended to practice it. My recreations were with the gun in the woods, or the gig in killing fish in the river, which abounded with perch, buffalo, pike, cat-fish, and sturgeon. At all the sports of those days I considered myself a full hand. I spent several months in the woods surveying Congress lands for Thomas Worthington, Esq., afterward governor of the state.

I finished my medical studies in the fall of 1800, and was admitted to practice. In connection with my preceptor, I visited and prescribed for many sick, and have vanity enough to believe that, had I continued, I would have made a respectable physician for the times. As I before remarked, not feeling at home in this profession, but being desirous of taking to the woods, I joined with three others and purchased a drove of fat cattle, and we started, in October, with them for the Detroit market. There were no roads, and we had to follow Indian paths from one village to another. We took the Indian path by Westfall to Franklinton, on the west bank of the Scioto, which has long since been outrivaled by the city of Columbus, and has gone into decay. Here we found several houses built by Dixon, Turner, Foose, Skidmore, and a few others. In consequence of the flies, which were exceedingly numerous and troublesome to the cattle in the woods, we remained here till November.

After leaving Franklinton we took the path to Delaware, where were the famous sulphur springs, which we reached the first day. Here, right around these ancient springs, we were obliged to sit on our horses all night to prevent the cattle from running back. The next day we reached the Sandusky plains. This was a rainy day, and in riding through the woods we were as wet as if we had been in the river; and in addition to all this, we had nothing to eat but a little corn-bread. We were chilled with the rain, and it was with the utmost difficulty we could start a fire. My companions despaired and began to wish themselves at home. My motto being *nil desperandum*, I rallied them, and persevering in hope against hope, at length the spark from the smitten steel took effect, and none but those placed in the same situation could appreciate our joy, kindled by the light of a blazing fire. Here, on the waters of the Scioto, we passed a tolerably-comfortable night. The next day we resumed our journey, and passed on through Upper Sandusky, Honey creek, and Lower Sandusky, till we reached the rapids of the Maumee, where we found a large Indian village. The inhabitants of this town had just finished their great fall dance and a drunken frolic, and were making preparations to start to their hunting-grounds. Being hungry and half starved, they demanded of us a steer for the privilege of driving through their country. I told them no, they could not have it, as the cattle were for the soldiers at Detroit. At this one of the Indians raised his rifle to shoot a steer, but riding instantly between him and the animal, I told him if he shot I would send a force of soldiers after him from Detroit, and he should be taken there to answer for his conduct. This had the desired effect, and we passed on unmolested. Continuing our journey, after a period of two weeks and five days, we arrived, with our drove, at the mouth of the river Rouge, five miles below Detroit, and in a few hours we found the end of our journey. The first thing, on arriving, was to effect a sale of the cattle. After six weeks, during all which time we lodged in a Frenchman's barn, we succeeded in selling our drove to a contractor of the army for a draft on the Government. Soon after the sale we left for home, with provisions sufficient to last us till we reached the Maumee rapids. Having arrived at this place, and our stock of provisions being exhausted, we found it impossible to purchase any; and taking a string of corn, on which we subsisted, together with some hazel-nuts, for two days, we arrived at Lower Sandusky. At this place we purchased of Whitaker a few quarts of flour and the half of a small deer. A short time before night we reached Honey creek, and concluded to stay there till morning. While my companions were engaged in disposing of the horses for the night, I kindled a fire and peeled some linn bark, and mixed up some flour to make what was called stick bread. This backwoods bread is made by peeling the bark off a stick, then wrapping the dough around it and turning it round before the fire, one end of the stick being in the ground. On this we made our evening's repast.

A short time after dark an Indian ran by our camp in great haste. His silence and conduct excited our suspicions that all was not right. As we had driven our stock to Detroit, it might be supposed, by the Indians, who were aware of this fact, that we might have money, and this, together with our horses, might be an object with some of the desperadoes that infested the Sanduskies. After we had partaken of our suppers, we caught our horses and took the path for Upper Sandusky. Pursuing our journey till midnight we came upon the camp of the Indian. He was much frightened at first, but he soon became composed, and we tarried all night together. The next day we resumed our journey, and, after passing through Franklinton, in a few days arrived safe at home.

In contrasting the present with the past, no one can fail to see what were the difficulties and dangers which the early pioneers encountered in traversing the country, and the courage and perseverance which were necessary in the various departments of life. Then there were no roads or means of transportation, and it took us nearly two months to perform the journey. Now, by railroad car and steamer, a drove of cattle could be transported in as many days from Cincinnati to Detroit, with greater facility. No one can read the discovery and settlement of this new country without being deeply interested. In reading of the adventurous struggles of the bold and hardy pioneers, an American becomes a party in all the thrilling scenes of border life. While contemplating the dangers of the wilderness, the terrors of savage war, the want and distress through which they passed, he is filled with admiration at their self-denial, and the perseverance which characterized them in surmounting the obstacles, enduring the hardships, and braving the dangers to which they were exposed, that they might turn this unbroken wilderness into fruitful fields and gardens, and transmit to posterity the inestimable blessings of civil and religious liberty. The pious mind can not fail to see a Divine hand overruling and conducting the whole. The people of the United States have more reason to be thankful to God than any other people; for "he hath not dealt so with any nation."

CHAPTER V.

BACKWOODS BIOGRAPHY.

If history be philosophy teaching by example, biography furnishes the examples which history records. I have already alluded to some of the early pioneers, and shall continue to weave into my narrative biographical sketches of such distinguished individuals of my times as I shall deem most interesting to my readers.

Captain Cassaday, of whom I have already spoken, was a native of Pennsylvania, and among the first intrepid adventurers to the cane-lands of Kentucky. He was a stout, well-formed man, and a valiant soldier. He settled about two miles from Stockton's Station, near where the town of Flemingsburg now stands. The place was called Cassaday's Station. At one time he was taken prisoner by the Indians. When a boy I have often heard him relate the circumstances connected with his captivity and escape. One day, while hunting in the woods, a party of Indians closed on him by surprise—for they were in ambuscade—and took him prisoner. They considered him a great prize; and, taking him across the Ohio river, they traveled, without stopping, two days in the wilderness. Having selected a place where to camp, they tied him to a tree; and, leaving him in care of an old Indian and some lads, they started out on a hunting expedition. By some means he succeeded in getting his hands loose, and, keeping an eye upon the old Indian and the boys, he next relieved himself of the tugs which were round his waist. The evening shades were gathering around the earth, and while the boys were picking up sticks for the fire, and the old Indian, wearied with fatigue, was nodding on his seat, Cassaday bounded from the tree, seized a gun and pouch, and before they had time to recover from their surprise, was lost to sight in the depths of the forest. The alarm was given; and the Indians returning, and finding their prisoner gone, started off in the direction he had taken. He knew his enemies could not be far off, and would soon be on his track. To elude their pursuit, he struck off in a northerly direction, which was in a contrary direction from home. When night came on he changed his course toward the Ohio river. He heard in the distance the Indians on his track, and the dismal howl of the Indian bloodhound, which was scenting out his way. The chase was continued till late at night, and he imagined again and again that his enemy was just upon him. Seeing a stream which ran in a southerly direction, he plunged into it, and, wading in its bed for some distance, crossed to the other bank, following it down some distance, when he would plunge in again, and continue wading down the stream. This he did to elude the scent of the dog, and it was the only thing that could have saved him. The pursuit was kept up all night, and the next day till evening, when, to his great relief, he reached the Ohio river, into which, without a moment's thought, he plunged, and commenced swimming for the other shore. Before he reached the middle of the stream his strength, which had already been taxed to its utmost, began to fail, and he began to despair of ever being able to reach the Kentucky shore. A thought of home and friends inspired him, however, with new courage, and he redoubled his exertions. The gun, which he had tied to his head, was pressing him down; his strokes became less frequent and more feeble, and he was about resigning himself to a watery grave, when it occurred to him that perhaps the water was not over his head. Accordingly he let his feet descend, and to his great joy he found the water only up to his shoulders, and, after resting a short time, he was enabled to wade out to the beach. When he reached the shore he was completely exhausted, and he sought a place for rest and safety. Worn down with fatigue, and having had no sleep nor food for the last two days, it was not long till he fell into a profound slumber. When he awoke in the morning his limbs were so stiff that it was with difficulty he could move them. He, however, arose from his resting-place, and, after seeking for something to satisfy the cravings of appetite, he journeyed toward home, which he reached in three days.

He was an active defender of the frontier settlers, a brave man, a valuable citizen, beloved and respected by all. He was subsequently chosen to represent the county where he resided in the Legislature of the state—a duty which he performed with credit to himself and satisfaction to his constituents.

Mercer Beason, another pioneer of those times, was one of our spies. He was a descendant of the family of Beasons who settled at an early day near the foot of Laurel Hill, where they laid out the village of Beasontown, now known as Uniontown. He was an active, fearless young man, above the medium stature. Bold and daring, he traversed the wilderness, encountering its dangers and hardships with an undaunted spirit. Many were the hazardous undertakings and perilous adventures of which he was the hero. He was the pride of his country. His fame spread far and wide, and his daring deeds struck terror into the hearts of the foe. He was one of nature's warriors; reared among the mountains, and breathing the wild air of liberty, his spirit soared aloft, unfettered and free, as the eagle of the Alleghanies. But, alas! the spoiler came, and that gifted, high-born son of the wildwood fell by the shaft of the demon Intemperance. Like Death itself, this demon loves a shining mark; and who does not weep over the early graves of heroism, genius, and learning, which have fallen by the hand of this fell destroyer?

Bazil Williams was a Virginian by birth, but was raised in Kentucky. He was one of the most active men of his age, with but one exception—the incomparable M'Cleland. He was an officer in Captain Joseph Colvin's volunteer company from Bourbon county, which joined the army of General Wayne. Having been in many skirmishes with the Indians, he learned their various arts and stratagems, and hence he was prepared to do effective service in the great battle on the Maumee. During this battle he was shot in the arm, but he never ceased fighting till the battle was ended and the victory achieved. G. Partee was also wounded in the thigh, but, like his brave officer, he fought on to the last of the conflict. Williams was eminently useful as a spy, and his fleetness of foot rendered him a great acquisition in carrying intelligence from one part of the country to another. It was said of him, that for a half a day's heat he could outrun any horse in the country, and it was considered useless for any man to try to catch him. It would seem, from the diversities of natural gifts which were possessed by the early pioneers, that they had been specially designed by Providence for the wants and necessities growing out of the border wars.

Duncan M'Arthur was a son of nature. He was tall in stature, with a giant frame. His hair was black as a raven, and his eyes dark and piercing. When excited there was an unearthly flash in his fiery eye which indicated a keen and daring spirit, restless and fearless. When I first knew him, in 1793, he was quite a young man, and was employed as a spy in company with Samuel Davis They were to range the country from Limestone to the mouth of Big Sandy. In their excursions they met with many narrow escapes. In 1794 he, with Nathaniel Beasley, was employed as a spy on the same ground, and they were often in great jeopardy of their lives. Traversing the dense forests that lined the banks of the Ohio, or gliding along in the swift canoe over its beautiful waters, with naught to disturb the repose of nature but the scream of the panther or the yell of the savage, as he would be startled from his camp by the dreaded approach of the white man, young M'Arthur grew up to manhood inspired with the wildness of the scenes around him, and disciplined to hardship by the toils he endured. After this he became a hunter for General Massie, and subsequently a deputy surveyor of the wild Congress lands. He finally bought up warrants, and located the land himself, till he became immensely rich as a landlord. He assisted General Massie in laying out the town of Chilicothe, and was among the first settlers of that ancient metropolis. He held many offices, both of a military and civil nature, and figured largely in the history of the western country during his day. He was a member of the state Legislature, several times a member of the Congress of the United States, Brigadier-General of the North-western army during the last war, and Governor of the state of Ohio. He was a kind neighbor and a valuable citizen. A poor backwoods boy, with nothing but a hunter's dress and rifle, he rose, by dint of indomitable perseverance and courage, from his obscurity to fill the highest offices in the gift of his countrymen.

Colonel John M'Donald, one of my early companions, was of Scotch descent. His father was connected with the army of the Revolution from its first organization up to the year 1780. John was born in Northumberland county, on the 28th of January, 1775. His father crossed the Mountains with his family in 1780, and settled at a place called Mingo Bottom, three miles below the present site of Steubenville. The Ohio river was then the extreme frontier, constituting the dividing line between the white and red man. No line, however, was sufficient to form a barrier against the invasions of both parties. The white man was as frequently the aggressor as the Indian, and many were the scenes of suffering, carnage, and massacre witnessed along this border line.

My young friend was reared amid all the dangers of a border war. In the year 1789 his father removed to Washington, Ky., where we were then residing, and soon after their arrival my acquaintance with young M'Donald commenced. Simon Kenton resided here also at that time. I have already given a sketch of his life, but can not forbear adding, that, although he could neither read nor write, he was regarded as the prince of the pioneers of this region of country. Bravery and daring courage were considered more essential elements of greatness in those days than learning, or wealth, or dignified titles. Kenton had a pleasant countenance and a sweet voice, yet of great compass and power. Unlike Daniel Boone, he was social in his manners. When engaging in battle he was prudent and cautious, but when the fight began he was bold and daring to excess. In the tumult of battle his clear, manly voice would roll over the combatants, like thunder, inspiring his men with courage, and striking dismay into the hearts of his foes. He was the teacher and captain of all the young men and boys in this part of the country. He was a master-spirit, and the prototype of young M'Donald.

The boys of those days were early brought into service; and as soon as they could hold up a rifle at off hand, take off a gun-lock and clean it, taking it apart and oiling it, and then putting it together again, were ranked with the hunters and soldiers of the day. It is almost incredible to relate the intrepid and desperate daring of the feats performed by mere boys. I will relate an instance which occurred with two boys with whom I was well acquainted. They were in the woods hunting the cows. It was in the fall of the year; and as hickory-nuts were very plentiful, they concluded to gather some and take them home. While thus engaged two Indians came upon them, and took them prisoners. With their prize they started off, traveling all night and the next day. At evening they stopped to camp. After taking their evening repast they made the two boys lie down between them. The eldest kept awake till all the company were locked in the fast embrace of sleep. He then quietly awakened his brother, and they stole softly from their resting-place. The elder brother then took a gun from one of the Indians and a tomahawk from the other. Placing the muzzle of the gun at the head of one of the Indians, he told his brother that the moment he should strike the other Indian he should pull the trigger. The deadly weapon gleamed in the light of the watch-fire, and in an instant was buried deep into the skull of the savage, while the sharp crack of the rifle sent the death-dealing ball into the brains of his companion. The one that had been tomahawked bounded and fell into the fire. The boys then made their escape, and, taking the Indian trail, they proceeded toward home, which in due time they reached in safety. A party started out with the eldest to visit the scene of slaughter, and found the Indians dead as reported. The name of these boys was Johnson. They grew up to be useful members of society, and joined the Methodist Episcopal Church—the eldest being a steward and the youngest a local preacher.

The first excursion of my friend M'Donald was taken with Kenton. Three men from near Washington went out on a hunting expedition, and encamped on the waters of Bracken, about ten miles from home. While they were out hunting a party of Indians came upon their camp, and placed themselves in ambush, to waylay the hunters on their return at night. The names of two of the hunters were Dan Figgans and Josiah Wood· the name of the other is forgotten. It was late when the party returned. As they were preparing their supper the Indians crept up stealthily, and fired, killing Wood and the one whose name is forgotten. Figgans, being unhurt, fled for his life. The Indians started in pursuit, with the most hideous yells. The race was most fearfully kept up, but Figgans distanced his pursuers, and at midnight reached Washington, where he alarmed his friends at Kenton's Station. This bold warrior immediately mounted his horse, and in a short time, having raised a company, started in pursuit. Young M'Donald was anxious to accompany them; but his father, thinking him too young, being but fifteen years of age, to be of any service, refused his consent. He was not, however, to be deterred; so stealing his father's rifle and horse, he started at full speed, and soon overtook the company. They arrived at the place about sunrise, and a most shocking scene presented itself to their view. One of the men had been scalped, and thrown into the fire, where he was nearly consumed; the other had also been scalped, and cut to pieces with the Indian hatchet. The party proceeded to the mournful work of depositing their remains in the ground; and ascertaining by the tracks of the horses that the Indians had directed their course for the Ohio river, they started after them. When they arrived at the river, they found that the Indians, without waiting a moment, had plunged in and swam across, thus cutting off pursuit. This dreadful sight had a tendency somewhat to cool the ardor of the youthful warrior, who, nevertheless, would have been glad of an opportunity for taking revenge upon the savage foe.

From this time M'Donald was constantly engaged with scouting, hunting, and surveying parties. In the spring of 1792 he joined General Massie's settlement at Manchester, twelve miles above Maysville. This was the third settlement on the north-west side of the Ohio river, above Cincinnati, or Losantiville, as the town was called. This infant settlement, together with the lives of all in the station, was in constant danger. Many and exciting were the scenes by which they were surrounded. Sometimes they were deeply depressed, and anon, when danger was over, their spirits rose exulting at the trials and conflicts through which they had passed. A report would sometimes come in, that one of their number had fallen by the hand of the enemy, which would cast a shade of sadness and gloom on all hearts; then again the intelligence that the bold and daring hunter had captured the foe, would inspire them with courage. Thus life was made up of constant alternations of hope and despondency. This constant warfare made the early settlers so familiar with scenes of blood and carnage, that they became, in a measure, indifferent spectators, and at the same time reckless and fearless of all danger. Scenes of horror that would have congealed the blood in the veins of those unaccustomed to them, would scarcely move the heart of the hardy pioneer.

In the spring of 1794 Colonel M'Donald and his brother Thomas joined General Wayne's army as rangers, or spies. The company of rangers consisted of seventy-two, of whom Captain Ephraim Kibby was commander. He was a true Jersey blue, fully adequate to any emergency growing out of his highly responsible position. It was the duty of the rangers to traverse the Indian country in every direction in advance of the army. This was not only a toilsome, but a dangerous work. The company was divided into small detachments, which started out in every direction, and, after scouring the country, returned and made their report to head-quarters.

The history of these times has been so often told that I do not consider it necessary to enter into any detail in regard to the many adventures connected with the rangers, and shall only record what has never yet been made a matter of public history.

Early in November of the year above mentioned, Mr. Lucas Sullivan, a land-speculator and surveyor from Virginia, collected a company of twenty-one men to go upon a surveying tour into the Scioto country. This was a hazardous undertaking. Notwithstanding the Indians had been severely beaten by General Wayne, a few months previously, yet the country was far from a state of peace. Attached to this company were three surveyors; namely, John and Nathaniel Beasley, and Sullivan, who was the chief. Young M'Donald was connected with this company. Every man carried his own baggage and arms, consisting of a rifle, tomahawk, and scalping-knife. While engaged in surveying, the hunters would go in advance as spies, and the surveyor, chain-carriers, and marksmen would follow in line, the whole being brought up by the pack-horse and the man who cooked for the company. It was his business to keep a good look-out, so that the enemy should not attack them in the rear. In this military manner was most of the surveying in Ohio and Kentucky performed. They did not carry any provisions with them, but depended on their rifles for a living, which seldom failed to afford them an abundant supply.

Having taken Todd's trace, they pursued their journey

till they came to Paint creek, at the old crossings. From thence they proceeded to old Chilicothe, now Frankfort, and thus on to Deer creek, where they encamped at the mouth of Hay run. In the morning Sullivan, M'Donald, and Murray went down to the mouth of Deer creek with the intention of taking its meanderings back to the camp. They had not proceeded more than a hundred rods till a flock of turkeys came flying toward them. M'Donald and Murray being on the bank of the creek, near to a pile of drift-wood, Murray, without reflecting a moment that the turkeys must have been driven toward them by some persons, slipped up to a tree and shot a turkey. He then slipped back, and as there were more turkeys on the tree, M'Donald slipped up to the position left by his companion. Just as he was about to fire, the sharp crack of a rifle fell on his ears, and turning instantly he saw poor Murray fall to rise no more. Looking in the direction from whence the messenger of death came, he saw several Indians with their rifles leveled at him. Quick as thought he sprang over the bank into the creek, and they fired but missed him. The Indians followed hard after him, yelling and screaming like fiends. Running across the bottom he met Sullivan and three others of the company. Sullivan instantly threw away his compass and clung to his rifle. Their only safety was in rapid flight, as the Indians were too numerous to encounter. As they ran the Indians fired upon them, one of the balls striking Colvin's cue at the tie, which shocked him so much that he thought himself mortally wounded. But he was a brave young man, and being fleet of foot, he ran up the creek and gave the alarm at the camp, stating that he believed all were killed but himself. Those at camp of course fled as soon as possible. M'Donald and his party ran across the bottom to the high land, and after running three miles struck a prairie. Casting their eye over it, they saw four Indians trotting along the trace. They thought of running round the prairie and heading them, but not knowing how soon those in pursuit would be upon them, and perchance they would get between two fires, adopted the better part of valor and concealed themselves in the grass till the Indians were out of sight. After remaining there for some time they went to the camp and found it deserted. Just as they were about to leave, one of the company espied a note stuck in the end of a split stick, to this effect, "If you should come, follow the trail." It was then sundown, and they knew they would not be able to follow the trail after dark. When night came on, they steered their course by starlight.

They had traveled a distance of eight or nine miles. It was a cold, dreary night, and the leaves being frozen, the sound of their footsteps could be heard some distance. All at once they heard something break and run as if it were a gang of buffaloes. At this they halted and remained silent for some time. After a while the fugitives could be heard coming back softly. Supposing that it might be their companions, M'Donald and M'Cormick concluded to creep up slowly and see. They advanced till they could hear them cracking hazel-nuts with their teeth. They also heard them whisper to one another, but could not tell whether they were Indians or white men. They cautiously returned to Sullivan, and the company, after deliberation, finally concluded to call, which they did, and found, to their joy, that it was their own friends who fled from them. They had mutual rejoicings at meeting again, but poor Murray was left a prey to the Indians and wolves. They now commenced their journey homeward, and after three days' travel, arrived at Manchester.

This disastrous enterprise, however, did not deter others from trying their fortunes. Soon after this, General

Nathaniel Massie collected a party of twenty-eight men, of whom M'Donald was one, to take a surveying tour on the head waters of the Little Miami and Paint creek. He took with him three assistant surveyors, namely, Peter Lee, William O'Banion, and Nathaniel Beasley, men of tried courage, and able to encounter any hardships. None but men of this stamp were adapted to such an enterprise, and hence the company was composed of such. A surveying expedition incurred more toil and danger than a scouting party or a regular army, the latter particularly, as it was always embodied and better prepared for defense. The surveying company was divided into bands, and each had its particular duties to perform; hence it was impossible to be always on the guard against the wily and revengeful Indian.

General Massie was a man of great energy of character, a brave and daring spirit of the times in which he lived. He was honest and upright in all his dealings with his fellow-men. He was not only just, but generous to a fault, the poor man's friend, the widow and orphan's benefactor. Pinching want, with haggard mien and downcast eyes, never went pining from his door. His house was the home of hospitality, and an asylum for the distressed. But, alas! like many high-souled, gifted, and generous men of all times, the demon Intemperance marked him as his victim, and

> "Like some ill-guided bark, well built, and tall,
> That angry tides cast out on desert shore,"

that noble spirit was wrecked. He died in 1813. Having neglected his business, which was in great confusion at his death, his heirs reaped but little benefit from his great estate.

Peter Lee, one of Massie's surveyors, was a native of Mason county, Ky. He possessed a large fortune, and was reputed a liberal and honest man. He was unostentatious in all his demeanor, and much respected by all who knew him. He remained a bachelor, as matrimony did not seem to have sufficient charms to lure him from the path of single blessedness. If to some it is not given to enjoy this estate, they may excite commiseration for their misfortune, instead of condemnation for their course.

Nathaniel Beasley, the youngest of the surveyors, has long since passed away from the ranks of the living, and been numbered with the dead. He served his country with great fidelity in many responsible stations. He was justice of the peace, county commissioner, and representative in the state Legislature.

In the war of 1812 he again shouldered his rifle in his country's cause, as commander of a battalion in two expeditions. He had, when we take into account the day in which he lived, and the training which he received, as few faults as any man. He was a plain, common-sense, self-taught, and self-made man. He possessed a thorough business capacity, had great honesty of purpose, and his industry and perseverance secured for him the esteem of all who knew him.

William O'Banion was the bravest of the brave, and one of the most fiery and impetuous spirits old Kentucky ever sent into the battle-field. After serving, with the greatest fidelity and courage, in various minor grades of rank as an officer in the army, he was promoted to the rank of lieutenant in the United States army. He was in the battle of Tripoli in Africa, and the first man that mounted the wall of a fortified town near Tripoli. Since his return from Africa I have not been able to learn any thing concerning his history.

Such were the men who constituted the leaders of the expedition; while the chain-carriers and marksmen were all well-tried backwoods hunters, brought up amid the perils of the border wars. Without beds, tents, or wagons, the ground covered with snow, and the weather intensely cold, they traversed the wilderness, and, gathering around their camp-fires, after the toils of the day, they would laugh, and sing, and talk as merrily as though at a backwoods wedding.

But to return to the biography of my friend M'Donald. In the year of 1799 he was married to Miss Catharine Cutwright, and in 1802 removed to Poplar Ridge in Ross county, where he now resides. He had eight daughters and one son, all of whom obtained respectable positions in society. He was elected several times a justice of the peace; also served as a militia officer, being captain, major, lieutenant-colonel, and colonel. When the war of 1812 broke out, he enlisted as a volunteer in the first regiment of Ohio volunteers, and received the appointment of paymaster-general. Immediately on the receipt of this appointment, he went to Dayton, the place of general rendezvous for the north-western army, and was subsequently appointed quarter-master of the regiment, and continued to perform the duties of both offices till the surrender of the army by General Hull. In the early part of the winter of 1812–13 he received the appointment of captain in the United States army, but did not resign his commissions in the militia. In July following he commanded a regiment of militia, and marched to the lake country, and served under the orders of General William Henry Harrison. He represented his county in both houses of the state Legislature. This young man, reared in the wilderness, subjected to all its toils and dangers, presented a specimen of manly courage, intellectual worth, and true greatness, worth a regiment of West Point cadets, and an example to all young men of the present day. I have been familiarly acquainted with him for upward of half a century. He is now, like myself, in the sear and yellow leaf of age, and soon the wintery winds will sweep us as the leaves from their parent tree, and we shall be gathered to our fathers. The latter part of his life has been spent in promoting the benevolent enterprises of the age, such as temperance, Sabbath schools, etc. His life has been one of excitement, toil, and conflict. His best years have been devoted to the interests of his country, and, though man does not, may God reward him for his conduct! He has written a most interesting and reliable history, called "Sketches of the West."

CHAPTER VI.

TRAGICAL OCCURRENCE—BRAVE BACKWOODS GIRL.

The dangers to which the early inhabitants of the Scioto Valley were exposed made their appearance on the death of Captain Herrod. He was among the number of those who raised the first corn in the prairie below Chilicothe, in 1796. He was a most respectable and worthy man, possessing great influence in the country, and beloved by all who knew him. Having removed to a farm a few miles west of Chilicothe, which he was engaged in clearing, an incident occurred, which created the utmost terror and alarm in the whole country, and spread consternation and dismay wherever the sad intelligence reached the sparse and scattered population. In the spring of 1803, as some persons were hunting in the woods, they found the body of a man scalped and tomahawked. This was recognized as the body of Captain Herrod; and it was supposed, from the manner of his death, that the fearful deed had been perpetrated by the Indians. It was also supposed that the Indians had recommenced hostilities on the whites. The treaty of peace concluded by General Wayne in 1795 had remained undisturbed up to this time. By whom or for what purpose Captain Herrod was thus brutally murdered, has never been ascertained, and remains wrapped in the profoundest mystery to this day. Various were the conjectures at the time. It was secretly hinted, and by some firmly believed, that the savage deed was done by a white man who had been an unsuccessful rival candidate of Captain Herrod's, for the office of captain in the Ohio militia. It was known that the bitterest envy rankled in his heart toward Herrod, and it was supposed that he sought to cover up the foul deed by adopting the Indian mode of human slaughter. Whether he was guilty or not, this was at least the general impression among the immediate neighbors; but, as no evidence of guilt was ever sought or found against him, he was allowed to pass without being taken. On the other hand, as little faith had been placed by the inhabitants in general in the treaty of the Indians, a large majority were disposed to charge the deed to them, and the death of Herrod was regarded as the forerunner of war. The account of his death, as if borne on the wings of the wind, spread with great rapidity all over the Scioto Valley, and the excitement and alarm produced among the citizens was most intense. Whole families, from five to fifteen miles apart, flocked together for purposes of self-defense. In some places block-houses were run up, and preparations for war made in every direction. The citizens of Chilicothe, though in the center of population, collected together for the purpose of fortifying the town. Sentinels were posted, and a vigilant guard kept, day and night. Rumor, with her overheated and affrighted imagination, and her thousand tongues, was busily engaged in spreading her alarms. At one time it was reported that Captain John, an Indian chief, with his warriors, had killed all the inhabitants of Darby; and again, that other settlements had fallen beneath the hand of the savage foe. The inhabitants living on the north fork of Paint creek were all collected at Old Town, now Frankfort, and among others was David Wolf, an old hunter, a man of wealth and some influence. He had settled on the north fork, twenty miles above Old Town. After remaining in the town several days, he employed two men, Williams and

Ferguson, to go with him to his farm, with a view of examining into the condition of his stock. When they had proceeded about six miles, and were passing through a prairie, they saw an Indian approaching them in the distance, and walking in the same path over which they were traveling. On a nearer approach it was found to be the Shawnee chief Waw-wil-a-way, the old and faithful hunter of General Massie during his surveying tours, and an unwavering friend of the white man. He was a sober, brave, intelligent man, well known to most of the settlers in the country, and beloved by all for his frank and generous demeanor. He had a wife and two sons, who were also much respected by their white neighbors where they resided, near the falls of Paint creek.

Waw-wil-a-way was frequently engaged in taking wild game and skins to Old Town, for the purpose of exchanging them for such articles as he wanted. He had left home that morning on foot with his gun for the purpose of visiting Frankfort, and meeting the company before named, he approached them in that frank and friendly manner which always characterized his intercourse with his white brethren. After shaking hands with them most cordially, he inquired into the health of each and their families. The salutation being over, Wolf asked him if he would not trade guns; and the chief assenting, an exchange was made for the purpose of examining previous to the ratification of the bargain. While this was going on, Wolf, being on horseback, unperceived by Waw-wil-a-way, opened the pan, and threw out the priming, and, handing it back, said he believed he would not trade with him.

Wolf and Williams then dismounted, and asked the chief if the Indians had commenced war.

His answer was, "No, no! the Indians and white men are now all one, all brothers."

Wolf then asked if he had heard that the Indians had killed Captain Herrod.

The chief, much surprised at the intelligence, replied, that he had not heard it, and seemed to doubt its correctness.

Wolf assured him that it was true.

"May be whisky, too much drink, was the cause of the quarrel."

Wolf replied, "Herrod had no quarrel with the Indians; nor is it known by whom he was killed, or for what cause."

Waw-wil-a-way said, "May be some bad white man kill Captain Herrod."

The conversation then ended, and the party making preparation to resume their journey, the chief again shook hands with all in the same friendly manner as at greeting. After he had proceeded on his way about ten steps, Wolf raised his rifle, and, taking deliberate aim at the Indian's back, fired, and shot him through the body. Waw-wil-a-way did not fall, although he knew his wound must prove mortal; nor did he submit to die as most men would have done in similar circumstances.

The illustrious Julius Cæsar, one of the most renowned warriors of imperial Rome, when attacked by superior numbers in the Senate Chamber, terrified at the approach of death, muffled his face in his cloak, and received the deadly thrust of Brutus; but the brave Shawnee chief, in the wild prairie of his fathers, which had been invaded by the white man, turned upon his ungenerous and cowardly assailants, determined to sell his life at as dear a rate as his hopeless condition would admit, raised his unerring rifle, and leveled it at Wolf, who jumped behind his horse. Williams's horse becoming frightened, and plunging about, left his body unprotected, and the unerring fire of Waw-wil-a-way's rifle told its tale of death

Williams was shot through the body, and fell dead in the path. The Indian then clubbed his gun, and, in a state of desperation, rushed upon Wolf, and with one blow felled him to the earth. Recovering, and being strong and active, he closed upon the Indian, and made an effort to seize him by the long tuft of hair on the top of his head. He had a shawl tied around his head in the form of a turban, and this being seized by Wolf, instead of the hair, he gave a violent jerk for the purpose of bringing him to the ground. The shawl giving way, Wolf fell on his back. At this the Indian drew his scalping-knife, and made a thrust at Wolf, who, seeing his danger, and throwing up his feet to ward off the blow, received the blade of the knife in his thigh. In the scuffle the handle broke off, and left the whole blade fast in the wound. At the same time Wolf made a stroke at the Indian, the blade of his knife entering the breast-bone. Just then Ferguson came to Wolf's assistance; but the Indian, taking up Wolf's gun, struck him on the head a most fearful blow, and brought him to the earth, laying bare his skull from the crown to the ear. Here the sanguinary conflict ended; and so rapid was the work of bloodshed that all was accomplished in less time than I have taken to relate it.

When the deadly strife ended, the foes of Waw-wil-a-way were all lying at his feet, and had he been able to have followed up his blows he would have dispatched them, for they were completely in his power. But his strength failed him, and perhaps his sight; for he must have been in the agonies of death during the whole conflict. It may be that the poor Indian relented, and that forgiveness played like a sunshine around his generous heart. He cast one glance upon his fallen foes; then turning away, he walked out into the grass, and fell upon his face amid the wild flowers of the prairie, where his heart, which never ceased to beat with kindness for the white man, at once and forever was still.

During the entire engagement he never spoke a word. Silently he acted his part in the fearful drama, as though moved by an invisible agency. The conduct of Wolf and his comrades was the most dastardly and mean, and deserves the execration of the world. They first attempted to disarm him by throwing the priming out of his gun, and then talking with him, and parting under the mask of friendship. Had Wolf and his companions supposed him to have been accessory to the death of Herrod in any way, he would have gone with them cheerfully to Old Town or Chilicothe, and given himself up to an investigation. But Wolf was determined on murder, and the blood of Waw-wil-a-way rests on his head.

Williams was found dead of his wounds. Wolf was carried home in a wagon, and the knife-blade extracted by a surgeon. Ferguson's wound was dressed, but both of these suffered much. The body of the chief was found where it fell, and it was pronounced by the surgeon—Dr. Edmiston—who examined his wounds, that either of them must have proved mortal. It seemed that Providence designed he should, in some degree, avenge his own death.

The death of this great and good Indian chief added fuel to the excitement which had preceded it. The Indians in the neighborhood fled in one direction, and the whites in another. Neither party knew what to do. All was dismay and confusion.

In this dreadful state of suspense and alarm, General M'Arthur and Governor Worthington, with a few others, mounted their horses and went into the Indian country near Fort Greenville, where they found a numerous body of Indians, among whom was the far-famed and celebrated chief, Tecumseh, or Shooting Star, as this name signifies. With these Indians a council was held. They related what had happened, narrating all the circumstances connected with the death of Captain Herrod and Waw-wil-a-way. The Indians declared they had no knowledge of these transactions, and reiterated their purpose to stand firm by the treaty made at that place. After some further deliberation between the parties, Tecumseh agreed to accompany them to Chilicothe, which he did. After their arrival, a day was fixed on which he would address all the people. At the appointed time a vast assemblage was convened. The interpreter for the occasion was a white man by the name of Riddle, who had been for many years a prisoner among the Indians. Governor Tiffin opened the talk, and after he had finished and sat down Tecumseh arose. His personal appearance was prepossessing. His figure was tall and commanding. Native dignity sat enthroned upon his massive brow; and while this son of the forest—this shooting meteor—poured out the bright flashes of wit and eloquence over the vast concourse, all was silent as the grave. With the strongest language, he spoke of the amicable relations subsisting between the Indians and their white brethren, and the determination of the former forever to abide by the treaty. He expressed a hope that it would be kept inviolate by both parties, and that brotherly love would be long and lasting as time between the white man and the Indian. When he concluded, the sachems shook hands in token of the friendship and fellowship existing between both parties. This interview allayed all alarm, and the people all returned again to their quiet homes and peaceful pursuits.

There was one exception, however, to the general tranquillity. Waw-wil-a-way, as before related, had two sons, who had, in obedience to their religion, vowed to be revenged on Wolf for the death of their father. According to the custom of the Indians, the nearest kin to the murdered man has a right, and it is made his duty, to kill the murderer whenever or wherever he could find him, unless the murderer purchased his life by a certain price agreed upon by the family. Wolf, hearing of the intentions of the sons of the murdered chief, took his family and removed to Kentucky, at the same time employing an agent to intercede with the young men. A negotiation was finally entered into, and the agent agreed to furnish each of the young Indians with a horse, a new saddle and bridle, and a new rifle. On complying with this condition, they agreed to bury the tomahawk and make peace with him and his forever. Wolf agreed to the proposition, and the time and place were fixed upon for the fulfillment of the contract.

A large concourse was assembled at Old Town, to witness the Indian ceremonies. A hollow square was formed, in which were Wolf and his horses and trappings, and the two Indians. The Indians, in relinquishing their claim to the life of the murderer, raised their hands toward heaven, invoking the Great Spirit, declaring that to him alone they transferred the blood and life of Wolf, forfeited by the death of their father. The scene was full of the most impressive solemnity, and many were moved to tears. In token of their forgiveness, they advanced and took Wolf by the hand—the same bloody hand which sent their beloved father to the grave and made them orphans. Then saluting him as a brother, they lighted the calumet, or pipe of peace, and smoked with him in the presence of the Great Spirit. They remained good friends ever afterward, and often visited each other.

I have selected the above as one of the many tragical occurrences of those days; and though some may think I ought to pass over such scenes of carnage and death, yet, as a faithful chronicler of the times in which I lived, I think it due to posterity to know through what perils their fathers passed, and what were the circumstances by which they were surrounded. The only way to judge correctly of human character, is to take into the account the circumstances under which it was developed.

The trials which our fathers and mothers endured in the early settlement of this country, and the fortitude evinced by them in the hour of danger, should never be forgotten by their sons and daughters. Before closing this chapter, I will relate an incident which occurred on Bear Grass, in Kentucky, near where the city of Louisville now stands. A gentleman by the name of Atkinson had removed, with his family, from some of the older settlements, to this place, and with his colored servants, had opened a farm. Before, however, the forests were leveled around him, or he had realized the bright anticipations in which he had indulged, he fell by the stroke of death. His wife and an only daughter, a beautiful and accomplished girl of fifteen summers, after his death, concluded to remain in their new home. The scene of the husband's and father's labors and death was rendered too sacred to be left for any slight or transient cause. On a grassy knoll, not far from the cottage, slept, in his long last sleep, the idol of their hearts. Thither they would repair, when the early spring opened the buds, and plant flowers. There, after the toils of the day, that lonely child would wander, to weep and pray; and often have the stars, those bright sentinels of heaven, looked down from the blue depths, to watch the devotions of the pure spirit lingering there.

About one year after this melancholy event, the daughter was out later than usual, accompanied by a faithful servant. Seeming unwilling to leave the spot where her heart's treasure was entombed, she tarried, pensive and sad, when suddenly she was startled by a low growl in the woods, apparently at a short distance from her. Fearing it might be some beast of prey, with which the woods were infested, she hastened home. So accustomed was she to visit her father's grave in the evening, her mother was not alarmed at her stay. When she entered the cottage, she was considerably agitated, and communicated the cause of it to her mother.

The servants occupied quarters close at hand, and as they were true and trusty, there was no great cause of fear on the part of the mother and her daughter; but, on retiring that night, they doubly barred the door of their rude habitation. After they had retired to rest, they were startled by an unusual noise in the yard. The mother sprang out of bed, and, adjusting her clothes, took down the rifle, which hung over the door, and after examining, cautiously, the load, and priming, she carefully opened the door, and stepped into the yard. She looked in every direction, but she could see nothing. She walked around the house, examining every corner, but still nothing was to be seen. She also passed around the cabin of the servants, but could not detect the cause of the noise. She returned into the house and set down the gun. Her daughter had arisen, and dressed herself, and was stirring up the fire. She assured her mother that there must be some wild beast about the house, as she distinctly heard its footsteps while she was out. Upon this, the mother resolved to go to the cabin, and wake the servant Dan, a bold and fearless negro. She accordingly went and waked him, and told him to get up, which he did as speedily as possible, and after putting on his clothes, he came out armed with a heavy stick. She directed him to go round the house one way, and she would take the other. Before they had proceeded ten steps, Mrs. Atkinson was seized by a huge bear. The negro immediately made a blow with his club at the head of the animal, and stunned him so that he let go his hold; but soon recovering himself, he commenced his attack on Dan, who kept up a running fight till he reached his lodge, which he did, and, slamming to the door, roused all the inmates. Having thus cut off his pursuit, the bear directed his course toward Mrs. Atkinson, and, just as she was entering the door of her house, caught her by her dress, and drew her toward him. At this critical moment the click of a gun-lock was heard, which was instantly followed by the sharp crack of a rifle; the bear relaxed his hold, doubled up, and rolled over at her feet, in the last struggle. An unerring aim had sent a ball through his heart.

The daughter was a witness of the conflict in the yard; but it was too dark for her to see to shoot, without the light of her fire, and whenever the enemy came within its range, his life paid the forfeit.

This intrepid act doubtless saved the mother's life. That brave, yet delicate, affectionate, and dutiful child became the high-souled, heroic woman. Her skill, judgment, and bravery were often, in after years, relied upon to guide the destiny of the infant settlements, during many severe conflicts in the dark and bloody ground. By marriage, this courageous backwoods girl became connected with one of the first and most ancient families of the south. Her descendants are numerous and respectable, inheriting the virtues and bravery of their mother, figuring largely in the military, civil, and political history of the west; and they have not forgotten the story of the bear.

Before closing this chapter I will relate another incident of backwoods bravery.

An aged lady, who died in Ross county some fifty years since, related to me the following circumstance: When she, with her family, went first to reside in Kentucky the Indians attacked their cabin, and shot her husband, wounding him so badly that he was unable to render any further assistance. They then tried to force the door No person being with her in the house but a mulatto boy, about seventeen years of age, they both flew to the door, and pressed all their weight against it. An Indian finally succeeding in getting his body partly into the house, she seized the hand-ax, and killed him on the spot. They then succeeded in closing the door and barring it. She then took her husband's gun, and, firing through the port-hole, shot another Indian dead in the yard. The other two—for there were four of them—then made preparations to descend the chimney; but no sooner had one of them entered the flue, than ripping open a pillow-case, she threw the feathers on the fire. This so suffocated and scorched the Indian that he fell into the fireplace, and the negro boy seizing him, he was soon dispatched by the old lady in the same manner the first aggresser was killed. There was but one Indian left, and fearing he would meet the same sad fate which befell his companions, he fled in dismay from the scene of conflict.

CHAPTER VII.

LIFE IN THE WOODS.

I WILL now return to my personal narrative. After the Detroit expedition, I spent the greater part of the winter in hunting. Having attained the age of twenty, I felt considerable uneasiness and indeterminateness in regard to my future course in life. There were many things to divert my mind, and much that was calculated to produce dissipation of thought. An abundance of youthful company, with every variety of diversions, such as huskings, quiltings, dancings, and plays of all descriptions, presented themselves and were urged upon my attention. All these, however, possessed not the charms of a hunter's life, and I was not long in making my election.

In company with three of my companions, I made preparations to start out upon a winter's hunt. We agreed to take no horses, and every man was to carry his own stock of provisions and cooking utensils. So taking a few corn-dodgers, one camp-kettle, about a quart of salt, a blanket apiece, and our hunting apparatus, we started for the woods. After two days' travel, we arrived at a place where there were bear signs in great abundance, but they were not fresh. Here we camped and started out to hunt. By this time our store of provisions was exhausted, and the leaves being dry none of us were able to kill any game. We tried hard the next day, but with the same unsuccessful result, except that one of our party killed a wild-cat. This we prepared for our camp-kettle, and when boiled it made us the first meal we had partaken of foi two days. I shall always think it was the toughest meal I ever ate.

Our object being to hunt bears, and finding that they had all left that section and gone in quest of mast, we resolved, if possible, to follow them. As there was no snow on the ground, and we could not track them, the only things we had to guide us in our search, were the branches and soft muddy places over which they had crossed. On the third day we concluded to take a large circle and make observations. It was cloudy, and the snow began to fall. About noon I fell in with two of my companions, and supposing it to be near night, as the clouds and snow had made it dark, we considered it time to look out for a place to camp. We differed about the course we should take, but finally yielding to the judgment of the oldest hunter, we traveled on till it began to be quite dark. Despairing of finding any game, we were about to stop and make preparations for camping, when our dogs treed a large raccoon. Being dark, we could not see the animal with any distinctness, and after several ineffectual shots, at length a ball found its way to the hapless victim, and he fell dead at our feet. This was, to us, a source of great joy. Three days, with only one poor wild-cat for three hearty hunters, was short fare; and the reader may be assured that a fat coon was very acceptable. We soon made preparations for a barbecue. A fire was made, and we could hardly wait till our game was roasted, till we were cutting and eating it. The coon was exceedingly fat, and we wished very much for some bread to catch the rich drippings.

Next morning the snow was a foot deep on the ground. My moccasins were worn out on the bottom, and I was obliged to peel lynn bark and make soles for them before I could proceed. After drying ourselves as well as we could, before our camp-fire—for we were much exposed to he snow during the night, and the only way we could keep at all comfortable with our scanty clothing, was to get the dogs to lie to our backs—we decamped.

We had not proceeded far till we came upon a large flock of turkeys, and killing as many as we could carry, for future use, we commenced retracing our steps, and, finding but little game, we changed the object of pursuit to that of deer. For this purpose we removed our camp to the large bottoms of Paint creek, where we hunted with good success, and had plenty to live on.

After getting all the skins and game that we could carry, we returned home.

The holidays, such, for instance, as Christmas and New-Year's, were spent in shooting-matches, dancing, and frolicking, at which, in the language of the back-woodsman, I made a whole hand. These diversions, as I before remarked, were not altogether suited to my taste or inclination. I was still undecided in regard to what course I should pursue in future life. If I went into the practice of medicine, I saw or thought I saw innumerable difficulties connected therewith. To be always with the sick and dying, and constantly to breathe an atmosphere of sighs and disease, was far from being agreeable to my feelings. Besides, the collection of the fees, which, of all others, are the most uncertain, added to the great responsibilities of the profession, with not one hour to call my own, seemed entirely too great an undertaking for me at that time. Then I would be totally deprived of the pleasures of hunting, whose peaceful enjoyments had the greatest charms for my youthful imagination. After weighing all these considerations, I finally resolved on adopting a hunter's life. This being settled, the next thing was to get me a wife suited to this mode of living, and, after taking advice from my mother in so important a matter, I made my choice. On the third day of March,

1801, I was accordingly married to Hannah Strane. My father having bought land in what is now Highland county, I resolved to move, and take possession. This section of the country was then a dense wilderness, with only here and there a human habitation. My father-in-law, being unsatisfied with his daughter's choice, did not even allow her to take her clothes, so we started out, without any patrimony, on our simple matrimonial stock, to make our fortune in the woods. With the aid of my brother John, I built a cabin in the forest, my nearest neighbor being three miles off. Into this we moved, without horse or cow, bed or bedding, bag or baggage. We gathered up the leaves and dried them in the sun; then, picking out all the sticks, we put them into a bed-tick. For a bedstead, we drove forks into the ground, and laid sticks across, over which we placed elm bark. On this we placed our bed of leaves, and had comfortable lodging. The next thing was to procure something to eat. Of meat we had an abundance, supplied by my rifle, but we wanted some bread. I cut and split one hundred rails for a bushel of potatoes, which I carried home on my back, a distance of six miles. At the same place I worked a day for a hen and three chickens, which I put into my hunting-shirt bosom, and carried home as a great prize. Our cabin was covered with bark, and lined and floored with the same material. One end of the cabin was left open for a fireplace. In this we lived comfortably all summer. Having no horse or plow, I went into a plum bottom near the house, and, with my ax, grubbed and cleared off an acre and a half, in which I dug holes with my hoe, and planted my corn, without any fence around it. I cultivated this patch as well I could with my hoe, and Providence blessed my labor with a good crop, of over one hundred bushels. Besides, during the summer, with the help of my wife, I put up a neat cabin, and finished it for our winter's lodgings. For the purpose of making the cabin warm, I put my corn in the loft, and now, if we could not get bread, we had always, as a good substitute, plenty of hominy. We had also plenty of bear-meat and venison, and no couple on earth lived happier or more contented. Our Indian friends often called, and staid all night, and I paid them, in return, occasional visits.

During the season several families settled in the neighborhood, and, when we were together, we enjoyed life without gossip and those often fatal bickerings and backbitings which destroy the peace of whole communities. Of all people on the face of God's earth, I despise a gossiping tattler, whose chief business is to retail slander from house to house, and ruin the peace of families. I would rather meet a lioness bereft of her whelps, a bear of her cubs, a hungry panther, or a revengeful savage, than a living human being in the form of a tattler, with smooth tongue and slimy feet. Though we had but little, our wants were few, and we enjoyed our simple and homely possessions with a relish the purse-proud aristocrat never enjoyed. A generous hospitality characterized every neighbor, and what we had we divided to the last with each other. When any one wanted help, all were ready to aid.

I spent the greater part of the winter in hunting and laying up a store of provisions for the summer, so that I might give my undivided attention to farming. As we had no stock to kill, and could not conveniently raise hogs, on account of the wild animals, which would carry them off, we were obliged to depend upon the product of the woods.

As the bear was the most valuable, we always hunted for this animal. This fall there was a good mast, and bears were so plentiful that it was not necessary to go from home to hunt them. About Christmas we made our turkey hunt. At that season of the year they are very fat, and we killed them in great abundance. To preserve them we cleaned them, cut them in two, and, after salting them in troughs, we hung them up to dry. They served a valuable purpose to cook, in the spring and summer, with our bear, bacon, and venison hams. Being dry, we would stew them in bear's oil, and they answered a good substitute for bread, which, in those days, was hard to be obtained, the nearest mill being thirty miles distant. Another great difficulty was to procure salt, which sold enormously high—at the rate of four dollars for fifty pounds. In backwoods currency, it would require four buck-skins, or a large bear-skin, or sixteen coon-skins, to make the purchase. Often it could not be had at any price, and the only way we had to procure it, was by packing a load of kettles on our horses to the Scioto salt lick, and boiling the water ourselves. Otherwise we had to dispense with it entirely. I have known meat cured with strong hickory ashes.

I imagine I hear the reader saying this was hard living and hard times. So they would have been to the present race of men, but those who lived at that time enjoyed life with a greater zest, and were more healthy and happy than the present race. We had not then sickly, hysterical wives, with poor, puny, sickly, dying children, and no dyspeptic men constantly swallowing the nostrums of quacks. When we became sick unto death, we died at once, and did not keep the neighborhood in a constant state of alarm for several weeks, by daily bulletins of our dying. Our young women were beautiful without *rouge, color de rose, meen fun,* or any other cosmetic, and blithesome without wine and fruit-cake. There was then no curvature of the spine, but the lasses were straight and fine-looking, without corsets or whalebone. They were neat in their appearance, and fresh as the morning, in their homespun, without the paraphernalia of a la Parisian wardrobe and toilet.

Young ladies did not then weep over the sickly sentimentalism of a Bulwer, or Dickens, or Eugene Sue, or become corrupted by the yellow-covered literature which is now, like the frogs of Egypt, infesting our land. They were not annoyed with any Don-Juan-puff-cigaros, with his long hair and face resembling a worn-out hearth-brush, and whose long ears indicated to what species of the *genus homo* he belonged. The hard-fisted, honest yeomanry of the country, instead of being the mere product of the tailor or hair-dresser, were nature's noblemen, and their associates.

I know it is said, "*Tempora mutantur, nos mutamer cum ilius;*" but I don't believe the doctrine. The ever-shifting phases of the times would prove a poor guide for any sensible man. And yet I would not be an insufferable croaker, and repudiate all progress—æsthetical, social, and intellectual—any more than I would reject progress in the physical sciences and religion. I would only protest against the needless and hurtful superfluities of fashionable life.

But a truce to this, and I will resume my personal narrative.

When the spring opened I was better prepared to go to farming than I was the last season, having procured horses and plow. Instead of the laborious and tedious process of working the land with a hoe, I now commenced plowing. Providence crowned my labors with abundant success, and we had plenty to eat and wear. Of course, our wants were few and exceedingly simple, and the products of the soil and hunting yielded a rich supply. Thus we lived within ourselves on our own industry, our only dependence being upon the favors of an overruling, bountiful Benefactor. We spun and wove our own fabrics for clothing, and had no tax, no muster, no court, no justices, no lawyers, no constables, and no doctors, and, consequently, had no exorbitant fees to pay to professional gentlemen. The law of kindness governed our social walks; and if such a disastrous thing as a quarrel should break out, the only way to settle the difficulty was by a strong dish of fisticuffs. No man was permitted to insult another without resentment; and if an insult was permitted to pass unrevenged, the insulted party lost his standing and caste in society. Many a muss or spree was gotten up, in which the best of friends quarreled and fought, through the sole influence of the brown jug.

It was seldom we had any preaching; but if a traveling minister should come along and make an appointment, all would go out to preaching. If the preaching was on a week-day, the men would go in their hunting-shirts, with their guns. On Sabbath the gun was left at home, but the belt and knife were never forgotten. When assembled all was attention and order, and no one was allowed to behave disorderly, as such conduct would have been punished, and the miscreant driven from decent society. Such was the high sense of honor and decorum, that a young woman would discard the society of any young man who would be guilty of overstepping the bounds of propriety.

We have fallen, however, upon different times. In the rapid march of civilization and refinement, we find young men, "nice young men," and, strange to say, young women, too, who can, on these occasions, with the most unblushing effrontery, desecrate the house of God, and disturb a whole congregation of worshipers, without eliciting any censure from a large majority.

I once went a considerable distance to hear father John Collins preach. When I arrived there the house was filled to overflowing. Being just able to crowd in the door, I stood listening, deeply interested with the soft, sweet tones of his silvery voice, as he described the love of God to man. Every sentence increased my interest, so that I would not have lost a word for a world. Just when my interest was wrought up to the highest pitch of intensity, a fellow, without sense or manners, commenced disturbing the congregation by talking and moving about. I told him two or three times to be quiet, but he still persisted. So I took him by the arm, and led him out some distance from the house, intending to give him a severe horsewhipping for his impudence and insolence; but he pleaded so hard and pitifully, and promised never to be guilty of so mean an act again, that I let him go.

At that time there were but few schools in the country, and they were like angels' visits. The schoolmaster was evidently abroad. The most of the children were, however, taught to read; as for writing, that was an accomplishment for which they had no use. Those who had the rare privilege of going to school generally graduated in a quarter. The Sabbath day was usually spent in visiting, hunting, and fishing; but notwithstanding this was the general practice when there were no meetings, I never could indulge in it, for two reasons: First, I was taught, from my youth up, to "remember the Sabbath day, and keep it holy," and my conscience would condemn me more for a breach of this commandment than for almost any other sin I committed. Second, I had a conviction that if I hunted on the Sabbath day I would have no luck all through the next week. I observed that those who made a practice of hunting on that day were always the most unsuccessful hunters.

I once broke this commandment of God. It was a most lovely day. The sun rose bright and clear. All nature rejoiced in his light. The birds sang sweetly their matin songs, and a holy quiet reigned around, save when an occasional hunter's gun would break the stillness, sounding as harsh almost as discord in heaven. Strange that I should, under such circumstances, be tempted; and yet I was powerfully, irresistibly tempted. I persuaded my wife to go to the nearest neighbor's, with a promise that I would soon follow. When she was gone, I took my gun, ran about a mile from home, and seeing a fine, large buck, I fired, and killed him; then taking out his entrails, I threw him over a log, and returned. When I arrived at home I began to feel safe in the reflection, that no one had seen me; but quick as lightning Conscience reared her terrific scepter, and uttered, in a voice of thunder, "*God has seen you, and you have shown that you fear man more than you do God.*" How much then did I wish my load back in my gun, and the buck alive, grazing in his own native forest! Wicked as I was, I was accustomed to pray for luck in hunting; and I believed then that God often heard and answered my prayers. Once, in particular, my brother John and myself had been hunting for three entire days without success, and were hungry as wolves. The leaves were so dry it was impossible for us to get near enough to any game to shoot it. Weary and faint, I prayed to God for help. My brother, being on the opposite side of a branch, as soon as I ceased praying, started up a buck, which ran directly toward me. I was as much impressed with the belief that God had sent him as that he sent the ram to the thicket on Moriah. After coming near to me, he stopped, and I shot him.

This fall a neighbor and myself, urged by our wives, went some distance to gather cat-tails to make them beds, as the leaf beds were nearly worn out. We entered upon the journey, and had not proceeded many miles till our dog started up a bear, and soon ran it up a tree. I remained there only a short time, when it let go and came down. I sprang from my horse and ran while the dogs were fighting, and forgetting to cock my gun, placed the muzzle of it against the bear and pulled the trigger, but it would not fire; so I threw it down, and taking my tomahawk was about to strike, when it broke loose and ran away. Soon after this we saw a large buck running across our track. I bleated; he stopped, and I shot him.

After gathering our bags full of cat-tails, we started, about sundown, to hunt a place to camp. Soon after we started, I heard the dogs after a bear. Leaving my horse with my companion, I ran half a mile and found a large bear treed by the dogs. It was getting dark, but taking as good aim as I could I fired and he fell, but was only wounded and regained his position. I loaded and fired again, and again he fell; but before I could reload he was up and fighting with the dogs. I ran up to him, placed my gun against his ear, and killed him. Here we encamped all night and feasted on the deer which we had killed, and in the morning we breakfasted on the bear's feet, which had been roasting in the ashes all night. This meal constitutes the richest conceivable delicacy. Some hunters think a beaver's tail is better, or the marrow from the joint of a buffalo, but I beg leave to differ. Those who have been living on puddings and confectionaries know nothing of these good things.

This was an unlucky year to me, as I lost all the property I had by going security, or appearance-bail, at court for one of my neighbors. It being forty miles to Chillicothe, I did not go to lift my bonds; and after judgment went against him he ran away, and they held me special bail for the debt, which I always believed was unjust. I knew nothing of the matter till the deputy sheriff came with an execution. I had in my possession one hundred acres of military land, and had made good and substantial improvements thereon, but all must go to pay the debts of another. It made a clean sweep; took all my land and all the money I had to the last farthing. I then vowed that I would never again, as long as I lived, go security for any living being. Right or wrong as this vow may have been, I have kept it to this day.

I consoled my wife as well as I could, and told her we were young, and had begun the world with nothing, and would do it again. I requested her to stay at home, and keep house, and I would take to the woods and hunt. Bear-skins commanded a good price—from three to seven dollars, according to the size and quality. I spent the winter mostly in the woods, and suffered much from lying out at night without bed-clothes or bed, only as I could make one out of dry bark. I wrapped skins around me and laid by the fire. It was a prosperous winter, and success, the most sanguine, crowned my days and nights of toil and privation. From the proceeds of my winter campaign, I was enabled to purchase as good a home as that from which the law had ejected me.

Thus I passed seven years, farming in the summer and hunting in the winter, and adding to my resources till I had a comfortable home, with every thing necessary to make a backwoodsman happy. But my neighbors became too numerous, and my hunting-grounds were broken in upon by the ax of civilization; game became scarce and hard to take; my ranges were broken up, and I had about come to the conclusion to go to a new country. It seemed as though my happiness depended upon a life in the woods—"the grand old woods," where Nature had erected her throne, and where she swayed her scepter.

Alone in the deep solitude of the wilderness man can commune with himself and Nature and her God, and realize emotions and thoughts that the crowded city never can produce. To be sure one has said, "A great city is a great desert;" but it is a desert of depraved humanity, where every one is wrapped up in selfishness, and guards himself against his neighbor while his heart rankles with envy at his prosperity, or his wild, unbridled ambition urges him on the reckless course of outstripping all his competitors. Not so in the woods. There pride, envy, selfishness, and ambition have no abode. The only evil spirit that haunts the woods is Melancholy. This will often steal upon the heart of those who have not found the satisfying portion which religion imparts. There are some scenes in the wilderness where a gloomy grandeur reigns around, and they often inspire like sensations in the mind of the beholder. Speaking of Melancholy, a certain poet says:

> "She dwells by a cave, where the cypress and willow
> Are gemmed with the tears that fall from her eyes
> The cold earth her bed, the flint-stone her pillow,
> Midnight her mantle, her curtain the skies;
> Her tresses are dark as the wings of the raven,
> Her robes are all jet, and her bosom is bare;
> Like a bark on the waves, 'mid the whirlwinds of heaven,
> She wanders distracted, or sinks to despair."

Unexcited by the chase, the hunter, especially if alone, is apt to become melancholy; and though sages may speak of "the charms of solitude," the mind, without some stimulus, would not be likely to discover them. Again and again have I felt this melancholy steal over me like a cloud over the face of the sun; and were it possible to write out my thoughts, conjectures, imaginings, hopes, fears, and temptations while alone in the woods, it would startle a reader unused to such scenes and associations Often a stirring adventure would break in upon the dead sea of thought or the whirlpool of passion, rousing the one or calming the other, and again the life would flow on in the even tenor of its way.

On one occasion my feelings underwent a sudden transformation by an incident which occurred. I had been brooding in melancholy over my bad luck, when a large she bear, started up by my dogs, broke the reverie. I shot at and wounded her; but she had attacked my dogs and was killing one of them. No time was to be lost, so I ran up and thrust my knife into her side. At this she released her hold of the dog and caught me by the leg. In my effort to get released I was thrown upon my back She then made an attack on me, and I felt that scarcely any thing short of a miracle could save me. Already I could see her wide, distended jaws ready to devour me. The dogs, though wounded, recommenced the attack, and succeeded in pulling her off, and thus saved me from death. Being released, I succeeded in killing my enemy. At another time, my neighbor was with me hunting coons. At night the dogs caught some animal in a grape-vine thicket. I ran in to see what it was, and stooping down found myself directly between the horns of a large buck, which had become entangled in the vine. I was now literally between the horns of a dilemma. My companion cut the ham-strings, and I took hold of one horn and placed my feet on the other for the purpose of throwing him. At this he made one lunge, broke the vine, and threw me some distance on my back. Had my feet slipped, I would doubtless have been gored to death.

Thus I have endeavored to give the reader some account of the scenes and trials through which I passed in the woods of the west.

CHAPTER VIII.

RELIGIOUS LIFE.

HAVING given some small account of my training in the woods, I will now go back and give the reader some account of my religious education. As I before remarked, I was raised by Presbyterian parents. As customary in that Church, a custom too, I would remark, worthy of all praise, I was taught the catechism. From this I learned that God, from all eternity, had elected some men and angels to everlasting life, and passed by the remainder, ordaining them to eternal death. This election and reprobation was unconditional. Though young, I could not see the reason or justice of such a procedure on the part of God, and it gave me a very unfavorable impression in regard to the character of the Supreme Being. I recollect, distinctly, of being harassed with fear, under the impression that God had decreed I should commit some crime, and be hung for it. Associated with this was the resolution, on my part, that if he had thus decreed, I would always be the enemy of God. These impressions arose from an inability, on my part, to reconcile the punishment of the creature for the commission of sins which God had decreed he should commit, and the justice of God in the infliction of that punishment.

One Sabbath afternoon my father called us up to repeat our catechism, as was his custom. After the lesson was over, he called me to him, and said, "James, do you pray?" I replied, "No, father, I do not."

"Why do you not pray, my son?"

"Because I do not see any use in it. If I am one of the elect, I will be saved in God's good time; and if I am one of the non-elect, praying will do me no good, as Christ did not die for them."

"But, James, you do not know whether you are one of the elect or non-elect; and, as God has wisely concealed this from you, you ought to pray, any how."

To this, of course, I could make no reply, without reiterating my former declaration of the needlessness of prayer.

This doctrine had well nigh-ruined me, and often I was harassed with doubt and temptation; and, at times, almost sunk into despair. Sometimes I was led to doubt the very existence of God. The Holy Spirit often convicted me, and I felt my lost and undone condition as a sinner. These convictions were deepened and strengthened under the prayers of my pious grandmother, an account of whose death I have already given. Not knowing how to seek the Lord, I remained in this wretched condition till I was fifteen years of age. At this time I had put into my hands Winchester's Dialogues, the design of which was to prove the final redemption from hell of all. This I read over and over again with great care, and it proved a sovereign balm to all my fears. It represented God as being so merciful, that it inspired a love for him, and I became a convert to the doctrine of the final restoration of all men to the favor of God. I read the Bible to establish my faith, and boldly advocated the doctrine with my Calvinistic associates, many of whom I was enabled to overcome with my arguments. I also took occasion to show up the glaring inconsistencies of the doctrine which saved or damned men arbitrarily. This, to me, was wholly incompatible with the attributes of justice and mercy. Many of my companions looked upon my views with favor, and were pleased with my profession of faith. Finally it got to the ears of my parents that I had become a believer in hell redemption; and the news also spread among the Seceders and Covenanters—all of whom were Old School Calvinists—that the pastor's son had become a renegade from the faith of his fathers. This brought me into a new field of conflict with older and wiser heads. One of the elders attacked me at a log-rolling, and I thought he would demolish me, and make me a butt for ridicule. I told him I was but a boy, and not able to controvert with him, but if he would answer one or two questions, I would be pleased. He agreed to my proposal.

Then said I, "Did Christ die for all men?"

"No, he did not die for any but the elect."

"Will the reprobate be damned?"

"Yes; God, for the praise of his glorious justice, has decreed their damnation."

"For what is the reprobate damned?"

"Because it is so decreed, even so, according to the good pleasure of God's will."

"But the Scriptures say the reprobate is damned for unbelief. 'He that believeth not, shall be damned.' Now, if Christ did not die for him, according to your system he is to be damned for not believing what is in itself not true. In other words, he is to be damned for not believing a lie."

At this he seemed confused, and finally became angry, and said if I was his son, he would soon whip such notions out of my head. I told him he could not, unless it had been decreed. After this I became very obnoxious to the high-toned Calvinists, and they looked upon me as very dangerous to their young people. This increased my prejudice, and excited my ambition, and I sought every opportunity to have my faith confirmed, so that I might successfully contend with my opponents. At some times my faith would waver, in spite of all my efforts to bolster it up, and my conscience would sting me with remorse. The thought that perhaps the doctrine was not true, and my soul would be lost, would produce the most intense emotion in my mind. At that time there were none of those last and worst of all editions of Universalism, namely, that all will be saved, no matter what they believe, or what they do, because there was no devil, and no hell; and, hence, none could go to a place which has no existence. Such doctrines not being taught, I could not, of course, embrace them; nor do I believe I was ever so ignorant or wicked, the worst day I ever saw, as to believe a doctrine so grossly inconsistent with reason and Scripture, so false in fact, and so dangerous in tendency; but I thought that if God had brought me into the world, without my consent, for his own purposes, it was no concern of mine, and all I had to do was to be honest, enjoy life, and perform the errand of my destiny.

Thus I entered fully and freely into all parties of pleasure, except gambling, and although I could hold a good hand at cards, yet to play for stakes I had no relish. Indeed, I was afraid of this, for I always thought I could see the devil presiding over such games. Dancing constituted my chief joy; to enter its giddy mazes, and enjoy its frenzied whirl, afforded me the most pleasurable excitement. Occasionally I would take a spree; would swear when angry; and fight, when insulted, at the drop of a hat. Backwoods boys were brought up to the trade of "knock down, and drag out."

In the midst of all this mirth and revelry I dared not think of death and eternity. The thought was appalling, and in my moments of calm reflection I would resolve upon a reformation of life. A strictly moral life I regarded as the only true religion; and I believed all who 'ed such a life would go to heaven.

Thus I lived thoughtless and wicked, resolving and re-resolving upon amendment, but continuing the same, or, rather, growing worse and worse, till I arrived at the twentieth year of my age. About this time a great revival of religion broke out in the state of Kentucky. It was attended with such peculiar circumstances as to produce great alarm all over the country. It was reported that hundreds who attended the meetings were suddenly struck down, and would lie for hours and, sometimes, for days, in a state of insensibility; and that when they recovered and came out of that state, they would commence praising God for his pardoning mercy and redeeming love. This exercise was accompanied with that strange and unaccountable phenomenon denominated the jerks, in which hundreds of men and women would commence jerking backward and forward with great rapidity and violence, so much so that their bodies would bend so as to bring their heads near to the floor, and the hair of the women would crack like the lash of a driver's whip. This was not confined to any particular class of individuals, but saint, seeker, and sinner were alike subject to these wonderful phenomena.

The excitement created by these reports, was of the most intense and astonishing character. Some thought that the world was coming to an end; others that some dreadful calamity was coming upon the country as a judgment of God on the nation; others still, that it was the work of the devil, who had been unchained for a season, and assuming the garments of an angel of light, was permitted to deceive the ministers of religion and the very elect themselves. Many of the preachers spent whole Sabbaths in laboring to show that it was the work of the devil, and nothing but the wildest fanaticism, produced through the means of an overheated and distempered imagination. They also urged their congregations not to go near these places, as they would be sympathetically affected, and would, in all probability, be led to indulge in the same wild and irrational vagaries. Their instructions and exhortations, however, were lost, and it seemed that the exposition only increased the desire of thousands to go and see for themselves.

In the month of August, 1801, I learned that there was to be a great meeting at Cane Ridge, in my father's old congregation. Feeling a great desire to see the wonderful things which had come to my ears, and having been solicited by some of my old schoolmates to go over into Kentucky for the purpose of revisiting the scenes of my boyhood, I resolved to go. Obtaining company, I started from my woody retreat in Highland county. Having reached the neighborhood of the meeting, we stopped and put up for the night. The family, who seemed to be posted in regard to all the movements of the meeting, cheerfully answered all our inquiries, and gave us all the information we desired. The next morning we started for the meeting. On the way I said to my companions, "Now, if I fall it must be by physical power and not by singing and praying;" and as I prided myself upon my manhood and courage, I had no fear of being overcome by any nervous excitability, or being frightened into religion. We arrived upon the ground, and here a scene presented itself to my mind not only novel and unaccountable, but awful beyond description. A vast crowd, supposed by some to have amounted to twenty-five thousand, was collected together. The noise was like the roar of Niagara. The vast sea of human beings seemed to be agitated as if by a storm. I counted seven ministers, all preaching at one time, some on stumps, others in wagons, and one—the Rev. William Burke, now of Cincinnati—was standing on a tree which had, in falling, lodged against another. Some of the people were singing, others praying, some crying for mercy in the most piteous accents, while others were shouting most vociferously. While witnessing these scenes, a peculiarly-strange sensation, such as I had never felt before, came over me. My heart beat tumultuously, my knees trembled, my lip quivered, and I felt as though I must fall to the ground. A strange supernatural power seemed to pervade the entire mass of mind there collected. I became so weak and powerless that I found it necessary to sit down. Soon after I left and went into the woods, and there I strove to rally and man up my courage. I tried to philosophize in regard to these wonderful exhibitions, resolving them into mere sympathetic excitement—a kind of religious enthusiasm, inspired by songs and eloquent harangues. My pride was wounded, for I had supposed that my mental and physical strength and vigor could most successfully resist these influences.

After some time I returned to the scene of excitement, the waves of which, if possible, had risen still higher. The same awfulness of feeling came over me. I stepped up on to a log, where I could have a better view of the surging sea of humanity. The scene that then presented itself to my mind was indescribable. At one time I saw at least five hundred swept down in a moment, as if a battery of a thousand guns had been opened upon them, and then immediately followed shrieks and shouts that rent the very heavens. My hair rose up on my head, my whole frame trembled, the blood ran cold in my veins, and I fled for the woods a second time, and wished I had staid at home. While I remained here my feelings became intense and insupportable. A sense of suffocation and blindness seemed to come over me, and I thought I was going to die. There being a tavern about half a mile off, I concluded to go and get some brandy, and see if it would not strengthen my nerves. When I arrived there I was disgusted with the sight that met my eyes. Here I saw about one hundred men engaged in drunken revelry, playing cards, trading horses, quarreling, and fighting. After some time I got to the bar, and took a dram and left, feeling that I was as near hell as I wished to be, either in this or the world to come. The brandy had no effect in allaying my feelings, but, if any thing, made me worse. Night at length came on, and I was afraid to see any of my companions. I cautiously avoided them, fearing lest they should discover something the matter with me. In this state I wandered about from place to place, in and around the encampment. At times it seemed as if all the sins I had ever committed in my life were vividly brought up in array before my terrified imagination, and under their awful pressure I felt that I must die if I did not get relief. Then it was that I saw clearly through the thin vail of Universalism, and this refuge of lies was swept away by the Spirit of God. Then fell the scales from my sin-blinded eyes, and I realized, in all its force and power, the awful truth, that if I died in my sins I was a lost man forever. O, how I dreaded the death of the soul; for

"There is a death whose pang
Outlasts the fleeting breath:
O what eternal horrors hang
Around the second death!"

Notwithstanding all this, my heart was so proud and hard that I would not have fallen to the ground for the whole state of Kentucky. I felt that such an event would have been an everlasting disgrace, and put a final quietus on my boasted manhood and courage. At night I went to a barn in the neighborhood, and creeping under the hay, spent a most dismal night. I resolved, in the morning, to start for home, for I felt that I was a ruined man. Finding one of the friends who came over with me, I said, "Captain, let us be off; I will stay no longer." He assented, and getting our horses we started for home. We said but little on the way, though many a deep, long-drawn sigh told the emotions of my heart. When we arrived at the Blue Lick Knobs, I broke the silence which reigned mutually between us. Like long-pent-up waters, seeking for an avenue in the rock, the fountains of my soul were broken up, and I exclaimed, "Captain, if you and I don't stop our wickedness the devil will get us both." Then came from my streaming eyes the bitter tears, and I could scarcely refrain from screaming aloud. This startled and alarmed my companion, and he commenced weeping too. Night approaching, we put up near Mayslick, the whole of which was spent by me in weeping and promising God, if he would spare me till morning I would pray and try to mend my life and abandon my wicked courses.

As soon as day broke I went to the woods to pray, and no sooner had my knees touched the ground than I cried aloud for mercy and salvation, and fell prostrate. My cries were so loud that they attracted the attention of the neighbors, many of whom gathered around me. Among the number was a German from Switzerland, who had experienced religion. He, understanding fully my condition, had me carried to his house and laid on a bed. The old Dutch saint directed me to look right away to the Savior. He then kneeled at the bedside and prayed for my salvation most fervently, in Dutch and broken English. He then rose and sung in the same manner, and continued singing and praying alternately till nine o'clock, when suddenly my load was gone, my guilt removed, and presently the direct witness from heaven shone full upon my soul. Then there flowed such copious streams of love into the hitherto waste and desolate places of my soul, that I thought I should die with excess of joy. I cried, I laughed, I shouted, and so strangely did I appear to all, but my Dutch brother, that they thought me deranged.

After a time I returned to my companion, and we started on our journey. O what a day it was to my soul! The Sun of righteousness had arisen upon me, and all nature seemed to rejoice in the brightness of its rising. The trees that waved their lofty heads in the forest, seemed to bow them in adoration and praise. The living stream of salvation flowed into my soul. Then did I realize the truth of that hymn I have so frequently sung:

"I feel that heaven is now begun;
It issues from the sparkling throne—
From Jesus' throne on high:
It comes in floods I can't contain;
I drink, and drink, and drink again,
And yet am ever dry."

I told the captain how happy I was, and was often interrupted, in a recital of my experience, by involuntary shouts of praise. I felt a love for all mankind, and reproached myself for having been such a fool as to live so long in sin and misery when there was so much mercy for me.

At length we arrived at home, and I told my wife what great things the Lord had done for me. While I spoke she commenced weeping, and began to seek the Lord. I also told my brother John, and soon the news spread through the whole neighborhood that Finley had obtained religion. The difficulties the Christian has to encounter have to be learned by experience. When I was converted, I did not conceive how it was possible that even a single shade of trouble could cross my peaceful breast. I soon found, however, that the

"World was no friend to grace,
To help me on to God;"

and that if I would reign as a king and priest with God and the Lamb forever, I must fight; that the only way to the crown was by the cross. There were no religious persons in the neighborhood, and no religious meetings to attend. Persecution began to be waged against me, and difficulties rose up on every hand; but still I strove to watch, and fight, and pray, determined never to give the battle over. I sent to my brother, and persuaded him and another young man to come and unite with me in holding prayer meeting, in the woods, on Sabbath. One has said,

"The groves were God's first temples;"

and here, with no eye to see, and no ear to hear, but the great Father, we held many meetings. Still I felt, deeply, the need of Christian society. I had commenced family prayer, and reading the Scriptures whenever I had a leisure moment. The backwoods Christian is shut up to his Bible; and I have wondered if the great multiplication of books has not had a deleterious tendency, in diverting the mind from the Bible; just as the multiplicity of benevolent associations has a tendency to divert the mind from the Church. This should not be; and, in fact, there is no necessity for it, for there is room for all good books and good associations, as auxiliaries.

I sighed for Church privileges, and communion with the people of God. I could not join the Presbyterian Church; for I did not believe in the doctrine of unconditional election and reprobation. I went to a New Light camp meeting, to see if I could find a home among that people; but when I heard their doctrine on the supreme divinity of Jesus Christ, I would not go with them; for I was well assured, if Christ was not God, he could not save me; and I had such a clear and powerful demonstration of that truth, in the conversion of my own soul, that I could never doubt, for a moment, that he was God, as well as man. So I bade them farewell, and returned home. The next denomination I visited, was the Shaking Quakers; but their worship seemed to me so ridiculous, I could not entertain a serious thought about joining them.

For a while I thought I would try and travel to heaven alone. Thus I continued for about eighteen months, during which time the prayer meeting was discontinued. My attention was directed to the immorality of some professors of religion, known by the name of Seceders, which had an unhappy effect on my mind. Some of them scarcely had the form of godliness; the power they never knew. One of them was carried home intoxicated, and the next Sabbath I saw him at the communion table. This, to me, was a great stumbling-block.

Shortly after my conversion I was exercised on the subject of preaching the Gospel, and so much so, that I could not rest, day or night. I thought it a temptation of the devil, and prayed to be delivered from it, but I could not shake off the conviction. I belonged to no Church, and consequently there was no way of getting into the ministry. I once opened my mind to a Presbyterian clergyman, and he gave it as his opinion, that I should study theology at least three years, before I could be at all qualified to preach. I thought it would be folly for me to make the attempt; and hence I resisted the call, till, from a state of robust health, I was reduced almost to a walking skeleton. I had lost all my comfort, and became gloomy and desponding. Religious exercises in my family became a great task and burden. One morning I went out into the woods, and there told my Maker, if I must preach the Gospel, or go to hell, that the latter must be my portion, as I had not the least qualifications for the work. Just then all comfort and hope left me, and I was so miserable that I wandered in the woods for months, not desiring to look upon the face of any human being. Family prayer was given up, and then followed, in the sad train of evils connected with backsliding, the abandonment of prayer altogether, and a return to my former companions. To mitigate, if possible, my wretchedness

I also returned to my former practices, and realized, with Virgil,

"Facilis descensus Averni."

The road to hell was easy of access, and rapid in descent. I went to a dancing party in the neighborhood. As dancing was one of my greatest besetments, I was the more easily beguiled by Satan to enter its magic circle. I had not been long there till a lady invited me to dance with her. I remarked that if she would get some one to dance with my wife, I had no objections to complying with her request. With much persuasion and effort on the part of several, they succeeded in getting her out on the floor, and I followed. After the conclusion of the first set, I felt no more compunction of conscience, and concluded I might as well live like other people, and that there was no harm in indulging in such innocent amusements; and if there was, we would all go to hell together in accomplished and genteel society. Not so, however, with my poor wife. She suffered extremely from a wounded conscience. wept nearly all night, and feared she had denied her Savior, and put him to an open shame.

Thus I pursued the way of sin, seeking happiness in its guilty pleasures, for a period of three years. My eyes were blinded, my heart hard as adamant. I had no peace, no hope, and was without God in the world. A thought of my former happiness would occasionally, in hours of cool reflection, steal over my spirit, like forgotten joys, pleasant but mournful; while the joys of the world were

"Like odor, fled as soon as shed."

I felt an aching void, that vanity could never fill; and often did I sigh for those halcyon days of my religious life when the morning dawn and the evening shades witnessed my devotions to God. But I had cast away my confidence, and relinquished my hold on heaven, in exchange for the short-lived pleasures of sin, and a desolate heart.

In the fall of 1808 brother John and myself started out on our fall hunt. We were on horseback, and following a narrow path. I was a few paces in advance; and, as we were winding up through the thicket, my gun, which was on my shoulder, went off suddenly. In the most awful suspense I ever experienced in all my life, I stopped, and listened to hear my brother fall from his horse. After the shock was over, fearing to look round, the long agony was broken by my brother, who had recovered from the shock, saying, "Brother James, I am not hurt." This relieved me for the moment, but my soul was soon tossed by the tumultuous ragings of despair. All my sins crowded upon me like so many demons of darkness; my disobedience to God, my backslidings all rose before me, and it seemed to me that hell was just at hand, and that soon I must plunge into its dismal abodes. No imagination, had it the fervor or flight of a Milton, or Dante, could conceive, or pen describe the horror of darkness and despair that enveloped my wretched, ruined soul.

CHAPTER IX.

RELIGIOUS LIFE CONTINUED.

Gloomily and sadly I traveled on in silence, under the mountain pressure of my spirit-burden, occasionally answering a question from my brother. After having arrived at our place of camping, we spanceled, belled, turned out our horses, and started to the woods in different directions, to hunt. Having obtained what I desired, which was to be alone—for the heart can only know and appreciate its own bitterness—I realized, if possible, an increasing intensity to my feelings of wretchedness, and my excited imagination filled the woods with demons of darkness. I thought I could feel their fearful proximity, and once turned round to see if I could not discover them on my track. Just then this temptation was suggested to my mind: "You are one of the reprobates; Christ never died for you; and God has raised you up, as he did Pharoah, to show his mighty power, in your eternal destruction. You had better kill yourself with your gun, and know the worst of your wretched state; for the longer you live, the more sin you will commit, and, hence, the greater will be your damnation." This temptation came with such tremendous force, it seemed irresistible, and I was on the point of yielding, when, doubtless, my heavenly Father, in mercy, interposed a thought of my family. "How," thought I, "will my dear wife and parents feel, when my body is found, perhaps mangled and torn by wild beasts?" Again the tempter assailed me with still greater power; so much so, that I came to the dreadful conclusion of falling by my own hand. While in the very act of preparation to commit the fatal deed, my blessed Lord—who has no pleasure in the death of a sinner—again interposed, and the following words came to my mind, as sensibly as if audibly pronounced: "There is yet mercy with God, if you will seek it." At this, I threw down the deadly weapon, fell on my knees, and prayed for mercy, confessing all my guilt and sin, and sacredly vowing, if God would restore my former peace, I would do any thing he would require: ay, that I would even try to preach the Gospel of his Son. I was not conscious how long I remained in this state of agony and prayer. When I rose from the ground, I picked up my gun, ran back to the camp, fired it off, rolled myself up in my blanket, and, throwing myself on the ground, lay there till my brother John, who hearing the report of the rifle, came into camp. When he arrived, finding me lying down, he asked me if I was sick, or what was the matter. He had a kind of presentiment that all was not right, and, hence, he hastened to the camp on hearing the report of the gun. I told him I did not know what was the matter with me; but ever since the gun had gone off in the morning, I felt as if he should die, and go to hell; and "O, my brother," said I, "if the ball had hit you, you would have been in torments before this time." This seemed to convict him deeply; and, as we were both unfitted for hunting, we determined on returning home.

Still I had no peace, and I prayed, and sought for mercy day and night. "The hand of the Lord was heavy upon me." I read the Bible, but it only increased my condemnation. I found no happiness in the society of any one, and fled to the woods every day. I did not dare to take my gun with me, for fear I should, in the hour of the power of darkness, commit suicide. Instead of this, I took my Bible; and although it flashed out in letters of fire my condemnation, still my heart clung to it as my only hope. The weather being quite cold, and having no exercise, I would crawl, feet foremost, into a hollow log, and there read, and weep, and pray. In this way I spent three weeks. My wife and friends became alarmed at my condition. No one understood my state of mind, and hence there were none to administer comfort to my sin-sick soul. I thought I had committed the unpardonable sin, and despair, with its gloomy horrors, was about settling down, in all its sullen power, upon my soul, when some friend put into my hands "Russel's Seven Sermons." This book I read with the most thrilling interest. I fairly devoured its contents, and endeavored to find from it some gleam of hope—

> "Some beam of day to shine on me,
> To save me from despair;"

and "as cold water to a thirsty soul, or good news from a far country," it proved a balm to my wounded spirit. Hope again sprung up in my heart, and I was comforted with the conviction that God would have mercy and abundantly pardon.

One day my wife manifested great anxiety to have me go with her to a Methodist prayer and class meeting about six miles distant, but my prejudices were so strong against that people that I could not think of such a thing. From the various reports I had heard concerning the Methodists, I believed they were the worst of all deceivers, and, if possible, they would deceive the very elect themselves. On my declining she was much affected, and went out and wept. This scene moved me, and I relented and told her to get ready, and I would get the horses and we would start. When we arrived there my presence seemed to strike all with dismay. I had been so wicked that they had all given me up to Satan, and I even bore the cognomen of "The Newmarket Devil." The general inquiry was, "What has brought him to meeting?" The time having arrived for meeting to commence, it was opened ov singing and prayer. I conformed to the rules, for I never was wicked enough, devil though I was, in the estimation of the people, to persecute the righteous, or show my ill-breeding and vulgarity by disturbing a worshiping assembly, nor would I suffer any one else to do it where I was without correcting them. After several prayers, the leader—Mr. Sullivan—rose and said, "We are now going to hold our class meeting, and all who have enjoyed this privilege twice or thrice will please retire, while those who have not and are desirous of being benefited by the exercises may remain." I was anxious to be benefited, and being favorably impressed, thus far, with the exercises, concluded to remain. My wife also kept her seat. The members of the class eyed me very closely, and I could easily tell by their furtive glances that my room would be better than my company. The leader, as is customary on such occasions, opened the speaking exercises by relating a portion of his own experience, in which he spoke feelingly of the goodness of God to his soul. After this he spoke to the rest in order, inquiring into their spiritual prosperity; addressing to them such language of instruction, encouragement, or reproof, as their spiritual states seemed to require. It was a time of profound and powerful feeling; every soul seemed to be engaged in the work of salvation. I was astonished beyond all expression. Instead of the ranting, incoherent declarations which I had been told they made on such occasions, I never heard more plain, simple, Scriptural, common-sense, yet eloquent views of Christian experience in my life. After all the members had been spoken to the leader came to me, and, in a courteous, Christian manner, inquired into my religious condition. To his kind inquiries I could only reply in tears and sighs; for I felt as if my very heart would burst with an overwhelming sense of my wretched state. Much sympathy was awakened on my behalf, and many prayers offered to God for my salvation.

After the meeting was over we returned home, and, as soon as I could put up the horses, I went out to the woods to pray. Thus I continued retiring, as usual, to the woods, and spending my time in reading the Scriptures and Russel's Sermons, and prayer, till Thursday, which I set apart as a day for solemn fasting, humiliation, and prayer. The most of the day was spent in the hollow log, reading the Bible, and praying. In the evening I came home, and, after attending to some duties, went out again to the woods, after dark, determined, if I perished, to perish at the feet of mercy. I selected, as a place for my supplications, a large poplar-tree, and, getting on the opposite side from the wind, I scraped away the snow, that I might kneel there. Here I prayed and wrestled till about midnight, when I felt comforted. My load of sin was gone, and the sensations of cold which I had experienced were also gone. The weather seemed pleasant, and balmy as spring. I arose, and went home, filled with gratitude to God, for his forgiving mercy and redeeming love. I had not received the direct witness of the Spirit that I was a child of God, but yet I knew my sins were pardoned. I found my wife waiting for me, and we retired to rest. Just at the break of day I awoke, and I shall never be able to tell the gratitude I felt to God, that I was permitted to awake out of hell; and I thought I would express my feelings to my wife, when, to my astonishment, I found her convulsed in sorrow. and bathed in tears.

I immediately arose for the purpose of going to my barn, to pray. Just as I passed the corner of the house on my way, suddenly God poured upon me the Holy Spirit in such a manner, and in such a measure, that I fell, my whole length, in the snow, and shouted, and praised God so loud, that I was heard over the neighborhood. As soon as I was able to rise, I returned to the house, and my wife having risen, I caught her in my arms, and ran round the house, shouting, "Salvation! salvation! God has again blessed me with his pardoning love." No doubt many would have said, had they seen me, "This man is drunk or crazy." But I was not "drunk with wine, wherein is excess;" but I was "filled with the Spirit." For an hour I could do nothing but praise the Lord. While thus exercised, I felt as though some one had spoken to me, "Go preach my Gospel." I instantly replied, "Yes, Lord, if thou wilt go with me." I did not stop to confer with flesh and blood, but hurried out, as fast as I could, to my nearest neighbor, and called all the family together, and told them all that God had done for my soul; and to all within my reach that day I proclaimed a risen Savior, who had power on earth to forgive sins. This produced a powerful excitement in the neighborhood. The next morning my brother William and his wife, on their way to a Christmas frolic, called, and I persuaded them to alight and warm themselves. They assented, and came in. So soon as they were seated, I closed the door, and commenced preaching to them repentance and remission of sins, and related what God had done for my soul. At this they wept; and, placing before them chairs, I told them to kneel down, and I would pray for them. They kneeled, and I poured out my soul to God in their behalf. This was the first mourner's bench I had ever seen or heard of. I persuaded them to abandon their design of going to the Christmas frolic, and go home, and seek the salvation of their souls. This they did, and, in a few days, found peace in believing. I then invited the Methodists to come to my house and hold prayer meetings; which they did.

Then I went to the place where the circuit preacher had an appointment. After preaching he held class meeting; at the close of which he gave an invitation to any who wished to join the society, on trial, to come forward and give him their hand. I concluded if my wife would join with me, I would give the Methodists a trial, and if I liked them, I would make that Church my home. Accordingly I went to my wife, and asked her if she would join; and on her assenting, I took her by the hand, and we went up together. Several others followed us, and the meeting closed.

I commenced, from this on, to hold prayer meetings in my own house; and had not kept them up one month, till nineteen of my relatives and neighbors experienced religion. In a short time a circuit preacher came into our neighborhood, and formed us into a class or society, and appointed me the leader. This was an entirely new thing to us all. We knew but little of the Methodists and their usages; and all we could learn from them, coming as it did through a prejudiced medium, only had a tendency to produce the same results in our own minds; but we were strangely and providentially brought in the way of that people, and now were connected with them in Church fellowship. Of those who composed the class, none but myself and wife had ever been in one; and, hence, class meeting to them was an entirely novel thing. I appointed a class meeting, the next Sabbath, at my own house. When the day arrived, the whole surrounding country appeared to be on the move. The people came from every direction, and filled the house and the yard, and the lane leading thereto. My father and mother both were there.

The time for meeting arrived. With palpitating heart and trembling limbs, I arose, gave out a hymn, which we all united in singing; then I poured out my soul to God in prayer, asking for grace and wisdom, to enable me to discharge the onerous duty which rested like a mountain upon me. After prayer I sang again, and then approaching my venerable father, who had been years in the ministry of the Presbyterian Church, I inquired how his soul prospered. He arose, and related his experience, the various trials through which he had passed, and the wonderful providences of God in his behalf. I then proceeded to my mother, who had previously been much afflicted at my having joined the Methodists; but she was a good woman, and when she found that her views of that people had been formed upon incorrect and prejudiced reports, she confessed her error, and gladly acknowledged them the people of God. From my parents I passed round to each one in the house, talking and singing, exhorting, and occasionally shouting the praises of God. After having led all in the house, I went out to the yard, and while passing round there among my neighbors, telling them what God had done for my soul, and how happy I was in religion, my father continued the meeting in the house by singing and prayer. From the yard I passed into the lane, speaking to all in course. Many would turn round, and lean on the fence, and weep. Such a time I never saw before, nor have I seen since. And many were convicted, and, from that hour, began to seek religion.

A few weeks after this general class meeting was held, I was required, by one of the preachers, to take a text, and try to preach. This, in my estimation, was getting along a little too fast; but, as an obedient son in the Gospel, I yielded to his entreaties, and endeavored to exhort the people. I had determined to face duty at all hazards; and, waiving my objections to the superior judgment of one who had been in the work, I resolved that I would try. While I exhorted sinners to flee the wrath to come, many wept, and shortly after were happily converted to God. I suffered extremely in mind from this effort, and the enemy came in upon me like a flood. I ran to the woods, wept bitterly, and promised the Lord, if he would forgive me, I would never do so any more.

Soon after this I was sent for, to go and hold a meeting at brother Fowler's, on Straight creek, fourteen miles distant. I dare not refuse, for my bitter experience before had taught me that if I refused to serve God in the Gospel of his Son, the same awful darkness would surround me. Accordingly I put on my hunting-shirt and moccasins, and, leaving my hunting apparatus at home, I started before day, through the woods. I arrived at the place of meeting, and was greeted by a vast concourse of people, who had congregated from all parts of the country to hear the backwoods preacher, or rather to hear the wild hunter preach. My soul sank within me at the sight, and I ran into the woods, and fell on my knees, invoking God, with all my heart, to grant me wisdom and strength for the great work before me. My prayer was, "O Lord, thou hast sent me, and now I pray thee to help me; for I am nothing, and helpless as a child! Glorify thyself in my great weakness." I then returned, and took the stand in the cabin, and announced my text as follows: "Repent ye therefore, and be converted, that your sins may be blotted out, when the times of refreshing shall come from the presence of the Lord." Acts iii, 19. Although I knew little concerning the theory of repentance, yet I had a deep and powerful experience. When I came to speak of conversion, and the blotting out of sin, with refreshing from the presence of the Lord, my soul fired with the theme, and the Holy Spirit shed abroad its hallowed influences, and the divine power pervaded every heart, so that all the house were more or less affected; some shouting salvation, and others crying aloud for mercy. The meeting lasted till evening, and I announced that, after a short intermission, we would have a prayer meeting. When the time arrived, the people came together again, and, during the exercises of singing, prayer, and exhortation, many were converted, and one brother professed sanctification. At this point the excitement increased, and several were taken with the jerks. The next day I went home through the woods, and was so happy that I sung and shouted alternately during almost the entire journey.

About this time I was visited by my old German friend, at whose house I was converted in Kentucky, and had a most delightful interview. He was deeply experienced in the things of God, and gave me much important instruction. He told me I was now a babe, and would frequently be alarmed, and, in trying to walk, would be easily thrown down; but, like the child learning to walk, I must not be discouraged, but get up and try again; that I must never suppose that my temptations and trials would be too great for me to encounter; but that, by endurance, I would grow stronger, and also more watchful. "The devil," said he, "is like the shepherd's dog in Germany. He will sometimes worry the sheep, but it teaches them to keep up with the flock." Revivals of religion he said were like a strong wind, which blows the trees all one way, but, as soon as the storm is over, the most of them will fly back. He said I had to be drilled, and go into the army, and, as a faithful soldier, fight against the world, the flesh, and the devil. "Now," said he, "you think all that profess religion are good people; but there are many hogs among the sheep, and you may be able to distinguish between them; for when a hog comes to a mud-hole, he will put his nose into it, and grunt, and lie down in it; but the sheep will go around it, as they do not like the mud. In your Christian life you will have many cloudy days. Then the devil will come to you, and ask you to settle accounts with him. He will accuse you of many things, and try to make you believe you are nothing but a painted hypocrite, and never had any religion. You must not settle with the devil at such times, for, if you do, he will assuredly cheat you; but tell him to go away till the clouds are gone, and your soul is happy, and then call on him." These with many other good things he said to me, and they were of essential service in after life.

Our congregations became so large that none of the cabins in the neighborhood could accommodate them. To obviate this difficulty, we collected together and put up a meeting-house; and the Lord continued to revive his work. During the month of March the quarterly meeting was held on our part of the old Scioto circuit at Hillsboro. To this meeting I resolved to go; and when the time arrived, quite a number of us started. Arriving at the Rocky fork of Paint creek, we found the stream over its banks, and, as it was impossible to ford, and no craft of any description being at hand, my company turned back. I was not, however, so easily discouraged. I had set my heart upon the meeting, and I was determined on getting there, at all hazards. Riding into the water, which had overflowed the bottoms, I came to a tree which had been washed out, and lodged across the main channel, connecting with another tree on this side of the creek. Riding to the hill out of the water, I took off the saddle and bridle, and turned my horse loose, then climbing up a sapling and bending it down, I tied them to the top, and let them swing up. Then I waded out to the tree, climbed up it, got into the top of the other, went down, passed over, and waded out to dry land. I was extremely wet and cold, but I fell on my knees, thanked God, and went on my way.

Just as I entered the meeting-house the presiding

elder—Rev. John Sale—was reading his text from the eighty-fourth Psalm: "The Lord God is a sun and shield: the Lord will give grace and glory; no good thing will he withhold from them that walk uprightly." I was greatly refreshed and benefited by this discourse. When he concluded, to my great astonishment, one of the preachers present called to me to come and exhort, and close the meeting. I was overwhelmed for a moment, and scarcely knew what to do: but I dare not refuse; so I went, and told my old companions in sin what great things the Lord had done for my soul, and what he was willing to do for each and every one of them. While I was speaking, the Lord blessed me abundantly, and many hard-hearted sinners wept. On Sabbath morning the love-feast was to be held. This was entirely new to me, as I never had been in one before. It was a most deeply-interesting occasion. As one after another spoke of the goodness of God, my soul swelled with gratitude and joy, and, being unable to contain myself any longer, I sprang from my seat, and shouted the praises of God with an overflowing heart. The excitement at this point rose to its greatest hight, and it was impossible to distinguish between the shouts of joy and the cries for mercy. I thought and felt as if heaven had come down to earth. In the afternoon the sacrament of the Lord's supper was administered; and as I never had partaken of this holy communion before, it was a time of great self-examination, and deliberate, solemn consecration to God on my part. I was much blessed in partaking of the emblems of the broken body and shed blood of my Redeemer.

A little circumstance occurred while I was at this meeting, which tended wonderfully to confirm my faith in regard to trust in God for temporal blessings. When I left home I had but fifty cents in my pocket, which I was taking to Hillsboro, for the purpose of paying a debt.

When the collection was taken up on Sabbath, a struggle ensued in my mind as to whether I should throw it into the treasury of the Lord or reserve it for the purpose of paying a just debt. I did not suppose that the payment of one debt would cancel another. On the subject of my indebtedness to the Gospel there was no doubt; but as I could not meet both demands at the same time, it was suggested that I pay the man to whom I owed the sum I possessed first. At the same time it was suggested that I contribute it to the support of the Gospel and trust the Lord. The latter suggestion prevailed, and I threw it into the Lord's treasury. The next morning a man came to me who owed me a dollar and a half, a debt which I had long regarded as lost, and never expected to receive one cent. I then said instantly, "Here is my fifty cents and a dollar in the bargain." So I paid my debt and realized that they who trust in God shall never be confounded.

From this meeting I returned home, found my bridle and saddle where I had left them, and my horse in the stable. About this time my old associates, who had tried every scheme to get me back to the beggarly elements of the world, as a last resort thought they would try persecution. They sought to lay every temptation in my way, and on all occasions abused and slandered me for the purpose of rousing me to anger. The grace of God, however, was sufficient, and failing to accomplish their purposes they became divided among themselves. On one occasion a wicked man came to the place where I was working on the road, in company with the neighbors of the district, and pushing me violently, cursed me for a Methodist dog. I stepped away and said nothing. At this another man stepped up to the one who had abused me and cursed him for a coward, remarking, "Six months ago you would no more have dared to do what you have done to Finley, than you would to put your head in the fire; for he would have knocked all your teeth down your throat in an instant; and if you insult him again I will whip you like a dog." This same man went, on election day, to another fellow who was in the habit of abusing me by the most opprobrious epithets, and said to him, "R., the Methodists had a council last night, and have come to the conclusion, that inasmuch as you are constantly abusing Finley, that if you do so again they have given him the liberty to give you a sound flogging, and they will not Church him for it. Now, I advise you as a friend, if you wish to keep a whole hide, to keep out of his way." At night he told me he had seen R., and related what he had said to him. I told him he did wrong, for the Methodists had done no such a thing. He said he knew that, but he was determined to cool the fellow off. I give these incidents as a specimen of some of the trials I had to encounter in the onset of my career as a Christian.

I was greatly exercised, at times, about my call to preach, and passed through some of the most severe conflicts, lasting for whole weeks together. I still held prayer meetings and exhorted, and occasionally tried to preach. My father had joined the Methodist Church, and frequently lectured and preached. On one occasion, at our meeting, he tried to reconcile the Calvinistic notion of imputed righteousness with Wesley's teaching, and put a construction on Wesley's words which, whether legitimate or not, was not Methodistic, according to my notion of things. As soon as he was through, I rose in the congregation and said, "Father, you can no more reconcile Calvin and Wesley than you can darkness and light, or error and truth, and there is no use of your trying to do so. Permit me to say, if you are a Methodist be one, and if you are a Calvinist be one, for I want truth to prevail every-where, and every man to be really what he is."

I felt somewhat unpleasant concerning this attack on my father, but I had great zeal for the truth which had made me free. This Scripture was also applied to my mind: "He that loveth father or mother more than me, is not worthy of me." After many hard struggles of mind in regard to giving myself up exclusively to the work of a minister of the Gospel, I settled into an acquiescence to the Divine will. I thought I could labor as a local preacher around the country, and enjoy all the benefits and blessings of domestic life; and yet I felt if it was woe with me if I did not preach the Gospel, that the same necessity which drove me into the field would compel me to constant labor.

CHAPTER X.

ITINERANT LIFE.

On the solicitation of many friends, and the urgent request of Rev. John Sale, the presiding elder, I consented, for a short time, to travel the Scioto circuit. I left home on the first day of May, 1809, hoping that in the fall there would be no need of my poor services, and I could return to the quiet pursuits of domestic life. My first appointment was at the house of brother William Lucas. When the hour for meeting arrived, I went to the woods and prayed most devoutly that no one might come to the meeting; but my prayer was not answered, for the people came from all directions, and it appeared to me that the cross was so heavy it would crush me to the earth. Nevertheless, I was obliged to take it up and bear it; and although my sermon was without form and void, yet God blessed the blundering effort and gave me favor in the sight of the people. I went on to the next appointment, and attended to the duties of a traveling preacher, but had no comfort. My mind, for three weeks, was constantly harassed by the enemy, and alternated between hope and despair. Thus I continued till I arrived at West Union, and here a fresh trial awaited me. The meeting was held in brother Shultz's house, and when I rose up to commence the exercises, who should confront me but Mr. John Campbell, a lawyer, subsequently a judge but now deceased, who had come expressly for the purpose of taking down my sermon in short hand! He was one of my former most intimate friends. My thoughts became confused; all my arrangements passed away from my memory. Had I not been impelled by a sense of duty too strong to be overcome by any temporal consideration, I never would have undertaken to preach at that time. But I had passed the Rubicon—had given myself wholly to the Lord, and was not going to take back what I had done. Lifting my heart to God for grace and strength, I commenced. I knew that, although in some of the sciences he was greatly my superior, in the science of salvation I had the advantage, and could instruct him in things concerning which he knew nothing. I accordingly took a passage of Scripture which led me to speak of the new birth, and this opened up the way for me to give a relation of my experience, and to show the goodness and power of God as manifested in my conversion. The sermon seemed to make a good impression on all in the house, and many were excited to tears.

I continued to travel and preach without any license whatever till August, when a camp meeting was held on Benjamin Turner's place, in the valley of Paint creek, where I received license as a local preacher in due form from the quarterly meeting conference, and my papers were made out and signed by the Rev. John Sale. The same conference recommended me as a suitable person to be received on trial into the traveling connection. While the preachers were gone to the annual conference, I continued on the circuit, filling the appointments in regular order. Every day I prayed most fervently that if it was not the will of God that I should devote myself exclusively to the work of the ministry, that he would shut the door against me at conference, and I very much desired that such a result would happen. Having finished my round I turned my face homeward, but I had no sooner reached my residence than my wife informed me that brother Collins had passed on his way from conference and had left a few lines for me. My heart beat violently as I opened and read the contents of the letter. It stated that I was appointed to Wills Creek circuit, to travel alone. Can it be possible, thought I, that the bishop has sent me to that charge alone, with all my ignorance and inexperience? The nearest appointment on the circuit was one hundred and thirty miles from home, and to move my family that distance would be a considerable undertaking; beside my utter want of qualification to superintend a circuit, made me feel extremely unpleasant. A great conflict arose in my mind, whether I should go or not. I supposed the bishop was not sufficiently acquainted with the facts in the case, and that the partiality of my friends induced him to make an appointment which never would have resulted from personal knowledge of my incapacity. I took the whole subject before the Lord in prayer. After family worship I went into the loom-house and commenced praying to God to give me some sure indication in regard to his will in this matter. I wrestled all night in supplication, but found no relief. Morning came, and I went into my house and sat down by the table, on which was the family Bible, almost distracted. I asked the Lord, if there was a promise in that book which would give me direction and settle the doubtful state of my mind, to direct me to it. On opening the Bible, the first passage on which my eyes fell was Deuteronomy xxxiii, 25: "Thy shoes shall be iron and brass; and as thy days, so shall thy strength be." This promise was applied to my heart by the Holy Spirit with tremendous power, and I shouted and praised God with all my soul. My doubts and fears all left me, and I told my beloved wife that I now had faith to believe that God would take care of me and guide me aright.

As soon as I could get all things in readiness I prepared to start for my circuit. I shall never forget the parting scene. It seemed to me that I was about to leave the world and part from all my relatives, and wife, and little daughter forever. After prayer I rose, embraced them all, mounted my horse, and started. After riding some distance, I came to a point where the road diverged, and desiring to take a last look at the loved ones behind, I turned and saw them weeping. It was a severe struggle with nature, but grace proved triumphant, and I journeyed on.

Several days' travel brought me to Zanesville, the principal appointment on my circuit. When I arrived in town it was raining hard. In lieu of an overcoat, to protect me from the storm, I had procured a blanket, and cutting a hole in the middle of it, I thrust my head through it and found it a good protection. Riding up to the door of one of the principal Methodists of the place, I asked for lodgings, informing the brother that the conference had sent me there as the preacher. Eyeing me closely from head to foot, he replied, "You look like any thing else than a preacher." I told him he should not judge too rashly, as he might, perhaps, think better of me on a closer examination, and I suggested the propriety, at least, of his giving me a fair trial. To this he assented, and I tarried with him. The next day being Sabbath, I preached, in the morning, in the log court-house, and, after leading the class, rode six miles to brother Joseph's, where I preached again in the afternoon and met class.

Wills Creek circuit was formed by the Rev. James Watts, and was computed to be four hundred and seventy-five miles round. Its route was as follows: Beginning at Zanesville and running east, it embraced all the settlements on each side of the Wheeling road, on to Salt creek and the Buffalo fork of Wills creek; thence down to Cambridge and Leatherwood, on Stillwater; thence to Barnesville and Morristown; thence down Stillwater, including all the branches on which there were settlements, to the mouth; thence up the Tuscarawas, through New Philadelphia, to One-leg Nimishilling; thence up Sandy to Canton, and on to Carter's; thence to Sugar creek, and down said creek to the mouth; thence down the Tuscarawas to William Butts's, and thence down to the mouth of Whitewoman; thence, after crossing the river, including all the settlements of the Wapatomica, down to Zanesville, the place of beginning.

I entered upon this work with great fear and trembling. No where, in all the round, could I find a place for my family to live, and hence I was driven to the necessity of building a cabin, which I located on the Leatherwood fork of Wills creek, fourteen miles west of Barnesville. After getting it ready for occupancy, I wrote to my father, requesting him to bring my family, and after a separation of four months we had the pleasure of meeting again. We took possession of our humble cabin, twelve by fourteen feet, which proved sufficiently capacious, as we had nothing but a bed and some wearing apparel. My funds being all exhausted, I sold the boots off my feet to purchase provisions with; and after making all the preparation that I could to render my family comfortable, started out again upon my circuit, to be absent four weeks.

Instead of taking a circuitous route to reach my appointments, I proceeded across the country through the woods, and after traversing hills and vales, without a path to guide me, I was thrown considerably out of my course. About sunset I struck a trace leading from Cambridge to Cadiz, and night overtaking me as I was following this path, I came to the cabin of an old Irish gentleman, a Roman Catholic. On entering this habitation in the woods, I found the family at their evening repast. They occupied one side of the fireplace, and a calf, which was busy eating a mess of pumpkins, occupied the other. I was invited to join in the evening meal, which I did with good relish, as I had eaten nothing during the day. After supper was ended I asked the old gentleman in regard to his nativity, his religious profession, etc. On his informing me that he was a Roman Catholic, I inquired how he got along without his confession. At this he became visibly agitated, and informed me he had not seen a priest for years; but that he was laying up money to go to Pittsburg to obtain absolution. I then asked him if he had ever experienced the new birth, or if he had been born again. To this question he seemed unable to give an answer, and manifested still more uneasiness. He asked me what I meant; for, said he, "I am now seventy years old, and never heard of such a thing in all my life." Becoming alarmed he called his son John. I told him he need not be excited, as I would do him no harm. He then asked me if I was a minister. I told him I tried to speak to the people and teach them the way of salvation by faith in the Lord Jesus Christ. The whole family seemed to be alarmed at the conversation; but I spoke kindly to them; and after their fears were somewhat quieted I took out my Bible, and reading a part of the third chapter of John, I spent an hour in explaining to them the nature and necessity of the new birth. The family listened to all I had to say with the most profound attention, and silence was only interrupted by their sighs and tears. After prayer we all retired to rest for the night.

In the morning, previous to leaving, the old gentleman invited me to preach for the neighborhood when I came round the next time, which I promised to do, enjoining on him and his family the necessity of prayer to God.

Nothing worthy of particular note occurred till I returned to this house. I found, at the time appointed, a large collection of people, and preached to them salvation in the name of Jesus. The Lord attended his word with power to the hearts of the people; many were awakened, and a good work began. Soon after the old gentleman experienced religion, and also his son John; and they, with other members of the family, joined the Church. The father lived a consistent life and died a happy death, and the son became a talented and useful exhorter.

Many were the difficulties I had to encounter in traveling this circuit. The country was new, and the people were generally ignorant and wicked. Sometimes while trying to preach, they would interrupt me by cursings and mockings, and frequently they would threaten me with chastisement, but none of these things moved me. My want of experience and conscious inability to preach the Gospel as a workman that need not be ashamed, led me to seek, with great earnestness, the sanctifying influences of the Spirit of God, and to devote every spare hour to the study of the Bible. My place of study was the forest, and my principal text-books the Bible, Discipline, doctrinal tracts, and the works of Wesley and Fletcher. Often, while in the woods reading my Bible on my knees, and praying to God for the wisdom that cometh down from above, was my heart comforted. My feeble efforts were abundantly blessed, and many seals were given to my ministry. The Lord revived his work at several appointments and opened my way, giving me access to the hearts of the people. At one time I made an appointment on Sugar creek, but when I came to it there was no house for me to preach in. Accordingly I called the people together under a large oak in a small prairie. The people, however, would not come near me, but stood in the plum bushes around, and I preached to them, in their hiding-places, Jesus Christ and the resurrection. At my second appointment they seemed less fearful, and I gained so much on their confidence that I ventured to make an appointment for my next round at Mr. Cory's house.

When I arrived the people had collected, and after preaching to them, I proposed holding class meeting. I began with an old German, named Baker, and afterward spoke to his son Jacob. While talking to Jacob, the old man exclaimed, "Jake, if you and I don't do petter, de tivel vill come and dakes us poth." He then wept bitterly. At this the divine power came down upon the hearts of the people, and many were awakened and converted to God. I formed a class, and appointed brother Corey the leader.

At another time, while preaching at brother Butt's, a German woman became awakened to a sense of her lost condition as a sinner, and it seemed, so great was her distress of mind, that she would go into despair. Her husband said I had bewitched her, and he was determined to shoot me, not for a witch, but a wizard. For this purpose he loaded his rifle with a charmed bullet, and went two miles for the purpose of waylaying me. Having reached the point in the road which I had to pass, he secreted himself in the bushes, and awaited my arrival. He was not long, however, in this position, till his mind was filled with dreadful thoughts; horrid visions floated before his excited imagination; demon shapes gathered around him, and he fled precipitately for home, in as much distress as his poor wife. They sent for brother Vulgamode and his wife to come and pray for them, which they did, and soon both experienced religion; and I had the pleasure of receiving them into the Church.

A painful incident occurred about this time. A brother S., who had been appointed leader of the class at White Eyes Plains, with some of the members of his class, was induced to go to a horse-race, where they became intoxicated. Soon after this he was taken sick, and, while suffering under disease, he made many promises, if the Lord would spare his life, to do better. The Lord heard his vows; the disease was rebuked, and his health began to return. Before, however, he was fully restored, he went to a corn-husking, and was again overcome by strong drink. He was carried, in a state of intoxication, into the house, and laid on a bed; and no further attention was paid to him till after supper, when the party began to clear the room for a dance. The room being small, it was necessary to remove the bed; but when they came to wake S. from his drunken slumbers, they found him dead. His soul had been summoned away. What an awful warning to backsliders and drunkards! Reader, have you departed from God by sin and transgression? Return, O return speedily, lest you be filled with your own ways. Remember God will not always be mocked. Have you been in the habit of drinking? Quit it instantly; go not where it is; "taste not, touch not, handle not," or you are gone forever. O, "look not upon the wine when it is red, when it giveth its color in the cup, when it moveth itself aright; for at last it biteth like a serpent, and stingeth like an adder." Death and damnation are in the maddening draught; therefore, fly from the insidious destroyer.

Another alarming judgment occurred in the case of M. P. about this time. He had embraced infidelity, and was a boasting disciple of Tom Paine. On a public occasion he was heard to say that he was a deliberate enemy of Jesus Christ, and would only live to oppose him and his religion; confirming the declaration by several awful oaths and imprecations. The following week he became suddenly deranged, and became such a furious madman that it was necessary to put him in close confinement. His haggard features and demon-like scowl were truly terrific, and his language was horrible and blasphemous beyond expression. He raved as though torn by a thousand furies, gnashed his teeth, and gnawed his blaspemous tongue, till exhausted nature yielded, and he gave up the ghost. I was invited to preach his funeral; and, in the fear of God, I endeavored to make what improvement I could of so awful a scene. It is not strange that those who abuse their reason in denying the existence of a God, should lose its proper exercise, any more than that those who abuse any physical organ should lose its use.

Once after preaching at White Eyes Plains, a messenger came to me and said there was a poor woman, who lived about five miles distant, who was anxious to see me. Accordingly I went, and, on arriving, found her in an open cabin, surrounded by four helpless children, all in the deepest poverty. Her husband had died, and was buried in the woods, a short distance from the rude, unfinished cabin which he had tried to rear for his family. My sympathies, already excited by the appearance of the family, were hightened in their intensity by the widow's sad tale of woe. All the money I had in the world was thirty-seven and a half cents. What to do I knew not. It occurred to me, that my thick, new, cloth leggins, which I wore over my buckskin pants, would make the eldest son a good, warm coat; and I was about untying them, when it was suggested that I could not possibly do without them; besides it was raining and cold, and I would be much exposed; I, however, overcame the temptation, pulled off the leggins, and gave them to the mother, telling her to make a coat out of them for her son; and then, giving her the small sum of money, and praying with the family, I departed. I had not gone a hundred yards from that desolate habitation till the Lord poured down upon me a blessing, and I shouted and traveled on in the rain. As night approached I reached the mouth of Whitewoman, which I crossed, and stopped at a tavern. I told the tavern-keeper I would like to stop with him, but had nothing to pay. He took my horse, and, after putting him in the stable, he came in and asked me who I was. I gave him my name and vocation. While I was drying my pants by the fire, supper was announced, which I ate with great relish. After prayers, and conversation on a variety of topics, I went to bed. While sitting, in the morning, by the fire, trying to rub some pliability into my now dry and hard leather breeches, the landlord came in and presented me with a fine pair of new leggins, and a dollar in the bargain. This kind act so filled me with gratitude to God that I made the barroom ring with shouts of praise. I realized the truth of that proverb, "He that hath pity on the poor, lendeth to the Lord; and he shall be repaid again."

Some time in June the Rev. James Quinn—the presiding elder of the district—sent brother John Strange, of blessed memory, to travel with me. He was then quite a youth, and had just entered the field as an itinerant preacher. His person was tall and slender, but graceful, and his manners prepossessing and engaging. Although he could not wear the armor of Saul, he soon learned to use the sling of David with admirable dexterity. He was unassuming and modest in all his deportment to his superiors; kind and conciliatory in all his bearing to his equals, and affectionate and amiable to all. He possessed a voice of unusual sweetness, compass, and power. His singing would entrance the hearts of listening thousands; and I have witnessed its effect as the silvery tones would rise, and swell, and fall upon the ear, like strains from heaven. He was not a literary man, in the ordinary acceptation of that term; but, like the backwoods preachers of those days, was self-taught; and, by deep communion with himself, and nature, and God, had acquired a knowledge of human nature and the springs of human action, that enabled him to wield a vast power over the minds of the thousands who crowded together to hang upon the moquence of his lips. He was one of nature's orators. When inspired with his theme, his eye kindled with unearthly fire, and his whole face gleamed with a heavenly radiance. When he described heaven, which he always did in the beautiful and impressive imagery of the Bible, the mind seemed transported to that bright world, and to wander, with rapture,

> "Among the bowers, and by the streams
> Of heaven's delightful shore."

When he would describe the dying Christian, so vividly would he bring before the mind the triumphs of the parting scene, that, like Bunyan when he saw Christian and Faithful enter the celestial gate, you would be constrained to wish yourself with them in that hour. When, by him, the violated law spoke out its thunders, he would rise to an awful sublimity; his brow would gather blackness; his eye dart fire; and, with the quick and significant gesture of his hand, he would indicate the doom of the finally impenitent, and startle the most hardened from their seats. He seemed to have lost all love of the world, and literally to have forsaken all for Christ. His whole soul was in his work; and having but one object, he was concentrating all his powers in its pursuit. I at once took him to my heart, and found him a faithful and affectionate co-laborer in the vineyard of the Lord. Our hearts were always in unison; and we never exchanged an unpleasant word or look for upward of twenty years' labor and acquaintance. He entered the ministry and pursued the work of an itinerant, as all young men who enter the field should do. Who ever heard John Strange say, "My work is too hard," or, "My circuit is too poor?" Although he had a slender frame and feeble constitution, subject to many afflictions, he seldom ever lost an appointment. Sick or well, he continued in the work, trusting in God, and laboring for the salvation of souls. He had taken his charge, and had resolved only to lay it down with his body, ceasing to work only when he ceased to live. He was my first colleague, my true yoke-fellow, my bosom friend. But he has done the errand of his Master, and entered into the joy of his Lord. He fought a good fight, finished his course, kept the faith, and obtained the crown of eternal life. After traveling thirteen years in the Ohio conference, he was transferred to Indiana, where he labored eight or nine years, and died in Indianapolis in 1832. Twenty-two years of his life were spent in the vineyard of the Lord; and many in eternity's morning will hail him as their herald to the land of bliss. A short time before his death he sent me the following message: "Tell my old friend, brother Finley, that all is well. I shall soon be at home. Glory to God for the prospect I have of meeting him there!" Yes, sainted one, I shall soon meet you in that upper, better sanctuary. I feel that the frosts of fifty winters, in the hard-fought field of itinerant life, will soon cause me to fade like the leaf of an Indian summer; and I shall sleep with my fathers and brothers on the bosom of my Savior and my God.

The first camp meeting ever held in this region of country was on the land of Mr. James Clark, on Tuscarawas river. This meeting produced a great excitement among all classes of people; and they came from all parts of the country to attend it. The Moravians, who resided a short distance above, were prohibited, by their good old priest, from attending; but, notwithstanding all the admonitions to prevent their attendance, when the time arrived for holding the meeting, many were there. Quite a number of these people experienced religion; and so powerful was the manifestation of the Spirit of God, that multitudes were converted, and hundreds went away deeply and powerfully convicted on account of their sins. As usual on all such occasions, the spirit of persecution was developed. Inroads made on the territory of darkness will always excite a sturdy conflict with the powers thereof; and the resistance to truth and righteousness more visibly manifests itself during a revival than at any other time. The power and genuineness of a work of God may be usually measured by the opposition it meets with from the world, the flesh, and the devil. The work of the Lord, however, went on, and the cause of Christ triumphed gloriously.

An incident occurred on this circuit in reference to our rules, which I will relate. At Lemuel Joseph's the class-leader had permitted a Lutheran, by the name of Mr. John Bowers, to meet in class from time to time, and have all the privileges of the Church, though he was not a member, and refused to join, assigning as a reason, that if he should leave the Lutheran Church and join any other, he would be guilty of perjury. His wife, also a Lutheran, was in the habit of attending and enjoying the same privileges. When I came to lead the class, I told them they could not remain unless they would join the Church, and they must leave. They went away much afflicted, and the whole class felt offended at me for the procedure. I told them they must not blame me. If they had any fault to find, they must attack the rules of the Church, which forbade their remaining; and besides, they must think me faithless to my trust, as the administrator of Discipline, if I would permit the rules to be violated under my own eye, when I had the power to prevent it. When I came round again Mr. Bowers and wife and mother were there again. After preaching I told them, as before, that unless they intended to join the Church, they must retire while we held class. At this the old lady left, but the old gentleman remained. While the meeting progressed, the Lord manifested himself to the people in great power, and we had a glorious time, so that the old lady, who was an attentive listener on the outside, thrust open the door, exclaiming with a loud voice, "My God, I can stay out no longer!" That day they all joined the class, and we had a season of great rejoicing. The members who were dissatisfied at the stand I had previously taken in carrying out the rules, now came to me and said, "You did just right."

Some years after I stopped to see the old people. As I approached the house, old brother Bowers was standing inside the bars; I said to him, "Brother Bowers, please let down the bars, that I may ride into the yard." "No," said he, "brother, you must let down the bars yourself. You made me lay down the bars once to get into the Church, now you must take down the bars and come into my house, and you shall be welcome." This man and his family were very consistent members of the Church and ornaments of their profession.

At the mouth of One-leg, in the bounds of my circuit, there lived a hunter and trapper. He spent the most of his time in the woods and mingled but little with society. He was looked upon by the neighbors as rather an object of dread than otherwise. As I had a long ride between my appointments, I concluded, one day, to take his cabin in my route and stop with him and his family, and perhaps I might be able to do them some good. Accordingly I rode up to his rude habitation and asked him if I could get something for myself and horse to eat. He cast a sour look at me and crustily replied, "I suppose you can." I got off my horse and walked in, and while his wife was making preparations for a meal, I looked up and saw his rifle suspended upon hooks over the door. Said I to him, "You have a good-looking gun hanging there." He replied, "Yes."

"Are you a good shot, Mr. Reeves?"

"I count myself among the very best."

"Do you think you can beat me?"

"Yes, with all ease, or any other man."

"I have some doubts on that subject."

"You can soon settle that matter after you get your dinner."

He then took down his rifle, put it in order, and made his target, and waited till I had partaken of my dinner, seemingly impatient to test my skill as a marksman. We walked out, and placing the target he stepped off the distance and said, "The first shot is yours." I took the rifle, and, taking deliberate aim at the center, fired. He reloaded and did the same, but I had beaten, as my ball was nearest the center. We fired again, and this time he had slightly the advantage, which seemed to cheer him much. We took another round, and my ball was the nearest the center. The whole six balls, so close were the shots, could have been fully covered by a quarter of a dollar. He was anxious to try it again, but I declined, saying, "If it suits your pleasure, wait till I come round my circuit again, and then, if you wish, we will try it over. I will then stay all night, and we will have more time." I said, also, "If you will tell your neighbors to meet here at three o'clock, four weeks from to-day, I will preach to them." I then returned to the house, got my horse, and proceeded on to my next appointment.

When I came round at the appointed time, I found all the men, women, and children of the settlements, within four miles, collected to hear me preach. I had great freedom, and during the discourse there was much weeping. I spoke affectionately to all about their salvation. After the congregation had dispersed, the trapper came to me and said,

"Excuse me, sir, I wish to go trapping; you can stay at my house till I return."

"But," said I, "let me go with you." To this he

assented. and getting his traps we started. On the way I proposed to take half the traps and set them, that we might see which had the best luck. He agreed to this, and we went on setting trap about. When a favorable opportunity presented itself I commenced conversing with him about the salvation of his soul and the souls of his family, and preached to him Jesus and his salvation. At first he scarcely knew how to take me; but seeing my earnestness and sincerity, at length he yielded to the power of truth, and he burst out into passionate expressions of grief. After setting the traps we returned to the trapper's home. I prayed with the family that night and also in the morning, and started on my way. On my next visit the trapper and his wife obtained the pardon and the peace of God, and I formed a class at his house and appointed him the leader.

One of the most tragical events ever recorded, occurred within the bounds of this circuit at the village of Gnadenhutten, March 8, 1782. The Moravian missionaries, whose zeal is unquenched by the snows of Lapland, and whose energy braves the burning sands of Arabia and Africa, had penetrated these western wilds before the white man had made his settlement, and had succeeded in establishing missions on the Tuscarawas, among the Delaware Indians. They had three stations on the river; namely, Gnadenhutten, Shoenbrun, and Salem. These villages were occupied by the Indians, all of whom had become Christianized, and were peacefully engaged in the various pursuits of civilization.

Several depredations having been committed by hostile Indians, about the time of which I am writing, on the frontier inhabitants of Western Pennsylvania and Virginia, they determined to retaliate, and a company of one hundred men was raised and placed under the command of Colonel Williamson, as a corps of volunteer militia.

They set out for the Moravian towns on the Tuscarawas river, and arrived within a mile of Gnadenhutten on the night of the 5th of March.

On the morning of the sixth, finding the Indians at work in their cornfield on the west bank of the river, sixteen of Williamson's men crossed over, two at a time, in a large sugar trough, taking their rifles with them. The remainder went into the village, where they found an Indian and squaw, both of whom they killed. The sixteen on the west side, on approaching the Indians, found them more numerous than they had anticipated. The Indians had their arms with them, which they carried not only for purposes of protection, but for killing game. The whites accosted them kindly, telling them that they had come for the purpose of taking them to a place where in future they would be protected in safety, no longer to be startled by the rude alarm of angry foes. They advised them to quit work, and go with them to Fort Pitt. Some of the tribe had been taken to that place in the preceding year, and were treated with great kindness by their white neighbors, and especially the governor of the fort, and returned to their homes with tokens of friendship and kindness. Under such circumstances it was not surprising that the innocent and unsuspecting Moravian Indians surrendered their arms, and at once consented to place themselves under the protection and control of Williamson and his men. An Indian messenger was dispatched to Salem, for the purpose of apprising their brethren of the arrangement, and then both companies returned to Gnadenhutten. On reaching the village, a number of mounted militia started for the Salem settlement, but ere they reached it, so great was the dispatch of the messenger, that they found the Moravian Indians at that place had already left their cornfields, and were on the road to join their brethren at Gnadenhutten. Measures had been previously adopted to secure the Indians whom they had at first decoyed into their power, and accordingly they were bound, and confined in two houses, securely guarded. On the arrival of the Indians from Salem—their arms having been secured without any suspicion of their hostile intentions—they were at once seized, fettered, and divided between the two prison-houses, the males in one, and the females in the other. The number thus confined in both houses, including men, women, and children, amounted to from ninety to one hundred.

A council was then held to determine how the Moravian Indians should be disposed of. This self-constituted military court consisted of both officers and privates. Williamson put the question whether the Indians should be taken, prisoners, to Fort Pitt, or *put to death*, requesting those who were in favor of saving their lives to march out of rank, and form a second rank in advance. Only eighteen, out of the whole number, stepped out as the advocates of mercy. In these the feelings of humanity prevailed; but in the others, constituting the large majority, humanity and justice were utterly extinct. They had deliberately come to the conclusion to *murder* the whole of the Christian Indians in their power. Among the doomed were several who had contributed to aid the missionaries in the work of conversion and civilization; two of whom emigrated from New Jersey after the death of their pastor, Rev. David Brainard. One Indian female, who could speak good English, fell upon her knees before Williamson, the commander, and begged most eloquently and piteously for his protection; but all her supplications and pleadings were unheeded by the heartless and dastardly wretch, who ordered her to prepare for death.

They had anticipated the cruel fate that awaited them, and their hymns of praise and fervent prayers ascended from their prison, during the whole of that eventful night.

to their great Father in heaven. Their prayers and tears, and their pleadings for mercy and protection were lost upon their white murderers, but they entered the ears of an avenging God. When the morning sun arose, the work of death commenced, and a scene of human butchery occurred, of sufficient enormity to move the heart most used to blood and carnage, and gather paleness on the cheek of darkness itself. One after another, men, women, and children were led out to a block prepared for the dreadful purpose, and, being commanded to sit down, the ax of the butcher, in the hands of infuriate demons, clave their skulls. Two persons, who were present at that time, and who related to me the fearful story, assured me that they were unable to witness, but for a short time, the horrid scene. One of these men stated that when he saw the incarnate fiends lead a pretty little girl, about twelve years of age, to the fatal block, and heard her plead for her life, in the most piteous accents, till her innocent voice was hushed in death, he felt a faintness come over him, and could no longer stand the heart-sickening scene. The dreadful work of human slaughter continued till every prayer, and moan, and sigh was hushed in the stillness of death. No sex, age, or condition was spared, from the gray-haired sire to the infant at its mother's breast. All fell victims to the most cold-blooded murder ever perpetrated by man.

There lay, in undistinguished confusion, gashed and gory, in that cellar, where they were thrown by their butchers, nearly one hundred murdered Christian Indians, hurried to an untimely grave by those who had but two days before sworn to protect them. God of humanity, what an act! But this was not enough. If possible, to highten its atrocity, the buildings were fired, and the timbers of their peaceful homes were made the fuel that consumed their lifeless bodies. When I stood beside this cellar, and witnessed its blackened and dilapidated walls, and learned with what fortitude those poor Moravian Indian brethren met their martyr fate, some of them praising God to the last, others, like their divine Master, praying for their murderers, none can tell the deep and overwhelming feelings of my soul. But, blessed be God! Satan can only go the length of his chain! The ax of persecution can only cut down the separating wall that lets the saint into heaven. The fires can only consume the mortality, from which the deathless spirit is evolved, and from whence it shall go, as in chariots of fire, to heaven.

At this settlement I found the Rev. Mr. Mortimer, who had charge of the Indians, and the Rev. George Godfrey Miller, who had charge of the whites in the Moravian reservation. Here I ventured to go and preach, and the Lord owned and blessed his word; many were awakened and converted. I formed a class, and appointed a leader. This rather displeased old father Miller, and he wrote me a letter, requesting me to leave the reservation, and not preach there any more. I sent him word that I could not do that; as my commission was to go into all the world, and preach the Gospel to every creature; and that, as soon as I was able, I intended to obey the Divine command; and if he had any thing to say, he must say it to my Master. I furthermore said, if he could ascertain from the Lord that my field of labor did not include the reservation, then I would comply with his request, and retire. The next week the old gentleman walked four miles, to brother Karr's, to meeting. I asked him to preach for us, which he did; and after meeting, at my request, he remained with us in class, where he received, with all of us, a powerful blessing. The whole class was in a flame of love and joy; and the old Moravian saint caught the fire, and shouted, as loud as any of us, the praises of God. After this, whenever he could, he worshiped with us, and never alluded to my leaving the reservation.

On this circuit there were four local preachers; namely, J. M. Round, John Willey, J. Myers, and James Sharrock; all efficient and useful ministers of the New Testament.

My first was perhaps the most interesting of all the years of my itinerant life. I kept a memorandum of the names, places, and date of all that joined; amounting to one hundred and seventy-eight in number, some of whom became preachers, and are now on the walls of Zion, proclaiming salvation in the name of the Lord.

CHAPTER XI.

LOST IN THE MOUNTAINS.

In the bounds of my first circuit lived sister Boarer, a history of whose wonderful deliverance, by Providence, was related to me with her own lips, and I will narrate it for the benefit of my readers.

Mrs. Boarer, the heroine and narrator of the story, was the wife of Mr. George Boarer, and was, by education and parentage, a Roman Catholic. Her parents were natives of Berkley county, Va., and, at the time, were residents of the country in the vicinity of Sleepy creek. Early on the morning of the 7th of January, 1800, she left home on a borrowed horse, to cross the Capon Mountains, to visit her aged parents. She took with her an infant child, a daughter, seven months old. The snow upon the mountains was three feet deep, and the weather was exceedingly cold. For defense, and company's sake, she took with her the house-dog, a very large spaniel. Having gained the top of the mountain range, she concluded to leave the great road, and, by a short cut, arrive the same night at her father's house.

She had, however, not proceeded far before she found herself bewildered, and, in consequence, becoming frightened. She dared not turn back, but wandered about through the mountain till night had settled its gloom over the world. She then dismounted; and having fastened her horse to a sapling, she prepared a place, as well as circumstances would admit, where to pass the night. The snow, as before remarked, was three feet deep; the darkness was profound, and the wind from the north-west broke in a hurricane above her. With no company but her child, and no protector but her dog, her condition was lonely beyond the imagination to conceive.

Fortunately, she had with her some extra clothing, in the shape of a cloak and a shawl. Removing, as well as she could, the snow from beneath a large tree, she took her apparel and made the best disposition possible with it; and, with her child and her dog, she composed herself for the night.

Sister Boarer stated to me, that for a week previous to undertaking this journey she was unusually exercised about her spiritual welfare, and very frequently took an old prayer-book and read it.

Now, far from her home, desolate and distressed, she felt the need of close communion with God. The prayers which she had read the week before came fresh to her mind, which she offered fervently to her Maker. The night was long and dreary, and she spent it without sleep. Very shortly after fastening her horse, the animal became uneasy, and breaking his bridle, started off at full speed. This greatly added to her misfortunes, for she had hoped by him to have reached some settlement the next day.

At length day dawned; and though, by the help of her clothing and her dog, she had kept herself and child from freezing, yet she was so benumbed by the cold as almost to be unable to walk and carry her infant daughter with her. This was Saturday morning. She now left part of her clothing, and made an effort to return to the point where she left the great road. After traveling till she was nearly exhausted, she concluded that, unless she reached the settlement, she must perish with the cold. Indulging the hope, however, that she might keep herself from freezing, or be found by some one, she thought it best to return to the spot where she passed the previous night

Accordingly, she started back, and, on her way, hung up her apron on a bush, and afterward a handkerchief, as signs of distress, in hope, though indeed but faint hope, that some passing hunter might see one or the other, and come to her relief. Late in the afternoon of Saturday, and with great difficulty, she regained her lodging-place.

But feeling now the dread of passing another night in so desolate a place, and summoning that indomitable spirit of courage, peculiar to her sex when in difficulty and danger, and seeing the sun fast declining, she determined to change her course; and make one more desperate effort to gain some settlement. Throwing off part of her apparel, in order to be less incumbered, she began again to contend with the snow, rocks, and caverns of the mountains, and at length came to a deep, narrow gorge, down the sides of which she could not descend with her child.

She looked up and down, but could see no place that offered an easier passage than the one before her. She hesitated a moment, but having no other alternative, she threw her child over, and then followed herself. By taking hold of the laurel bushes on the opposite side of the ravine, she managed to crawl up to the place where her child lighted, which, to her great joy, she found uninjured, save by a slight scratch on its face, caused by its falling on the crust of the snow. Resuming her journey, she came upon a hog-path, which led to a cleft of shelving rocks where these animals were accustomed to sleep.

She had now traveled—as was afterward ascertained—one mile and a half. Here she might have remained sheltered for the night, but fearing the return of the half starved hogs, and that herself, her child, and her dog, might all become a sudden prey to their voraciousness, and her family never learn their fate, she immediately resumed her march, and, weary and faint, made her way about three hundred yards off, to the side of the mount ain. Finding her stockings entirely cut up by the crust of the snow, and her limbs, and ankles, and feet all bleeding, she yielded the struggle, and under some pine bushes hard by, she obtained a place to sit down; but the snow sinking beneath her, rendered her situation most critical and desperate.

She took care to wrap her clothes around her feet and body as well as she could; then clasping her babe warm to her bosom, she committed herself to God.

Her faithful dog had not left her, and this night would lie down just where she bade him; sometimes on her feet and limbs, and sometimes at her back, changing alternately, as if to keep her from freezing. During the night she fell asleep, being exhausted with the labor and with want of food. This night it snowed and blew, till the new fall of snow was ten inches deep on the top of the former. When she awoke she heard the chickens crowing at the foot of the mountain, and the dogs barking, so near was she to a house; but the wind was blowing directly from them to her, which proved extremely unfavorable to her. About the same time she thought she heard the people feeding their cattle. She called as loud and as long as she could, but no one came to her relief. This morning she found that her feet and limbs were badly swelled, and the skin, in many places, broken.

This discovery went home to her heart, and she commenced to make her peace with God, and gave herself up to die. She thought if her infant child were dead, she, too, could die in peace; but to leave it to perish with cold and hunger, was a thought more than a mother's heart could bear. She laid the little thing down to freeze to death before she should die herself, but when it wept. she would take it up and clasp it to her bosom. Despairing at last to make herself heard, as the wind continued to blow violently in a contrary direction, she resorted to another expedient. It was this: She pinned her child's bonnet around the dog's neck and sent him to solicit help. The poor animal, as if perfectly understanding her meaning, started off immediately, and was afterward tracked to the house nearest to his distressed mistress, and then to a mill; but, it being Sabbath day and extremely cold, the dwellings were all shut up and no one saw him, and in an hour or two he returned and took up his station. When it was becoming about feeding time she commenced calling again, and a man on the top of a stack of hay heard her, and told his wife that he heard something on the mountain making a noise like a person in distress; and he went to a neighbor and told him the same thing; to which the latter, however, only replied, "I suppose it must be a panther." This night was likewise spent in making her peace with God, and she stated to me that if she had perished that night she had no doubt but that she would have gone to heaven. Part of the night was spent in great anxiety about her child. Her faithful dog, as he had done before, kept close to her, and would lay down precisely where told to. This circumstance, in connection with that of being covered with snow, kept her from freezing to death.

In the morning, which was Monday, she commenced calling, the third time, for help. Her clothes were frozen to the ground, and kept her from rising, and her exhaustion was complete. She called like one yielding to despair; but the wind being now favorable, a man who was feeding his stock heard her voice, as also did his wife in the house, who was intimately acquainted with the distressed heroine of our narrative, and who said to her husband, "If Polly Boarer was near, I should say it was her voice." James Smith and John M'Intyre took their guns, and mounted their horses and started, but were deceived in their course by the echoes of Mrs. Boarer's voice. They hunted nearly all day, and returned home, and were about putting up their horses, when Mr. Smith heard the same plaint of distress. The sun was about an hour high, and the long, lingering beams, striking from the far horizon upon the snow-clad wilds, inspired feelings of the deepest gloom and solitude.

They started again, but the feeble cry of the perishing woman had ceased, and, just as the men were taking a wrong direction, she said that she felt an indefinable, mysterious feeling come over her, which seemed to say that if she only would call again, help would come to her. She, therefore, called once more, and was heard, and found.

But a new difficulty now arose. She was frozen to the ground, and was almost lifeless, and her faithful dog refused to let the strangers approach. At length, however, he was pacified. She had not shed a tear till this moment of her rescue. But now the tears fell, like raindrops, from her eyes. She was speedily conveyed to the nearest house, where she became insensible, and remained so for twenty-four hours. The flesh fell or rather peeled off her limbs, and many of her toes came off; so that she was unable to walk till the following August—a period of over six months. Her husband supposed that his wife was safe at her father's, and her father never thought that she had started to visit his family. The horse, after becoming free, did not return home; so that there was no suspicion felt in regard to her safety.

I leave the reader to his and to her own reflections on this incident. I have heard the mother and the daughter tell, in love-feast, what I have here imperfectly told you. How true, and how applicable in every condition of life—in poverty or in health, in prosperity or adversity, in sunshine or in storm, in plenty or in distress—that declaration of the merciful Keeper of our race, "My grace is sufficient for thee!"

CHAPTER XII.

THE DOOMED CHIEFTAIN.

During this summer an event occurred, on the circuit adjoining the one which I traveled, of a tragical and melancholy character; and, as I propose, in connection with my own biography, to furnish the reader with a cotemporaneous history of the times in which I lived, I will relate the circumstances connected with that event.

On the evening of the first day of June six Wyandott warriors went to the house of Mr. Benjamin Sells, on the Scioto river, about twelve miles above the spot where now stands the city of Columbus. They were equipped in the most warlike manner, and exhibited, during their stay, an unusual degree of agitation. Having ascertained that an old Wyandott chief, for whom they had been making diligent inquiry, was then encamped, at a distance of about two miles further up, on the west bank of the river, they expressed a determination to put him to death, and immediately went off in the direction of his lodge.

These facts were communicated, early on the ensuing morning, to Mr. John Sells, who now resides in the village of Dublin, on the Scioto, about two miles from the place where the doomed Wyandott met his fate. Mr. Sells immediately proceeded up the river, on horseback, in quest of the Indians. He soon arrived at the lodge, which he found situated in a grove of sugar-trees, close to the bank of the river. The six warriors were seated, in consultation, at the distance of a few rods from the lodge. The old chief was with them, evidently in the character of a prisoner. His arms were confined by a small cord, but he sat with them without any manifestation of uneasiness. A few of the neighboring white men were likewise there, and a gloomy-looking Indian, who had been the companion of the chief, but now kept entirely aloof—sitting sullenly in the camp. Mr. Sells approached the Indians, and found them earnestly engaged in debate. A charge of "witchcraft" had been made, at a former time, against the chief, by some of his captors, whose friends had been destroyed, as they believed, by means of his evil powers. This crime, according to the immemorial usage of the tribe, involved a forfeiture of life. The chances of a hunter's life had brought the old man to his present location, and his pursuers had sought him out, in order that they might execute upon him the sentence of their law.

The council was of two or three hours' duration. The accusing party spoke alternately, with much ceremony, but with evident bitterness of feeling. The prisoner, in his replies, was eloquent, though dispassionate. Occasionally a smile of scorn would appear, for an instant, on his countenance. At the close of the consultation it was ascertained that they had reaffirmed the sentence of death which had before been passed upon the chief. Inquiry having been made, by some of the white men, with reference to their arrangements, the captain of the six warriors pointed to the sun, and signified to them that the execution would take place at one o'clock in the afternoon. Mr. Sells went to the captain, and asked him what the chief had done. "Very bad Indian," he replied, "make good Indian sick—make horse sick—make die—very bad chief." Mr. Sells then made an effort to persuade his white friends to rescue the victim of superstition from his impending fate, but to no purpose. They were then in a frontier situation, entirely open to the incursions of the northern tribes, and were, consequently, unwilling to subject themselves to the displeasure of their savage visitors by any interference with their operations He then proposed to release the chief by purchase—offering to the captain, for that purpose, a fine horse, of the value of three hundred dollars. "Let me him see," said the Indian. The horse was accordingly brought forward, and closely examined; and so much were they staggered by this proposition, that they again repaired to their place of consultation, and remained in council a considerable length of time before it was finally rejected.

The conference was again terminated, and five of the Indians began to amuse themselves with running, jumping, and other athletic exercises. The captain took no part with them. When again inquired of as to the time of execution, he pointed to the sun, as before, and indicated the hour of four. The prisoner then walked slowly to his camp, partook of a dinner of jerked venison, washed, and arrayed himself in his best apparel, and afterward painted his face. His dress was very rich—his hair gray, and his whole appearance graceful and commanding. At his request the whole company drew around him at the lodge. He had observed the exertions made by Mr. Sells in his behalf, and now presented to him a written paper, with a request that it might be read to the company. It was a recommendation, signed by Governor Hull, and, in compliance with the request of the prisoner, it was fixed and left upon the side of a large tree, at a short distance from the wigwam.

The hour of execution being close at hand, the chief shook hands in silence with the surrounding spectators. On coming to Mr. Sells he appeared much moved, grasped his hand warmly, spoke for a few minutes in the Wyandott language, and pointed to the heavens. He then turned from the wigwam, and, with a voice of surpassing strength and melody, commenced the chant of the death-song. He was followed closely by the Wyandott warriors, all timing, with their slow and measured march, the music of his wild and melancholy dirge. The white men were all likewise silent followers in that strange procession. At the distance of seventy or eighty yards from the camp they came to a shallow grave, which, unknown to the white men, had been previously prepared by the Indians. Here the old man kneeled down, and, in an elevated but solemn tone of voice, addressed his prayer to the Great Spirit. As soon as he had finished, the captain of the Indians kneeled beside him, and prayed in a similar manner. Their prayers, of course, were spoken in the Wyandott tongue. When they arose, the captain was again accosted by Mr. Sells, who insisted that, if they were inflexible in the determination to shed blood, they should at least remove their victim beyond the limits of the white settlements. "No!" said he, very sternly, and with evident displeasure, "no—good Indian fraid—he no go with this bad man—mouth give fire in the dark night—good Indian fraid—he no go! My friend," he continued, "me tell you—white man bad man, white man kill him—Indian say nothing."

Finding all interference futile, Mr. Sells was at length compelled, reluctantly, to abandon the old man to his fate. After a few moments' delay, he again sank down upon his knees, and prayed, as he had done before. When he had ceased praying he still continued in a kneeling position. All the rifles belonging to the party had been left at the wigwam. There was not a weapon of any kind to be seen at the place of execution, and the spectators were, consequently, unable to form any conjecture as to the mode of procedure which the executioners had determined on for the fulfillment of their purpose. Suddenly one of the warriors drew, from beneath the skirts of his capote, a keen, bright tomahawk, walked rapidly up behind the chieftain.

brandished the weapon on high for a single moment, and then struck with his whole strength. The blow descended directly upon the crown of the head, and the victim immediately fell prostrate. After he had lain awhile in the agonies of death, the Indian captain directed the attention of the white men to the drops of sweat which were gathering upon his neck and face, remarking, with much apparent exultation, that it was conclusive proof of the sufferer's guilt Again the executioner advanced, and, with the same weapon, inflicted two or three additional and heavy blows.

As soon as life was entirely extinct, the body was hastily buried, with all its apparel and decorations, and the assemblage dispersed. The Wyandotts returned immediately to their hunting-grounds, and the white men to their homes.

Around the spot where his bones repose, the towering forest has now given place to the grain field; and the soil above him has, for years, been furrowed and refurrowed by the plowshare. The Wyandott nation, to whom the old chief belonged, never afterward were reconciled to the tribe that killed him.

CHAPTER XIII.

ITINERANT LIFE CONTINUED.

AT the conference which was held November 1, 1810, I was appointed to Knox circuit. This circuit was taken from Fairfield circuit at the conference held in Cincinnati on the thirtieth of September, 1809, and, of course, this was the second year of its existence. Though a large circuit, still it was not so large as Wills Creek. It commenced at the mouth of Licking opposite Zanesville, and embraced all the settlements on that stream up to Newark; thence up the south fork of Licking to Holmes's, and on to Granville, extending as far as Raccoontown, now Johnstown; thence on the north fork to Robinson's mill and Lee's, on to Mount Vernon and Mitchell Young's; thence down Owl creek to Sapp's and John's, and down to the mouth of Whitewoman; thence down the Muskingum, including the Wapatomica country, to the place of beginning. It took four full weeks to travel around this circuit. It was well supplied with local help, there being eight local preachers living within its bounds, as follows: James Smith, John Green, —— Rapp, Joseph Pigman, James Fleming, Joseph Tharp, —— Parks, and —— Pumphrey. Six of these were from Virginia, and the other two from Monongahela. At that time they were all pious men, and devoted zealously to their Master's cause.

I commenced my first round with much fear and trembling, and most ardently did I pray for Divine guidance and protection. At some of the appointments, I was permitted to witness the fruit of my labors in the awaken ing and conversion of sinners to God.

At Bowling Green the Lord visited us with a great and powerful revival. Many souls were converted and made to rejoice with a joy unspeakable and full of glory. Multitudes were also added to the Church, and the people of God were greatly refreshed in spirit. But as it is in almost all revivals so in this—the devil was roused from his slumbers in hearing the prison-doors fly open and the chains fall off from the captives, and like Giant Despair, in good old Bunyan's Pilgrim's Progress, he hastened to defend his castle. During our night meetings the emissaries of Satan cut the people's clothes with scissors as they engaged in prayer. They also cut the saddles and bridles of the horses. This, however, only increased the zeal of God's people, and drove them more closely to the Lord and to each other.

A great and glorious work also broke out at Mount Vernon. At this place there lived an Indian woman, who was united in marriage to a man who had been a prisoner in the tribe to which she belonged. She was in the habit of attending our meetings, and seemed to take a great interest in all our exercises. On one occasion, after preaching, she staid in class, and when I came round I spoke to her on the subject of her soul's salvation. She wept and said, "Me too bad, me no love get good, me too much sin, me sick, me no sleep, me no eat, me walk all night, me no look to Great Spirit; he no love me, me so bad." I told her to pray to the Great Spirit and he would bless her. I asked her if she did not love her child when it did bad and then was sorry for it. "O yes, me love my child." Then said I, "God will pity, and love, and save you when you cry and are sorry for your sins." At this she went away weeping as though her heart would break. At the next meeting of the class she came again, but, instead of being filled with sorrow and anguish, she was happy in the love of God. When she arose to speak, she said, "Me no more sorry; me no more sick; me happy, happy, happy; my husband, he pray to Great Spirit, and cry too, and he happy; den we go togedder."

She was an interesting woman. Her dark, raven tresses fell in glossy ringlets over her shoulders, and her large, dark, lustrous eye beamed with the joy of heaven. She was the happiest creature, I think, I ever beheld. Though she spoke broken English, she was cultivated and graceful, and one of the finest specimens of nature's children that could be found in the western wildwood.

This year we had two camp meetings on our circuit, and they were both attended with great power. At the last one which was held, we were favored with both of our Bishops, Asbury and M'Kendree. During the progress of this meeting, the greatest and most wonderful displays of the Divine power were manifested, and many were savingly converted to God.

Brother Samuel Hamilton was converted at this meeting, and soon became a flaming herald of the cross. In a short time he entered the traveling connection, and has been engaged in effective, laborious service till within a few years past, when, in consequence of ill-health, he was obliged to abandon the work he loved so well, and take a superannuated relation.

Brother Gavit was also converted at this meeting, and still lives to bear witness to the power of Divine grace in changing the heart. He resided in the town of Granville, which had been settled by a company from New England, of the old stock of Calvinistic Puritans. He was a confirmed Deist, and had been rooted and grounded in infidelity for many years. In this town resided an old sea captain with his wife and two daughters. The captain was a confirmed drunkard, and was spending all his property in the gratification of this monster appetite. At a town meeting, Mr. Gavit was appointed his guardian—a most wholesome arrangement. Every conceivable means was used by the guardian to break up the habit of the captain, and every inducement was offered to get him restored to sobriety. All, however, proved in vain. As a last resort, he took him to camp meeting; for, although he had no faith in religion, and cared not for any of its exercises, he believed, from what he had seen and heard, that the Methodists had some process by which they could transform a drunkard into a sober man.

The time at length arrived, and, with much moral suasion and physical force, he succeeded in getting Mr. B. into the carriage, in company with himself, Mrs. Gavit, and their eldest son. On Saturday they arrived on the ground, and pitched their tent that evening. In the mean time the captain stole away from their observation, and became intoxicated. Mr. Gavit went and brought him into the tent. A strict watch was now kept over him, lest he should again run away. The Sabbath passed away, and B. became perfectly sober. In the evening God opened heaven, and let down glory on the encampment. A praying circle was formed; and Mr. Gavit, taking the captain by the arm, said, "Let us go into the circle, for I have brought you here to get you converted, and now is the time."

I saw them coming; and as they approached, he asked me if they could get in. I made a way for them in the crowd, and they passed in. After succeeding in getting as close as possible to those who were engaged in leading the exercises, Mr. Gavit said to the captain,

"Who will you have to pray for you?"

"I don't want any one to pray for me," he replied.

"But you must get down on your knees, and have the prayers of this people."

Seeing he was resolved, and knowing the determined character of the man, he said,

"Well, if I must have prayer, I would just as soon have Mr. C., the class-leader, pray for me, as any one."

The leader was soon brought, and Mr. G. said to the captain,

"Now get down on your knees."

He replied, "I don't like to do that, unless you will kneel with me."

In an instant both were on their knees, and the class-leader began to pray, with all the faith and fervency of his soul, for the salvation of both. The power of God came down, and, in less than two minutes, Gavit fell prostrate on the ground, and screamed for mercy, like one in despair. This frightened the captain, and, springing from his knees, he fled through the crowd, and made his escape. We carried G. out of the crowd, and brought his wife and son, but could not get the captain to move a step from the tent. We prayed with G. all night, during which time his wife and son were powerfully convicted. They all continued to pray and seek religion, but did not find peace.

The time arrived for the meeting to close, and Mr. G. and family made their departure for home. A heavy load was at his heart, and he was loth to leave the ground. While on the way, so insupportable did his burden of sin become, that he ordered his son to stop the carriage, and they all got out and held a prayer meeting by the roadside. During this meeting, the son was converted, and the captain became powerfully convicted, and began to cry for mercy. They again resumed their journey, the son shouting, the father and mother praying, and the captain weeping. On their journey they were stopped at Newark, and invited to prayer meeting; at which Mr. G. and his wife both found peace in believing, and went on their way home, giving glory to God. Shortly after this the captain was happily converted. When I came round I formed a class, consisting of these four persons; and this was the introduction of Methodism into Granville. All these lived happy Christians. Mr. G. had two younger sons that embraced religion, and became efficient and useful traveling preachers.

We were not only favored, at this camp meeting, with the presence of our beloved bishops, but also by the presence of the Rev. Robert Manley, a flaming herald of the cross. and pioneer of the Gospel in the west. I shall never forget the first time I saw him. At a camp meeting, held at brother John Collins's, on the east fork of the Little Miami, in the year preceding the one about which I am writing, I had the pleasure of an introduction to this devoted and talented minister, by brother Collins, who represented him as his spiritual father.

When he arose in the stand, all eyes were turned toward him. Instead of giving out a hymn, as is customary on such occasions, before preaching, he commenced, in a full, clear, and musical voice, singing that exceedingly-impressive, spiritual song,

"Awaked by Sinai's awful sound,
My soul in guilt and thrall I found;
I knew not where to go.
O'erwhelmed with guilt, and anguish slain,
The sinner must be born again,
Or sink to endless woe."

Before he had finished singing the fourth verse. the power of God came down, and pervaded the vast assembly, and it became agitated—swelling and surging like the sea in a storm. It seemed as if the glory of God filled the entire encampment. At this meeting, it may be said, the power of Manley reached its culminating point Never did he preach with greater eloquence and power nor were his efforts ever crowned with greater success

But his work was done. Shortly after the meeting closed he was taken sick, and called from labor to refreshment and rest in heaven, by the summons of his Master.

"Servant of God, well done;
Rest from thy loved employ:
The battle's fought, the victory won;
Enter thy Master's joy."

During this round I made an attempt to preach in the town of Newark. This place was notorious for its wickedness; and, as no house was opened for me, I was obliged to preach in the bar-room of a tavern. Fearing the citizens would cut my saddle, or shave my horse, I hid him in the bushes. When I stepped into the door I found the room full; and many were crowded around the bar, drinking. It looked to me more like the celebration of a bacchanalian orgie, than a place for the worship of God. But I had made an appointment; and I must fill it at all hazards; and, as the Gospel was to be preached to every creature, my mission extended to every place this side of hell. I procured a stool, and, placing it beside the door, got upon it, and cried out, at the top of my voice, "Awake, thou that sleepest, and arise from the dead, and Christ shall give thee life." For thirty minutes I labored to show the audience that they were on their way to hell, and as insensible of their danger as though locked fast in the embrace of sleep. I assured them that hell would soon awaken them. When I had done warning them of their danger, and inviting them to Christ, I returned to the bushes, found my horse, and rode to brother Channel's. The bar-room folks made search for me, but I was gone. They sent me word, if I came again they would roast me; but, notwithstanding, I made another appointment in the court-house.

On my next round, fearless of the threats of the bar-room hearers, I preached in the court-house, to a more orderly congregation, and formed a class. At this place I continued to preach regularly during the year, and was permitted to witness some fruits of my labors.

On one of my tours down the north fork of Licking, one evening I heard, not far from me, the report of a rifle, and instantly heard some one scream as if shot. It was getting dark, and I rode on to brother Robinson's, and, after being there a short time, a messenger came and informed us that a man had been shot up the creek. We immediately started for the place where he was reported to have been shot, and found the track and blood in the snow. We traced the wounded man as far as the creek, which he had crossed, and, following him by the blood which had spurted from his wound at every jump, as from a stricken deer, for about one mile, where we found him in a cabin, with a family. He was shot through the body; but, being in a stooping position, the ball escaped his vitals. The man who shot him was a neighbor; to whom the wounded man had been a great friend. He had loaned his murderer a sum of money; and for simply asking the payment of a part of it, the debtor determined on killing him, for the purpose, doubtless, of getting clear of the whole debt. It appeared, from the testimony of the wounded man, that he had followed him a mile, and made several attempts to shoot, but was deterred, from some cause or other, till he arrived at that fatal spot. We bound up his wounds in the best manner we were able, and, after praying with him, returned home. A similar case occurred a few years since, in the melancholy death of Dr. Parkman, of Boston. O, the wickedness of the human heart! Who can know it?

Soon after our second camp meeting a glorious work commenced at the house of brother John's. After preaching, and meeting class, the company separated, and went in different directions, to their homes. On the way, a young woman, who had been convicted at the meeting, fell down in the road, and greatly alarmed those who were with her. They scarcely knew what to do; but finally came to the conclusion to take her back to the place of meeting. She was the sister of the lady at whose house the meeting was held; and when the circumstance of her having fallen on the way home was noised abroad, the whole neighborhood came together. The religious portion commenced singing and praying; and, while engaged in these exercises, the power of God came down upon them, and many were smitten by the Divine influence, and fell to the floor, crying for mercy. The intelligence of this excitement spread in every direction; and great multitudes, from a distance, flocked together to see this wonderful thing. The young woman—Eliza Hankins—still remained insensible, without exhibiting any signs of life. Fears were entertained by some, that she would never recover from this state; but, after remaining apparently lifeless, for the space of thirty-two hours, she sprang instantly to her feet, and commenced singing and shouting alternately. Her face seemed lighted up with an unearthly radiance; and, as she spoke of Jesus and heaven, in strains of the most inimitable eloquence and sweetness, the whole congregation was overwhelmed, and we felt ourselves in the presence of a superior being, rather than that of an artless, unsophisticated country girl. This gave a fresh impulse to the work of God, and the exercises resembled those of a camp meeting more than any thing else. The meeting lasted ten days, increasing in interest and power; and there were at least one hundred happily converted to God.

An incident occurred during this meeting worthy of particular note; and, as it belongs to a class of frequent occurrence in the early days of Methodism in this country, I will narrate it. A young man had come to the meeting, who seemed to have been possessed of the devil. His ravings and blasphemy shocked all who heard him. He boastingly exclaimed that he defied the power of God; and that those who had fallen were overcome by the influence of fear, or nervous weakness. While this stout-hearted young man was listening to the fervid eloquence of the young woman before described, he sprang suddenly from his feet, and fell his whole length on the floor. Had he been shot through the heart, he would not have fallen more suddenly, or been more lifeless to all appearance. Here was a marked demonstration of the power of God, in irresistible conviction; and I determined to watch the issue closely. His companions in sin were terribly alarmed, and many of them hurried away. After lying a short time, the limbs of the young man became perfectly rigid, and remained in this state for eight hours, when they relaxed, and he was seized with convulsions of such an intense and powerful character, that it seemed as though he must die from the agony. While thus torn, as the demonized young man in the Gospel, till the hearts of all were wrung with sympathy at his sufferings, and some began to fear the consequences, instantly he sprang to his feet, praising God for his salvation, and exhorting all his friends to seek an interest in the Savior. His conversion was a matter of astonishment to all. One man, who was inveterately opposed to the revival, said that it was the work of the devil. I replied, "If it be a work of the devil, when this young man recovers from this state he will curse and swear as formerly; but if it be a work of God, his oaths and curses will be turned into prayers and praises." When the gainsayer witnessed the wonderful change wrought on the young man, he was confounded, and went away.

The Lord crowned our labors this year with abundant success. Upward of two hundred were added to the

Church I left this circuit as I did my first one, with many tears, and knew not how strongly my heart was attached to my brethren till I was called to separate from them.

At the conference held in Cincinnati in 1811, E. Bowman was appointed to be my successor. This was a sad appointment. He no sooner arrived than he commenced sowing the vile seed of Arianism and Socinianism, which spread over the whole circuit. It was not long till it sprang up and produced its deadly fruit. James Smith, John Green, and other local preachers embraced this heresy and joined the New Lights. Green soon backslid, lost the comforts of religion, and, as I learned, became a drunkard—broke the hearts of and beggared his once happy family. Rapp also embraced the doctrine, and lost the grace of God out of his heart.

Henry Haines, once a good man, full of faith and good fruits, went off with them, and soon after became deranged and hung himself. Mody was also among the number of apostates from the faith. He erected a distillery, lost all his beautiful property at Bowling Green, ruined his interesting family, and died a most horrible death. Others, who left in this heresy, became Universalists and infidels. Never was that Scripture more clearly fulfilled than in the case of these unfortunate men—"they have chosen their own way and I will choose their delusions."

It is now more than forty years since this sad heresy prevailed, and its desolating effects are yet to be seen. The history of this one man, intrusted with the care of souls, but who proved faithless, is an illustration of the proverb, "One sinner destroyeth much good." Let all beware how they depart from sound doctrine. The first digression from the old and beaten path of truth is attended with danger, and no one can tell whither he shall wander, or what will be his end, who departs from the good and the right way. A few years after Thrap and Fleming went off with the Radicals. Pigman, Parks, and Pumphrey, only three out of nine local preachers on the circuit, remained faithful to their high calling. They lived for many years to preach the Gospel in destitute settlements, and do good in every department of the Church for which they were fitted, and having finished the work assigned them, they entered into rest. While the "memory of the wicked shall rot; the righteous shall be had in everlasting remembrance."

Brother Cratzer, the person with whom I boarded, and one of the most devoted of Christians, and talented and useful exhorters, fell into this fatal error and became a New Light preacher. But, alas! like his deluded companions, he departed from God and reaped the bitter fruits—poverty, sin, and death! The memory of these men should prove as beacons to warn all of the dangerous rocks on which they wrecked their hopes.

On this circuit lived old brother Carpenter, whose son Samuel has since become a useful local preacher. Brother Carpenter resided in St. Albans township, and, being invited, I went to his house and preached. This was the first sermon ever preached in the township.

On Owl creek there lived a Universalist, who like the most of them, was full of controversy; and to hear him talk, one would imagine that he considered himself able to overturn all orthodoxy, and even "wiser than seven men who could render a reason." He always came to our meetings, and invariably pressed me to go home with him. I was considerably annoyed by the fellow, and one day, for the purpose of getting rid of him, agreed to accompany him home. He was a real backwoods hunter, rough and uncouth in his manners. He lived about four miles from the appointment, and we started through the woods, traveling. part of the time, a cow path. When we arrived at his cabin, which was situated in a corn-patch, and only about sixteen feet square, I said to him, "Bill, what shall I do with my horse?" "Tie him to the fence," he replied. "Well, but what shall I give him to eat?" "Feed him with cut up corn," said he. It was too late to retreat, so I went into the cabin, and his wife prepared some venison in backwoods fashion, and we partook of our supper. As soon as we had finished our repast, Bill got down his old Bible and said, "Now I have got you, and you will be obliged to argue with me on the subject of religion. I have been waiting for an opportunity for a long time to have a controversy with you." "No," said I, "Bill, you have not a sufficient amount of sense to hold an argument on any religious subject. You brought me here as a Methodist preacher, and I must instruct you and your family; so call in all your children and we will have prayers." Notwithstanding all his excuses and pleadings I insisted upon the course I had adopted, and his wife and children were called in, and I read the Scriptures, explained, and applied the truth to all, and then prayed to God for their salvation. I trust the poor wife and children were benefited, if the redoubtable Bill was not. After spending a rather unpleasant night in the loft of the cabin, among the chickens, I arose in the morning, had prayers with the family, and departed. Bill never after annoyed me with invitations to go home with him.

At the Cincinnati conference, which I have already alluded to, I was appointed to Fairfield circuit. A mistake in the Minutes represents brother Isaac Quinn as having been appointed to this circuit in charge. Brother Quinn was on the Tombigbee circuit with William Houston. These brethren were both elected delegates to the General conference of 1812. They both came up from that conference, but did not return. In June brother Quinn came home sick, with his brother James, and remained till the next annual conference.

This circuit received the name of Fairfield in 1809, and had been traveled the two preceding years by brother Ralph Lotspiech. He was of German descent, born in Virginia, and raised in Tennessee, where he was converted to God and called to preach the Gospel. He was extremely meek and unassuming in all his manners and deportment, deeply pious, and always wore a serious air. In his discourses he wept much, and from this circumstance was called, by his brethren, the "weeping prophet." His pulpit labors were characterized with close practical application to the consciences of his hearers, and attended with good results wherever he ministered. While traveling Deer Creek circuit he was attacked with sickness, which was unto death. Realizing that his work was done, he called his colleague to his bedside, and told him to get a piece of paper and make an inventory of his property. Though he had but little, he felt it his duty to "set his house in order" before he died. The task, which was a short and easy one, being completed, and his assets and liabilities reckoned up, he said, "Well, after paying my debts there will be one hundred dollars left, and that will support my wife and almost helpless children [two of them being twin babes] for one year, and then God will provide. Now," said he to his colleague, "my work is done; turn me over with my face to the wall." This being done, he commenced singing in soft but sweet and plaintive tones,

"Great spoil I shall win
From death, hell, and sin;
'Midst outward affliction,
Shall feel Christ within.
And when I'm to die,
Receive me, I'll cry;
For Jesus hath loved me,

I can not tell why;
But this I do find,
We two are so joined,
He'll not live in heaven,
And leave me behind."

The last strain was finished, and the soul of the "weeping prophet" went out, with his last song, to that bright world where "there is no death, neither sorrow nor crying; but where God shall wipe the tears from all eyes." How rich must heaven be in pure and sainted spirits, who have, in the lapse of six thousand years, gone up to people its bright abodes!

This circuit was large, having twenty-five appointments, and I increased the number to thirty-eight before the expiration of the year. It extended from the town of Putnam, on the bank of the Muskingum, opposite Zanesville, ten miles west of Lancaster, and from the head waters of Licking to the falls of the Hockhocking, including all the settlements on Jonathan's creek and Rush creek. It embraced parts of five counties; namely, Muskingum, Licking, Fairfield, Perry, and Ross. I traveled round this circuit every four weeks, and formed fifteen new societies. The local preachers were John Goshen, Jesse Stoneman, —— Park, —— Newman, —— Bright, Jesse Spurgeon, and Martin Fate. Spurgeon went off with the party of Methodists organized in Cincinnati by the Rev. William Burke. Stoneman, Park, and Bright lived, labored, and died in the Church. Brothers Goshen and Fate are still living, advanced in years, but laboring on the walls of Zion. Robert Manley, the first missionary to the Muskingum, died on this circuit the year before I came, full of faith and the Holy Spirit.

Among the more prominent of the old Methodists on this circuit, were Edward Teal, William Hamilton, and Benjamin Smith, the latter being mighty in faith and prayer Robert Cloud also lived within its bounds. The strongest societies were on Rush creek, at Hamilton's. Cooper's, Hog Run, and Thomas Ijam's. Many strong men and mothers in Israel had emigrated and settled in these neighborhoods. I never shall forget the true-hearted Christian kindness and affection with which I was received and treated by the good, simple-hearted class at Hog Run. They took me in when a stranger, and comforted me by their counsel and prayers. It is with no ordinary feelings of affection that I call these brethren to remembrance. Brother Pitzer and family were especially endeared to my heart. He has long since entered into rest, and his widow and children have emigrated to the far west. As I before remarked, I labored alone on this circuit till after the General conference, which was held in May, when brother Isaac Quinn came on, with feeble health, from the south, and, as far as circumstances would permit, labored with me.

This year will long be remembered as the one in which this whole region was shaken by a mighty earthquake. On the night of the twelfth of February, I was awakened by the rocking of the house in which I slept. It seemed as if my bedstead was on a rough sea, and the waves were rolling under it, so sensible were the undulations. Slight shocks were felt almost every day and night for some time. One day, while I was preaching a funeral, the house began to rock and the cupboard doors flew open. The people became alarmed and commenced shrieking and running. It was a time of great terror to sinners.

The greatest shock was felt on the sixteenth day of the month. It commenced at ten o'clock and lasted fifteen minutes. I was then in the town of Putnam, opposite to Zanesville, where the Legislature was then in session. It was reported that the steeple of the state-house vibrated some five or six inches, like the pendulum of a clock. It was a time of the most awful suspense. Consternation sat on every countenance, especially upon the wicked, who fled into the streets, clinging one to another, and crying for mercy. In the town of Putnam there lived a sister Gardiner, a woman of great piety, and who was often persecuted for shouting, which she often did, not only at meetings, but at home, while engaged in her daily domestic avocations. On this day, while the houses were rocking and the chimneys falling, as though the dissolution of all things was at hand, sister Gardiner ran out into the street shouting and clapping her hands, exclaiming, "Glory, glory, glory to God! My Savior is coming! I am my Lord's and he is mine!" Thus she showed her enemies, who were loudly crying for mercy, that her religion, however much despised, could stand the test of so awful an hour.

Although we had some favorable indications, before this event, of a revival, it contributed greatly to increase the interest on the subject of religion. Multitudes who previously paid no attention to the subject of religion, now flocked out to meeting, and the power of God was manifested, not only in the earthquake and the fire, but in the still small yet powerful voice. The number of converts was great, and the work extended almost every-where. The most signal manifestation of Divine power was at Rush creek, at the house of David Swazy. The neighborhood had been notorious for wickedness, and, especially, for drunkenness. The young people seemed to devote all their time to mirth and revelry; but now, instead of threading the giddy mazes of the dance at the sound of the viol till past the noon of night, the meetings were crowded with anxious souls, and the cry of penitence, which wakes the harps of angels, and the songs of joy from happy converts, were the only sounds that broke upon the stillness of the night air.

On one occasion I stood upon a table in a new cabin

and cried out, "For the great day of his wrath is come and who shall be able to stand?" That night will never be forgotten in time or eternity. Many hardened sinners fell, before the power of God, like those slain in battle Many also found pardon and salvation in the blood of the Lamb.

On my next round, after preaching at this place, I was about to meet the class—a thing which I never neglected—when one of the brethren came to me and said, "Mr. H., the great distiller of whisky, is here with his party, and they have determined to break into class meeting." I placed old brother Hooper at the door, and charged him to keep it shut and let no one pass without permission As our meeting progressed the members became happy, and began to sing and shout most lustily. This attracted the attention of old brother Hooper, and he became more interested in the meeting than watchful of the door. In the mean time H. came, lifted the latch, opened the door, and walked in. He had no sooner got in than brother Hooper reclosed the door and stood against it, fearing the others would follow the example of their leader. The great champion of whisky and infidelity was now in a hot place, and he seemed to be at a loss to know what to do. I went up to him, and kindly laying my arm around his neck began to recommend to him my loving Savior. At this he became somewhat enraged, but I held on to him and continued to press my entreaties. Presently he began to tremble from head to foot, like an aspen leaf. Still encouraged, I poured the truth upon him, and his agitation increased, and letting go my hold he screamed out with all his might and fell his whole length upon the floor. At that moment the excitement in the room was intense, and it seemed as if heaven and earth had come together. The noise might have been heard a mile distant. At this point brother Hooper opened the door and cried to those outside at the top of his voice, "Glory be to God, H. is down, H. is down!" The rush to the door, of those from without, was such as can not be described. As they came rushing forward they fell upon one another in the doorway, and so completely blocked it up that none could pass either way. The excitement rose to a tremendous hight, and it was impossible to close the meeting. Those who had not fallen under the power of conviction ran to their horses and fled with the greatest precipitancy and consternation to their homes. The meeting lasted till sunrise the next morning. Several were converted, and H. joined the Church, though he did not experience a change of heart. Had he given up his distillery he doubtless would have been converted; but God will not hear those who regard iniquity in their hearts, or hold unrighteousness in their hands. He went away, and, as I believe, lived and died a manufacturer of the accursed poison. Some good, however, resulted from his conviction, as it completely cured him of his disposition to annoy and persecute the people of God.

Richard M'Mahan, an amiable, talented, and eloquent young preacher, who traveled Knox circuit one year before, died at the house of brother John. Feeling that the vows of God were on him, and he must not stoop to play with earthly flowers, he turned away from all the endearments of home and entered the rugged field of itinerant life. He bore hardness as a good soldier; and though the conflict was severe, it was short and glorious. Away from home and kindred, in the wilderness, he yielded up his spirit to God. It was a calm and quiet evening of summer. All nature seemed hushed into stillness, while in that cottage in the wilderness the youthful herald of the cross was sinking to rest. Already had he passed the land of Beulah, breathing the air and hearing the songs of the celestial city, and now there remained for him nothing but the passage of Jordan. As he neared it the heavenly glory gleamed upon his brow; and no sooner did his feet touch the waters than an angelic convoy bore him safely home.

Again and again have I visited the grave of this sainted one. It was in the woods—a lone, sequestered spot, where Solitude herself might have chosen a seat; and yet, to me, no place could have been more favorable to religious meditation. No pen could describe my feelings the first time I visited it alone. The forest cast its deep shade around. Scattered here and there were wild flowers, which, one has said, are the alphabet of angels, whereby they write on hills and plains mysterious truths. Around the grave was placed a rude inclosure. Here I read my Bible on my knees, and prayed, and sang, and often did it seem to me that I was quite on the verge of heaven.

CHAPTER XIV.

ITINERANT LIFE CONTINUED.

As fruits of the revivals this year may be reckoned seven interesting young men, who were subsequently called of God to preach the Gospel—James and Jacob Hooper. Henry, Samuel, and Job Baker, Samuel Hamilton, and Cornelius Springer. They all entered the traveling connection, and labored with zeal and success for many years. The latter, however, went off in the Radical secession, and became the editor of a paper which was adopted as the organ of Radicalism for the west. This sheet contained many bitter things against the government of the Methodist Episcopal Church, representing it as an oligarchy, and the bishops, presiding elders, and preachers as so many tyrants, lording it over God's heritage. The transition from schism to railing is easily made, and he, unfortunately for himself and many others who left the Church, which had taken them from obscurity and nursed them into character and importance, lost sight of their vocation of calling sinners to repentance and feeding the flock over which they were placed as shepherds, and spent their time and exhausted their talents in laboring to break down the fold from which they had escaped. I shall not, however, bring against them any railing accusations; "to their own Master they stand or fall." Many of them were doubtless sincere, good men; but they were wonderfully misled by a few disappointed, and, consequently, disaffected leaders.

Samuel Baker closed his earthly labors in great peace,

and entered into rest. Job Baker located, studied medicine, and went south. Since then I have not heard any thing concerning his history. Jacob Hooper traveled various circuits till his health failed, when he located, and continued, as far as circumstances would allow, to labor in the vineyard of his Lord. He yet lives, I believe, a good man and faithful minister. James Hooper still remains effective, and there is, perhaps, no traveling preacher in the connection who is more devoted to the missionary and Sabbath school cause, the latter particularly claiming his most earnest and faithful attention. Samuel Hamilton, till within a few years, has been a most laborious and efficient traveling preacher. For many years he served the Church as a presiding elder. Few sons in the Gospel have lived to graduate among the fathers with more fidelity or honor. Though now worn down with toil and halting to the tomb, he is calmly and patiently waiting the call of his Master to enter into rest. May his setting

"Sun in smiles decline,
And bring a pleasing night!"

Henry Baker also lost his health on the rough and toilsome field of itinerant life. It seemed to him that his mission was at an end, and following the leadings of Providence, he commenced the study of medicine, which he prosecuted with vigor and success. In due time he was admitted to practice, and by dint of application and skill rose to eminence in his profession. He became the favorite physician of some of our older bishops. After practicing medicine for several years and his health being somewhat restored, he felt the returning fires of itinerancy glowing within his heart, and he accordingly re-entered the traveling connection, where he remains to this day, a sound doctrinal and practical divine.

So extensive and powerful was the revival on this circuit, that in the short space of three months three hundred souls were converted and brought into the Church. I have in my journal all their names, together with the classes with which they were connected, and the date of their joining. A great majority of these ran well in the Christian course, held out to the end, and received the victor's crown; some, however, turned back to "the beggarly elements of the world," and thus brought a reproach on the goodly cause.

This year I commenced preaching at Mr. John Dillon's iron-works, on Licking, about six miles from Zanesville. Mr. Dillon was a member of the society of Friends, or Quakers, and strongly attached to that denomination. He had married a lady in Baltimore who was a Methodist; but the influence of the husband, as, alas! it too often proves, so far as the Methodist Church is concerned, overcame her denominational attachments, and she joined the Quakers. Some years afterward, however, by way of reprisal, they were both taken in the Methodist net. Brother Dillon has been for many years an acceptable and useful class-leader in the Church. During his life he has been extensively engaged in commerce and manufactures. He is a man of talent and enterprise. His indomitable energy and perseverance have enabled him to breast reverses in fortune and business, under which thousands would have been irretrievably ruined. The town of Zanesville, where he lived for many years in a beautiful mansion on the bank of the Muskingum, the home of hospitality and kindness, is indebted to him for much of its prosperity. He took a lively interest in whatever pertained to agriculture and was calculated to develop the resources of the country, as his official acts in the agricultural board of that county will show. He was also a warm friend of temperance and the cause of colonization. Deeply devoted to the Church, he has ever been ready to advance her institutions. Mrs. Dillon, his partner, several years since entered into rest. She could always be distinguished in the Church, even in the latter day of Methodist refinement, by her neat but rich Quaker dress. She was a lady of education and refinement, and ardently attached to the Church; and though called, from her position in life, to mingle with the first class, yet never was ashamed of the humble society to which she belonged. Her parlors were always open to prayer and class meetings. Every member of the family embraced religion at one time and another during life, and joined the Church. Four of the children have died; namely, Keziah, Lloyd, Margaret, and Elizabeth. They all, I believe, died in the full assurance of faith, and in the hope of a glorious immortality. The sufferings of Lloyd were protracted and severe; but he bore them with the most exemplary patience and fortitude to the last, frequently rejoicing in hope of the glory of God. Margaret—the gifted and accomplished Margaret—who early gave her heart to God and consecrated herself devotedly and exclusively to his service, like one of earth's choicest flowers, too bright and beautiful to last, was also called to join the company of the early dead in that better land. She was smitten before her life had reached its prime, and, sanctified by suffering, ripened for heaven. That the loving in life in death might not be divided, her younger sister soon followed her to the brighter mansions above. May all the members of this household form an unbroken family in heaven! Two of the sons are traveling preachers—the elder a member of the Ohio conference, and the younger a missionary on the shores of the distant Pacific.

But to resume my narrative. At Dillon's iron-works there were many who were grossly addicted to habits of intoxication. My first appointment was at Mr. Dick's tavern, and the prospect was any thing but encouraging. While I was trying to preach many were engaged in drinking and swearing. On reproving them for their conduct, one fellow turned round, with his glass in hand and a leering look, and said, "You go on with your business of preaching and we will mind ours." However, the Lord can work and none can hinder; and notwithstanding the unpropitious circumstances, one of those miserable men was awakened, and, seeking, found religion. I formed a class consisting of John and Jacob Hooper, J. Dittenhiffer, the new convert, brother Cooper and wife, and Samuel Gassaway, a colored man. These were all in the employ of Mr. Dillon, at the furnace. At one time I went down to the furnace, and, standing on a large salt kettle, delivered a temperance speech. After I was through, I took a vote and voted all kinds of intoxicating drinks out of and from around the furnace, and pledged them to keep them out forever. I then went to work and got up a subscription to build a hewed log meeting-house. Mr. Dillon gave a lot of ground, and I raised enough, in one morning, to pay for the building. In a short time the timbers were all upon the ground and preparations were being made for a raising. At this stage of progress, Bishop M'Kendree came along on his western tour, and we solicited him to preach the dedication sermon. This, of course, was altogether anticipatory, as the corner-stone had not yet been laid. At that time, however, we were not such sticklers for order, and so our venerable Bishop took his stand upon the rock on which the church was to be built, and preached a most powerful sermon from that memorable text, "On this rock I will build my Church, and the gates of hell shall not prevail against it.' It was a soul-refreshing season, and many were awakened and converted to God, while the hearts of believers were greatly blessed. In progress of time this house was finished, and remained a place for divine worship for many years. Subsequently it was taken down and removed about one mile distant, where it was re-erected and continued as a temple of grace. That humble edifice remains to this day, and its walls still echo the sound of thanksgiving and the voice of praise. In this neighborhood a gracious work of God was carried on, and another broke out a few miles distant under the labors of a local brother—Rev. John Goshen. The place had been proverbial for wickedness and opposition to godliness. This laborer in the vineyard sought out this field of wickedness, and took it into his work. He continued to labor, and weep, and pray over the devoted inhabitants till the Lord heard and revealed his arm of power. The devil's kingdom was terribly shaken by the conversion of the great champion of wickedness, Mr. Savage. The practices of drunkenness and gambling ceased, and fear and trembling came upon the most vile and hardened sinners, and many were brought to realize that Christ had power on earth to forgive sins. These two revivals, like fires in a prairie, continued spreading till they met, and the reformation was truly great and glorious. One of the greatest, if not, indeed, the greatest, sources of wickedness and misery resulted from the manufacture, sale, and use of intoxicating liquor; and the evil, lamentable to be told, existed in the Church as well as elsewhere. Ardent spirits were used as a preventive of disease. It was also regarded as a necessary beverage. A house could not be raised, a field of wheat cut down, nor could there be a log rolling, a husking, a quilting, a wedding, or a funeral without the aid of alcohol. In this state of things there was great laxity on the subject of drinking, and the ministers as well as the members of some denominations imbibed pretty freely. The only temperance society that then existed, and, consequently, the only standard raised against the overflowing scourge of intemperance, was the Methodist Church. The General Rules of the society prohibited the use of intoxicating drinks as a beverage, and only allowed their use when prescribed as a medicine by a physician. No other denomination having prohibited the use of ardent spirits as a beverage, it followed, as a necessary consequence, that all persons who refused to drink were called, by way of reproach, Methodist fanatics. But few came out publicly against this monster evil, and manufacturers, venders, and users were out against the Church. I often met with opposition for my advocacy of the cause of temperance. On my first round I was taken into a room at one of my stopping-places, where there was a ten gallon keg. I asked my host, who was said to be a pious man, what the keg contained, and he replied that it was whisky, and that he had procured it for the purpose of raising a barn with it. I asked him if he did not know that this drink was the worst enemy of man, and that it might occasion the death of some person, and be the cause of a great deal of swearing, and, perhaps, fighting. I further asked him, if he did not know that God had pronounced a curse against the man who putteth the bottle to his neighbor's mouth and maketh him drunken. At this he became excited and angrily said, "There is no law against using whisky, and I'll do as I please."

"Very well," said I, "it is a poor rule that won't work both ways. If you do as you please, I will do as I please; and unless you take that keg out of this room I will leave the house, for I would rather lie out in the woods than to sleep in a Methodist house with a ten-gallon keg of whisky for my room-mate." I furthermore said, "Now, sir, if any thing transpires at your barn-raising of an immoral nature, through the use of that infernal stuff, I will turn you out of the Church."

He refused to move the keg, and I took my horse and went to another place. At my appointment, the next day, I took occasion to preach against the use of ardent spirits in any form, except prescribed by a physician. As soon as I was done, an old exhorter came up to me and said, in a fierce and angry tone, "Young man, I advise you to leave the circuit and go home, for you are doing more harm than good; and if you can't preach the Gospel and let people's private business alone, they do not want you at all."

I replied, "I will not go home; and I have a mission from God to break up this strong-hold of the devil. By his help I will do it, despite of all distillers and aiders and abettors in the Church."

Those of my brethren who were alive to God stood by me, and I drew the sword and threw away the scabbard, resolving to give no quarters and to ask no quarters in this war of extermination. An old and respectable Methodist, who had been in the habit of taking his morning dram for years, and who kept his bottle locked up in his trunk, came to reprove me, stating that he was in the habit of drinking, and had been so for years, and he was not aware that he was any the worse for it. I told him it was a great mercy that he had not become a drunkard, for I had never known a man who was in the habit of drinking regularly that did not become a drunkard. He said that he had a constant headache, and was obliged to use stimulants for it. I told him it was that very thing which gave him the headache; and if he would follow my advice and quit the use of whisky and tea till I came round again, which would be four weeks, and he was not cured of headache, then I would submit to his using such stimulants.

The old gentleman made a pledge and kept it, and when I came round, before I arrived at the house he came out and told me he was well, having had no pain in his head for the last two weeks. He became a thorough-going temperance man, and proved a valuable auxiliary to the cause. Encouraged in my efforts to promote the cause of temperance, I suffered no opportunity to pass that I did not improve in portraying the physical, social, and moral evils resulting from intemperance. I dwelt particularly upon its sad and ruinous effects in a religious point of view, and made strong appeals to the religion and patriotism of my congregation. Frequently I would pledge whole congregations, standing upon their feet, to the temperance cause; and during my rounds I am certain the better portion of the entire community became the friends and advocates of temperance, and on this circuit alone, at least one thousand had solemnly taken the pledge of total abstinence. This was before temperance societies were heard of in this country. It was simply the carrying out of the Methodist Discipline on the subject. My efforts, as a matter of course, awakened the ire and indignation of the makers and venders of the ardent, and their curses were heaped on me in profusion. They would gladly have driven me from the country if they could, but this was beyond their power. One of the greatest distillers in the land said I was worse than a robber, as I had prevented him from selling whisky to the harvesters, and his family was likely to suffer. The craven-hearted wretch did not think of the broken-hearted wives and beggared children his distillery had made. This distiller had a field of grain to cut, and he invited all his neighbors to help him. They came at the appointed time. Before the company commenced reaping he offered the bottle to the leader, and then to all the rest, but no one touched, tasted, or handled the accursed thing. After they had reaped the first through, he tried them all again, and with many entreaties besought them to drink, but they still persisted in refusing. At this he became angry, and swore that they should all leave the field; for if they would not drink his whisky they should not cut his grain. They paid no attention to him, but went on reaping; whereupon he ordered them out of his field, and swore he would prosecute the first man who dared to trespass by cutting another inch of his grain. Still they kept on reaping, and he went off with his bottle, swearing vengeance. His friends finished the field, shocked up the grain, and went home. This circumstance gave a fatal blow to whisky in that neighborhood at that time and for years afterward. God at last caused victory to turn upon the side of temperance, and the Church was delivered from the deadly evil.

This year a camp meeting was held at the Rushville camp-ground. At this meeting we were blessed with the presence of both of our beloved Superintendents—Asbury and M'Kendree. A row was raised, on Saturday, by about twenty lewd fellows of the baser sort, who came upon the ground intoxicated, and had vowed they would break up the meeting. One of the preachers went to the leader for the purpose of getting him to leave, but this only enraged him, and he struck the preacher a violent blow on the face and knocked him down. Here the conflict began. The members saw that they must either defend themselves or allow the ruffians to beat them and insult their wives and daughters. It did not take them long to decide. They very soon placed themselves in an attitude of defense. Brother Birkhammer, an exceedingly stout man, seized their bully leader, who had struck the preacher, and with one thrust of his brawny arm crushed him down between two benches. The aiddecamp of the bully ran to his relief, but it was to meet the same fate; for no sooner did he come in reach of the Methodist than, with crushing force, he felt himself ground on the back of his comrade, in distress. Here they were held in durance vile till the sheriff and his posse came and took possession, and binding them, with ten others, they were carried before a justice, who fined them heavily for the misdemeanor.

As soon as quiet was restored, Bishop Asbury occupied

the pulpit. After singing and prayer, he rose and said he would give the rowdies some advice. "You must remember that all our brothers in the Church are not yet sanctified, and I advise you to let them alone; for if you get them angry and the devil should get in them, they are the strongest and hardest men to fight and conquer in the world. I advise you, if you do not like them, to go home and let them alone."

The work of the Lord commenced at this point, and meetings were kept up without intermission till Tuesday morning. Upward of one hundred were converted to God and joined the Church. Many more gave in their names, and they were handed over to the leaders, to be presented to the next preacher who should come upon the circuit. At the close of the camp meeting we left for conference, which was held in Chilicothe, October 17, 1812.

This year there was an increase in the membership of the western conferences, of three thousand, three hundred and sixty-two whites, and one hundred and eighty-one colored—making a total of three thousand, five hundred and forty-three. The number in the whole connection amounted to ten thousand, seven hundred and ninety. Twenty-three preachers were admitted on trial into the traveling connection.

An incident occurred at this conference which I shall never forget, and I think some of my brethren will bear equally lively recollections. Bishop Asbury said to the preachers, "Brethren, if any of you have any thing peculiar in your circumstances that should be known to the Superintendent, in making your appointment, if you will drop me a note, I will, as far as will be compatible with the great interests of the Church, endeavor to accommodate you." I had a great desire to go west, because I had relatives which called me in that direction, and it would be more pleasant to be with them; so I sat down and addressed a very polite note to the Bishop, requesting him to send me west.

My request, however, was not granted; for when the appointments were read out, instead of hearing my name announced in connection with some western appointment, I was sent one hundred miles further east. To this, however, I responded amen, and after the adjournment of conference I said to the Bishop, "If that is the way you answer prayers, I think you will get no more prayers from me." "Well," said he, smiling and stroking my head, "be a good son in the Gospel, James, and all things will work together for good." I have found that those who are the most in the habit of praying for appointments, are those who are generally most disappointed; for if their prayers were answered, it would be against the prayers of whole Churches, who pray to be delivered from them.

At the General conference, which was held in May, 1812, the old Western conference was divided into Ohio and Tennessee, and parts of Kentucky belonged to each conference. It was the last time that many hearts, which were united as David and Jonathan, were to meet in conference together, and great sorrow was felt at parting. When the hour came we united in singing the hymn,

"Blest be the dear, uniting love,
Which will not let us part;
Our bodies may far off remove,
We still are one in heart."

Then taking the parting hand, we took a hearty, warm farewell, inspired with hope that when the toils of life were over, we should meet again in the communings of that better world.

The name of my circuit was West Wheeling, in the Ohio district. Jacob Young was appointed presiding elder of the district. St. Clairsville, the capital of Belmont county, was the center and metropolis of my circuit. The number of members returned was four hundred and sixty-two; but this number was ascertained on the principle of guessing—a Yankee mode of computation that don't exactly suit western mathematics. The careless manner by which the preacher in charge too frequently arrives at the numbers in society, can not be too severely censured. My custom, on the first round, was to get all the class-books, and in the presence of the leaders take down all the names in my memorandum, kept for that purpose, and when any were removed, expelled, or had died, I would mark my book accordingly. Thus, without recourse to the class-books, at the end of the year, I could tell exactly the numbers in society.

I removed my family to St. Clairsville. The society here had many pious people in it, though some were in a backslidden state. At one of my appointments there lived a very pious sister, who had been raised a Roman Catholic, but had been converted and lived in the enjoyment of religion. She could not read a word, and had never seen a Bible, as she had been taught it was an extremely dangerous book, and not to be read or touched. This sincere, simple-hearted woman went to confession, and, as she supposed, received the pardon of her sins by priestly absolution. She was happy in the belief that her father confessor would open to her the gates of heaven; that as he had the keys of St. Peter he could open or shut heaven at his pleasure; that whosoever he blessed was blessed, and whosoever he cursed was cursed. This poor woman said she feared the priest more than she did God. Being called at one time to mourn the loss of a beloved child, her grief became extreme, and she found no rest day or night. She imagined that God had taken her child as a punishment for her wickedness. She prayed with great earnestness to the Virgin Mary and other saints. She also subjected herself to the severest penance, and said over her ave Marias. Her dreadful state of mind continued, so that she neither ate nor slept, and fears were entertained that she would become deranged. At length she concluded to pray to God to help her. For the purpose of praying to God she ascended the side of a mountain, and there, far from human vision, she fell on her knees and poured out her heart in prayer to God. Her language was, "O God, have pity on a wretch like me!" She repeated this petition for some time, and was about to abandon herself to despair, when she saw, as she described it, a dark and heavy cloud, which had rested upon her, pass away, and she was surrounded with a glorious light. All her distress left her, and the anguish of her heart was turned into joy. She thought she must die, so much was she burdened with excessive happiness. After a while she returned home and continued happy all day and all night. The next day, while sitting at her wheel spinning, Satan tempted her and darkness again surrounded her. In this state of mind she fled again to God in prayer, and was happily delivered from the snare of the devil.

Hearing of a Methodist meeting in the neighborhood, she went, and there, for the first time, did she hear the Gospel preached and salvation by faith in Jesus proclaimed. Then she beheld the glory of God as it shone in the face of Jesus Christ. Soon after this she joined the Church, and ever after remained one of the most consistent and happy Christians. She was poor, in regard to things of this world, but rich in faith and spiritual enjoyments. Once while my colleague and self were talking in her house of the goodness of God and the comforts we enjoyed, she let the stick, with which she was stirring the mush, fall into the fire, and startled us with a loud shout of glory. I was alarmed at this sudden outcry, and supposed sister E. was scalded, but in a moment I understood all perfectly plain. She continued praising God till near midnight. She would often shout on her horse, letting go the reins and clapping her hands. Once she attended a popular meeting of another denomination. The rain obliged all persons present to crowd into one room. The preacher was eloquent in discoursing about Jesus and his love, in dying for our guilty race. As his heart warmed with the theme, sister E. caught the fire, and being unable to suppress her emotions, she shouted aloud the praises of God. This greatly alarmed the preacher and disturbed the whole congregation, and the old lady was carried out. As it was still raining she was put into an empty corn-crib, where she walked about shouting and singing—

"No changes of season or place,
Would make any change in my mind;
For prisons would palaces prove,
If Jesus would dwell with me there."

In this neighborhood the Lord commenced a great and glorious work, and many souls were converted. There were also revivals at G. B.'s, on M'Mahon's creek, at A. Scott's, on Wheeling creek, on Pipe creek, and in Dilley's Bottom. At all these places there were many manifest evidences of the power of grace in renewing the heart.

About this time there flourished in this section of the country a halcyon preacher by the name of Abel Sargent. He formerly resided near Morgantown, Virginia, and was a Universalist preacher; but receiving a new revelation, in which he said he held converse with angels, and he was made the medium of communication to the world. His doctrines did not differ very materially from the Universalist creed, except that he taught the annihilation of the wicked. The regenerated soul, he taught, was a part of God; and when the body died there was a resorption of the soul into God. He did not believe in any devil, in a place of future torment, nor in a judgment. He went about the country with his twelve apostles, mostly women, preaching and pretending to raise the dead. One of his followers, in the bounds of my circuit, declared that he could fast as long as the Savior did—forty days and forty nights. This, he said, he was enabled to do, because the divinity was in him. To prove it he commenced the work of fasting, and persisted in abstaining from food for sixteen days, when he died. The halcyon declared that he would resuscitate himself after three days, and they kept his body till decomposition had progressed so far that they were compelled to bury it out of their sight. This, like all other species of fanaticism and superstition, had its day and produced some excitement on the circuit, but nothing that resulted very disastrously to the cause of religion.

This year the war spirit unfortunately entered into many professors of religion, and as soon as they caught it they began to lose their religion. Many that once walked with us to the house of God and took delight in the services of religion, now marched off in rank and file to become disciplined in the arts of war. Several, who had been saved from drunkenness by the Church, returned to their evil habits as "the dog returns to his vomit, and the sow, that was washed, to her wallowing in the mire." Wars and rumors of wars are peculiarly fatal to the mild and peaceful spirit of the Gospel; and when the Prince of peace shall obtain his dominions, "swords shall be beaten into plowshares and spears into pruning-hooks, and nations shall learn war no more."

The local preachers on this circuit were Vachel Hall, James Starr, Amos Sparks, David M'Masters, and Archibald M'Elroy. One of these, brother M'Masters, went off in the Radical secession, though he was a good man. Like many others, he was led astray by designing men. He died soon after joining the Radical Church, and has, no doubt, entered into rest. Brother M'Elroy entered the traveling connection. He was an Irishman, and came to this country at an early day. He was one of the most zealous and devoted in all the itinerant ranks. He seemed to have had a peculiar aversion to Calvinism, and scarcely ever failed, in his discourses, to present some of its most odious features to the attention of his audience. He would denounce the heaviest terrors of the law upon the doomed head of the sinner, and was regarded, in his day, as one of Sinai's thunderers. He was a faithful and efficient Methodist preacher, and died in his work.

One of the best class-leaders I ever saw, lived on this circuit. His name was M'Coy. Classes too frequently lead the leader; not so, however, with M'Coy's; he always led and governed his class. M'Coy was converted in Ireland, under the labors of Wesley, when but a boy. His master, to whom he was apprenticed, being a Roman Catholic, would lock him out at night while absent at class meeting. Often has he slept all night in the cow-house. I never met with a man in all my life who was so deeply experienced in the things of God, and he had the only methodized class that ever I became acquainted with. He would take no frivolous excuse for neglect of class, and there were no gaddings about on Sabbath among his members; no going to soirees of fashion and pleasure. He allowed no family to live without prayer. No one who neglected the communion, or indulged in the use of intoxicating drinks, could remain in his class without reformation. All the rules of Discipline were carried out in his class. No steward or preacher was allowed to say a word to his class on the subject of money. All the steward had to do was to let him know how much his class had to pay, and at the quarterly meeting it was promptly handed over to the board. None in the class were allowed to say, "I am too poor to pay any thing." On one occasion, as I was passing along, I overtook Jane Craig, a poor old Irish woman, who was on her way to town to sell some sewing thread. I said to her, "Aunt Jane, where are you going on foot?"

"Going to sell this thread to get quarterage."

"But you are too poor and too old to pay quarterage."

"Bless God for poverty. I have none of the world, and there is nothing to take my mind off of Jesus, my blessed Savior. I should feel very unhappy and ungrateful if I did not give something to help on the cause of my blessed Master. My good leader tells us that without faith it is impossible to be saved, and this faith must be active and fruitful; for a dead faith is worth nothing either for time or eternity, and in the day of judgment our faith will be proven by its fruits. The happiest day I have, is when I am trying to earn something for the support of the Gospel." She would not receive her quarterage as a gift from another, but resolved that it should be the product of her own hands. The conduct of this woman ought to shame many members of the Church. She did not belong to that class of Methodists who thank God that their religion costs them nothing.

This was a year of great spiritual benefit to me. Our quarterly meetings were occasions of great power, and multitudes of all denominations, sects, and conditions would come out to preaching. Once at a meeting of this description, when the house was crowded and the power of God was divinely manifested, I was called on by brother Young to exhort. Being much blessed, I suppose I raised my voice to its highest pitch and struck the book-board with my hand. At this a young lawyer—Charles Hammond—who had a considerable reputation for talents, became alarmed, and, urging his way through the crowd to the door, fled for his life. On my next round the sexton found in the pulpit a very neatly-turned maul with a slip of paper wrapped around the handle, which was directed to me. After meeting it was presented, and on the paper were the following verses:

"Thus saith the Lord, the preacher now
 Must warn the people all,
And if you can not make them hear,
 I'd have you use this maul.

Your hand, dear sir, is far too soft
 To batter on the wood;
Just take this maul, it is but small,
 And thunder on the board.

Lift up your voice and loudly call
 On sinners all around,
And if you can not make them hear,
 Take up this maul and pound."

CHAPTER XV.

ITINERANT LIFE CONTINUED.

At the conference held at Steubenville, September 1, 1813, Barnesville and West Wheeling circuits were united. I had for my colleague the aged and venerable minister, Michael Ellis. It was a full six weeks' circuit; and, as father Ellis lived in the bounds of the West Wheeling part of the circuit, I removed my family to Barnesville. This end of the circuit was new; and that part of it which lay between Barnesville and Marietta was a wilderness without roads, settled principally by hunters. I took this part of the work, as I considered it too hard for my colleague. During the year we had revivals in many places, and were much encouraged to labor in the vineyard of the Lord. The local brethren were at their posts, filling the Sabbath appointments, and assisting at our revivals like men of God baptized for the work.

An incident occurred on one of my excursions in the wilderness part of my circuit, which I will relate. I was traveling along a solitary path through the woods, and all at once I came upon an old man of the most grotesque appearance, trudging along at a slow rate, half bent, with an ax and two broomsticks on his shoulder. As I approached him I said, "Well, grandfather, how do you do?"

He was a German, and replied, "It ish wall."

"You have too much of a load to carry."

"Yes, but I can go not often."

"Where do you live, old friend?"

"Shust dare," pointing to a small cabin on the hill-side.

"You seem to be poor, as well as old."

"O yes, in dis vorld I has noting; but in de oder vorld I has a kingdom."

"Do you knew any thing about that kingdom?"

"O yes."

"Do you love God?"

"Yes, mid all my heart, and God love me."

"How long a time have you been loving God?"

"Dis fifty years."

"Do you belong to any Church?"

"O yes, I bese a Metodist."

"Where did you join the Methodists?"

"I jine de Metodist in Maryland, under dat grate man of Got, Strawbridge, on Pipe creek, and my vife too; and Got has been my father and my friend ever since; and I bless Got I will soon get home to see him in de himels."

By this time I felt my heart burn within me; and, having arrived at the Bethel, I stopped, and went in. His wife, who was also quite aged, was sitting by her wheel, spinning tow. I told them I was a Methodist preacher, and was more than happy to meet with them. There was but one little chair in the cabin; but, though destitute of furniture, every thing I saw looked neat and clean. I inquired into their history, and learned that they once owned property in Maryland; but they sold it, and came out west, for the purpose of benefiting their son. They bought a tract of land containing fifty acres, and improved it so they could live comfortably. In the mean time their son grew up, and became restless and uneasy; wished to leave home, and make his fortune elsewhere. To quiet him the old people made him a title to the farm, and took his obligations to maintain them as long as they lived. In a short time, however, the unnatural son sold the land, took the money, and left for the west; since which time they have never heard of him. Being obliged to leave their home, they went into the woods, built their little cabin on Congress land, and obtained a livelihood by making brooms and baskets. They had an old Bible, well-worn, and a hymn-book, which bore similar marks of use Here, in this cabin alone, they held their meetings; class meeting on the Sabbath, and prayer meetings morning, noon, and night. They had rich enjoyment. They talked about religion, as if they had been the inhabitants of the heavenly Canaan. We sang and prayed together; and such a meeting I had not enjoyed for years. I realized, in my very heart, that I would not have exchanged their lonely little cabin for the most sumptuous palace on earth, without God. It was distressing to look at their apparel, and yet their faces were radiant in the midst of their rags. I took down my saddle-bags, and gave the old servant of God all the wardrobe I had with me, and then, with many blessings, bade these happy saints adieu. When I arrived home I reported the case to the brethren and sisters of Barnesville, and they went to work, and made up two horse-loads of clothing, meal, and meat, and dispatched it to them. O what a lesson I learned from this Simeon and Anna! their humility, patience, entire and happy resignation to the providence of God! Thus they lived happy in God while they lived; and after a few years, they went rejoicing home to heaven.

On this circuit there lived a man by the name of D., who had led the daring and adventurous life of a backwoods hunter without God, and consequently without hope in the world. He was drafted, in the war of 1812, to go on a tour of duty at a block-house on one of our western stations. This was a frontier station, and Indians were all around them. One morning he arose, and, with some of his companions in arms, he cautiously opened the door, and they went down to a spring for the purpose of performing their morning ablutions. Just as they arrived at the spring they were fired upon by Indians, and two of their number fell dead in their tracks. D. wheeled instantly, and saw the Indians rushing from their covert to intercept the path, and cut off retreat to the block-house. At the same time he saw two Indians draw up their guns to shoot him. His only hope of life consisted in running to the block-house, and instantly he sped with the most desperate fleetness. He reached the door, and threw himself his whole length into it, to escape, if possible, the balls of the enemy. Just as he fell, they fired, and one of the balls passed through his leg. Those in the house caught him, and pulled him in, shutting the door with much difficulty before the Indians arrived. The battle now began; but, as there were four or five Indians to one white man, it was necessary to use great precaution. They were well protected, as the house was closely notched down, and well chincked. Several Indians were shot through the port-holes. During the battle D. lay wounded and bleeding near the wall. While there he saw an Indian trying to push in the chincking with the muzzle of his gun, so that he might shoot him; but he placed his well foot against it, and kept it in its place. At that moment he saw how near he was to eternity, and then rushed upon him, like a mountain torrent, his sins. While overwhelmed with a sense of his guilt he saw also the goodness of God, in preserving his life in the terrible events of that day. While he lay there he vowed to God, if he would spare him he would renounce all his sins, and lead a religious life the remainder of his days. This promise he kept faithfully; for, after returning home, he joined the Church, obtained religion, and ever afterward lived a consistent and useful life.

During this year there was a great revival of religion

on Duck creek. The people were poor, but contented and happy, and enjoyed religion in all its simplicity and power. Men in the winter came to meeting with their moccasins and hunting-shirts, and women with their linsey-woolsey gowns, and bareheaded; and in summer, barefooted. O how, they could pray, and sing, and shout!

Early in the spring my colleague resolved on visiting this part of the work, and having obtained a guide I yielded to his wishes. In the morning we took breakfast together, and I said to him, "Father Ellis, you had better eat hearty, for you are going into a wilderness, where your fare will be backwoods indeed, perhaps coons or opossums." "My dear brother," said he, "I can not eat dogs or cats." The first house he arrived at was brother Dye's, who had, that morning, killed a bear and two cubs. As they were lying in the yard, father Ellis walked around them, and dryly said, "They have the very foot of a negro, and the tusks of a dog." The old gentleman had a gracious meeting with the brethren in the wilderness; and when he returned, he said they were the happiest and most simple-hearted people he had ever seen.

The year was one of great prosperity. Multitudes were taken into the Church. Notwithstanding the prosperity on some of the circuits, there was only an increase, in the district, of about two hundred; and in the whole connection the increase was only thirty-six. The previous year there had been a decrease of three thousand. This great decrease in the membership was attributed to the war. This excitement, all-pervading and demoralizing as it was, operated disastrously to religion. Nor could it be otherwise. A spirit so directly averse to the spirit of the Gospel—which breathes peace on earth, and good-will to man—if allowed to take possession of the Church, would eat out all godliness.

A camp meeting was held this year, near to the place

where Fairview now stands. At this meeting many were converted. On Sabbath afternoon it seemed as if the windows of heaven were opened, and there was a revival of pentecostal times. The shouts of saints and the cries of sinners were mingled together, and went up to heaven

Here we had our trials and conflicts, as well as our triumphs. A son of Belial and a few of his associates, instigated by Satan, went into the pulpit, and commenced abusing the preachers and members. They were invited down by one of the preachers, whereupon the leader drew a pistol, and aimed it at him, and was about firing, when a friend, who was standing close by, suddenly threw open the pan of the lock, and then, seizing the bully by the shirt-collar, threw him on his back, and dragged him, reluctantly, into the preacher's tent, where he was disarmed, and a magistrate sent for. The party, seeing how it fared with their leader, were suddenly taken with a leaving; and when the prisoner called upon his faithless allies, to go his security, they were all missing. At this he commenced weeping, and praying, and pleading. He said, if it were himself only that was to suffer, he would not care. "But that it should break my mother's heart, is more than I can stand. Pity my poor mother, for God's sake," said he. On condition that he would never disturb a congregation again, he was released, and soon he left the encampment; and there were no more disturbances after that. Father Ellis and myself closed our labors on this circuit, with the consoling reflection that we had not labored in vain; but that souls had been converted, and the borders of Zion enlarged. We were also comforted in the assurance that the Church had grown in grace and spiritual knowledge. We wound up our circuit abors, made the necessary preparation, and started for conference, which was to be held in Cincinnati, September 8, 1814.

This year I was appointed to Cross Creek circuit, and had for my colleague the Rev. Archibald M'Elroy, of whom I have already spoken. Our circuit included the towns of Steubenville, Cadiz, Mount Pleasant, Smithfield, and several other villages, embracing all the country in Jefferson, part of Harrison, and Belmont counties. It took four full weeks to travel round it, with an appointment for every day and two for the Sabbath. The membership was large, amounting to nearly one thousand. We had to preach thirty-two times every round, and meet fifty classes. Thus, it will be seen that we had no time for "visits, modes, and forms," to attend parties of pleasure, loaf around stores, offices, and shops, read newspapers and chat about farms, horses, hogs, and cattle, or the politics and the various speculations of the day. My colleague was a stout-built, hale, and hearty Irishman, of fine native talents, a zealous and fearless, outspoken Christian minister. He was frank in his manners, blunt and honest in all his demeanor. He called things by their proper names, was shrewd in argument, and always ready to make war on the enemy in every shape. We met soon after conference and arranged our work, resolving to enter upon it, trusting in Him who hath said, "Lo, I am with you always, even unto the end of the world." At our first quarterly meeting, at which brother Young was present, we had a refreshing time from the presence of the Lord. The meeting closed on Monday, and all went home under the injunctions of a solemn covenant to live and labor for the salvation of souls. I met all the classes, made new papers, changed negligent and unprofitable leaders, appointed prayer meetings, waked up the local preachers and exhorters, and started every thing to work. As might be expected, the hit birds began to flutter, and there was a considerable of religious gossip among a certain class. Some scolded, others cried tyranny, oppression, etc. Brother M'Elroy joined heartily with me, and all the pious members were cheered at the prospect of a return to discipline again. The next round the leaders' meetings were held and the delinquents reported, and visited, and by our next quarterly meeting things put on quite an encouraging aspect. Revivals had broken out in many places, and the work of the Lord went on gloriously. This waked up opposition, and the heavy but sluggish artillery of Calvinism was brought to bear upon our ranks. I gave my colleague charge of this wing of the opposition. I was present, on one occasion, when one of the Calvinist ministers attacked my colleague. He was an Irishman, and hence, in that respect, Greek met Greek. The point of debate was in regard to the secret and revealed will of God. M'Elroy contended that if God had a secret will, from the very necessity of the case we must be ignorant of it; for if we knew it, it would be no longer secret. He also denied that the Bible taught such a doctrine. The Calvinist replied, "Your sophistry must give way to matter of fact." The matter of fact to which he referred, was the case of Abraham. God had commanded him to offer up his son Isaac, and the revealed will of God was evidently that Isaac should be slain as a sacrifice, but the secret will of God was of an entirely opposite character. "Now," said the Calvinist, with an air of pride and conscious triumph over his antagonist, "your system of error falls to the ground." The Methodist rejoined, "I am sorry, for your sake, though not for the truth's sake, that your matter of fact turns out to be matter of fiction. Had you paid half as much attention to the Bible as you have to the Assembly's Catechism, you would not have assumed that to be a matter of fact, which has in reality no existence. You say that only a part of the Divine procedure, in the case of Abraham, was revealed, and that related to the peremptory command to slay his son. But what are the facts? God commanded Abraham to slay his son. While in the act of obeying, another command is given entirely reversing the former. Neither of these purposes of God were secret, inasmuch as they were both revealed."

Many interesting incidents are connected with the life of this eccentric minister.

The new meeting-house in Steubenville had been left in an unfinished condition, and it was put under contract and soon completed. At the dedication, a gentleman of the town, with eleven others, presented a very handsome copy of the Bible for the use of the pulpit, with a request that a sermon should be preached from Revelation xxii, 21. Their request was complied with, and it pleased God to pour out his Spirit in a wonderful manner. Eleven out of the twelve who gave the Bible, were converted to God and joined the Church. This work spread till the whole town was under its influence. I procured a local brother to fill my appointments, and remained with my colleague for some time. Our meetings continued day and night. One morning, before breakfast, I was sent for to pray with eight families, many of whom I found lying on the floor crying for mercy. The influence of this revival extended to other Churches, and many were brought from darkness to light, and from the bondage of Satan to the liberty of the children of God. One hundred and thirty joined on probation. The revival flame spread, and at many other appointments on the circuit there were manifest displays of Divine power in awakening and conversion. It was not long till all the waste places of Zion were restored, and the Church became the garden of the Lord.

In the town of Smithfield there was no society of Methodists. It was settled principally by Quakers; and though there were many good people in it, yet there were many very wicked. My colleague and I met here every two weeks, and we resolved on preaching here. A gentleman by the name of S. gave us the use of his house as a place of worship, and it was not long till he who opened his door for the worship of God, received the blessing of God in his heart. The Lord revived his work here, and in a short time we had a society of seventy members; and so large were our congregations, that the place was much too small for us. I divided the circuit between my colleague and self for the purpose of reading the Rules, which we did once a quarter. While brother M'Elroy was reading the Rules at a certain place, called Irish Ridge, where his congregation was mostly composed of his own countrymen, he took occasion to contrast their condition with what it was in the mother country. Said he, "You Irishmen remind me much of the Israelites when they were in Egypt. They had taskmasters, and were obliged to make their tale of brick, finding their own straw. When you were in Ireland your taskmasters took all your living and only left you a few potatoes to eat, and these ye often salted with your tears; but God has opened up a way for you across the briny deep, and brought you and your wives and children into a land which flows with milk and honey, and ye have good homes, while your dinners now every day are better than your best wedding dinners in the old country. Ye have grown fat, and your eyes stick out like Jeshurun's. When ye cross the fence with your sickles to reap down the golden harvests, instead of reaping the sheaf and bringing it as a wave-offering to the Lord, you must have your bottle of whisky, and cry out, 'Come, boys, we'll all jist take a dram. Sure an' it'll hurt no body,' and in an hour or two ye are all half-seas over." This lecture so offended many of his countrymen that they protested against being so abused, and manifested a great deal of feeling against their preacher, so much so that they were ill at ease under the reproof.

Their "Irish" had got up so high that M'Elroy wrote me the following letter:

"DEAR BROTHER,—Woe is me, for my mother brought forth a man of strife. My hand is against every man, and every man's hand is against me. I have pulled the bottom out of the hornet's nest at L.'s meeting-house, and if you don't come and cooper it in no one knows where they will swarm to."

After all our increase this year, we returned but sixty-seven more than the preceding year. This, however, was to be accounted for by the numbers that were laid aside for breach of rules, and others who fell away under the influence of the mania that prevailed in regard to banks and speculations in real estate. The Church was, however, in a healthy state, and prepared to take care of those who had been taken into her fold and placed under her watch-care. To me it was a pleasant and profitable year. One of the young men who joined the Church became a traveling preacher. Two others were called, I have no doubt, to the same work, but they heeded it not; turned away and went back—became poor, dissipated, trifling men. I. C. Hunter was faithful to his calling. He gave himself up wholly to the work of the ministry. In youthful zeal he preached the Gospel of Christ, and like a valiant soldier, he died with his harness on. Brother Hunter was one of the most honest, fearless, and independent men I ever knew. He was a sincere and unfailing friend, prompt in the discharge of every duty, and ready to fill any post assigned him by the Church. He was for many years presiding elder, and sustained that relation to the Church when attacked with his last sickness. In the town of Gallipolis, where he resided, he was called to pass through the dark valley, but he was calm collected, and fearless. Trusting alone in the merits of Jesus, he entered the valley and was lost to earth, but found in heaven. His body lies in a quiet, peaceful rural cemetery, near the town of Burlington, on the Ohio river. There, undisturbed, may his ashes rest till the archangel shall wake them into that new and beautiful form which the saints shall have at the resurrection!

Many who resided on this circuit have long since finished their course and entered into the rest that remaineth for the people of God. The society in Steubenville was characterized for zeal and consistency, but, unfortunately, strong as the fold was it was broken down, and many of the influential members went off with the Radicals. This unhappy state of things was brought about by the very shepherds who were placed over the fold. They rent the Church and had not the courage and consistency to go with the straying. There was, however, a remnant left, and in the course of several years the Church regained, in a good degree, what she had lost.

I must not omit to mention—chronicling, as I am endeavoring to do, the times—the almost universal spirit of speculation which prevailed, and to which I have already alluded. A money mania seemed to have seized, like an epidemic, the entire people. Every body went to banking. Within the bounds of our circuit there were no less than nine banking establishments, seven of them within the county of Jefferson, and one of them said to have been kept in a lady's chest. All these were engaged in issuing paper, while every incorporated town, village, or company went to work to issuing notes. But it did not stop here. Tavern-keepers, merchants, butchers, bakers—every body seemed to have become bankers. This fever not only raged in this vicinity, but throughout the entire west. It proved fatal, in a greater or less degree, wherever it spread. Before it subsided, another mania sprung up, to which we have also alluded; namely, the laying out of new towns. So great was the excitement, that towns were laid out at almost every cross road within a mile of each other, and on the tops of barren hills. It was no matter where they were located, plots were made, advertisements were stuck up, lots were sold, and magnificent squares left for public buildings. After this rage subsided, it is not to be wondered at that society was left in a deplorable condition. The imaginary riches of the speculator flew away like the morning cloud, and from a state of high excitement the community relapsed into a state of stagnation. A perfect paralysis seemed to have come upon every department of business, and all who had entered into these speculations were entirely bankrupt. Discontent and dissatisfaction prevailed every-where.

About three weeks previous to the conference, I left the circuit to accompany Bishop M'Kendree and assist him with his pack-horse. On the pack-horse he carried the most of his movables, such as clothes, books, manuscripts, minutes of conferences, etc. It would look rather strange to see a Methodist bishop, in this country, now on horseback, though I heard of one, the other day, on a mule in California. Our first stopping-place was Cambridge, where the Bishop preached at twelve o'clock. From thence we traveled on to Zanesville the next day, and held meeting again. Thus we continued on our course, passing through Somerset, Lancaster, Chilicothe, Hillsboro, Xenia, and Springfield, holding meetings at all the places but Somerset. Here I left the Bishop and rode on to Mechanicsburg, where the brethren were holding a camp meeting—the first held in this section of country. This entire region was overrun with New Lights, and every thing that could be persuaded to go under the water was immersed. This was all the rage, and the highest ambition of the preachers of that faith, was to get the people dipped. The novelty of a camp meeting called out immense multitudes, and among them the New Lights

Those who know any thing about this people, especially their preachers, know that, like the doctor who was death on fits, they are great on argument. There were two things specially against which they leveled their artillery, and these were, first, Church government, and, secondly, creeds, etc. The reader must not suppose, from this, that they were a Church without any government or belief whatever. Far from it; their great central doctrine was immersion, which included regeneration. This one idea seemed to have swallowed up all other forms of faith and worship.

Bishop Asbury came to this camp meeting on Saturday, in company with his traveling companion, the Rev. J. W. Bond. No sooner was it known that he had arrived, than there was a general move toward him. All seemed to be anxious to see a bishop, and they pressed around him so closely that it was difficult to get him into the preachers' tent. After he was housed, the people crowded round the door by hundreds. He remarked to me, on witnessing the curiosity of the people, "You might as well have an elephant in your camp as to have me." It seemed to annoy him, to have them gazing at him in such numbers; and to relieve him I requested them to retire from the tent, and the Bishop would preach for them, perhaps, the next day, when they all could have an opportunity of seeing and hearing him. Brother Bond, his traveling companion, desiring to visit his friends at Urbana, I took charge of the Bishop, and made him as comfortable as circumstances would allow. On Sabbath the Bishop preached, and the vast concourse had an opportunity of judging for themselves in regard to the ability of the Methodist prelate.

That day the Gospel was preached in demonstration of the spirit and power of God. During the meeting many were converted and joined the Church. At the close of the meeting I started, with the Bishop, for Springfield, where we arrived Tuesday afternoon. We stopped with a Methodist family. As we passed through the parlors we saw the daughter and some other young ladies dressed very gayly. The daughter was playing on the piano, and as we moved through the room we doubtless elicited from those fashionable young ladies some remarks about the rusticity of our appearance; and the wonder was doubtless excited, where on earth could these old country codgers have come from? The Bishop took his seat, and presently in came the father and mother of the young lady. They spoke to the Bishop, and then followed the grandfather and grandmother. When the old lady took the Bishop by the hand he held it, and looking her in the face, while the tear dropped from his eye, he said, "I was looking to see if I could trace in the lineaments of your face, the likeness of your sainted mother. She belonged to the first generation of Methodists. She lived a holy life and died a most happy and triumphant death. You," said the Bishop, "and your husband belong to the second generation of Methodists. Your son and his wife are the third, and that young girl, your granddaughter, represents the fourth. She has learned to dress and play on the piano, and is versed in all the arts of fashionable life, and I presume, at this rate of progress, the *fifth* generation of Methodists will be sent to dancing-school." This was a solemn reproof, and it had a powerful effect upon the grandparents. The first Methodists were a peculiar people in their personal appearance and manners, and could be distinguished from the world at a single glance. Their self-denial led them to the abandonment of all the lusts of the flesh. They were simple-hearted, single-eyed, humble, and devoted followers of the Savior. They loved God devotedly and one another with pure hearts fervently; and though scoffed at by the world, hated and persecuted by the devil, they witnessed a good profession of godliness and faith.

The conference was held in Lebanon, and Bishops Asbury and M'Kendree were both present. The session was one characterized by great harmony among the preachers. It lasted seven days, at the expiration of which we all received our appointments. I was sent back to the same circuit, with Joseph Powell for my colleague. Brother David Young was appointed presiding elder of the district; but as he had business requiring his attention in East Tennessee, I was drafted to make the first round of appointments, and my place was supplied in my absence. It was with some considerable difficulty I consented to attempt the task, yet with great depression of mind I entered upon the work on the eighth of November. I was made to realize my trust in God and the necessity of greater spiritual power. I prayed with earnestness for the baptism of the Holy Spirit, and in reconsecrating my heart to God I felt the power divine. O the ineffable richness and extent of divine love! May my soul ever bask in its infinite ocean! At the first quarterly meeting, during the holy communion, the Spirit was poured out in rich effusion.

Here I met with brothers Waterman and Ruark, and on Monday the thirteenth, rode in company with the former to Hubbert, and stopped at brother Parrish's, where I spent the evening in reading and prayer.

Tuesday 14*th*. I rode through Hartford to brother J. Leech's, on Shenango. This was a lonesome road, and I was much tempted and tried in mind. I prayed all the day to be delivered, and did find some relief.

Wednesday 15*th*. I rode through Meadville, on French creek, to Gravel run. Here I put up at brother Ford's. Living, in this county, is very hard, there being but little for man or beast. This day I am not so tempted. I slept well and arose early to offer myself to God without reserve.

Thursday 16th. I rode to brother King's on the flats of French creek, three miles from Waterford. Here I was comforted and felt a blessed hope of heaven.

Friday 17th. I rode through Waterford to R. K.'s—himself and wife were formerly Methodists. I exhorted them to seek the Lord and set forward again to run the race set before them. I prayed with them, and went on to Erie. This town occupies a handsome site, and has a good harbor for vessels. Here I met with brother L. Lane, the preacher on this circuit, and tried to preach, at night, to a number of hardened sinners.

Saturday 18th. Set forward for North-east, and stopped at brother Russel's. This family loves the Lord.

Sunday 19th. I tried to preach to a large congregation from Acts iii, 19. The Lord helped me, and we had a gracious season. I trust the fruits of this meeting will be seen in the gates of heaven, when all time has an end.

Monday 20th. Rode through Canadeway, now Fredonia, to brother Baldwin's. In family prayer the Lord visited us in mercy, and our prospects of a better world were greatly increased.

Tuesday 21st. Rode sixteen miles further down the Lake to brother Webb's. This is a new country; every thing scarce and dear, and hardly to be had at all—corn two dollars per bushel, wheat three dollars per bushel, flour sixteen dollars per barrel, and pickled pork twenty-five cents per pound. These new settlers must learn to live by faith, and many of them have, and are a people zealous of good works. Here, according to the best calculation, I am about two hundred and fifty miles from home, and yet here is the same throne of grace, the same Savior, and Christians of the same spirit and heaven's calling.

Wednesday 22d. This day I preached to an attentive, weeping congregation, after which I baptized six by immersion, and it was a solemn time, and afterward visited a sick brother. He was happy in God his Savior, and was resigned to his will, waiting to depart and be with Christ, which is far better. This evening rode five miles to a neighborhood on Silver creek, where the Lord is graciously reviving his work, and many of these new settlers have been converted to God. It has been the observation of my life, that new countries and new settlements are the most favorable to revivals of religion. Many who have lived under the preaching of the Gospel in old settlements, and might have lived and died there without religion, when thrown into a new country, from their old associates and other hinderances, turn to God and live.

Thursday 23d. This morning I felt much revived and encouraged. My communion with God was sweet; yes, sweeter than honey or the honey-comb. I spent part of the forenoon in visiting the young converts, and in praying with them. At twelve o'clock I tried to preach to a large, attentive, and weeping congregation, and, I trust, not in vain, and baptized six by immersion, and several joined the Church. It is in accordance with the religious education of these people that no one must kneel in prayer, at least till he has determined to be religious; then he must get religion, and then be baptized, and that by immersion, and then join the Church, and then take up his or her cross in prayer and conversational class or love-feast meetings. In the afternoon we rode twelve miles to brother Baldwin's, and had a good night's rest.

Friday 24th. Started for Chatauque Lake in company with brother Lane, and after traveling several miles through a swampy country, we arrived at a brother Southworth's, where quarterly meeting is to commence to-morrow.

Saturday 25th. This day it began to rain, and looked as though a storm was on hand. I sought, before the mercy seat, for a suitable preparation of heart for the duties which lay before me, and I felt the Lord precious to my soul. At twelve o'clock I tried to preach from Matt. viii, 11, 12, and it was a very open time with me; the Lord helped me. There was a great move in the congregation; saints rejoiced, and sinners cried aloud for mercy. After preaching we held our quarterly meeting conference. There were two appeals, and we got them adjusted satisfactorily. At five brother Smith preached, and I exhorted after him, and then we held a prayer meeting; and the shouts of new-born souls were heard before it closed.

Sunday 26th. At nine o'clock our sacrament commenced, and we had a good time. But Satan was enraged at our love-feast: one of the old men's sons, who was kept out, became enraged, and tried to break open the door, and then went to a window and broke it, and hurt an old man much. God's judgments will overtake him before long. I was told he will curse his mother and father to their faces. Notwithstanding this interruption, the meeting was one of interest and power. At twelve I commenced preaching from the first Psalm, and the three first verses I read for my text. During the time of my preaching, in which I laid it down as heavy as I could on the sinner, some one called me a liar. Satan was enraged to the very highest pitch; his kingdom was shaking, and I felt that God, and heaven, and angels, were with us, and on our side, and the devil's kingdom trembled. Such was the constancy of the rain, that few could leave, and we had a house-full. All night was spent in exhortations, singing, and prayer. It was a night never to be forgotten.

Monday 27th. I rode to North-east, and preached to a dull, hardened set of sinners, from Prov. xx, 4.

Tuesday 28th. Rode to brother Stone's, and put up to rest till to-morrow. Sister Stone is an old lady, and a well-tried Christian. She embraced religion in early life, and became a member of the Methodist Episcopal Church when it was a reproach and by-word; but she knew in whom she had believed, and walked with God in newness of life. She is now a mother in our Israel, and we Methodist preachers find in her a mother, and her house a welcome home. For years after this I made her house my home, when I could reach it. She sent for 'Squire Reese and his wife to spend the afternoon, and we had a comfortable time. We mingled our prayers together, resolved to live for God, and strive for heaven.

Wednesday 29th. This day I feel at peace with God, and all men. At two o'clock I tried to preach to the people from Heb. ii, 3, and some were awakened to see their condition, and to pray. May the work of life penetrate the inmost hearts, and bring forth fruits unto holiness, that the end may be eternal life!

Thursday 30th. This morning my soul is staid on God. I rode to Erie, where I saw the vessels which Commodore Perry took from the enemy when he conquered the British navy on Lake Erie. They were literally torn to pieces. The Niagara is the largest, and seems to have received the hottest fire. They all lay out in the basin, sunk, a mile from the town. From Erie I rode to brother Randall's, on Conneaut, where our next quarterly meeting is to be held—thirty-two miles up the Lake.

Friday 31st. At twelve o'clock our meeting commenced. I tried to expound John xii, 21, 22. Brother Ira Eddy exhorted. In the quarterly conference we had a good time, stirring each other up to faith and good works. In the evening brother Stantliff preached, and brother Westlake exhorted. This was a time of great power. On the Sabbath I tried to hold forth from John vi, 50. At the close, some fell, others shouted, and some were in a rage. At night the Lord's people were filled with his heavenly presence in an astonishing manner; and while some were shouting and praising God in the house, others were in the yard giving glory to God in the highest.

Monday I rode forty miles to brother Skene's, and next day to brother J. Leach's, and preached in old Salem meeting-house; thence to Beaver-town, where we had a good quarterly meeting; thence home to Steubenville, where I found my family all well, and glad that my service as presiding elder was at an end.

In a short time I took my circuit, to my great comfort. At my own quarterly meeting we had a time of grace and mercy. Our Smithfield class had grown so that there was no place to hold us. I then resolved to try to put up a meeting-house; but ground must first be obtained, and I went to the proprietor and asked to buy a place suitable for a meeting-house. He then promised he would let me have a place suitable, and would select it by the time I returned. When I returned there was no lot found, and he could not let us have any. I then made application to a man who made no pretensions to religion, and he told me I should have a lot; and he took me to the lot on which the Church was built, and gave it me for forty dollars. I set to work, and, scarce as money was, in one round I collected the amount and got the deed. Then the money must be raised to build. Five hundred dollars were necessary. This time it was hard work. But it must be done; and to begging we went. Those who could not give money gave trade. I got from the sisters more than the half of it, in linens, yarn, thread, socks, stockings, flax, and feathers. So I traded and persevered, till, by the help of God, I made it up; and we got a house, and dedicated it to the service of God. We had the following preaching-places; namely, Steubenville—here we spent the whole Sabbath—Hale's meeting-house, Edward Taylor's, Scarlott's, Davis's, Moore's, Long's meeting-house, Baker's, Kent's, Evans's, Hinde's, Cadiz, Dickerson's, Roberts's, Holmes's meeting-house, Cramlett's, Smithfield, Hopewell meeting-house, Scott's, Dean's, Permar's, and another I do not recollect.

This year we had to train those who had joined the year before; and this we labored to do by requiring a strict attention to class, prayer meeting, family, and private prayer, and especially the last two. We admitted of no exemption. Many excuses were made about family prayer; but the rules required it, and the family required it, and Christianity required it. Some were borne with for a season; but if they repented not they were excluded for neglect of duty. The leaders were all instructed to watch over the observance of the Sabbath, and report any who should desecrate the day by doing ordinary work, buying, selling, or running about when they ought to be at Church. The leaders pretty generally did their duty, so that those who were not in earnest seeking the Lord, the place became too strict for them, and they retired; and, notwithstanding all the difficulties we had to contend with, we were able to return forty net increase. We closed our year's labor with a camp meeting on Lost run. This was a season of the gathering together of the people, and they came, many of them, in the spirit of the work. It commenced with singing and prayer meeting, which continued almost day and night, in some part of the encampment, till it closed. How many were converted none could tell. About one hundred gave in their names as probationers, but were not returned on the Minutes. Thus closed my second year on this circuit. I was much attached to the people both in and out of the Church.

I started to conference, at Louisville, in Kentucky, in company with Bishop M'Kendree. At Chilicothe we fell in with Bishop George, crossed the Ohio at Maysville, and at Paris we parted. Bishop M'Kendree went through Georgetown and Bishop George through Lexington, to meet the Shelbyville camp meeting the Saturday and Sabbath before conference. At this place was collected nearly one-half the conference. Such a crowd and so much feasting was going on that little good was done. We retired in the afternoon to a farm-house, and staid all night. Next day we started for the seat of the conference, where we arrived. The session of the conference was opened on the 3d of September, 1816.

This closes my diary for that time, and I give it to the reader just as it was entered in my journal.

CHAPTER XVI.

ITINERANT LIFE CONTINUED.

At the conference all the Bishops were present—M'Kendree, Roberts, and George. Bishop Asbury had ceased his labors, and followed his beloved Coke to heaven. It was an interesting session to both preachers and people. One day a messenger came to me and informed me that Bishop M'Kendree wished to see me at his room. I went accordingly, and when I arrived he said, "I am going to put you in charge of the Ohio district." I told him candidly I thought he might make a much better selection; and, besides, I was entirely too young in the ministry for such a post. "Well," said he, "you must go and learn. You are not too young to learn." Accordingly, when the appointments were read out, my name stood in connection with the Ohio district. I felt exceedingly depressed, and groaned under the load; but I resolved, God being my helper, to enter the field and do the best I possibly could under the circumstances. My district embraced eight circuits, extending from the mouth of Captina, on the Ohio river, to the lake at the mouth of Huron, including the state of Ohio, all the Western Reserve, all western Pennsylvania, from the Ohio, and Alleghanies, and western New York, as far down as Silver creek, below Fredonia. On this field of labor were ten traveling preachers and a membership of four thousand and fifty. My first round of quarterly meetings commenced October 19th and 20th, at Leesburg, on Tuscarawas circuit. The next was on Beaver circuit, at the Falls of Big Beaver, on the 26th and 27th Grand River and Mahoning, at Hartford, Western Reserve, on November 2d and 3d; Erie circuit, at Oil creek, on the Alleghany river, in western Pennsylvania, November 9th and 10th; Chatauque circuit, at Broken Straw, November 16th and 17th; Shenango circuit, at Jackman's meeting-house, four miles below Pittsburg, November 23d and 24th; Steubenville circuit, at Long's meeting-house, November 30th and December 1st; West Wheeling, December 7th and 8th, at Andrew Scott's, near Wheeling. The most of these quarterly meetings were seasons of great interest, and attended with Divine manifestations. It was customary, in consequence of the newness of the country and the sparseness of the population, to hold prayer meetings at different places, on Saturday night of the quarterly meeting. These meetings were attended with great good, and when they would all meet in love-feast in the morning, and speak of the blessings received at different places where the meetings were held, it would kindle the spirit of piety; and I have no doubt if this practice had been continued it would have resulted in vastly more good to the Church than the preaching of Saturday night. A custom prevailed at these meetings which was strange to me. No one was called on to pray. The leader would say, "If any of you feel like taking up the cross and delivering your mind, do so." Sometimes three or four would commence at once. This was altogether upon the voluntary principle. The practice was carried into the public meetings, and if any one male or female felt inspired, no matter who was preaching, they would rise and deliver their impressions. While I was preaching one Sabbath, at a quarterly meeting, a sister rose and commenced delivering her mind at the top of her voice. This sudden and unexpected outburst startled me, and I did not know what to make of it. I told her.

however, to hold up, and if, after I was done my sermon, she wished to exhort, she should have the opportunity, as I thought one at a time was quite enough. She took her seat, and many were much tried because I stopped her. After this I was not again interrupted by a female prophet. I thought the practice a wrong one, and contrary to that decency and order which should characterize the worship of God, and quoted the language of St. Paul in regard to women teaching in the Church, and expressed a hope that the Spirit would not move any more to speak on such occasions. The people had another practice which I greatly disliked; namely, that of keeping open doors at love-feasts and class meetings. I took strong ground against this practice, and found that among the New England Methodists there was much opposition, as they desired to have all their neighbors, good and bad, enjoy all the advantages connected with their select meetings. I labored to show the impropriety of such a course. We were exhorted not to give that which was holy to dogs, or to cast our pearls before swine.

But these were not the only difficulties we had to contend with. In almost all the towns, Calvinism and Universalism had intrenched themselves. A Calvinist minister was stationed in almost every town, and the Presbyterian influence was so great that Methodism could scarcely live. What few Methodists there were, could not hope to rise above the occupation in the Church of hewing wood and drawing water. When they were few and despised, Presbyterian dignity could not stoop to a recognition of them; but when the number increased, and the fervent Gospel appeals of the "circuit rider" waked up the town, then the gentleman in black would call and inquire into the "religious interest" that seemed to be abroad in the town, and speak of the much greater attention which was shown to preaching in his congregation, and suggest the holding of a union meeting; and such a union! Save the mark! Presbyterian union, formed for the sole purpose of using the Methodists in advancing Presbyterianism! I plainly told my brethren I had nothing against the Presbyterians; I loved them, but I loved Methodism more, and, as we had a shop of our own, we would not work journey-work any longer. I exhorted them to hold their own prayer meetings and class meetings, and attend to their duty, and God would revive his work in his own way. "In your union meetings," said I, "you can not pray aloud; and if one of you should get happy, you must quench the Spirit; or if you take a Methodist shout, they will carry you out as a disturber of the peace; besides, you dare not even to say amen above a whisper."

This short, homely address, brought down many bitter things on my head, and waked up a spirit of controversy. I carried the Confession of Faith with me, and whenever the doctrine of the horrible decree was denied, I would produce the old Saybrook platform in my congregations, and read for the satisfaction of the hearers. My course in this regard gave great offense. Some of my opponents seemed to affect great astonishment that I should have the effrontery to expose the tenets of Calvin. Such conduct was insufferable; but I was not Servetus, and so passed unhurt amid the howlings of the enemy. This course soon waked up the popular mind, and inquiries and investigations were made, which resulted most favorably to the Methodist cause. I exhorted the preachers to scatter the doctrinal tracts; Wesley on Predestination, and Fletcher's Checks; and, in the mean time, many were awakened and converted.

The second round of quarterly meetings commenced in January, and closed on the first and second of March In this round I suffered much with a cold, which I ha(

contracted from exposure to the chilling blasts of the northern lakes. Our meetings were all attended with the presence and power of God, and the preachers were all in the spirit of revivals. At North-east we had a most glorious time, both among saints and sinners. The snow was about two feet deep, and continued for a long time. affording great facilities for sleighing, which were improved. Vast numbers came to church, and many were converted. At this place I visited the grave of the Rev. Thomas Branch, a native of Preston, Connecticut. He entered the traveling connection in 1800, in the New York conference. He labored in the vineyard of his Lord with great acceptability and usefulness to the people. His health failing him, and thinking that a change of climate would improve it, he asked for and obtained a transfer to our conference, and was appointed, with brother David Young, to Marietta circuit, in 1812. He progressed in his travels as far as North-east, in Pennsylvania, where he was obliged, from increasing disability, to desist from his labors, and seek rest. But his work was done, and his rest was to be the rest of heaven. My feelings were of a peculiarly-solemn cast, as I stood by that lone grave of the stranger minister, in a strange land. His meek and quiet spirit won for him the friendship of all. Indeed, it may be said,

> "None knew him but to love him,
> None named him but to praise."

And though he died away from home, and his eyes were closed by stranger hands, they were, nevertheless, the hands of affection.

The last round of quarterly meetings for the year were camp meetings, with few exceptions. A quarterly meeting was held at Long's, which was called the great quarterly meeting, and is so remembered to this day. My brother, John P. Finley, was present at this meeting. On the Sabbath he took for his text but one word, and that word was *Mercy*. God was truly with us in mercy. The whole assembly was melted down under the genial influences of the spirit of the text. It was my lot to follow and I took for my text *Justice*. As I progressed, the convicting power of God fell on the people, and before I was done more than twenty stout-hearted sinners threw themselves upon the altar, and cried for mercy. Among the number was a rough, stalwart old sea captain. It seemed as though all the dark spirits of the deep had seized him. I never saw a man in so much distress and agony of mind in all my life before. The conflict, however, though terrible and awful, was not of long duration. In a short time mercy came and touched his heart, and opened his eyes, and unloosed his tongue, and he spoke the language of heaven. Before the meeting ended more than fifty were converted.

Our quarterly camp meeting commenced at Canadeway, or what is now called Fredonia, July 24, and lasted four days. Brothers James M'Mahon and Smith accompanied me to labor in word and doctrine. At this meeting we expected from the wicked much opposition, as they collected together a band the previous year, and drove the people away. The brethren this year fenced in the ground with hemlock brush, leaving two gate-ways, one of ingress and egress, and the other leading to the spring. One of the rules for the government of the encampment was, that at the sound of the trumpet, at nine o'clock at night, all were to retire to their tents, and those who had no place to lodge were required to leave the ground. At dark the rabble gathered, and one of their number was designated as their captain by a piece of white paper attached to his hat, and a white club in his hand. The company made but little disturbance till preaching was over. Seeing that there were indications of hostility on their part, I blew the trumpet, and requested all to go to their tents, while those who had none were to leave the ground.

The captain of this banditti refused to go, and summoned his men to go to his aid. I ordered the constable to take the captain a prisoner; but he swore he would knock down the first man that touched him. He had hardly finished the declaration till I seized him and threw him on the ground, and, disarming him, gave him over into the custody of the officer. His company, seeing the fate of their captain, fled in dismay from the ground. In a conversation I had with the prisoner I learned what his plans were, and how sadly he was disappointed in not being able to carry them out. He pleaded so hard for mercy, and promised so faithfully never to engage in such a wicked work again, that I let him go. We kept up a watch all night, fearing they might return; but they did not disturb us. Some were in favor of an attack; but one of the company reported that, as I was a Kentuckian, I carried a long dirk in my waistcoat, and that I would as soon stab a man as not.

The hour for preaching had arrived, and, as there were rumors coming in from various quarters, that the rowdies were gathering, I preached on the subject of civil and religious liberty. Of course this led me to speak of our Pilgrim forefathers, and the dangers and sufferings endured by them in crossing a wintery deep to plant the standard of equal rights on this desert soil; and that they might

> "Leave unstained what here they found—
> Freedom to worship God"—

they pledged their lives, their fortunes, and their fame. I remarked, if there were any in whom flowed the blood of the patriot sires of '76 present that day, who would protect us in the exercise of our religious rights and privileges, to come over on our side, and defend us from the rabble. Just at that moment Judge Cushing, who was sitting in the congregation, rose, and addressing the audience, said, "I have fought for this liberty, and I will maintain it with my life; and I give due notice, as a servant of my country, that I will enforce the laws of the state of New York to the utmost against any one who shall disturb this people in their worship." From this on, the meeting was the most orderly one I had attended.

The Sabbath morn broke upon the earth in all its sacred stillness. All nature seemed to rest calmly in the light and beauty of that Sabbath morn. At an early hour the trumpet summoned us to the concert of prayer. Brother M'Mahon commenced the morning services, and preached at eight o'clock in demonstration of the Spirit and power. I followed at eleven o'clock, and brother Smith at five. At every coming together of the people the work of the Lord progressed with power, and during the night, in the tents, many were born into the kingdom of God. This meeting exerted a good influence upon the whole surrounding country. So clear and powerful were the conversions, followed up, as they were, by consistent religious lives, that the mouths of gainsayers were stopped.

A singular case was brought before the quarterly meeting conference at Nelson, which I will relate. A local preacher had been suspended on charges preferred against him by a Mr. M'Intosh. The parties having presented themselves, I called for the papers in the case. The accuser refused to hand them over, and contended that he had the only right to read them. I told him if he did not hand over the papers to the secretary of the conference I would dismiss the case. After some consultation, he finally gave them, with much reluctance, to the secretary. The testimony seemed quite voluminous, the papers numbering from one to twenty. On examining these papers I found that they were all written with one hand, which excited my suspicion that all was not right. I asked the preacher if he was prepared for his trial. He replied that he had received no notice of the taking of the testimony contained in those depositions, and that it was not taken either in the presence of himself or the preacher in charge. My suspicions of a villainous attempt to ruin this brother, were confirmed by this development. I noticed that some had made their marks, being unable to write, and I called one of them in. To this Mr. M'Intosh strongly objected. I then turned to the witness and said, "Will you please to state what you know of this matter?" "Why, sir," said he, somewhat surprised, "I know nothing about it." I then proceeded to read what had been signed by him as his testimony. He was still more surprised, and positively denied ever having said such things, and that what was there written was entirely contrary to what Mr. M'Intosh had read to him. At this the accuser demanded the papers as his property, and on my refusing, he began to swear that he would have them, and threatened to sue me. I told him his papers were a piece of forgery, and if he did not keep perfectly quiet, I would have him prosecuted for forgery. I had the papers filed with the conference papers. The decision of the committee was reversed in the case of the persecuted brother, who felt like a man taken out of a dreadful pit. Thus ended this case. It was a foul, dark plot to ruin the reputation of a minister; but God overruled it, and the guilty were brought to light.

The next quarterly camp meeting was held at Gravel run, and commenced the first day of August. These meetings were attended with great good; for whatever may be said now about the propriety of camp meetings, when churches are scattered all over the country, and whole conferences are included in what was then embraced in a district, it is very certain that they proved of essential service to the Church. Many were converted tha otherwise would not have heard the Gospel; besides, backsliders were reclaimed, and believers were quickeneo and built up in Christian faith.

An English officer, who had heard of camp meetings, but never saw one, came down from Erie to gratify his curiosity. He kept a journal of all the meetings, noting down every thing in the order in which it occurred. Being disposed to allegorize, he compared the Church to an army making an attack on the army of the world. The army of the Church was under the command of Immanuel, and that of the world under Diabolus. Every meeting was regarded as an engagement with the enemy, and the number of converts were reported as the loss in Diabolus's army. Those who joined the Church were represented as recruits. The great battle was fought on Sabbath night. It was a close and hot engagement, lasting all night. The army of Diabolus was attacked in front, flank, and rear, and literally cut to pieces, so that, in military parlance, there was a total defeat, a perfect rout of horse, foot, and dragoons. Immanuel's troops kept the ground, without the loss of a single officer or private soldier, and triumphant victory perched on the banner of the cross. The officer said he would carry the report which he had written to England, and show his countrymen how Americans conducted a holy war.

Our next encampment was on Beaver circuit, at Zuver's camp-ground, and commenced the eighth of August. At this meeting we expected to be interrupted by the rabble, as great threats had been made by them in reference to the camp meeting. A young militia captain, however, in company with eleven young men, came to our assistance, and offered their services to keep order. As none of them were professors of religion, I felt somewhat suspicious of them, and thought it might perhaps be a mere ruse to get us into difficulty. After I had examined into the character and standing of the young men, I fully acquiesced in their proposition; and they did their duty most faithfully, securing the most perfect order to the whole encampment.

At this meeting we were assisted by that veteran pioneer preacher, Dr. Shadrach Bostwick, who had for fourteen years labored in the itinerant field. He entered the traveling connection in 1791, and traveled successively the following circuits: Milford, Talbott, Bethel, Flanders, Elizabethtown, Cambridge, Saratoga, and New London. He then traveled as presiding elder four years on Pittsfield district. In 1803 he was sent as a missionary to the Western Reserve, and formed a circuit called Deerfield. During his second year on this circuit, he married and located. He studied medicine, and after he had mastered the science entered upon the practice. During all the time he continued to preach, as circumstances would admit. He was a most amiable man, and had a lovely family, beloved and respected by all. Such was his piety, and uniform consistency of character, that he won the affection and esteem of all. His letters breathe an ardent spirit of piety. I have several, which I shall keep as precious mementoes of affection. As David and Jonathan, we were one in life, and I trust in death we shall not be divided.

The young men who volunteered their services to protect us from the rabble, were nearly all converted before the meeting closed.

The camp meeting for Steubenville circuit commenced on the twentieth of August. This was the largest camp meeting we had this year. On Sabbath there was such an immense crowd of people, that little could be done, except preach. Dr. Doddridge, an Episcopal preacher, but who had once been a Methodist traveling preacher, was at the meeting, and preached on Sabbath. His speech be trayed him, for it was very evident to any practiced observer that he had been in Methodist harness. He preached with life and power, and he evidently felt quite at home. It is somewhat remarkable that many of our preachers have entered the Protestant Episcopal Church. I have known quite a number take the frock and bands. Some who were neither very learned or eloquent, nor particularly pious, have entered the "succession," and bettered their condition vastly, so far as mere temporalities are concerned; and, instead of traveling circuits, or filling some of the more humble stations in the Methodist Church, have mounted at once to the zenith, and fill the pulpits of metropolitan churches. Verily, this is an age of progress. I knew an English local preacher, a watch-maker, who, after failing to get into the Ohio conference, joined "the Church," and at once went up to the highest pulpit in our land. Their popularity in the Episcopal Church, however, is readily accounted for. The fervor and freshness of the Methodist element will attract attention, and win admiration, though buried in the folds of the gown, or the forms of the Church.

Great allowances are to be made in behalf of many of our brethren, before whom loom up drearily in the distance want and poverty; "for," as Gen. Harrison said, in describing a traveling preacher, "their condition is just the same as though they had taken the vow of poverty." There are a few exceptions, however, to this rule. Some Methodist preachers I have known, who, notwithstanding their scanty allowance, have managed, maneuvered, and speculated with such admirable, productive skill as to amass property. But I hesitate not to say, that the great mass of them live poor, die poor, and leave their families to the charities of the Church. Some I know who have spent a fortune for the privilege of traveling circuits, at a salary of twenty-five dollars a year, while their wives lived in log-cabins, and rocked their children in sugar-troughs.

The meeting was one of great interest. The preachers seemed to have been recommissioned to preach the Gospel.

The next camp meeting was at West Wheeling. This was the last of the round, and finished the labors of the year. We were favored with the presence of the venerable Bishop M'Kendree, who preached with more power than I had ever heard him preach before. The work of the Lord was wonderfully revived, and meetings were kept up night and day, embracing all the exercises of singing, exhortation, and prayer. Vast numbers were awakened and converted. All were at work. Men, women, and even children spoke with new tongues and sung new songs.

At the conference held in Zanesville, September 3, 1817, I was reappointed to the Ohio district, with the following brethren: Beaver circuit, Jacob Hooper and Samuel Baker; Erie circuit, Ira Eddy; Grandview and Mahoning, D. D. Davidson and Ezra Booth; Chatauque, Curtis Goddard; Steubenville, Samuel Hamilton, William Knox, and Calvin Ruter; Tuscarawas, James M'Mahon; Huron, John C. Brooke.

In the true spirit of Gospel ministers, these brethren went to their respective fields of labor. Great were the toils and hardships they were called to endure. The winter was extremely severe, the cold being almost beyond endurance; yet the Lord crowned the labors and sufferings of his ministers with success. The country was but sparsely settled; the rides were long and roads rough; the fare hard and provisions scarce; but in the midst of all God was with them. The Huron circuit was the newest, and, consequently, the most difficult field. When Mr. Brooke went on to the circuit there were twenty-five preaching-places, but he was enabled to increase the number, so that it was necessary to divide the circuit; and I sent the Rev. Alfred Brunson, then a local preacher, to the fire-lands, or Huron port, for the purpose of forming a new circuit. The labors of a circuit preacher then bore but little resemblance to the labors of the circuit preacher now. To preach once every day, and lead class after having traveled from ten to thirty miles, and two or three times on Sabbath, and leading class, with the privilege of being home three days out of thirty, was somewhat different from having no week-day appointments, and being able to reach them from home every Sabbath morning, and return again at night a good part of the time. And we rejoice that the labors have decreased, and our churches have increased with such rapidity as to require such a division of labor. Ministers now have more time for study and pastoral work, and a man who, in view of all these facilities, proves himself a drone, had better leave the work of the Lord to more faithful hands.

On the land of Dr. Clark, near the portage, was held, this year, the first camp meeting that was ever known in this part of the country. There was quite a large collection of people. The brethren in attendance were M'Mahon, Davidson, Booth, and Brooke. The word preached was attended with power to the hearts of the hearers There were many places on this frontier circuit where persons lived who had never heard a sermon, and, probably, but for the camp meeting, never would have heard one, but would have lived and died as destitute as the heathen of interior Africa. Mr. Howe, in his History of Ohio, says, "The first sermon preached in Medina township was by an Episcopal clergyman;" but it was a fact that Mr. Brooke had preached there the year before, and had a regular oreaching-place. This account reminds me of a statement made by a verdant young missionary from Princeton, or Yale, some years since, who, in describing the moral desolation that reigned in the "far west"—Ohio and Indiana—stated that there were, in a certain county, only two efficient ministers of the Gospel in a population of ten thousand; that is, there were two Presbyterian preachers, and they were the only ones that deserved the name, while there were a half dozen Methodist preachers and several of other denominations. Some denominations we wot of would claim every thing. It has been asserted that the Sabbath schools organized in this country were by Presbyterians and Episcopalians, when it is a historical fact that, years before their own date, Bishop Asbury and his coadjutors had established them. So in regard to temperance. Old Dr. Beecher, "the great western missionary," as he is called in the east, having penetrated the wilderness as far as Cincinnati, becomes the apostle of temperance, when Methodist preachers had pledged whole congregations to total abstinence throughout the length and breadth of the land. But "*transeat*," and we will persevere, notwithstanding, in trying to do good. Whether it were we or they, it matters little, so the work is done, and our "*efficiency*" will be best judged by posterity.

An incident occurred illustrative of a certain class of preachers of that day. At a quarterly meeting held in Major Gaylord's barn a sharp-featured man came, on Saturday, and took his seat. I was advised that he was an orthodox clergyman. I tried to preach a free grace sermon on Revelation xxii, 17. After I had finished the discourse I invited him to come forward and conclude the meeting. Instead of doing so, he rose up in his place and said, "Let us pray." After congratulating the Lord on his greatness and the power of his righteous decrees, which never could be altered, he began, in the plenitude of his benevolence, to pray for the poor, ignorant, misled people and their instructors, informing the Lord that they were doing more harm than infidelity itself and hindering the progress of the pure Gospel. When he was done, I asked him, in the presence of all the people, who those ignorant, deluded people and their instructors were to whom he alluded in his prayer. He hesitated. "Did you," said I, "mean the Methodists, and their doctrines?" To all this he answered nothing. "Then," said I, "come out to-morrow, and I will show up the gross and irreconcilable inconsistencies and absurdities of unconditional election and reprobation." When the time arrived, there was a great crowd. I took the Saybrook platform, and read the creed, and brought it to the test of the Bible. The whole audience was greatly excited, and when I closed, the people gathered in groups every-where and entered into controversy, which continued till the next meeting hour arrived. I then preached the true doctrine, that Jesus, by the grace of God, had tasted death for every man, and that all might be saved. This was the beginning of a glorious revival; seventy-five professed to find peace in believing, and the joys of religion. In those days the Calvinists believed that they were doing God service in attacking Methodist preachers, and they would have driven them from the country, if they could have done it. Frequently I have been attacked by two or three at a time. I could invariably silence them by asking a few questions.

The Lord was pleased to give great success to the labors of the preachers on the Ohio district, this year, by the awakening and conversion of many precious souls. On Mahoning circuit two hundred were added to the Church. The work commenced at a camp meeting, held in Deerfield in July, 1818. During the meeting there were no perceptible evidences of revival, though all the meetings were solemn, and the word was preached in demonstration of the Spirit and power; but shortly after the meeting closed, the bread which had been cast upon the waters began to show itself; or, in other words, the seed which was sown sprang up and produced a speedy and abundant harvest. In the course of three months the society increased from sixteen to upward of one hundred. Among the converted were some of the principal men of the town—Dr. J. Manary, who became a zealous minister of the Gospel, Judge Day, and many others that I might mention.

After the session of conference in Steubenville, I visited this part of the work, and was astonished to find what God had wrought in Deerfield and the neighboring towns. The work spread like fire in a prairie, and at every meeting victory turned on Israel's side. I held a two days meeting in brother Manary's barn, and the work was powerful and overwhelming. All opposition seemed to have ceased, or was borne down by the tide of religious influence. The following May I attended quarterly meeting in the same place, and there were at least five hundred persons in the barn at love-feast. In this meeting the saints lifted up their voices in praise to God, and the sighs of penitence, mingled with the songs of joy, were grateful to angelic ears. Old Dr. Bostwick, of whom I have already made allusion, was present at the meeting, and seemed as Moses on the summit of Pisgah. He saw by faith the land afar off, and with shoutings exclaimed, in the language of the poet,

"'Tis grace that supports, or glory would crush me."

It was supposed that at least fifty souls were happily converted to God during this meeting.

On the fourth of June a camp meeting commenced at Lexington, on Erie circuit. All came together in the spirit, and the work commenced at the first meeting,

The Divine influence kindled and spread in every heart On Sabbath many were awakened to a sense of their lost condition, and were prompted to cry for mercy. The evening was set apart for a prayer meeting, and many came forward to the mourner's bench, and were converted to God by scores. Among the number was a native of France. This poor old soldier of Napoleon Bonaparte had wandered out into the western wilderness, houseless and homeless, without a knowledge of God. He had stood in the thickest of the battle, breasted the hottest fire, and heard the deafening roar of the artillery without trembling; but when he came to hear the thunders of Sinai, his lip quivered, his knees trembled, and he fell in the battle of the Lord. After sueing for mercy, and crying for quarters all night, it pleased God, at the rising of the sun, to pour upon him pardoning mercy. No sooner had heaven come down into the heart of the old, worn, and weary veteran, than he arose, and his whole face beamed with joy. His shouts of praise, ascribing glory to King Jesus, were truly remarkable. In broken English he tried to tell the bystanders what God had done for his soul. He told them he had eaten bread in three kingdoms, and that morning he was eating bread in the fourth, even the bread which comes down from heaven. "I fight," said he, "under de Emperor Napoleon, but now me fight under de Emperor Jesus. Vive le Emperor Jesus!" The conversion of this Frenchman was so clear and powerful, that infidelity itself was abashed and confounded. Great good was accomplished at this meeting.

On the tenth of June our camp meeting for Lake circuit, fourteen miles below Erie, commenced. A camp meeting had never been held in these parts before, and many were induced, out of mere curiosity, to attend the meeting. The meeting commenced under favorable auspices, and many were awakened and converted. Sabbath, however, was the great day of the feast. When the preacher addressed the vast congregation, from Rev. xx, 12—"For the dead, small and great, shall stand before God; and the books shall be opened; and another book, which is the book of life; and the dead shall be judged according to their works"—there was not one inattentive soul on the ground. The whole congregation was melted into tears, and deep groans, and cries for mercy were heard, bursting forth from hearts convinced of sin and judgment. Occasionally shouts of victory and triumph were heard from the pious, who waited the happy change. The evening was devoted to praying and laboring with mourners. After the ring was formed, and we commenced our address to the throne of grace, the Holy Spirit fell on us, and multitudes within and without the ring fell under the shocks of Divine power. Many mariners from the port of Erie were there, and some of them became the subjects of awakening grace. I heard one say to the sheriff, "Mr. B. is down, crying for mercy." To this he replied, "If the Methodists can make him a better man, it is more than the commonwealth of Pennsylvania can do, for he has been in nearly all the prisons of the state." This called my attention to Mr. B., whom I found in great distress, earnestly seeking the salvation of his soul. I gave him all the instruction I could, and soon the light of heaven broke on him, and the Sun of righteousness arose with healing in its beams. He was soundly converted, and what fines and imprisonments could not accomplish, the grace of God amply secured. He lived and died a good man.

Of the multitudes slain on that evening, many were made alive by the power of God.

From this camp meeting I passed to the Chatauque circuit, and commenced a camp meeting on Broken Straw, a branch of the Alleghany, June the 18th. At the commencement of this meeting I was much discouraged, but the Lord was greater to me than all my fears; and never did I have a more clear and satisfactory demonstration of the fact that man's extremity is God's opportunity. Sabbath morning arrived, and as the sun was gilding the eastern sky, the trumpet called us to the concert of prayer. While we were looking up to heaven for a blessing, God graciously poured out his Spirit, and we realized the opening of the gates of life. Preparatory to preaching, I walked out into the wilderness, or, rather, desert, for the ground was covered with rocks, for the purpose of meditation. While reclining among the rocks and fern, which grew in great abundance, I heard a sound which, to the practiced ear, carries more terror perhaps than any other. It was the rattle of death. The weather being exceedingly warm, I had taken off my shoes and stockings, and my feet being somewhat elevated, exposed my legs. Looking in the direction of the alarm, I saw the glaring eyes and forked tongue of the Americana horribilis, within a foot or two of me. It was coiled, and ready for a strike. The great Creator has so formed this dreadful creature that it can not strike without warning, and this doubtless saved my life, as it has the life of thousands. Seeing my danger, I instantly sprang, and, with one bound, was far beyond the reach of its deadly fangs. After dispatching the rattlesnake, I returned to the camp, thankful to God for deliverance.

During the day the work of the Lord went on with power, and many were saved by the regenerating grace of God. Monday morning we held a solemn communion, and I think it was the most glorious season I ever beheld. The most hardened sinners trembled and wept, and looked on while the followers of Him who, in Gethsemane and on Calvary, drank the bitter cup, were commemorating his dying love.

I held three camp meetings this year before conference, at which many were born into the kingdom, and made the happy partakers of saving grace. All the preachers, traveling and local, were at their posts, and labored with zeal and fidelity. Ira Eddy was recommended as a suitable person to be received into the traveling connection, and he was received.

Some remarkable incidents occurred at this camp meeting, two of which I will relate.

Two men from different parts of the country, with their companies, came to the meeting with the avowed purpose of disturbing the people of God in their worship. One of these men was from the mouth of the Chatauque Lake, and the other from the Alleghany river. The former, Capt. W——x, brought with him a supply of whisky. Both these men came into the congregation and took their seats. While the minister was preaching, the Holy Spirit attended the word, and Capt. W. was smitten, like Elymas, the sorcerer, with blindness. An awful feeling came over him as the horror of darkness surrounded him. He felt as if God was about to call him to judgment; and although he had been a Universalist, and had tried to believe and teach others the delusive doctrines, yet he now felt himself hanging over the fearful gulf, and nothing but life's brittle thread kept him from dropping into perdition. He afterward remarked that his feelings were awful beyond description. After some time his sight returned, and he arose and left the congregation. Notwithstanding his conviction, his stubborn heart was unwilling to yield, and obstinately persisting in the rejection of mercy, he resolved to seek oblivion in the cup.

But the most potential draughts of the maddening poison could not obliterate the traces of the Spirit's conviction from his heart. Soon, with redoubled force, the power of God again came down upon his sin-smitten soul. Unable to bear the deep and utter wretchedness which drank up his spirits, he resolved, if God did not kill him, to return home. While on his way home the constraining Spirit of God operated so powerfully, that he was forced to cry out in the bitterness of his soul for mercy. He did not reach home till some time in the night; and when he did arrive, his family were much alarmed. No sooner did he enter the house than he fell upon his knees, and continued his cries for mercy. The alarm was so great that the whole neighborhood was soon collected together. All night that man cried to God, and just as the gray streaks of morning were breaking out from the chambers of the east, the Lord in mercy spoke peace to his soul. His family, and many of the neighbors, were convicted, and the result was, the conversion of thirty in that neighborhood, whom I subsequently organized into a class, and made the Captain's house a preaching-place.

The other, W. N., was powerfully awakened on Sabbath, and being unable to withstand the powerful influence, he fled for his home. Just before reaching the door of his habitation, he was struck down by the power of God, and was carried into the house by some of the family. Soon the alarm spread, the neighbors were collected, and a messenger was dispatched to the camp-ground, a distance of nine miles. Two or three brethren went to the house, and found him in a convulsed and speechless state. Soon after their arrival, he seemed to awake to consciousness, and exclaimed with a loud voice, "O, hell! hell! hell!" He then fell away into the same unconscious state. His countenance bore all the deep-marked traces of despair. The brethren sang and prayed alternately, and those who watched his features could discover the deep emotions of his soul. At times a faint ray of light would kindle on his cheek, but soon it was gone, and like the lightning from a stormy cloud, which shocks the soul and disappears in darkness, it only rendered his features more gloomy It seemed as if despair would settle down sullenly upon him. After hours of religious exercise, such as singing and prayer, deep, agonizing prayer to God in behalf of the struggling soul, all at once the dark cloud passed away, his countenance was lighted up with an unearthly radiance, and opening his eyes he exclaimed, "O, heaven! heaven! heaven!" Then springing to his feet he shouted, "Glory! glory! glory!" Many were awakened and converted in this house. He related the exercises of his mind, during his unconscious state, afterward. He said his mind was as bright and clear as ever it was; that he distinctly saw hell and its miseries. He felt he was doomed; but just as hope was leaving him, he saw the Savior pleading for him. During this plea he said his suspense was awful beyond expression; but when it was ended, and mercy obtained, he saw heaven and glory open upon him.

This year five brethren were admitted into the traveling connection; namely, Samuel Adams, Samuel Brockunier, Edward Taylor, James Smith, and Dennis Goddard. Conference was held at Steubenville, and, being the presiding elder, it became my duty, with the preachers of the circuit, to find places for the preachers during the session. A request was handed to me by one of the stewards, from a gentleman of wealth, that I would send him one of our most talented ministers, and he would cheerfully keep him during conference. The gentleman was a member of the Episcopal Church, and had a worthy family, rather more than ordinarily refined, and enjoying all such elegancies of life as a country village would afford. Wishing to gratify him, I sent Russel Bigelow to be his guest. Now, Russel was dressed in plain, homespun apparel, cut and made with as much skill as home could furnish. It was not exactly that *a la mode* which suits fashionable life

The young miss in the parlor cast many side-long glances at the young preacher, who diffidently sat composing his features, and gazing upon the various objects around him. Meeting the steward, Mr. —— said, "I do not think you have treated me right in sending me such a common, homespun-looking man." At this the steward came to me in great haste, saying Mr. —— was displeased. "Well," said I, "his request has been complied with; he asked for a talented man, and I sent him the most talented man we have. Go and tell him that I wish him and his family to go out to the Presbyterian church to-morrow and hear him preach, and then if they are dissatisfied, I will remove him."

Sabbath came. The minister in homespun ascended the desk; all eyes were upon him. "How finely he reads!" says ——. "What distinct articulation!" said Mr. —— to his lady, as they sat in the pew. "Dear me," said the daughter, "how beautifully our country preacher reads poetry!" Then followed his prayer; and when, with warm heart, he prayed for the families who had with generous hospitality thrown open their houses for the entertainment of God's servants, the silent tear and half-suppressed sigh told of his power over the heart.

He preached, and it was only as Russel Bigelow, of sainted memory, could preach. Indeed, it is said he exceeded himself on that occasion. The effect upon the hearers was powerful, and upon none more so than his worthy host and family, who took him home, and sent for me to ask my pardon, remarking that he had never heard such a sermon in all his life. He said to the steward on Monday, "Why do you not keep your ministers better clothed? You ought not to have a man of such talents as Mr. Bigelow." That day he ordered for him a fine suit of clothes.

CHAPTER XVII.

BACKWOODS PREACHERS.

THE following graphic description of backwoods preachers, furnished me by a friend, serves not only to illustrate the manner in which many preachers were manufactured in early days, but will convey some idea of their character and talents:

A Presbytery of the Cumberland Church had assembled in one of the valleys of the Cumberland range. It was a season of spiritual drought, and the Churches had suffered from famine. The members of the ecclesiastical body then collected in their semi-annual convocation were mostly weather-beaten veterans—men who had braved the earlier difficulties of the denomination to which they were attached, when, about twenty years before, it had seceded from the parent stock, to erect a banner in Zion with a new device. They were in all about twenty persons, of whom a little more than half were preachers, the rest ruling elders of congregations, who were there to represent the local interests of the Church sessions.

This meeting was at a solemn crisis; for the Church was troubled, and the way before her was shrouded in darkness. The love of many had waxed cold. Defections had occurred. Some who were once masters in Israel had withdrawn, carrying off weighty influence and leaving perplexities behind.

Others were threatening to dissolve the Church unless radical changes were made in doctrines and polity. Alarming coldness prevailed in regard to candidates for the ministry, none having offered for several sessions, and those already in charge giving but little evidence of a disposition to advance or an ability to labor in the work which they had professed to love. Presbytery, however, was unusually full, nearly every Church session being represented, and not one of the ordained ministers absent. The deliberations were opened, as usual, with prayer by the moderator, an aged servant of God; and it was observed by those skilled in such things, that there was great liberty given him when he entreated "that the God of the harvest, in infinite mercy, would send more laborers into his harvest."

The usual formalities being ended, the opening sermon was preached by the same person. His subject comprehended the character and importance of a call to the Gospel ministry, and was treated with much earnestness. The morning hour being ended, the body adjourned to early candle-lighting. A considerable crowd had assembled upon this novel occasion, and it was under their hospitable roofs that the members found welcome reception. Few, indeed, of the mountain cabins in the vicinity but what received one or more upon that occasion, glad to be permitted to talk of the Savior to those who rarely had such opportunities of hearing the Gospel. Night brought them all back again to the house of gathering. It was a singularly wild and startling scene to one who has not mixed in the different phases of frontier life. The building in which the meeting was held was a plain log-cabin, the dwelling of one of the elders, and only selected on account of its being the largest in the vicinity. There were the beds and the furniture of the whole family, no unprolific one at that, stowed around a room but twenty feet square.

Upon those beds, and upon seats made by laying split puncheons upon cross logs, was seated the company of men, women, and children, ministers, delegates, and all, each glad to endure a process of compression for a few hours, in the expectation of an intellectual reward.

It had been before arranged that this night's meeting should be devoted to candidates for the ministry. A call was, therefore, made "to all who had felt impressions to preach to come forward and converse with Presbytery on the subject." Every one must undergo this peculiar ordeal who inclines to enter the ministry; and there are no traditions in the Church more entertaining than those which tell how the ministers who are now *burning and shining lights* made their first awkward and unpromising exhibit before Presbytery.

The call being made by the presiding officer, three persons arose to their feet. Of the first and second it will be unnecessary here to speak. The third had stood partly concealed in a dark corner of the room, while the others were relating the particulars which induced the Presbytery to accept them as probationers; but now he stepped forward and faced the moderator. His appearance excited a universal start of surprise even among that unsophisticated audience, accustomed to great peculiarities of dress and rudeness of manner. Let the reader imagine a person dressed in what is styled *copperas cloth;* that is, a cloth home-spun, home-woven, home-cut, and home-sewed, dyed in that bilious hue which is formed by copperas, alum, and walnut bark, and made into coat, vest, and breeches.

To this add brogans of home-tanned, red leather, tied with a leather thong, covering immense feet, made—both feet and brogans—for climbing hills, and you have the portrait of a *mountain boy;* able at full run to scale a bluff, to live upon the proceeds of his rifle for support, and to whip any lowland fellow in the state. Such was the person who left his dark corner and came into the full blaze of the pine-knot fire. He was weeping bitterly and, having no handkerchief, the primitive arrangement for such cases provided was necessarily adopted. He stood silent for a minute, every beholder awaiting with intense curiosity the announcement of his business, then, clearing his throat, commenced, "I've come to Presby——," but a new flood of tears impeded his efforts to speak. The moderator kindly remarked, "And what did you came to Presbytery for, my good friend? Take your own time and tell us all about it; don't be alarmed; be seated; nobody will hurt you. Come, now, tell us what you come to Presbytery for." The stranger was emboldened by this to commence again, even the third and fourth time, but could never proceed further than "I've come to Presby——," and the storm of his soul prevailed.

Here one of the members suggested that he had better retire with some one, and communicate his wishes privately; for as yet no person imagined his true errand, but rather supposed that he was laboring under some spiritual difficulty, which he would needs have settled by the meeting. But to this hint he resolutely demurred, replying "that he'd get his voice d'reckly, please God;" and so he did; and he rose up, straightening his gaunt, awkward form, and then such words as passed his lips had never before rung through that assembly.

I shall not attempt—nor could I do it, for want of a report—to quote his own words; but the oldest minister present declared, years afterward, that they *scorched and burnt wherever they fell.* A sketch of his subject will be sufficient here. It seems that he had lived all his days in ignorance and sin, without an hour's schooling, without any training either for this world or the next, without any knowledge of the affairs of humanity, having sprung up like one of the cedars on his own mountains, and with as little cultivation. Thus he had passed more than twenty years, laboring in a humble way for support, and at times pursuing the pleasures and profits of the chase.

A few months back he had accidentally fallen in with a traveling preacher, who had lost his way among the mountains, and, by several miles' travel, had put him in the right track.

The minister, interested at the oddity of his appearance and his intense ignorance of every thing religious, devoted the hour to a sketch of this world's condition, buried in sin, his own perilous state, and the value of his immortal soul, and concluded by kneeling with him, at the root of a tree, and pleading with God for his spiritual regeneration. They parted, and met no more, but the influence of that meeting parted not. The Spirit which dictated the good man's effort, abode henceforward in the temple of his heart. A voice began to whisper in his ears, "Repent, repent; why will ye die?" A load, a weight of mountains, pressed upon his soul. Sleep forsook his eyelids. His ax rusted by the pile; his rifle hung, dust-covered, on the wall.

The simple-hearted neighbors, ignorant as himself, pronounced him deranged; the younger portion called it love; a few, not slanderous, but suspicious, thought, in a private way, it might be liquor. The man himself sought religious meetings, but they were few and distant, and he heard no echo to the voice within him, and he still returned hungry and dissatisfied.

The people of a certain town will not soon forget the apparition of that awkward and ill-dressed man who visited their churches, to plant himself in front of the pulpit, and to listen to the exercises with all that attention which the criminal upon the gallows bestows upon the distant horseman, who, perhaps, brings him the expected reprieve. It was in the midst of a camp meeting fervor that he at last found peace; and there his frantic ejaculation, "I've got it, I've got it!" was like the world-wide Eureka of the Syracusan, when his grand discovery first electrified his own breast.

Then he came home to tell his neighbors what the Lord had done for his soul. Forsaking all other duties, he wandered from cabin to cabin, and, wherever he found a hearer, he called upon him to forsake his sins. His ardor increased every day.

Soon his rude but forcible illustrations began to tell upon the hearts of those simple mountaineers, as the words of a second John Baptist, crying out, "Prepare ye the way of the Lord, make his paths straight."

And yet he seemed to have no idea that he was called to preach. Such thought as that of entering the ministry did not enter his breast. Although his heart overflowed with the one subject, and he declared his determination to speak that subject to others, so long as he lived, yet it was only as a friend counsels friend that he expected to do it—no more. How could *he* become a preacher? He couldn't read a hymn or a text; he hadn't means to buy decent clothing, or pay for a session's schooling. But he was guided right, for he fell in with a gentleman who was botanizing among his native hills, and had the good fortune to spend a Sabbath in his company. This man, a profound observer of human nature, and a friend of his species, was struck with the peculiarities of the case, and, although no professor in a religious way, yet he felt convinced that the hand of might was here. He, therefore, advised him to apply to some religious association, before which he could lay open his heart, and be understood.

The results of this counsel we have seen in his coming to Presbytery, and presenting himself, a stranger to all, in the manner before described. This history, much elaborated, he gave out with a volubility that took away the breath.

The pine fire blazed low; the dipped and shapeless candles simmered themselves into torrents, unobserved by the hearers, while all sat spell-bound at the recital. With uncouth gestures, words barbarous as the African's, alternately crying and laughing, as he wandered from his first agony to his final triumph, and shouting till his voice rang back from the hill-side, the mountain boy enchained each heart, till its very pulsations might be heard. There was not a dry eye in the assembly. The gray-haired moderator sobbed aloud. The more excitable joined, from time to time, in his shouts, as the words of victory rung in their ears; and when, after a sentence of great length, he declared that "glory was begun in his heart," and that "God alone had done this work within him," not one who was experienced in such announcements but declared his conviction that it was even so—the hand of God was there.

A brief consultation ensued, and then, by general consent, George Willets was duly received as a candidate for the holy ministry. The next event in his history will carry us more than ten years forward.

Much may be said about camp meetings, but, take them all in all, for practical exhibition of religion, for unbounded hospitality to strangers, for unfeigned and fervent spirituality, give me a country camp meeting against the world.

It was not many years ago that I was traversing the hills in that vicinity in search of some rare specimens of *crinoids*, that could only be found thereabouts. My wallet hung heavily by my side—for the *crinoidea* abound all through that range—and my steps were perceptibly shortening as I toiled up the hill which separated me from my boarding-house, when I was overtaken by a horseman, who, as soon as he approached abreast of me, dismounted without a question, and asked me to *ride and tie* with him. The proposition was so bluntly made as to leave out all possibility of refusal, and I at once acceded to his request. On we jogged together, and before I knew what I was about, I found myself giving him a somewhat tedious report of my day's labor, even to the preciseness of specifying the peculiar species gathered.

He heard me patiently through—I laugh at myself now when I think of it—and then, with the most singular earnestness, inquired if I thought such labor redounded to the glory of God! Although taken all aback, as the sailors say, by the oddity of the association, yet I was not ill-read in the arguments of Buckland, Silliman, and Paley, and I replied that divines of the greatest eminence consider the study of nature as the study of the first revelation of God. He was struck with the remark, hackneyed as it was, and labored to draw me further out; but, feeling some diffidence upon this branch of my profession, I declined further debate, and changed the handle of the conversation into his hand. He took it, and it was then all about Jesus Christ and his religion, and how much that religion is needed in the world, and how well every kind of talent fits in the spiritual temple not made with hands, and a great deal more to the same purpose. Arriving in sight of my boarding-house, he asked me, in a most humble and winning tone, if I would join him in a wayside prayer; and as I could not, for the life of me, refuse, we kneeled together, and he prayed for the "learned and interesting stranger," that he might be led to the foot of the cross in an early day, and find, with a vision sharpened by faith, that the "revelation of grace" far exceeds the "revelation of nature" in its displays of the wisdom, power, and love of God. We parted then, neither having inquired the name or residence of the other.

A few days afterward the Bethel camp meeting commenced, and I did not fail to be there. I arrived just before sundown Saturday evening, and before any religious excitement had commenced. The meeting opened, as usual, on Friday by a sermon at night. On the next day the custom requires a morning sermon, and another at candle-light, while upon the Sabbath not less than three are expected by the crowded audiences that cover the camp-ground on that day.

The scene, as I approached it, was highly interesting, and my note-books are crammed, page after page, with memoranda that fairly sparkle with such leaders as—*vivid—rare—contrast of colors—clear heavens—solemnity, etc.;* but it has been better described in the series styled, Needles from my Needle-Book," in M'Makin's Courier, than I could do it; so I desist. As I rode up I was met at the gate of the camp-ground by a crowd, black and white, who asked the privilege to entertain me and my horse, with as much earnestness as hack-drivers on a steamboat wharf. Resigning myself to one with whom I had some previous acquaintance, I took a lounge with him around the inclosure, and then it was time for supper. This bounteous meal is of the flesh-pots of Egypt, being mainly composed of *hog-meat*—pardon the title; we see no vulgarity in it here—in all shapes of cookery, mutton, beef, and hecatombs of cold chickens. The sermon was preached by a third-rate man, all the heavy caliber being reserved for next day. The same choice was made for the eight o'clock sermon the next morning. There is a cant phrase used in dividing our camp meeting preachers· namely, *eight o'clocks* and *eleven o'clocks,* the latter being the intellectual Sampsons of the occasion. Long before the latter hour, I had seated myself at a convenient point to see and hear—to *see* the audience and *hear* the preacher.

The blowing of the horn called every one, young and

old, to the stand, and by their eagerness it was plain that something was expected beyond the ordinary; and I congratulated myself upon having secured so favorable a location, to gain the full advantage of it. I should have observed that this location was directly under the pulpit, leaning, in fact, against it, and I was, of course, debarred from seeing the countenance of the speaker. There is some little awkwardness, too, connected with that particular seat, for if the minister chance to prove a *pulpit-thumper*, as many do, you might be suddenly aroused by the fall of a pitcher of water, or the big Bible, upon your cranium, as I have more than once beheld it.

The opening services, which are usually short at camp meetings, were soon passed over, for it is plain that this class of preachers look upon them as lightly as Napoleon estimated the Tirailleur service, and they hasten up the artillery.

The text was announced in a voice that I immediately recognized as that of my traveling friend of a few days previous. I rejoiced at the omen. His subject of discourse was embraced in the single word "Consider," and led off by the odd remark, that if we would read the Bible diligently we could find it there, so he thought it unnecessary to point out chapter and verse! It is immaterial for me to follow him through his divisions and exhibitions of the subject. My purpose is simply to show what the *mountain preacher-boy*, for it was he, had done with himself in ten years, during which he had been devoted to the calling of a minister. His first half year had been spent in school, and although his educational progress had hardly been such as his friends anticipated, yet by preaching nights and Sundays, and exhorting all the time, he had got up a revival of religion in the school which swept like wildfire, and brought in scores to the fold of the Church.

At the next Presbytery he came up to beg leave to occupy a circuit, and despite of his limited acquirements—for as yet he could barely read a text or write a copy—that body had regard to the peculiarities of his case, and licensed him. That constituted the true commencement of his career; from this hour he was a man in the Master's work. It has been often remarked among the Methodist denomination, that the circuit is the true college of the young preacher. It proved so in the case of George Willets. His idiosyncrasy was to tell a thing as soon as he learned it; and while he could preach at night the Scripture that he had studied through the day, he made unbounded improvement. His memory proved retentive; his ideality was highly vivid; perseverance attended him as a shadow, and unlimited love for the souls of the world kept him up, and kept him going. There was never a better combination of native talent for the pulpit, but literary training was wanting.

In sheer desperation the Presbytery concluded at last to ordain him, and did so, although by a breach of the Church's rule as to literary qualifications. It happened that the occasion on which I first met him was his first sermon since his ordination, and that for the first time in his life he was to officiate in the administration of the Lord's supper.

The whole tenor of his discourse was to show sinners *where they stand, and where they might stand.* There was much eloquence, remarkable originality, even to coarseness, for I recollect that one of his comparisons introduced *fighting-chickens* and their owners; powerful appeals to the human heart, which he had read as a master; but best of all, a vein of tenderness so pure, so gentle, that hundreds of us were lost in tears. The peroration was tremendous. How such a voice could come from mortal ungs, I am not physiologist enough to explain, but it raised us to our feet like a trumpet, swayed us to and fro, to follow, as I suppose, the directions of his hand; and at the closing appeal "for mourners to come forward and be prayed for," such a rush was made that I could not have withdrawn from my position with less than Amalek's strength, and was compelled to endure such compression as I never before experienced.

At the hour of communion-service I heard him depicture the scene "on that dark, that doleful night,"

"When power of earth and hell arrayed
Against the Son of God's delight;"

and truly I had never before *seen* the face of the Man of sorrows, nor *heard* him speak. Will the reader forgive the personal allusion, when I say that, cynic as I may be, *or may have been*, that effort brought my inmost soul to declare that "almost thou persuadest *me* to be a Christian." At night that *mountain voice* again spoke upon us, and ere I left the next morning a large accession, in the way of new converts, was joyfully announced to the congregation.

Since that period I have often sat under the ministry of George Willets, and never but to admire the inexhaustible fertility of a soil that lay fallow for so many years. Maturity of intellect is upon him. The vagaries of his youthful exercise in the pulpit have been conquered, but the eloquence, the originality, the gentle vein of Christian love he retains.

I have been furnished with another sketch of a backwoods preacher, which I will give:

Immense was the gathering at the Methodist camp-ground near Springfield, on the second Sunday of September, 1832. A powerful magnet had attracted this great mass of people from their homes in many counties a hundred miles round. The new presiding elder, a late arrival from Kentucky, an orator of wide-spread and wonderful renown, it was known, would thunder on that day. The glittering prestige of his fame had lightened before him, and hence the universal eagerness to hear one concerning whom rumor's trumpet tongue discoursed so loudly.

Morning broke in the azure east, bright and beautiful as a dream of heaven; but the ex-prodigy had not made his advent. Eleven o'clock came—the regular hour of the detonation of the heavy gun of orthodoxy—and still there was no news of the clerical lion. A common circuit preacher took his place, and, sensible of the popular disappointment, increased it by mouthing a miserable failure. The vexed and restless crowd began to disperse, when an event happened to excite afresh their curiosity and concentrate them again denser than ever. A messenger rushed to the pulpit in hot haste, and presented a note, which was immediately read out to prevent the people from scattering. The following is a literal copy of that singular epistle:

"DEAR BRETHREN,—The devil has foundered my horse, which will detain me from reaching your tabernacle till evening. I might have performed the journey on foot; but I could not leave poor Paul, especially as he has never left Peter. Horses have no souls to save, and, therefore, it is all the more the duty of Christians to take care of their bodies. Watch and pray, and don't let the devil get among you on the sly before candle-light, when I shall be at my post

"Your brother, —— ———."

At length the day closed. The purple curtain of night fell over the earth from the darkening sky. God's golden fire flashed out in heaven, and men below kindled their watch-fires. The encampment, a village of snowy tents, was illuminated with a brilliancy that caused every leaf to shine and sparkle as if all the trees were burnished with phosphorescent flame. It was like a theater. It was a theater in the open air, on the green sward, beneath the starry blue, incomparably more picturesque and gorgeous than any stage scenery, prepared within walls of brick or marble, where the elite of cities throng to feast their eyes on beauty and their ears on music of silvery sound.

Presently a form arose in the pulpit, and commenced giving out a hymn, preliminary to the main exercises, and every eye became riveted to the person of the stranger. Indeed, as some one said of Burke, a single flash of the gazer's vision was enough to reveal the extraordinary man, although, in the present case, it must, for the sake of truth, be acknowledged that the first impression was ambiguous, if not enigmatical and disagreeable. His figure was tall, burly, massive, and seemed even more gigantic than the reality from the crowning foliage of luxuriant, coal-black hair, wreathed into long, curling ringlets. Add a head that looked as large as a half-bushel, beetling brows, rough and craggy as fragmentary granite, irradiated at the base by eyes of dark fire, small and twinkling like diamonds in a sea—they were diamonds of the soul, shining in a measureless sea of humor—a swarthy complexion, as if embrowned by a southern sun, rich, rosy lips, always slightly parted, as wearing a perpetual smile, and you have a lifelike portrait of Mr. —— ——, the far-famed backwoods preacher.

Though I heard it all, from the text to the amen, I am forced to despair of any attempt to convey an accurate idea of either the substance or manner of the sermon which followed. There are different sorts of sermons—the argumentary, the dogmatic, the postulary, the persuasive, the punitive, the combative, "in orthodox blows and knocks," the logical, and the poetic; but this specimen belonged to none of these categories. It was *sui generis*, and of a new species. It might properly be termed the waggish.

He began with a loud and beautifully-modulated tone, in a voice that rolled on the serene night air like successive peals of grand thunder. Methodist ministers are celebrated for sonorous voices; but his was matchless in sweetness as well as power. For the first ten minutes his remarks, being preparatory, were commonplace and uninteresting; but then, all of a sudden, his face reddened, his eye brightened, his gestures grew animated as the waftures of a fierce torch, and his whole countenance changed into an expression of inimitable humor; and now his wild, waggish, peculiar eloquence poured forth like a mountain torrent. Glancing arrows, with shafts of ridicule, *bon mots*, puns, and side-splitting anecdotes sparkled, flashed, and flew like hail till the vast auditory was convulsed with laughter. For a while the more ascetic strove to resist the current of their own spontaneous emotions, the sour-faced clergy frowned and hung their heads, and all the maidenly saints groaned as with unspeakable anguish at such desecration of the evangelical desk. These, however, soon discovered that they had undertaken an impossible achievement in thinking to withstand the *facetias* of Mr. ———. His every sentence was like a warm finger, tickling the ribs of the hearer. His very looks incited to mirth far more than other people's jokes, so that the effort to maintain one's equilibrium only increased the disposition to burst into loud explosions, as every school-boy has verified in similar cases. At length the encampment was in a roar, the sternest features relaxed into smiles, and the coldest eyes melted into tears of irrepressible merriment. Mather's best comedy or Sheridan's funniest farce was not half so successful. This continued thirty minutes, while the orator painted the folly of the sinner, which was his theme. I looked on and laughed with the rest, but finally began to fear the result as to the speaker.

"How," I exclaimed, mentally, "will he ever be able to extricate his audience from that deep whirlpool of humor? If he ends thus, when the merry mood subsides, and calm reflection supervenes, will not the revulsion of feeling be deadly to his fame? Will not every hearer realize that he has been trifled with in matters of sacred and eternal interests? At all events, there is no prospect of a revival to-night; for were the orator a magician, he could not change his subject now, and stem the torrent of headlong laughter."

But the shaft of my inference fell short of the mark; and even then he commenced to change, not all at once, but gradually, as the wind of a thunder-cloud. His features lost their comical tinge of pleasantry; his voice grew first earnest, and then solemn, and soon wailed out in the tones of deepest pathos; his eyes were shorn of their mild light, and yielded streams of tears, as the fountain of the hill yielded water. The effect was indescribable, and the rebound of feeling beyond all revelation. He descanted on the horrors of hell, till every shuddering face was turned downward, as if expecting to see the solid globe rent asunder, and the fathomless, fiery gulf yawn from beneath. Brave men moaned like sick infants, and fair, fashionable women, covered with silken drapery, and bedight with gems, shrieked as if a knife were working among their heart-strings.

Again he changed the theme; sketched the joys of a righteous death—its faith, its hope, its winged raptures, and what beautiful angels attended the spirit to its starry home—with such force, great and evident belief, that all eyes were turned toward heaven, as the entire congregation started to their feet, as if to hail the vision of angels at which the finger of the preacher seemed to be pointed, elevated as it was on high to the full length of his arm.

He then made a call for mourners into the altar, and five hundred, many of them till that night infidels, rushed forward and prostrated themselves on their knees. The meeting was continued for two weeks, and more than a thousand converts added to the Church. From that time the success of Mr. —— —— was unparalleled, and the fact is chiefly due to his inimitable wit and masterly eloquence that Methodism is now the prevailing religion in Illinois.

"In what college did he graduate? Surely, it must have been a mighty *alma mater* to develop such a son."

You are more than half right, my good questioner. Mr. —— ——, like most preachers of his sect, received his education in the great universal university, the same that produced Moses, Homer, Plato, Shakspeare, Franklin—that weaver of garlands from the lightning's wing—Washington, and Patrick Henry. High up on the mountain top, deep down in the lowest valleys, far out on the rolling billow, there he studied and toiled together, in the most glorious of all schools—the free school of self-culture!

"But did he graduate?"

Ay, and nature's own hand wrote his diploma with a pencil of living light, and stamped it with a seal of fire, the immortal fire of true genius.

Mr. —— became an itinerant at eighteen, with no learning from books save what he derived from the pages of his Bible and collection of hymns. Year after year he continued to travel the wild circuit of the frontier, earning annually but a hundred dollars for labors painful as a slave at the oar. But his vocation afforded him an excellent opportunity for meditation, and even reading. In his long journeys from one appointment to another, he was alone, with nothing around him but woods and waters, birds, mountains, sun, moon, and stars. Furthermore, he bought him books of literature and science, and pored over them as he rode along, with an ardor and perseverance such as perhaps never was witnessed within the stone walls of a college. Thus he mastered mathematics, logic, physic, law, and several languages, ancient and modern. O, believe me, believe all human history, there is no teacher like the student's own hard-working intellect, urged on to action and guided in its efforts by the omnipotence of an unconquerable will.

"Why did not this western prodigy achieve for himself a more extended renown? Why did he not climb to the loftiest stations in the Church? If this narrative be true, he ought, before now, to have been a bishop, at least."

The statement of a few facts will solve the problem. Let it be remembered, then, that the Methodist Episcopal Church is a hierarchy, in which the dispensation of clerical honors rests exclusively with the bishops and General conferences of itinerants, where the laity and local preachers are unrepresented, and, consequently, have no voice. Hence, in that sect, popular eloquence, and other showy qualities, have never been found sufficient passports to the pre-eminent distinctions of authority and office, but often to the reverse. The bishop's gown must be worn by steady, austere devotion, not by brilliant oratory or profound and varied learning.

On this perilous rock Mr. —— ——'s lofty vessel was shivered into atoms of a hopeless wreck. He made no pretensions to superior sanctity; nor was it manifested in his conduct and demeanor, whether in the pulpit or in private life. Indeed, he was distinguished by one very unclerical peculiarity—combativeness in the superlative degree. His battles, though always apparently in the defensive, were as numerous as the celebrated Bowie. The only difference was this, that Bowie fought with deadly weapons, while Mr. ——— used but his enormous fist, which was as effective, however, in the speedy settlement of belligerent issues as any knife or pistol ever forged out of steel. Let the reader judge from the following anecdote.

At a camp meeting upon one of his early circuits there was a great collection of rowdies. They were both intoxicated and armed with clubs, dirks, knives, and whips; and they swore they would break up the meeting. At eight o'clock, on Sunday morning, Mr. ——— was appointed to preach. When about half through his discourse two well-dressed young men marched into the assembly, with loaded whips, and hats on, and, standing up in the midst of the ladies, began to laugh and talk. The preacher requested them to desist; but, in reply, they cursed him, told him to mind his own business, and refused to sit down. Mr. ——— then called for a magistrate; but, although two were present, they were both afraid to interfere. The preacher then descending from the stand, told the magistrates to command him to take the rowdies, and he would do it at the risk of his life. He advanced toward them; they ordered him to stand off. One of them struck at the preacher's head with his whip, when the latter closed in with the rowdy, and jerked him off the seat. A regular scuffle now ensues; the congregation is all in commotion. The preacher throws his prisoner, and holds him fast; threatening that unless he is quiet, he will be thoroughly pounded. Meanwhile the mob rushes to the rescue, and an old drunken magistrate comes up, and orders Mr. ——— to let his prisoner go. He refuses. The officer swears that if he does not release the rowdy, he will knock him down. The preacher tells him to crack away. The drunken justice makes a pass at Mr

——, who parries the stroke, seizes the officer by the collar and hair, and, by a sudden jerk forward, brings him to the ground, and jumps upon him; telling him, as he told the rowdy, to be quiet, or he should be well pounded. A general melee ensues. The mob knocked down several magistrates and several preachers. Meanwhile Mr. —— placed himself at the head of the friends of order, and he and the ringleader of the mob meet. The rowdy attacks the preacher with the intention of knocking him down; but, by the force of his last pass, the side of his face is turned toward the preacher, who gives a sudden and well-directed blow in the burr of the ear, and drops him to the earth. Whereupon a general rush is made upon the mob by the friends of order, and the rascals are knocked down in every direction. In a few moments they wheel and flee to the four winds, with the exception of about thirty prisoners, who are marched off to a vacant tent, and placed under guard till Monday, when they were tried, and fined to the utmost limits of the law. The old drunken magistrate was fined with the rest, and cashiered.

The mob being vanquished, the whole encampment, as might be expected, wore the aspect of mourning. There was no attempt to resume preaching till evening; and such was the confusion that no one was willing to preach even then. But Mr. —— felt his spirit stirred within him, and said to the elder, "I feel a clear conscience, for, under the circumstances, we have done right; and now I ask to let me preach." "Do," said the elder, "for there is no other man on the ground that can do it."

The trumpet was blown, and there was a general rush to the stand. The preacher called upon them all to pray, if they ever prayed in their lives. He took for his text, "The gates of hell shall not prevail." His voice was strong and clear, and his speech was encouraging. In a few minutes the power of God fell wondrously upon the congregation; the people fell in ranks, and in all directions, and hundreds were presently like dead men on the field of battle. Loud wailings for mercy were heard from prostrate sinners, and a general shout of Christians rolled up on the evening air as the voice of many waters. The meeting lasted all night—all of Monday and Monday night, and two hundred souls were converted and joined the Church.

A thousand other incidents, equally material and interesting, are related as to Mr. ———'s adventures in Kentucky and Illinois. Many of them are probably fictitious; but those genuine alone, if collected, would be sufficient to stock at least two volumes of romantic reality.

Such was the backwoods preacher; and biography teaches us the mighty influences of circumstances in molding the characters and fixing the destinies of individual men. Had that splendid genius been cast on the tide of war or thrown into the fiery vortex of the revolutionary era, his name might have been a signal of doom to quaking nations, his renown might have blazed like a comet through all time.

CHAPTER XVIII.

THE YOUNG MISSIONARY AND THE ROBBER.

The following account of a missionary from one of the eastern states, who had completed his theological studies and received his commission to labor in the west, has been furnished me for publication. Like many who come from the east, he was wonderfully ignorant of the west. He had seen, occasionally, an article in some of the three or four religious periodicals of that period, about the far west, and with a benevolent desire of doing good to the destitute and scattered pioneers of this remote and then scarcely-known region, had traveled on horseback from his native village, preaching on Sabbaths, as occasion offered, during his long journey. Ohio was then "said to be" a land of moral desolation; Indiana was "supposed" to be many degrees lower in the scale of civilization; and the new state of Illinois was imagined to be situated very near the jumping-off place. A vague and somewhat doubtful impression existed as to the locality and character of Missouri; and Kentucky was known abroad by report for its fighting and gouging propensities, while the population were characterized as "half-horse, half-alligator, and a touch of the snapping-turtle."

Among the vague and rather indistinct impressions of the character and habits of the frontier adventurers, that floated over the mind of the young missionary, were those of robbery and murders.

During the period of inquiry and anxious meditation about devoting his life as a missionary of the cross, in the wilds of the west, the idea of robbery and murder occupied no minor place in his imagination. Still, with commendable resolution, and a martyr spirit, he resolved to hazard even life, with the sacrifice of every earthly comfort, to preach the Gospel, and introduce the meliorating influences of civilization among a people who belonged to the same nation with himself, and who might eventually exert a controlling influence over the destinies of the republic.

It was a cloudy and cold day in the month of December, that our missionary friend was seen crossing an arm of the Grand Prairie, east of the *Okau,* as the Kaskaskia river by abbreviation—*au Kas*—and French accent had been called. He had traveled a long distance that day, by following a devious and obscure trail, or "bridle path," now through a skirt of timber, then across the point of a prairie, without seeing a log-cabin, or any other sign of a human residence. Night was fast approaching. The landlord where he was accommodated with "private entertainment" the preceding night, had directed him on a "blind trail" to a fording place across the Okau, beyond which, and in the same direction, was the town of G——, to which he was journeying. But horse and rider were fatigued with long fasting and a hard ride, and the missionary could form no conjecture how far it might be from a settlement which he had hoped to reach before nightfall.

Anxious, and somewhat bewildered, he looked in each direction for signs of a human habitation, when an uncouth specimen of humanity appeared on horseback, coming in a rapid movement, and a diagonal direction, across the prairie, toward the path of the missionary. As the man approached, his personal appearance, dress, and equipage, manifested no friendly design. His head was covered with the skin of the prairie wolf, with tail hangin-

behind. His outer garment was neither a coat, frock, nor *blowse.* In western parlance, it was a hunting-shirt, made of dressed deer-skin, with the cape and side-strips curiously notched and fringed, but to the missionary it had an alarming aspect.

Over it hung a powder-horn and bullet-pouch, and around his body was a leathern belt, in which was thrust a formidable knife. A loaded rifle carelessly lay across the rider's shoulders.

Nor was his personal appearance in the least degree prepossessing. He sported a black beard of three weeks' growth, and dark, elfish locks of hair could be seen beneath the skin-cap. His countenance, from constant exposure to the weather, was swarthy, and a rough, stalwart frame seemed, to the alarmed missionary, of gigantic proportions. It had braved the storms of more than forty winters.

Every indication painted most vividly on the perturbed imagination of the missionary the danger that hung over him. The first impulse was to urge his horse into a flight. A second thought convinced him of the hopelessness of the attempt, and breathing a word of prayer to heaven for protection, he felt to submit to his fate, with a gleam of hope that the desperado, who was but a few yards from him, might, peradventure, spare his life.

The salutation that struck on his ears, in a harsh, guttural voice, conveyed no consolation to his mind, and only served to increase his alarm.

"Hallo, stranger! what are you about there? Where are you a riding?"

The reply was given in the language of weakness and submission, and something was added, with indistinct utterance, about giving up his horse and equipments if his life might be spared. Learning, on further inquiry, that his route was across the river, to a settlement some fifteen or twenty miles distant, the supposed robber replied, in a voice by no means mild and attractive, "You can't get there to-night; besides the old ford is washed away, and you can not find the new one. *I can fix you.*"

The term "fix" had an ominous import; but the exact degree of outrage implied in this new form of speech was not very clearly understood by the missionary. But there was no alternative. He was alone and wholly unprotected; he was small in stature, of a slender make, had no weapons but spiritual ones, and successful resistance was hopeless. He knew not the path to the river, and were he to attempt flight the death-dealing rifle might stop him. So he turned, as directed, into the trail, and followed the guide. As they slowly rode in "Indian file" through the tall grass, with points of timber and brushwood for the space of two miles, the missionary drew a fancy picture, on his imagination, of a cave and a band of robbers, who would soon "fix" him or determine his fate. He breathed more freely when he found only a single cabin, a rough-looking stable for horses, and a cornfield of a few acres, with no signs of accomplices.

"Light, stranger, and take your saddle-bags. I'll *fix* your horse."

Taking his saddle-bags on his arms, as directed, he entered the cabin through a low door-way. Here was a woman and three children; but their personal appearance and dress might or might not indicate danger to the traveler. On her head was a covering of coarse cotton, called, in the language of a past generation, a "sun-bonnet." It nearly hid her face from human observation.

Reaching forward a stool, the only salutation given was, "Take a seat by the fire, stranger."

Recollecting what Ledyard and other travelers had said of the humanity and hospitality of the female sex, the missionary mused on the probabilities of escaping with his life, feeling a degree of reconciliation to the loss of his horse, his saddle-bags, and the contents of his purse, which last contained but a few dollars for traveling expenses. In his saddle-bags were divers articles of apparel which he could spare, and there was the pocket-Bible, the gift of a mother now in heaven, a hymn-book, and a small package of neatly-written sermons, which had cost him several months' labor, and, as he fancied, were admirably adapted to disperse the clouds of ignorance that brooded over the inhabitants of Illinois.

In the mean time, the settler, hunter, or robber, in whatever vocation he might appear, had replenished the fire with some logs of dry hickory, while the busy housewife was preparing the homely meal.

It consisted of fried venison-steak, corn-dodgers, and highly-flavored coffee, with the appurtenances of fresh cream and excellent butter.

The missionary, who had eaten nothing since early dawn, and was cogitating whether feminine humanity would not afford him a morsel in the corner where he sat, was startled with the invitation, "Sit by, stranger, and take a bite."

If surprise and gratitude were the first emotions, amazement followed, when the apparent robber implored the blessing of God in a sonorous voice, closing with an expressive *amen.*

Bewildered and confused, the missionary forgot to eat, till repeatedly reminded by the now apparently-hospitable landlord and his kind-hearted wife that he did not eat. "Perhaps he was not used to such fare. Would he take a sup of milk?" He did not seem to regain his appetite till the officious housewife brought on her platter of honey, gathered from the hollow sycamore, and made divers apologies that her larder contained nothing he could eat.

After supper, the landlord commenced religious conversation with the inquiry, "Are you a professing man, stranger?" The question relative to Church membership was propounded in a novel form, and did not convey to the mind of the missionary exactly the idea intended.

"You looked mightily *skeered* when I found you in the prairie. I reckon you were a sort of lost?"

Still the replies were vague and confused, and it was not till the owner of the cabin, in a loud and animating tone, struck up the favorite hymn of the followers of Wesley—

"A charge to keep I have,
A God to glorify—
A never-dying soul to save,
And fit it for the sky"—

in which his wife joined—that the minister was relieved from his perturbation, and could converse calmly. The hymn was followed by a characteristic prayer, in which the "stranger" was affectionately remembered at the throne of mercy, to which the wife responded with several audible groans. Conversation followed the evening obligation, during which the missionary disclosed his profession and his object in traveling, and received due reproof for his previous backwardness. But he had not the heart to tell his fears and sufferings from the apprehension of robbery and murder from a kind-hearted local Methodist preacher, in a backwoods disguise, who was the first man to preach the Gospel to the scattered population on the borders of the Grand Prairie, east of the Okau.

Next morning the missionary led in prayer, and, after an early breakfast, the hospitable preacher saddled his own horse, with that of the missionary, and piloted him to the "new" fording-place across the river, several miles in the direction toward G——.

Giving the parting hand, with a severe but affectionate

grasp, the valedictory was, "Now, stranger, you know where my cabin is; don't pass without giving me a call, and stay long enough to give the people a preach."

The missionary found a field of labor in a new and growing village, among a population quite as intelligent and virtuous as the people of his native state, and a church edifice, a Sabbath school, and Bible class rose under his labors.

The Methodist preacher, whom his brethren at quarterly meeting never suspected of having been mistaken for a robber, in due time doffed his wolf-skin cap and leather hunting-shirt, became clad in cotton garments, spun and wove by his industrious wife, made a large farm, prepared spacious "camping ground" for the annual consecrations, and witnessed the conversion of many sinners under his own labors.

The missionary acknowledged to the writer, when he revealed, in a somewhat confidential manner, the story of his fright, that he was but half educated when he came to Illinois.

Both these men had their appropriate spheres of usefulness, to which they were fitted by nature, habits, education, and grace, and both, many years since, received the plaudit, "Well done, thou good and faithful servant, enter thou into the joy of thy Lord."

CHAPTER XIX.

THE MARTYR PREACHER.

The vows of God were on him. Hearing a voice which none else could hear, that called him to leave home, and kindred, and country, and seeing a hand which none else could see, that beckoned him onward, young Richmond Nolley bade adieu to all the endearments of a happy home, and entered the rough and toilsome field of itinerant life. Though he had a slender and delicate frame, and a feeble constitution, he did not stop to confer with flesh and blood, but, buckling on the harness as a faithful soldier, he went forth, at the command of his Master, to glorious war. He was one of nature's amiable children; such a one, like Summerfield or Cookman, whom all must love. To know them is to love them. Innocent, amiable, unsuspecting, and guileless, their nature is lost in the great depths of humanity, and their whole life is one of self-sacrificing devotion to the interests of the human race. They live, like their divine Master, for others, and not for themselves. Name, and fame, and fortune, are all ignored in Christ, and they are a practical exemplification of the apostle's doctrine of self-consecration to God. Of such, a cold, covetous, selfish, mammon-loving world is not worthy; and the wonder is not that they die early, but that God should allow them to stay here as long as they have been permitted to stay. I have a distinct and vivid recollection of the fate of Nolley. I was then but young myself in the ministry, and had passed through some rough and trying scenes in itinerant life; but in all my experience as a minister, I had heard of nothing like it. The impression made upon my mind was deep and powerful. His deep devotion, his youth, his delicate constitution, the circumstance of his dying alone and unattended in the wilderness, was like a wave of wormwood over my soul, rolling its bitterness. How did I wish that, instead of that frail form being exposed to the fatigues of that fatal journey, it had fallen to my lot, as one reared amid such scenes would have been likely to have survived the perilous mission. But I must not anticipate. The history of this young preacher is short, but full of incident.

He was born in Virginia, though the date of his birth is not exactly known. At an early age his father removed to the state of Georgia. But little is known of his early life, except that he possessed those remarkable traits of character which were so fully developed in after life. About the year 1806 he was made the happy subject of the converting grace of God, and united himself with the Methodist Episcopal Church. It was not long after his conversion that the inward monitions of the Spirit were felt, urging him to enter his Lord's vineyard, and engage in the work of calling sinners to repentance. In matters of such solemn import, the Spirit rarely moves upon the heart of the individual in advance of the impressions of the Church; and he scarcely begins to feel it his duty to exhort sinners to flee the wrath to come, and be saved from their sins, before he is invited by the Church to exercise his gifts. Some run before they are called. Of such are those who profess to be called of God to preach the Gospel, but who, notwithstanding all their efforts, can not convince the Church of that fact. Generally speaking, the voice of the Church is the voice of God, and what is done in her holy councils is ratified in heaven. It was soon discovered that young Nolley had a vow upon him, and that to grace was added gifts which, if allowed to be properly exercised, would soon be productive of fruit to the honor and glory of God.

One year after his conversion, he was admitted into the traveling connection, and sent to Edisto circuit, in South Carolina. So rapidly did the powers of this youthful herald of the cross develop themselves, that his next appointment, being but the second year of his ministry, was in Wilmington, North Carolina; and the succeeding year to the more responsible station of the city of Charleston, the capital of South Carolina.

A city life not proving congenial to his health, and the pastoral labors connected therewith being more than his frail constitution could bear, the next year we find him on Washington circuit, in the state of Georgia. In 1812, in compliance with the request of the bishop, he went on a mission to Tombecbee. After passing through a wilderness of three hundred and fifty miles, embracing many savage nations, during which he was subjected to all kinds of hardships, such as swimming deep rivers and creeks, often destitute of food, sometimes lost in the depths of the forest, exposed to wild beasts or savage men, and lying out with nothing but the earth for his bed and the dark vault above for his covering, he at last arrived at the place of his destination.

Here, on this distant and toilsome field, he spent two years in laboring most indefatigably for the glory of God and the advancement of the Redeemer's kingdom. Thousands would have lived and died in this frontier region, without having heard of salvation, had it not been for the itinerant system of a Church which had the men of nerve to carry it out. And while the "successors of the apostles" were sitting in their gas-lighted saloons, reclining on their rich velvet-cushioned Elizabethans, discoursing pathetically about the moral wastes of the west, and the inefficient ministry, Nolley and his coadjutors were carrying the bread of life to starving, dying thousands, and peopling heaven with little less than the redeemed of heathen lands. If Princeton, Yale, Union, and Rochester, were emptied to-day, and scattered among the destitute of our frontier settlements, how long do you think, gentle reader, it would take them to acquire the efficiency of a backwoods itinerant in getting souls converted to God?

On this mission, where appointments were as far apart as conferences now are long, or as would embrace an entire circuit, he never lost an appointment. He never stopped for wet or cold. The invisible hand beckoned him onward, the inaudible voice urged him forward, and often without a horse he would take his saddle-bags on his shoulders and walk to his appointments. In regard to the hours of sleep, he carried out to the letter the rules of the father of Methodism, and at early morn, while many were locked fast in the embrace of Morpheus, he was up with the lark, at his morning orisons. It is reported of him, that he most diligently instructed the children, in every place—a duty, alas! too often neglected by many who have declared before God and the world that they would attend to it. The poor slave was not forgotten in his daily ministrations. Every day, almost, found him in the hut of the sable son and daughter of Africa, teaching them the religion of Christ, and the way to heaven; and had it not been for the labors of just such faithful men, "Uncle Tom's Cabin" would have been devoid of every element of interest. But not only did he instruct the children, and labor and pray with the slave, but at every house, among parents and masters, with the young and the old, the rich and the poor, the bond and the free, he endeavored to make full proof of his ministry by "warning every man, and teaching every man in all wisdom, that he might present every man perfect in Christ Jesus."

In this great work he often met with opposition; he was threatened and execrated; but for revilings and persecutions he returned blessings, and his tears and prayers often disarmed persecution, and sent trembling to the stoutest heart. He was on the Tombecbee mission when the Indian war raged with the most relentless fury, and the unprotected whites fell in every direction beneath the murderous tomahawk and scalping-knife of the savage. When the people had all taken refuge in forts, and were afraid to visit their plantations, the intrepid missionary, as if conscious of immortality till his work was done, unarmed and unattended, went from fort to fort, and preached the Gospel as a visiting angel of mercy. By these, and other acts of Christian kindness, he enthroned himself in the hearts of all the people, and his name will be a household word in time, while his deeds will live forever.

His untiring zeal and devotion, which prompted him to many exposures, preyed heavily upon his delicate constitution, and it seemed, to all human appearance, that he must quit the itinerant field. Reduced almost to a shadow, with pale, attenuated features, he was found among his brethren at the conference, after the year's toil had ended. His dauntless spirit would not allow him to desist from labor, and seek that rest which was essential to his restoration. Determined, as it seemed, to run on and burn out, like the arrow of Ascestes, which took fire in its flight and vanished in the immensity of heaven, so he, as a flaming herald of the cross, on fire of a quenchless zeal, pressed on to the mark of the heavenly prize.

Receiving an appointment on the Attakapas circuit, in the state of Louisiana, he entered upon the work, and for one year encountered toils and hardships which would have broken down a more rugged constitution. Still he counted not his life dear to him; but, in the midst of long and tedious rides, muddy and almost impassable roads, deep waters, with weariness and faintness, with fastings and watchings, he journeyed on. The peculiarities of the work made it necessary, in the estimation of the bishop, for him to return to the circuit next year, and, without a murmur or a sigh, he started out again for his distant field.

He was accompanied by a fellow-missionary across the Mississippi and through a vast swamp. The difficulties they had to encounter were almost incredible, and, coming to a place where they must separate, after embracing each other, with mutual benedictions, they parted.

It was in the latter part of November, and it was a dark, cold, rainy day. Arriving at night at the house of a friendly man, where he staid till morning, imparting the comforts of religion to its inmates, he departed on his journey. Across his path there lay a large swamp and deep creeks, and not a single white man was to be found between that and the place of his destination. Alone he traveled on till evening, when he found himself at an Indian village. Having to cross a creek before night, and apprehending from the rains that it would be swollen, he employed an Indian to go with him. When he arrived on its banks, he found it, as he anticipated, a full and angry flood, rushing tumultuously along. There was no alternative but to cross or remain with the savages; so he chose the former, and, leaving his valise, saddle-bags, and a parcel of books with the Indian, he urged his horse into the stream. No sooner did his noble charger strike the furious current than he was beaten down the flood. The noble animal battled courageously with the tide; but before the other shore was reached, horse and rider were far below the landing-place of the ford, and, the banks being high and precipitous, it was impossible for the horse to gain a foothold or make the ascent of the other shore In the struggle to do so the rider was thrown, and, grasping the limb of a tree which extended over the stream, he reached the shore. The horse swam back to the side of the stream from whence he started.

The missionary directed the Indian to keep his horse till morning, and he would walk to the nearest house, which was distant about two miles. He traveled through the woods about one mile, wet, cold, and weary. Unable to proceed any further, and conscious, perhaps, that his work was done, and he had at last fulfilled the errand of his Master, he fell upon his knees* and commended his soul to God.

There, in that wild wood of the far west, alone with his Master and the ministering spirits that encamp around the saints, Richmond Nolley, the young missionary, closed his eyes on earth to open them in heaven.

When he was found he was lying extended upon the wet leaves, his left hand upon his breast and the other lying by his side. His eyes were closed, and the gentle spirit left a smile upon his pallid cheek ere it passed away to that bright and beautiful world, where the wicked cease to trouble and the weary are at rest.

* The indentations made by his knees were left on the ground close by, to mark the spot where he made his last prayer.

CHAPTER XX.

ITINERANT LIFE CONTINUED.

THE Steubenville conference of 1818 lasted eight days, and was a most interesting season. I was reappointed to the Ohio district, and, after conference, started with my brethren to my field of labor. All the preachers seemed disposed to do and suffer the will of God in the discharge of the duties growing out of their vocation.

For some years Bishop M'Kendree had been interested in the various tribes of Indians, and was anxious to have missions established among them. A work of grace having commenced among the Wyandotts, at Upper Sandusky, through the instrumentality of a colored exhorter—J. Stewart—the Bishop made an engagement with my brother, John P. Finley, to go among them and teach the youth to read and write, and to preach to the adults. Brother Montgomery was appointed to labor among the Indians in company with Stewart, and for his support a collection was taken up of five and ten dollars from the preachers. At this conference the Bishop asked me if I would not go there and labor as a missionary. I remarked that I did not think I had the necessary qualifications, and that there were others who would do vastly better. I thought I had not sufficient patience to teach school. After some further conversation on the subject we parted, but not without a strong impression made upon my mind by the remarks of the Bishop, that at some future day it was his intention to send me to that work.

We had a fine time on the district during the winter. The area of Immanuel's kingdom was enlarged. As fast as the people moved into the country the preachers visited them, and soon as they had their cabins reared, they commenced preaching and forming societies. The camp meetings during the latter part of the year were attended with success. In many places the novelty of such scenes as are presented by worshiping God in the grove attracted the attention of many, and produced a good impression. But few can look upon a camp meeting scene and not be moved. Such a scene as is presented by an encampment at night, to one who has never witnessed any thing like it before, must be impressive. To look upon the long ranges of tents surrounding a large area, in each corner of which bright fires are lighted up, and then from tent and tree to see innumerable lamps hung out, casting their lights among the branches and illuminating all the ground, would remind one of the descriptions given of an oriental wedding scene, when, at midnight, the cry is heard, "Behold, the bridegroom cometh! Go ye forth to meet him." Then the sound of the trumpet, and the gathering together of thousands, who pass to and fro with lights and torches, all has a tendency to awaken the most solemn reflections. And when the holy song rises from a thousand voices, and floats out upon the stillness of the night air, the listener must feel that surely such a place is holy ground. These camp meetings were seasons of special mercy to thousands, and many who came to curse remained to pray for salvation and seek an interest in the blessed Savior.

The conference this year met in Cincinnati, August 7, 1819. Many of the fathers of our Israel were with us. These holy shepherds, having been traveling extensively in the intervals of conference, passing through the circuits, and stations, and districts, proclaiming salvation, meeting classes, attending love-feasts, and stimulating the younger preachers in their work, kindled a flame of love to God in every heart. The itinerants caught the holy fire, and thus, newly baptized with the unction from above, went out with fresh zeal into the vineyard of their Lord. These backwoods bishops traveled from Maine to Georgia and from the Atlantic to the Mississippi, on the farthest bounds of western population, encountering every hardship; and their annual visits were looked for by preachers and people, saint and sinner, with the greatest anxiety and pleasure.

Nothing occurred at this conference to mar the peace and harmony which prevailed in the itinerant ranks. Delegates were elected to the General conference which was to be held in the following May, and, the business being finished, each preacher started to his field of labor.

This year I was appointed to the Lebanon district, which was bounded as follows; namely, on the south by the Ohio river and on the north by the lakes, including all the territory in Michigan. My district included the Indian mission at Upper Sandusky; and, although the mission is not named in the Minutes of that year, I was nevertheless chosen as superintendent. I made an appointment for a quarterly meeting for this mission at Zanesfield, on the waters of Mad river, the 13th and 14th of November. See Methodist Magazine, 1820, page 35. Here the reader will find an account of the first quarterly meeting ever held among the Indians.

I commenced my work by attending two camp meetings, one of which was six miles west of Springfield. This was a local preachers' camp meeting, at which there were present, I think, about twenty local preachers. As radicalism had begun to show itself, there was a considerable of prejudice against the traveling preachers. Brother John Strange, of blessed memory, was my conductor; and he remarked to me on the way, that it was highly probable we would meet with a cool reception, as the local brethren were very much prejudiced against my predecessor. However, we journeyed on, and arrived at the camp-ground on Friday afternoon. We said but little to any one. On Saturday afternoon brother Joseph Tatman was deputed to take me aside and examine me in regard to my views of Church government. He attended to his duty in a very Christian manner, and I presume the expositions I gave him of Methodist polity were satisfactory, as I was waited upon, and invited to preach on Sabbath at eleven o'clock.

The preaching hour arrived, and I was enabled to preach with liberty. The Lord attended the word, and many were awakened and converted to God before the exercises connected with that hour closed. From that time I witnessed nothing but the kindest feeling toward me.

The next Saturday and Sabbath the camp meeting commenced at Mechanicsburg, and this was a time of the greatest display of God's power in the awakening and conversion of sinners. After this I commenced my round of quarterly meetings. At every meeting I set myself to work to find out the exact state of religion among the officiary; and, to enable me more fully to do so, I took a list of all the names, and went into a regular class meeting examination. This was a novel procedure, but it was made a great blessing to every official member, and before I had passed around my district twice, it was all on fire. O, what blessed times! The fire was soon carried out by preachers, exhorters, leaders, and stewards, and by spring the whole Church throughout the vast field of my labor was in a blaze.

In the month of April I left for General conference, which was to be held in Baltimore, in company with brother John Collins. After twelve days of hard riding, we reached the seat of the conference, which commenced its session the first of May. As conference progressed, it was discoverable that there existed, unhappily, some discordant elements in the body. The east seemed to be arrayed against slavery, and the south against pewed churches. There was also another question which was of a somewhat exciting character, and which appeared to carry every thing before it. I allude to the election of presiding elders. A resolution proposing a change of the Discipline, so as to make the office of presiding elder elective, was offered by the Rev. Daniel Ostrander, and the resolution was discussed with great zeal and ability. The conference seemed so equally divided, it was hard to tell which side would gain the victory. The bishops and presiding elders were mostly committed to the old plan of appointing presiding elders; and as the latter usually constituted the delegation, there was a prospect of the rule being retained; but so vigorously did the friends of the new measure contend for a change which they deemed most in accordance with the genius of American Methodism, that it was confidently hoped they would succeed. Before coming to a vote, a compromise was proposed by the Rev. Ezekiel Cooper, of the Philadelphia conference, that there should be a committee of nine appointed to consult and report. This committee reported, that in the appointment of presiding elders, the bishop should have the power to nominate two or three men for each district, and the conference should choose from among these the presiding elder. This report passed by a large majority. Rev. Joshua Soule, who had been elected bishop previous to this action, refused to be ordained, unless the conference would reverse its action. The reason he gave was, that in his opinion the action of the conference was unconstitutional, and he could not administer discipline under it. Bishop M'Kendree, who was unwell, and was not in conference at the time of the passage of the report, came in afterward with a strong remonstrance against it, and hoped the conference would not urge its operation till it had been sent round to all the conferences, and its constitutionality decided. After debating the question of reference for two or three days, it was, finally, by a very small majority, suspended for four years.

At this conference the rule was adopted which required Methodist churches to be built with free seats. This was a quite exciting topic. When the question was raised whether the rule should be advisory or mandatory, it was decided that it should only be regarded as advisory, and, hence, such a caption was given to it. I recollect distinctly hearing the Rev. D. Ostrander say, in open conference, that it would not be twenty years before, under that very rule, some conference would restrict the stationing power. And I have lived to see the fulfillment of that prophecy, in the action of the Ohio conference of 1850 at Chilicothe.

The General conference having adjourned, we backwoods preachers directed our course homeward, and wending our way over the mountains, we reached once more the delightful valleys of the west.

We wound up our year's work with a round of camp meetings. Some of these were attended with unusual manifestations of Divine power. Of such were Rattlesnake, Honey creek, and Union camp meetings. At the latter we had the services of our beloved superintendents, M'Kendree and Roberts. The gathering of the people was immense. They came together in the spirit of prayer, and not for the purpose of making a display, such as might be called a religious picnic, where families vie with each other in showing off to the best advantage, but to worship God exclusively, without any regard to "visits, modes, and forms." And such realized the desire of their hearts. The work commenced at once, and continued day and night with increasing power, and over one hundred and fifty were soundly converted to God. Milford camp meeting was also a time of great power, there was a mighty shaking among the dry bones. A leader of infidelity, renowned for his advocacy of error, was awakened and converted, and sent out by the Spirit to bear testimony to the truth of that religion which he had reviled White-oak camp meeting was held at Indian hill, and was the most powerful one I had attended on the district How many were converted I am not able to say, but the number was large. On Sabbath I baptized one hundred persons before nine o'clock, by sprinkling and pouring. Brother G. W. Light wrote down the names as I announced them, and gave them to me. Among the number is the name of our beloved and lamented William B. Christie, of whom I intend saying something hereafter. The Revs. Augustus Eddy and Charles W. Swain, both young preachers just entering upon their ministerial life, were at this meeting.

Strait creek camp meeting was held soon after, and was attended with mighty power. On Sabbath morning, while brother John Collins was praying, the Holy Spirit came down on us as a rushing, mighty wind, and more than one hundred fell under the power of God; and such a time of weeping and rejoicing I never saw before. We were much annoyed by the rabble, who were set upon us by men professing to wear the garb of Christian ministers, but more frequently by the whisky-makers and venders themselves. Few men, in their sober senses, could be induced to disgrace themselves by interrupting the worship of God, and those few must be besotted and imbruted to a degree past recovery, who would cut to pieces the harness, saddles, bridles, tents, etc., of the worshipers, and howl around the encampment like skulking wolves Such creatures were sometimes handled pretty roughly by the conservators of the peace, and they learned often, by sad experience, that the way of the transgressor was hard.

I was solicited this year to send a minister to Detroit. After some considerable difficulty, I obtained Rev. P. B Morey, and sent him, with instructions to gather up the scattered members, and form the nucleus of a circuit. Brother Hecock, from Upper Canada, had been laboring two years in the shore settlements, among the destitute population. Brother Morey returned, and brought with him a plan of his circuit; but having contracted the fever and ague, he was unwilling to go back.

The conference this year was held in Chilicothe, and we were favored with the presence of all our bishops, M'Kendree, Roberts, and George. The session was characterized with great harmony, and the conference business was transacted with great dispatch. The increase in the membership in the Ohio conference this year, was five thousand, nine hundred and twenty-two.

At this conference I was returned to the Lebanon district, and my range was from the Ohio river to the lakes, including Detroit and the new settlements on the peninsula, besides the Wyandott mission. The Rev. John P. Kent was sent to Detroit circuit, which extended from the Maumee Rapids to Lake St. Clair.

It was late in the fall when I left the white settlements to attend my first quarterly meeting at the Maumee Rapids. There was not a single habitation of a white man from the old Indian boundary on the Scioto till we reached the Rapids. In this route there were three Indian settlements—Upper Sandusky, Big Spring, and Tawawatown, on a branch of the Carrion river. Through this wilderness I urged my way. I had a dismal journey through the Black Swamp. Two nights I lay out in the woods, during all which time I did not see the face of a human being. By the help of God I at length reached my appointment. How changed the country and inhabitants since I passed through in 1800 with the drove of cattle! From a wild, desolate region, where savages roamed, now could be seen fruitful farms, where could be found peaceful Christian families, in whose houses were erected altars to the God of the Bible. I was hailed, by preacher and people, with gladness, as one that bringeth glad tidings to the ends of the earth. I had the honor of being the first presiding elder that set his foot on the Miami of the lakes, and had the privilege of holding the first quarterly meeting, love-feast, or sacramental meeting ever held in this now densely-populated country. Our meeting commenced under the most favorable auspices. The few who came together—and there were some who had come the distance of seventy-five miles—sat together in heavenly places in our Lord Jesus Christ. The banner of Divine love was spread over us. Our meeting commenced on Friday night and continued till Tuesday morning. Several professed religion and joined the Church. The brethren were much refreshed and built up in holy faith. After visiting many of the settlements, I returned through the wilderness to the Big Spring, where I held a meeting with the Wyandotts. Here the subject of a mission school was taken under consideration by the principal men of the nation; and they had been encouraged to think they might have two—one at Upper Sandusky and the other at this place. I showed them the impracticability of organizing two schools, in consequence of the expense attending them, and that they must send their children all to one place. We had a very pleasant and profitable meeting; but no kind of Church organization. All were permitted to join in the exercises who felt disposed. The religion of the natives seemed to be a kind of national religion. There being no Church organization and no rules of discipline, none were called to an account for disorderly conduct. It was perfectly obvious to me, in this state of things, that we would be unable, as a Church, to accomplish much of any consequence unless we could organize the Indians into a Church and administer all the ordinances of religion and all the rules of Discipline.

During the winter the work progressed most gloriously on the district, and multitudes were converted to God. In the spring I started for the purpose of visiting more thoroughly my Detroit charge. The trip was a very adventurous one. When I arrived at Lower Sandusky the summer freshet was at its highest. I traveled alone to the Muscalange creek, and the water covered the entire valley from hill to hill. Unable to proceed any further, I went back to the town at Lower Sandusky, and hired a Frenchman to pilot me through to the rapids of the Maumee. When he came to the creek he said it was impossible for us to get through; so we returned, and I directed my course up the river to Fort Ball. Leaving my horse with a friend, I hired two young Indians to take me to the mouth of the river in a bark canoe, so that I might at this point get on board the steamer Walk-in-the-Water on Friday morning.

Setting sail in our frail canoe, we darted down the rapid river, and, when we came to the Sandusky Falls, we sped over them like a bird. Night overtaking us before we reached the mouth of the river, we concluded to tarry all night with an old Frenchman by the name of Poscile, who occupied a miserable shanty on the bank, and lived principally on muskrats. The place was dreadfully infested with fleas and musketoes. My comrades joined in partaking of our host's hospitalities; but I was not sufficiently hunger-bitten to eat muskrats. To protect myself from the foes which swarmed around me I sat all night on a box. When daylight came we pushed off our canoe and paddled on. As we reached the bay we found the wind blowing fresh from land and the waves rolling too high for our little bark. The bay was five miles wide, and, notwithstanding the boisterous weather, the Indians were for going directly across. To this I objected; and we finally agreed to take the east side and coast around. Several times our canoe filled with water, and we had to run ashore, pull it out, and turn it over—then relaunching, put to sea again. A more serious disaster befell us when we got within two hundred yards of the shore at Goat Island. A sudden squall upset our bark, plunging us all in the deep. Being unable to right up our vessel without something more substantial than water on which to rest our leverage, we swam with our boat to the shore. Here we took our canoe on our shoulders, and carrying it about a mile, we launched again and re-embarked. We paddled on, battling with the waves, and finally arrived within four miles of Portland. Taking my saddle-bags on my shoulder, I walked to town, almost exhausted for the want of something to eat. Here I stopped at a tavern, and, ordering a room with a fire, I emptied my saddle-bags, and, spreading their contents, with my clothes, before it, went to bed and slept till the sun arose next morning. Getting up, I found all my things tolerably well dried, except my books, and, after taking my breakfast, I got on board the boat, and arrived at Detroit on Saturday morning, where I put up with my old friend, Mr. Jeremiah Dean. At this place I received a letter from brother Kent, informing me of his sickness at the Rapids, and his inability to be with me. In that letter he informed me that he had given out appointments for me every day during the week, except Saturday and Monday. Thus you see, dear reader, I had work enough. The weather was excessively hot; but, notwithstanding, we commenced our meetings. Having no church, we worshiped in the old council-house, and the Lord was with us of a truth. Governor Cass, my old friend, treated me with great respect and hospitality, and also his estimable lady. Indeed, God seemed to give me favor in the eyes of all the people. The soldiers who were stationed here treated me with much respect, and many of them were awakened under preaching. Of all places in the world, a military station is the most unfavorable to religion; and hence there was but little fruit manifested. Several came forward for prayers and were converted to God. Had not appointments been given out for me, the meeting could have been kept up all the week to great advantage. Brother Abbott furnished me a horse, and I started on Tuesday to fill the appointments which had been made. That day I preached twice, and swam the river Ruse three times. I then went to two or three places out north and preached as far as Pontiac. Returning to Detroit, I spent another Sabbath of great interest and profit to myself and many others. My soul was much united to the dear people; for they seemed to be as sheep without a shepherd. On Monday I left for Upper Sandusky. When I arrived at Portland there was no conveyance for me to Lower Sandusky. After considerable search I found an Indian, whose horse I hired. The plan was for me to ride and the Indian to walk or run, as the case might be. Accordingly we started. The Indian would run on ahead in a long trot, and then, stopping, he would say, "Good horse; how much you give for him?" I would tell him I did not want to buy. He would then run on again a mile or two, and, stopping, would ask the same question. This he continued till, becoming tired of his questions, I told him I had no money. "You lie," said he, pointing to my saddle-bags. Then said he, "How much you give?" I said, "May be ten dollars." Becoming incensed at this, he exclaimed, "You rascal!

you Kaintuck! you rascal! you cheat Indian!" Shortly after this we came within hearing of several camps of Indians. As we advanced we found them in a drunken spree, singing, dancing, and hallooing as if all bedlam had broke loose. He asked me to turn in here and get some "lum." "No," said I, "you come on." "No: me go, and quick come." As soon as he was gone I cut a stout hickory stick and put the Indian pony to his best. Soon I heard the Indian yelling behind me; but he was not able to overtake me till I reached Lower Sandusky. When he came up he commenced abusing me and charging me with a disposition to run off with his horse. I told him he must stop his abuse, as I would have no more of it. "Did I not give one dollar for the use of your horse?" "Yes." "Well," said I, "here is a half dollar besides, to get your dinner with." At this he turned his tune, and said, "You good man; you no Kaintuck; you my friend!"

From this place I got a conveyance to Fort Ball, where I found my horse, and traveled on to the Reservation, where I met the chiefs and principal men and women of the Wyandott nation. I drew up a petition for them to send to conference, which was to be held at Lebanon. Vide History of the Wyandott Mission.

This year brother Morey was admitted on trial into the traveling connection, and appointed to Detroit circuit, where he promised great usefulness to the Church; but it pleased Him who holds the stars in his right hand, to call him from labor to reward. The Minutes of this year show an increase in the conference of one thousand, six hundred and three. This was one of the best years of my itinerant life. A petition was sent this year to the bishops for me to be stationed at Detroit. This petition was signed by Gov. Cass, the Messrs. Hunts, and principal citizens. In the petition they pledged themselves to pay all the expenses, and support me, besides building a church. It was confidently believed by them, that their prayer would be heard; but Bishop M'Kendree thought the Indian mission of more consequence than Detroit, or any other place that might want me. Bishop Roberts was in favor of sending me to Detroit, and the matter continued in suspense till late in the conference. My own judgment and feelings led me to Detroit, because I believed that at that time all the English inhabitants of the place would have joined the Church. But the senior bishop prevailed, and I was sent among the Indians. With regard to my moving to Sandusky, and my labors connected with the Wyandott Indians, I need only say, that the reader can refer to the work on the Wyandott mission, and to the Magazines of '22, '23, '24, etc. These, however, give but a brief history of my labors and trials. Much is unwritten, but I hope to furnish some things in this biography which are worthy of remembrance, and full of incident. In the fifth volume of the Methodist Magazine, you will find a letter to Rev. J. Soule, which will give some account of my removal.

There being no missionary funds at that day to furnish an outfit to the missionary, I left home in Warren county the eighth of October, with two wagon-loads of household goods, farming utensils, and other needful apparatus for the commencement of my work. After eight days' hard traveling, we arrived at the Indian nation, and took shelter in a cabin newly raised, without chinking or daubing, destitute of either chimney, window, or door. Here my family had to live till I could build one. There were six in the mission family—two young women, two young men I had hired, and myself and wife. I went to work to build a cabin for the winter. The first week three of my hired hands left me. Another calamity happened. While we were cutting down a tree for a house-log, a limb struck brother George Riley on the head, and I thought him dead for some time. Placing him on the wagon, I drove three-quarters of a mile, and then bled him before he revived. All alone I worked every day, from daylight till dark, till my hands were so sorely blistered I could not sleep at night. The marks of my fingers were left on the timbers and logs from the blood which flowed all day. In the course of a week brother Riley was able to help me. On Sabbaths I preached at the council-house, and held class meetings with all who would stay. On the fourth of November we moved into our winter cabin, without window or door, but we hung a blanket up for a shelter. Soon as we took possession of our new home, a widow, who had no means of sustaining her Indian children, presented us with four. We could not refuse to take these poor children of the forest, thus thrown by Providence upon us.

Sister Harriet Stubbs, of blessed memory, volunteered to leave as peaceful and happy a home as could be found in the state, with every thing to make her happy, and become the matron and instructor of the poorest of the poor outcasts, trodden under foot by vicious white men. She was a sister-in-law of the Hon. Judge M'Lean, of Ohio; and although reared in the tenderest manner, yet she forsook all the advantages and blessings her station in life secured, and espousing the cause of God's poor, fled to the relief of suffering humanity. She possessed more courage and fortitude than any one of her age and sex, that I have been acquainted with. It was but a short time till she, the intrepid female missionary, was the idol of the whole nation. They looked upon her as an angel-messenger, sent from the spirit-land to teach them the way to heaven. They called her the pretty red-bird, and were only happy in the light of her smiles. This most amiable young lady took charge of the Indian girls, and began to teach them their letters, and infuse into them her own sweet and happy spirit.

As spring came, some of the girls were so far advanced as to read and speak English tolerably well. No sight was more calculated to affect the heart than to see that young, lovely, and accomplished girl surrounded by Indian maidens, gazing into her deep-blue eyes, and reading the love that glowed there for them, and hanging with breathless attention upon her lips, as she endeavored to cultivate the powers of these children of the forest, and lead them up to the civilization of Christianity.

We spent the winter in making preparations for building a house for the family and the school. All this we did ourselves. We did not make the Indians our hewers of wood and drawers of water. So constantly was I engaged, that I did not eat a single meal of victuals by the light of the sun, except on Sabbath, during the whole winter. We first cut our logs, then hauled them to the saw-mill, where we staid day and night and sawed our lumber. Brother Riley sawed all day, and I hauled the lumber home on a wagon with two yoke of oxen; and, after returning, we sat up and sawed alternately all night. So we continued till we had all the lumber we wanted to build a house twenty-four by forty-five feet, and two stories high.

In the spring I hired the splitting and putting up of ten thousand rails, and also hired two hands to put in our spring crop. Our school, in the mean time, increased to thirteen children; but, as yet, we had no school-house. Our beloved sister had a booth made in the yard, where she taught her little flock daily. While we were doing all we could to lay the foundation for a large school by which to instruct the nation, we also labored to bring them to God. It required great wisdom to manage affairs so as not to prejudice the Indians. All the savage part of the nation were laboring hard to keep them in the Indian faith, and every effort was made to get those who had made a profession of religion to go back to heathenism. In addition to this, whisky-sellers were increasing to an alarming extent, and I saw it was necessary to have a more thoroughly-organized state of society to resist these encroachments. So I resolved, in direct opposition to some of the friends of the mission, to form a society on Methodist principles. I accordingly drew up a few articles in reference to attending meeting, family and private prayer, the observance of the Sabbath, and total abstinence from all intoxicating liquors. These things I explained so fully that they were perfectly understood; and then I made an effort to form a class, which resulted only in bringing out seven who were willing to live by rule. The temperance rule made a great stir among the whisky-traders, and they tried to convince the Indians that in thus putting their names on paper, they had signed away their Indian liberty, and had become the slaves of the white man. The lines, however, were drawn, and the national religion, which allowed a man to be drunk one day and very religious the next, was entirely broken up. The head chief and his secretary of war, Warpole, commenced holding meetings every Sabbath, for the purpose of worshiping their Indian god. Their ceremonies consisted in dancing, feasting, drinking, and their chief-priest was called upon to preach or rehearse the traditions of their Indian god, and the mighty works and wonderful words of their ancient warriors in the day of battle. This at first drew many to worship with them. The next Sabbath I expounded my rules, showed the beneficial effects they must produce if faithfully kept, and then opened the doors of the Church. That day ten more joined—all of them of the most influential of the nation. Four of them were principal chiefs, Between-the-Logs, Mononcue, Hicks, and Peacock. This separation gave an impulse to the Christian party, and caused many to investigate religion. The old faith was shaken. At one time I was sent for in the afternoon to go in haste to Between-the-Logs. When I arrived I found the parties had met to investigate the religion of the Bible. After a few Indian ceremonies, such as eating hominy and smoking, the subject was introduced by Bloody-Eyes, a notorious old drunkard. It lasted all night and till nine o'clock the next morning, when the council broke. It would take a small volume to communicate the transactions of that night. The speeches of some of these sons of the forest were truly wonderful. But suffice it to say that my adversaries, particularly the old chief, confessed themselves headed in every proposition.

CHAPTER XXI.

GREAT REVIVAL IN THE WEST.

In the spring of 1800 one of the most astonishing and powerful revivals occurred that has ever been known in the western country. This was also the most extensive revival that perhaps ever was witnessed in this country. It was marked by some peculiarities which had not been known to characterize any revival in former times. The nearest approximation to it, of which I can form any conception, was the revival on the day of pentecost, when thousands were awakened and converted to God under the most exciting circumstances.

The commencement of the revival is traceable to the joint labors of two brothers in Cumberland county, Kentucky, one of whom was a Presbyterian and the other a Methodist preacher. They commenced laboring together, every Sabbath preaching, exhorting, and praying alternately. This union was regarded as quite singular, and excited the curiosity of vast multitudes, who came to the places of meeting to hear two men preach who held views in theology supposed to be entirely antagonistic. Nothing was discoverable in their preaching of a doctrinal character, except the doctrine of man's total depravity and ruin by sin, and his recovery therefrom by faith in Christ. All were exhorted to flee the wrath to come, and be saved from their sins. The word which they preached was attended with the power of God to the hearts of listening thousands. The multitudes who flocked from all parts of the country to hear them, became so vast that no church would hold them, and they were obliged to resort to the fields and woods. Every vehicle was put in requisition; carriages, wagons, carts and sleds. Many came on horseback, and larger crowds still came on foot.

As the excitement increased, and the work of conviction and conversion continued, several brought tents, which they pitched on the ground, and remained day and night for many days. The reader will here find the origin of camp meetings.

In the spring of 1801 Bishop M'Kendree was appointed presiding elder of the Kentucky district; and being thus brought in contact with this wonderful work, he was prepared to form a correct judgment of its character. That there were extravagances that constituted no part of religion, he was prepared to admit, but that it was all a wild, fanatical delusion, he was very far from conceding. Nay, he believed that it was the work of God's Spirit on the hearts of the people, and that thousands were genuinely converted to God.

These meetings began to follow one another in quick succession, and the numbers which attended were almost incredible. While the meetings lasted, crowds were to be seen in all directions, passing and repassing the roads and paths, while the woods seemed to be alive with people. Whole settlements appeared to be vacated, and only here and there could be found a house having an inhabitant. All ages, sexes, and conditions, pressed their way to the camp meeting. At these meetings the Presbyterians and Methodists united. They were held at different places. On the 22d of May, 1801, one was held at Cabin creek; the next was held at Concord, in one of my father's old congregations; the next was at Point Pleasant, and the succeeding one at Indian creek, in Harrison county. At these meetings thousands fell under the power of God, and cried for mercy. The scenes which successively occurred at these meetings were awfully sublime, and a genera.

terror seemed to have pervaded the minds of all people within the reach of their influences.

The great general camp meeting was held at Cane Ridge meeting-house. This house was built for my father, and here was my old home. I have elsewhere described this meeting, or, rather, attempted to do so. Language is utterly impuissant to convey any thing like an adequate idea of the sublimity and grandeur of the scene. Twenty thousand persons tossed to and fro, like the tumultuous waves of the sea in a storm, or swept down like the trees of the forest under the blast of the wild tornado, was a sight which mine own eyes witnessed, but which neither my pen nor tongue can describe.

During the religious exercises within the encampment, all manner of wickedness was going on without. So deep and awful is man's depravity, that he will sport while the very fires of perdition are kindling around him. Men, furious with the effects of the maddening bowl, would outrage all decency by their conduct; and some, mounted on horses, would ride at full speed among the people. I saw one, who seemed to be a leader and champion of the party, on a large, white horse, ride furiously into the praying circle, uttering the most horrid imprecations. Suddenly, as if smitten by lightning, he fell from his horse. At this a shout went up from the religious multitude, as if Lucifer himself had fallen. I trembled, for I feared God had killed the bold and daring blasphemer. He exhibited no signs whatever of life; his limbs were rigid, his wrists pulseless, and his breath gone. Several of his comrades came to see him, but they did not gaze long till the power of God came upon them, and they fell like men slain in battle. I was much alarmed, but I had a great desire to see the issue. I watched him closely, while for thirty hours he lay, to all human appearance, dead. During this time the people kept up singing and praying. At last he exhibited signs of life, but they were fearful spasms, which seemed as if he were in a convulsive fit, attended by frightful groans, as if he were passing through the intensest agony. It was not long, however, till his convulsions ceased, and springing to his feet, his groans were converted into loud and joyous shouts of praise. The dark, fiend-like scowl which overspread his features, gave way to a happy smile, which lighted up his countenance.

A certain Dr. P., accompanied by a lady from Lexington, was induced, out of mere curiosity, to attend the meeting. As they had heard much about the involuntary jerkings and falling which attended the exercises, they entered into an agreement between themselves that, should either of them be thus strangely attacked or fall, the other was to stand by to the last. It was not long till the lady was brought down in all her pride, a poor sinner in the dust, before her God. The Doctor, agitated, came up and felt for her pulse; but, alas! her pulse was gone. At this he turned pale, and, staggering a few paces, he fell beneath the power of the same invisible hand. After remaining for some time in this state, they both obtained pardon and peace and went rejoicing home. They both lived and died happy Christians. Thousands were affected in the same way.

These camp meetings continued for some time, the Presbyterians and Methodists uniting together as one in the army of the Lord. Some ministers had serious doubts concerning the character of the work; but its genuineness was demonstrated by the fruits. Men of the most depraved hearts and vicious habits were made new creatures, and a whole life of virtue subsequently confirmed the conversion. To all but Methodists the work was entirely strange. Some of the peculiarities had been witnessed before by the preachers, and they were enabled to carry it on.

These meetings exhibited nothing to the spectator unacquainted with them but a scene of confusion, such as scarcely could be put into human language. They were generally opened with a sermon or exhortation, at the close of which there would be a universal cry for mercy, some bursting forth in loud ejaculations of prayer or thanksgiving for the truth; some breaking forth in strong and powerful exhortations, others flying to their careless friends with tears of compassion, entreating them to fly to Christ for mercy; some, struck with terror and conviction, hastening through the crowd to escape, or pulling away from their relations, others trembling, weeping, crying for mercy; some falling and swooning away, till every appearance of life was gone and the extremities of the body assumed the coldness of death. These were surrounded with a company of the pious, singing melodious songs adapted to the time, and praying for their conversion. But there were others collected in circles round this variegated scene, contending for and against the work.

Many circumstances transpired that are worthy of note in reference to this work. Children were often made the instruments through which the Lord wrought. At one of these powerful displays of Divine power, a boy about ten years old broke from the stand in time of preaching under very strong impressions, and having mounted a log at some distance, and raising his voice in a most affecting manner, cried out, "On the last day of the feast Jesus stood and cried, If any man thirst, let him come unto me and drink." He attracted the main body of the congregation, and, with streaming eyes, he warned the sinners of their danger, denouncing their doom, if they persevered in sin, and strongly expressed his love for the salvation of their souls, and the desire that they would turn to God and live. By this time the press was so great that he was taken up by two men and held above the crowd. He spoke for near an hour with that convincing eloquence that could be inspired only from heaven; and when exhausted, and language failed to describe the feelings of his soul, he raised his handkerchief, and dropping it, cried, "Thus, O sinner, will you drop into hell unless you forsake your sins and turn to God." At this moment the power of God fell upon the assembly, and sinners fell as men slain in mighty battle, and the cries for mercy seemed as though they would rend the heavens, and the work spread in a manner which human language can not describe.

We will now try to give something in reference to the manner and the exercise of mind of those who were the subjects of this work. Immediately before they became totally powerless, they were sometimes seized with a general tremor, and often uttered several piercing shrieks in the moment of falling. Men and women never fell when under this jerking exercise till they became exhausted. Some were unable to stand, and yet had the use of their hands and could converse with companions. Others were unable to speak. The pulse became weak, and they drew a difficult breath about once a minute. In many instances they became cold. Breathing, pulsation, and all signs of life forsook them for hours; yet I never heard of one who died in this condition, and I have conversed with persons who have laid in this situation for many hours, and they have uniformly testified that they had no bodily pain, and that they had the entire use of their reason and powers of mind. From this it appears that their falling was neither common fainting nor a nervous affection. Indeed, this strange work appears to have taken every possible turn to baffle the conjectures and philosophizing of those who were unwilling to acknowledge it was the work of God. Persons have fallen on their way home from meeting, some after they had arrived at home, others pursuing their common business on their farms, and others when they were attending to family or secret devotions. Numbers of thoughtless, careless sinners have fallen as suddenly as if struck by lightning. Professed infidels, and other vicious characters, have been arrested, and sometimes at the very moment when they were uttering their blasphemies against God and the work, and have, like Saul, declared that to be God's work which they so vehemently persecuted.

I trust I have said enough on this subject to enable my readers to judge how far the charge of enthusiasm and delusion is applicable to this work, unequaled for power and for the entire change of the hearts and lives of so many thousands of men and women. Lord Lyttleton, in his letter on the conversion of St. Paul, observes, and I think justly, that enthusiasm is a vain, self-righteous spirit, swelled with self-sufficiency and disposed to glory in its religious attainments. If this be a good definition, there was as little enthusiasm in this work as any other. Never were there more genuine marks of that humility which disclaims the merits of its own works, and looks to the Lord Jesus Christ as the only way of acceptance with God. Christ was all and in all in their exercises and religion, and their Gospel, and all believers in their highest attainments seemed most sensible of their entire dependence upon Divine grace; and it was truly affecting to hear with what anxiety awakened sinners inquired for Christ as the only Physician who could give them help. Those who call this enthusiasm ought to tell us what they understand by the spirit of Christianity. Upon the whole, this revival in the west was the most extraordinary that ever visited the Church of Christ, and was peculiarly adapted to the circumstances of the country. Infidelity was triumphant, and religion at the point of expiring. Something of an extraordinary nature was necessary to arrest the attention of a wicked and skeptical people, who were ready to conclude that Christianity was a fable and futurity a dream. This great work of God did do it. It confounded infidelity and vice into silence, and brought numbers beyond calculation under the influence of experimental religion and practical piety.

It is generally known that in the early settlement of Kentucky, the regular Baptists were by far the most numerous body of Christians. It is also known that they adhered most rigidly to the doctrines of unconditional election and reprobation, together with the final and unconditional perseverance of the saints. The same may be said of the Presbyterians, who firmly maintained and preached these doctrines till the commencement of this revival. Indeed, the doctrine of unconditional election and reprobation was so generally taught by these denominations, that there was rarely found any one sufficiently fearless and independent to call them in question. They had taken deep root, and it might be said the doctrines of Calvin had filled the whole country. During the prevalence of these doctrines, supported as they were on all sides by polemical divines, whose religion seemed to consist almost entirely of a most dogged and pertinacious adherence to the creeds and confessions of faith, which had been handed down from orthodox Puritan fathers, it was not a matter of surprise that professors of religion, losing sight of the weightier matters of the Gospel, while they attended to its "anise, and mint, and cummin," would fall insensibly into antinomianism. The inconsistency of the doctrines of Calvin became the subject of the sarcastic sneers of infidels, and the inability of these Churches to reconcile their doctrines with the justice of God and the present order of things, made fearful inroads on the cause of Christianity, and strengthened the hands of the wicked. The friends of the truth were few. They were without influence, and much persecuted; but, notwithstanding, they lifted up their voice.

It was at this juncture, and under these circumstances, that it pleased the Lord to look down upon the western country. Man's extremity was God's opportunity, and the wonderful manifestation of Divine power swept away antinomianism, and infidelity, and every refuge of lies. There were some in the Presbyterian Church who did not preach a partial Gospel, but who lifted up their voice like a trumpet, and invited all to come to Jesus for salvation, assuring them that he died for fall. Of this number was that man of God, Carey Allen. As a missionary he was "a flame of fire," and thousands were awakened under his fervent, soul-stirring appeals.

Not long after the revival commenced, several of the Presbyterian ministers renounced Calvinism, and being persecuted by their brethren, they left the Church, and organized a new Presbytery, which was called the Springfield Presbytery. As is often the case with those who separate from the Church because they judge it needs reformation in doctrine or discipline, so these brethren, unfortunately, did not stop *in media res*, but rushed to another extreme. They ran into gross errors and heresies, as was seen in their apology for renouncing the jurisdiction of the Synod, the tract on the atonement by Mr. Stone, in 1804, and their sermons. Methodists and Presbyterians both saw that an enemy had come in, and was sowing tares broadcast over the field, and they retired to their own stands, and defended their own doctrines.

The party which had separated were styled Newlights, but they have subsequently taken the name of *Christian*. In June, 1804, these preachers dissolved their Presbytery, and drew up a very curious paper, which they signed, entitled "The last Will and Testament of the Springfield Presbytery." Of the six ministers who signed this paper, two went back to the Presbyterian Church, three joined the Shakers, and one the Campbellites. They published to the world, in the paper above alluded to, their belief; or, in other words, their non-belief, for they renounced all creeds, confessions of faith, and standards of doctrine, and started out on a crusade against all the Churches.

Several of these ministers were my school-mates in other days, and I felt a lively interest in them; so much so, as the reader will find, in the relation of my religious life, given in the preceding pages, I went to their camp meeting on Eagle creek to join them. By a personal and confidential interview with one of the preachers, a former old class-mate at my father's academy, I learned that they did not believe in the doctrine of the Trinity, nor in total depravity, nor in the atonement, as held by orthodox Churches. Honest David Purviance, in his life, comes out boldly, and proclaims the doctrines of the Newlight Church.

This heresy spread and prevailed. The early settlers of Kentucky were most skeptical on the subject of religion. The more influential classes of citizens were infidel in sentiment, and they labored to bring all to their views. To accomplish their wishes more fully, they employed an Englishman to take charge of their seminary of learning at Lexington. He had an extensive library, and, from his position, exerted a great influence in society. Subsequently, the principal of the seminary was elected Secretary of State. The Governor, Mr. Garrard, was a celebrated Baptist preacher, and a gentleman of much respectability and influence. It was not long till the Secretary succeeded in converting the Governor to his faith; and, having accomplished a result so desirable to the infidel party, the next thing was to get the Governor to publish a tract on the doctrine of the Trinity. This made considerable noise. In 1802 the Rev. Augustin Easton and Governor Garrard commenced a meeting on Cooper's run, in Bourbon county. Here they proclaimed publicly the Arian and Socinian doctrines. The wavering separatists were excited and encouraged wonderfully by this movement, as is evident from their own confession and subsequent course. These unfortunate people—New lights—from the time they first began to preach their doctrines, were beset in their meetings with those wild exercises that have been alluded to. See Benedict's History of Baptist Church, vol. ii, p. 252.

These strange exercises that have excited so much wonder in the western country came in toward the last of the revival, and were, in the estimation of some of the more pious, the chaff of the work. Now it was that the humiliating and often disgusting exercises of dancing, laughing, jerking, barking like dogs, or howling like wolves, and rolling on the ground, manifested themselves. To add to their misfortune, being ripe for such a catastrophe, a company of Shakers from New York found their way among them, and proselyted their most talented and useful preacher and not a few of their members. These fanatics for a season went on with a tremendous influence, threatening to sweep all before them. But they, like all other wild and visionary people, had their day.

If the reader should desire to find what the Newlights, or Christians, teach, he will best obtain it from their own works. I refer the reader to Barton Stone's exposition, in pamphlet form.

The wild vagaries adopted by the Newlight preachers of Kentucky prepared them to gulp down all the ridiculous tenets of Shakerism, and this produced a general skepticism in that state, that, I fear, will not be done away for generations. It may seem strange that all grades of Arians and Socinians have adopted immersion as the only mode of baptism, and regard it as constituting a title to heaven.

The new isms that followed this great revival were many, and it seemed as if Satan had taken advantage of the excitement to drive the bewildered into darkness and the sanguine into error and folly. The Shakers drew off hundreds with them. Elder Holmes rose up with his pilgrims, and started out in quest of the Holy Land. He had many followers, and, after wandering about for some time, died on an island in the Mississippi river, and his band dissolved. Elder Farnum, also another fanatic, pretended to have received the spirit of immediate inspiration, and raised a party called the "screaming children." After flourishing for a season, this association dwindled away. Next came A. Sargent and his twelve disciples—all women. It was spread over the country that he was inspired and conversed with angels daily, from whom he received revelations. Then Elias Hicks, the Quaker, espoused Arianism, and split the Quaker Church, spreading confusion and schism every-where among the Friends.

Last, but not least in the train of evils, came Kidwell with the last edition of Universalism. He taught that there was no hell, no devil, no future judgment; that it was impossible for any one to commit any crime in this life that would possibly shut him out of heaven; that all souls at death enter at once into the heavenly state, and are happy with God forever, no matter how they have lived in this world.

CHAPTER XXII

NARRATIVE CONTINUED.

I CONTINUED at the Wyandott mission till the fall of 1827, having been engaged in the work of this mission for a period of five years. The reader will see that when I visited that nation there were but few who professed Christianity, and none who were members of the Church and regular observers of its ordinances. From a small Church organization, which I was enabled to effect, the society gradually increased till its numbers amounted to two hundred and sixty, and these were divided into classes. For an account of the condition and prospects of the mission just before I was called away from it, I refer the reader to the report of Judge Leib to the Secretary of War, which was made to the Government in 1826, as found in the "History of the Wyandott Mission," pp. 367; 368.

At the conference of 1827 I was appointed to the Lebanon district, where I labored two years, and at the end of which time I was sent to Cincinnati station. The Radical secession had taken place under the administration of my predecessor, the Rev. John F. Wright, and Cincinnati was any thing else but a desirable appointment. After remaining in the station two years, I was placed upon the district, and after remaining two years, was returned to the station, and the Rev. Thomas A. Morris succeeded me on the district. In the mean time, brother Morris being appointed editor of the Western Christian Advocate, I was again placed on the district.

After this I was appointed to Chilicothe district, where I remained two years, at the expiration of which time I was sent to the Lebanon district, where I remained three years. My next appointment was Dayton district, where I labored four years.

Many incidents occurred during my labors on these respective fields; but it would be impossible to relate them, as it would occupy entirely too much space.

During my labors on the Dayton district an incident occurred which I must relate, because it is due to the many to whom I promised an account of it that it should be published in my biography.

It was in the summer of 1842. Worn down with fatigue, I was completing my last round of quarterly meetings, and winding up the labors of a very toilsome year. I had scarcely finished my work till I was most violently attacked with bilious fever, and it was with great difficulty I reached home. The disease had taken so violent a hold on my system that I sank rapidly under its power. Every thing that kind attention and medical skill could impart was resorted to, to arrest its ravages; but all was in vain, and my life was despaired of. On the seventh night, in a state of entire insensibility to all around me, when the last ray of hope had departed, and my weeping family and friends were standing around my couch waiting to see me breathe my last, it seemed to me that a heavenly visitant entered my room. It came to my side, and, in the softest and most silvery tones, which fell like rich music on my ear, it said, "I have come to conduct you to another state and place of existence." In an instant I seemed to rise, and, gently borne by my angel guide, I floated out upon the ambient air. Soon earth was lost in the distance, and around us, on every side, were worlds of light and glory. On, on, away, away from world to luminous worlds afar, we sped with the velocity of thought. At length we reached the gates of paradise; and O, the transporting scenes that fell upon my vision as the emerald portals, wide and high, rolled back upon their golden hinges! Then, in its fullest extent, did I realize the invocation of the poet:

"Burst, ye emerald gates, and bring
To my raptured vision
All the ecstatic joys that spring
Round the bright Elysian."

Language, however, is inadequate to describe what then, with unvailed eyes, I saw. The vision is indelibly pictured on my heart. Before me, spread out in beauty, was a broad sheet of water, clear as crystal, not a single ripple on its surface, and its purity and clearness indescribable. On each side of this lake, or river, rose up the most tall and beautiful trees, covered with all manner of fruits and flowers, the brilliant hues of which were reflected in the bosom of the placid river.

While I stood gazing with joy and rapture at the scene, a convoy of angels was seen floating in the pure ether of that world. They all had long wings, and, although they went with the greatest rapidity, yet their wings were folded close by their side. While I gazed I asked my guide who they were, and what their mission. To this he responded, "They are angels, dispatched to the world from whence you came on an errand of mercy." I could hear strains of the most entrancing melody all around me, but no one was discoverable but my guide. At length I said, "Will it be possible for me to have a sight of some of the just made perfect in glory?" Just then there came before us three persons; one had the appearance of a male, the other a female, and the third an infant. The appearance of the first two was somewhat similar to the angels I saw, with the exception that they had crowns upon their heads of the purest yellow, and harps in their hands. Their robes, which were full and flowing, were of the purest white. Their countenances were lighted up with a heavenly radiance, and they smiled upon me with ineffable sweetness.

There was nothing with which the blessed babe or child could be compared. It seemed to be about three feet high. Its wings, which were long and most beautiful, were tinged with all the colors of the rainbow. Its dress seemed to be of the whitest silk, covered with the softest white down. The driven snow could not exceed it for whiteness or purity. Its face was all radiant with glory; its very smile now plays around my heart. I gazed and gazed with wonder upon this heavenly child. At length I said, "If I have to return to earth, from whence I came, I should love to take this child with me, and show it to the weeping mothers of earth. Methinks, when they see it, they will never shed another tear over their children when they die." So anxious was I to carry out the desire of my heart, that I made a grasp at the bright and beautiful one, desiring to clasp it in my arms, but it eluded my grasp, and plunged into the river of life. Soon it rose up from the waters, and as the drops fell from its expanding wings, they seemed like diamonds, so brightly did they sparkle. Directing its course to the other shore, it flew up to one of the topmost branches of one of life's fair trees. With a look of most seraphic sweetness it gazed upon me, and then commenced singing in heaven's own strains, "To Him that hath loved me, and washed me from my sins in his own blood, to him be glory both now and forever. Amen." At that moment the power of the eternal God came upon me, and I began to shout, and, clapping my hands, I sprang from my bed, and was healed as instantly as the lame man in the beautiful porch of the temple, who "went walking, and leaping, and praising God." Overwhelmed with the glory I saw and felt, I could not cease praising God. The next Sabbath I wen to camp meeting, filled with the love and power of God. There I told the listening thousands what I saw and felt, and what God had done for me, and loud were the shouts oi glory that reverberated through the forests.

Though years have rolled away since that bright, happy hour, yet the same holy flame is burning in my heart, and I retain the same glorious victory. "Halleluiah! for the Lord God omnipotent reigneth."

Being entirely restored to health, I went to conference, and was sent on the Zanesville district. Here, after many years, I returned to the same place from whence I started as from a point to travel round my first circuit. Old brother Spangler, whose hospitalities I first, and often subsequently, enjoyed, has long since left us, and I trust is now in heaven. Some of his family remain. David Spangler, Esq., a talented lawyer, resides in Coshocton. He was always a stanch friend of his father's people; and the same may be said of Isaac Spangler, a distinguished physician of Zanesville. Several of the daughters were Methodists, and perhaps are living still. Then Methodism was small and feeble, but Jacob has arisen and become strong. This city has some of the firmest Methodists: Moorehead, and Millis, and Howard, and the Coxes, Brush, and others, are an honor to any Church. Long may they live to honor God and Methodism!

I remained on the Zanesville district two years, and, at the request of the directors of the Ohio penitentiary, was appointed chaplain to that institution, where I remained three years and a half. A full account of my labors in that institution the reader will find in "Prison Life."

In 1850, my health being feeble, I took a superannuated relation, in hopes that rest would prepare me again for active service.

The next year I was made effective, and appointed to Yellow Springs. Again I took rest for another year, and now, in the 72d year of my age, I have charge of Clinton-street Church, Cincinnati.

In the year 1845 the Wyandott nation, whom I adopted as my people, and who constituted me a chief of one of their tribes, were removed to the Indian territory beyond the Mississippi.

It is a melancholy reflection, that all those powerful tribes which once inhabited these plains, roaming at freedom where we now reside, and who sped with their light canoes over the surface of our rivers, the monarchs of all they surveyed, have now no claim whatever even to the graves of their fathers. A dark and dismal fate rests upon them, and in their native land they are rapidly fading away beneath the gaze of the pale face.

Mrs. Catharine Walker, the amiable and talented wife of the Rev. Geo. W. Walker, has written some beautiful lines occasioned by the removal of the Wyandotts; and knowing that they will be interesting to my readers, I subjoin them. They are thus appropriately introduced by the writer:

"But solemn thoughts intrude upon these pleasing reflections of the past. Many of those veteran warriors, who became soldiers of the cross, have been called by the Captain of their salvation, to lay down their arms in the Christian warfare, and go to that rest which remains for his people, gathered from every nation, kindred, tongue, and people. But the remnant of brethren and children which they left below, and with whom they suffered and worshiped here, where are they? They had comfortable homes and fertile lands, and were enjoying all the blessings of the Gospel in civilized life; but the white man coveted their possessions, and they must go to the far-off western wilds, again to be exposed to all the temptations and trials incident to savage life. May the God of missions be with them!

"Go, fated Indian, to the farthest verge
Of earth's remotest shore;
There let the night-bird sing thy dirge,
When thy weary wandering's o'er.

Go sit upon the ocean's brink,
And in its solemn moan,
Fit music for thy broken heart,
Forget thy distant home.

But the white man's foot is on thy track,
As the blood-hound seeks the hare;
Then arise, and scale some barren rock,
For the white man will not spare.

Go dwell upon some craggy peak,
Where the eagle makes her nest,
And eternal snows are drifting down—
There thy weary foot may rest.

Away from where thy kindred sleep,
Beneath a frigid sky;
Where the wintery blast will freeze thy tears—
There lay thee down and die.

Cast not a look to thy native land,
But to that blissful shore,
Where oppression's sigh is never heard,
And thou shalt weep no more."

CHAPTER XXIII.

SKETCH OF BISHOP ASBURY, THE FOUNDER OF AMERICAN METHODISM.

In the autumn of 1771 Francis Asbury, after a voyage of two months in crossing the Atlantic, landed on our shores. His place of debarkation was Philadelphia. The venerable founder of Methodism, who had already been here on a mission, but had returned without having accomplished, to any great extent, the objects for which he came, and who still felt his heart stirred within him for the spiritual welfare of his brethren in this far-off, western world, made a call for volunteers at the conference in Bristol. This call was responded to by Francis Asbury.

That Providence which has ever presided over the Church perhaps was never manifested more signally, so far as Methodism in America is concerned, than in the selection, at that time, of an agent whose peculiar fitness for the work of organizing, giving direction, and imparting efficiency to the system of means already set in operation for evangelizing this continent, was so marked. His early religious training, under the guardianship of a pious mother, to whose memory he pays a merited tribute, and the formation in youth of those habits of piety which enter so essentially into the elements of all true greatness in Christian character, admirably qualified him for the work upon which he was about to enter. And here we would remark, that few men, either in Church or state, have been distinguished for goodness or greatness whose early religious training has been neglected.

Young Asbury was early inspired with religious emotions, and his youthful mind was imbued with religious principles ere he had passed the first decade of his life. His autobiography informs us that he was a diligent student of the Bible at seven years of age. The brutality of his schoolmaster, though it drove him from school, had the effect of driving him to God in prayer and of increasing his love for the Scriptures, thus exemplifying the truth that the wrath of man sometimes works out the purposes of God. At the age of fourteen he was awakenened under the sermon of a Methodist preacher, to whose meeting he was directed by his mother. In regard to this meeting he says, "I soon found it was not '*the Church;*' but it was better. The people were so devout—men and women kneeling down, saying amen. Now, behold! they were singing hymns. Sweet sound! Why, strange to tell, the preacher had no prayer-book; and yet he prayed wonderfully! What was yet more extraordinary, the man took his text and had no sermon-book. Thought I, this is wonderful indeed! It is certainly a strange way, but the best way."

To a great degree, a cold, heartless, and Christless theology characterized the sermons of "the Church" at that day. In the providence of God, through the instrumentality of Methodism, a warm spiritual life was infused into these dead forms, and awakening power roused them into action. No sooner had he felt the power of regenerating grace, and had come up to the possession of that "confidence and assurance in Christ" of which he heard the Methodist preacher speak, and which appeared to him, at that time, wholly inexplicable, if not a species of fanaticism unwarranted by the Bible, than he felt an irrepressible desire to communicate the glad and joyous intelligence to others. Nor was it long till, at his father's house, he held a meeting, and poured out the treasures of his full heart upon the consciences of those who were present, several of whom were awakened and converted.

At the age of seventeen he became a local preacher, and traveled extensively, visiting every place within his reach, and preaching from three to five times every week.

When he had reached his majority he gave himself up deliberately and fully to God and his work. About this time he felt his heart strangely drawn toward America, and made it a matter of constant and earnest prayer that he might be directed, in this respect, in all things agreeable to the will of God. Having consecrated himself wholly to the Lord, he was prepared to enter upon any work Providence should assign him, or visit any field, however distant; yet he was careful to ascertain the indications of Providence in that regard, lest, as he says, "he might run before he was sent."

Methodism had already been planted in America. The work of God which, under the Wesleys and their coadjutors, had spread throughout England, Wales, and Ireland, resulted in the organization of societies and the raising up of holy men to preach the Gospel to the scattered and persecuted flocks in those countries. Several of these emigrated to America, and among the number were Embury Webb, Strawbridge, Williams, King, Boardman, and Pilmoor. These men were instrumental in preaching the Gospel and planting Methodism in New York, Frederick county, Md., Norfolk, Philadelphia, and elsewhere. As heralds, they had prepared the way, and the seed which they sowed was, by the providence of God, cast in good places, and, like the "handful of corn on the top of the mountain," has been springing up and multiplying, till, like the cedars of Lebanon, the spacious branches and goodly fruit now spread over all the land.

Asbury, upon his arrival at Philadelphia, immediately entered upon his work. He was gladly received by the brethren, and hailed as a colaborer in the great field. To an untiring zeal he added the most consummate prudence He was a Methodist both in spirit and practice, adopting for his own government a most rigid method, by which he divided his time between prayer, study, preaching, traveling, and even extended his *regime* to eating and sleeping, and labored to impress upon preachers and members all the peculiarities so important to Methodist economy. He had not been long in this country till he received a letter from Mr. Wesley, appointing him general assistant of the work. This honor he received with a meekness characteristic of the man. The Church was then small and feeble, and Methodism was a term of reproach; but still it was an honor to have the leadership of that little and despised band. The motives to ambition which now exist were not then to be found. To travel from thirty to forty miles a day in rain or snow, over rough roads, on horse back, and preach twice or thrice, sometimes without food, and at night find shelter in a log-cabin or a barn, or frequently in the wilderness without any shelter, did not offer many inducements to aspirants for episcopal honors. There was then no "college of bishops," whose support was secured by a mammoth Book Concern and Chartered Fund, and who could in a few days reach their most distant appointments on velvet cushions, in cars supported by gutta percha springs, or in floating palaces, which plowed the deep at the rate of twenty knots an hour. Notwithstanding all this, however, we are thankful—truly thankful—that there has been a change, and, above all, that Methodism has kept pace with the mighty progress of this enterprising age. It is with a spirit of admiration that we can look up to those venerable and holy men who occupy the bench of bishops, with the most implicit confidence in their piety and fidelity and with a certain knowledge of the fact that their office is no sinecure, but one which calls for and receives at the hands of the present incumbents a greater amount of self-sacrificing devotion than that of any other office in Church or state.

And we rejoice, too, that we have a Book Concern—a mammoth Concern, if the reader please—taking rank with any individual Concern in the country, and larger, by far, than any similar Church establishment.

In 1784, in company with Dr. Coke and others, Asbury was consulted in regard to the propriety of organizing the societies into an independent Methodist Episcopal Church, with superintendents, elders, and deacons. In regard to the superintendency, his reply was, "If the preachers unanimously choose me, I shall not act in the capacity I have hitherto done by Mr. Wesley's appointment." The result of the conversation was the call of a General conference to meet in Baltimore the ensuing Christmas. At this conference he and Dr. Coke were unanimously elected to the superintendency. Till this time Asbury was an unordained minister, and as the Church had now taken a separate existence, it was necessary he should receive orders, for the purpose of perpetuating the ministry and of conferring upon those who gave evidence of a call and qualification to preach the Gospel the authority to administer the sacraments. Accordingly, Dr. Coke being a presbyter of the Church of England, assisted by two elders, successively conferred upon him the orders of deacon and elder, and at the same time, by the imposition of hands, set him apart for the office of a superintendent in the Methodist Episcopal Church.

Soon after conference he started out upon his work, traveling on horseback, in one journey, five hundred miles, and preaching on the way. He relates a pleasing interview which he had in this journey with General Washington, who gave him, without hesitation, his opinion against slavery.

In that early day of the Church in this country, the subject of collegiate as well as academical and common school education was not lost sight of by the pioneers of Methodism. Coke was an Oxonian himself, as well as the founders of Methodism, and the project of founding a college in this country was dear to his heart. Although Asbury was not what is denominated a classical scholar, so far, at least, as the literary degrees *in cursu* are concerned, yet it is evident from his journal that he was well versed in the original language of the New Testament and possessed of a good share of critical acumen in pulpit exegesis. As a lover of learning and a devoted student of Biblical and theological literature, he readily sympathized with the Doctor in the enterprise of founding a college, and gave it his countenance and hearty support. At the laying of the corner-stone of Cokesbury College at Abington, he delivered an eloquent discourse from the following words of the seventy-eighth Psalm: "We will not hide them from their children, shewing to the generation to come the praises of the Lord, and his strength, and his wonderful works that he hath done. For he established a testimony in Jacob, and appointed a law in Israel, which he commanded our fathers, that they should make them known to their children: that the generation to come might know them, even the children which should be born; who should arise and declare them to their children: that they might set their hope in God, and not forget the works of God, but keep his commandments: and might not be as their fathers, a stubborn and rebellious generation; a generation that set not their heart aright, and whose spirit was not steadfast with God."

From this it could be seen that, whatever our enemies may say to the contrary, our Church in this country, from its earliest organization, has given unmistakable evidence of her appreciation of and devotion to the interests of sanctified literature. This we trust, however, to make appear more fully and at large in the biographies ot our distinguished men of the past and present, with which we hope to enliven our pages and edify our readers.

Methodist preachers have hitherto been regarded, by a certain class, not only as destitute of education themselves, but as enemies of learning, especially of a learned ministry, and have frequently been slighted, if not sneered at, by those who had no other qualification for the ministry, and were not particularly burdened with that. On a certain occasion Asbury visited New Haven, the seat of Yale College. The appearance of a Methodist preacher there excited curiosity, and he had many students out to hear him, besides President Styles and other clergymen. When he had finished his discourse not one of the clergy deigned to speak to him. This reminded him of Whitefield's remark to Boardman and Pilmoor at their first coming to America: "If ye were Calvinists ye would take the country before ye." Notwithstanding this cold neglect, he visited the college chapel at the hour of prayer and expressed a desire to inspect the interior arrangements; but no one invited him. This is not the first time, nor has it been the last, that these self-styled "efficient" ministers of the Gospel have shown their boorishness in the treatment of Methodist preachers. In this respect, however, "*tempora mutantur,*" and they have been obliged to change with the times. To such conduct, however, toward Methodist preachers there are honorable exceptions—men of strength, and power, and piety, who do not consider it a want of self-respect, or a lowering down of dignity, or a sacrifice of caste, to associate with and treat the humble "circuit rider" with Christian respect.

Cokesbury College, the child of those two distinguished men whose names it bore, opened into life as a bright and beautiful boy, the pride and joy of its parent's heart. It was truly and emphatically the child of the Church. Bright, however, as were its prospects, and favorable as were the auspices under which it entered upon its career, yet, like the most precious things of life, often the earliest doomed, it was, in the providence of God, only allowed a brief destiny. Though early smitten, and the Church was called upon to mourn over the ashes of Cokesbury College, yet its spirit survived, and its metempsychosis may be seen in the numerous institutions of learning with which the Church is blessed in all parts of the country.

While Asbury manifested so much interest in schools and colleges, he did not neglect a personal attendance upon the instruction of the children in families, but diligently catechised them in every house where he went. This important part of a Methodist preacher's duty, and one which enters into the solemn injunction of his ordination vows, occupied a more prominent place in the good Bishop's ministrations and those of the early pioneers of Methodism, perhaps, than of the preachers of the present day.

It may be remarked that Sunday schools are vastly more extended, efficient, and systematic in their operations now than at that period, and this may constitute the reason for such laxity in regard to the catechetical instruction of the children by the preachers. This, however, should not be, as no Sunday school instruction can supply its place or prove an excuse sufficient to justify the shepherd in neglecting to feed the lambs of his flock. While on this subject we may take occasion to remark, that Asbury early identified himself with the Sunday school cause, and that to him is justly due the honor of having established the *first* Sunday schools in America. In a pamphlet which professes to give the origin and history of Sunday schools in America, it is stated "that the first

Sunday school organization in the United States of which we have any authentic record was the *First-Day or Sunday School Society*, which was established in Philadelphia in 1791." Now, it is a fact well authenticated, but strangely overlooked, that Bishop Asbury organized a Sunday school in Hanover, Virginia, in 1786, *five years before* the one in Philadelphia; and it is also a fact that one year before this organization the Minutes of the conference contain the following questions and answers:

"*Question.* What can be done to instruct poor children, white and black, to read?

"*Answer.* Let us labor as the heart and soul of one man to establish *Sunday schools* in or near the place of public worship. Let persons be appointed by the bishops, elders, deacons, or preachers to teach *gratis* all that will attend and have a capacity to learn, from six o'clock in the morning till ten, and from two o'clock in the afternoon till six, where it does not interfere with public worship. The council shall compile a proper school-book to teach them learning and piety."

The subject of our sketch was a man of most pacific spirit, and while he was removed from every thing like intolerance on the one hand, he was ready to go all lengths, where integrity and principle were not compromised, to conciliate the esteem of those who were in any degree alienated or felt themselves aggrieved, and spared no labor or sacrifices to cast oil upon the troubled waters of partisan strife. Nothing grieved him more than the unhappy excitement and division gotten up by O'Kelly and his coadjutors. In answer to the complaints alleged against him for exercising his episcopal prerogative, in preventing O'Kelly from becoming a fixture in a certain locality where he had worn out all his influence and usefulness, he says, "I have little to leave except a journey of five thousand miles a year, the care of more than one hundred thousand souls, and the arrangement of about four hundred preachers yearly, to which I may add the murmurs and discontent of ministers and people. Who wants this legacy? Those who do," he adds, "are welcome to it for me. The Methodists acknowledge no superiority but what is founded on seniority, election, and long and faithful services. For myself, I pity those who can not distinguish between a Pope of Rome and an old, worn man of sixty years who has the *power given him* of riding five thousand miles a year on horseback, at a salary of eighty dollars, through summer's heat and winter's cold, traveling in all weather, preaching in all places, his best covering from rain often but a blanket, the surest sharpener of his wit hunger, from fasts voluntary and involuntary, his best fare for six months of the twelve coarse kindness, and his reward, from too many, suspicion, envy, and murmurings all the year round."

Such, however, were only occasional shadows darkening his otherwise bright and happy pathway. His general experience may be summed up in his own words: "Close communion with God, holy fellowship with the Father and his Son Jesus Christ, a will resigned, frequent addresses to a throne of grace, a constant and serious care for the prosperity of Zion, forethought in the arrangements and appointments of the preachers, a soul drawn out in ardent prayer for the universal Church, and the complete triumph of Christ over all the earth."

As an evidence of his sincere attachment and disinterestedness, it may be remarked, that he never made an appointment of any of the preachers either with a view to afflict them or to gratify any feelings of personal prejudice on the one hand, or of affection on the other, nor would he allow such influences from his council to bear upon the appointment of any of the preachers.

The preachers were dear to his heart, and he da

made them the subject of his prayers and tenderest solicitude. To his care for the preachers might be added the care of all the Churches. By correspondence and otherwise, when he could not visit them personally, he kept himself posted in regard to all the interests of Zion. The conferences then were usually seasons of great religious interest, and as the miscellaneous business was small at that time compared with the present, the regular minute business was soon dispatched, and more time was allowed for religious exercises.

The worth of souls lay near his heart, and he was not satisfied unless he was conscious sinners were awakened and converted through his instrumentality. Once, after having traveled hard through a western wilderness, to reach a quarterly meeting on his way to a distant conference, he was unusually tempted at not having seen, for some time, any direct evidence of his personal labor in the conversion of souls. He felt inclined to the belief that his mission had expired, and he had better retire from the work. With this depression of spirit he entered the love-feast on Sabbath morning, in a rude log chapel in the woods, and took his seat, unknown to any, in the back part of the congregation. After the usual preliminary exercises had been gone through with by the preacher, an opportunity was given for the relation of Christian experience. One after another testified of the saving grace of God, and occasionally a verse of some hymn was sung, full of rich and touching melody. The tide of religious feeling was rising and swelling in all hearts, while a lady rose whose plain but exceedingly neat attire indicated that she was a Methodist. Her voice was full and clear, though slightly tremulous. She had traveled many miles to the meeting, and her feelings would not allow her to repress her testimony. She remarked that she had not long been a follower of Christ. "Two years ago," said she, "I was attracted to a Methodist meeting in our neighborhood by being informed that Bishop Asbury was going to preach. I went, and the Spirit sealed the truth he uttered on my heart. I fled to Jesus, and found redemption in his blood, even the forgiveness of my sins, and have been happy in his love ever since.

'Not a cloud doth arise to darken my skies,
Or hide for a moment my Lord from my eyes.'"

She sat down, and ere the responses which her remarks had awakened in all parts of the house had died away, Bishop Asbury was on his feet. He commenced by remarking that "he was a stranger and pilgrim, halting on his way for rest and refreshment in the house of God, and that he had found both; and," said he, with uplifted hands, while tears of joy coursed each other freely down his face, "if I can only be instrumental in the conversion of one soul in traveling round the continent, I'll travel round it till I die."

As an Englishman, he loved his father-land, and frequently expressed his grief at the war which then existed between England and the United States; yet he had adopted the latter, and, though many of the preachers had returned to England, unwilling to sympathize with the cause of American liberty, he warmly espoused it, and was firm in his adherence to the republicanism of Washington. On the occasion of receiving a letter from Mr. Wesley on the subject of the war, he remarks, "I am extremely sorry that the venerable man ever dipped into the politics of America. My desire is to live in love and peace with all men, to do them no harm, but all the good I can. However," he adds, "it discovers Mr. Wesley's attachment to the government under which he lives. Had he been a subject of America, no doubt he would have been as zealous an advocate of the American cause. But some inconsiderate persons have taken occasion to censure the Methodists in America on account of Mr Wesley's political sentiments." As a further evidence of his republicanism, it may be remarked, that at the New York conference in 1789 he offered for the consideration of that body the following proposal; namely, "Whether it would not be proper for us, as a Church, to present a congratulatory address to General Washington, who has been lately inaugurated President of the United States, in which should be embodied our approbation of the Constitution, and professing our allegiance to the government." To this the conference unanimously acceded, and an address was prepared and read by Asbury to Washington and his cabinet. To this address the President made a reply, expressive of thanks for the stand taken by the Church in the cause of American liberty. The address and the answer were published in the papers of the day, and soon after other Churches followed the example.

For Washington the Bishop had a high regard, which was strengthened by a personal acquaintance of many years; and when the sad intelligence came to him that the father of his country was no more, he entered the following in his journal:

"Slow moved the northern post on the eve of New-Year's day, and brought the heart-distressing information of the death of Washington, who departed this life December 14, 1797. Washington, the calm, intrepid chief, the disinterested friend, first father, and temporal savior of his country under Divine protection and direction! A universal cloud sat upon the faces of the citizens of Charleston; the pulpits clothed in black; the bells muffled; the paraded soldiery; a public oration decreed to be delivered on Friday, fourteenth of this month; a marble statue to be placed in some proper situation; these were the expressions of sorrow and these the marks of respect paid by his feeling fellow-citizens to the memory of this great man. *I am disposed to lose sight of all but Washington.* Matchless man! At all times he acknowledged the providence of God, and never was he ashamed of his Redeemer. We believe he died not fearing death. In his will he ordered the manumission of all his slaves—a true son of liberty in all points."

It is with a very ill grace, to say the least of it, that certain partisan theologians have charged the early Methodist preachers with being opposed to the war with Great Britain and the republican principles of which Washington was the great champion. We admit that some of them did manifest opposition, and prudently returned to England; but that the great body of them were firm and zealous supporters of the republic, none but the most hopelessly prejudiced can entertain a reasonable doubt. With Asbury, the great apostle of Methodism in America, this was particularly the case, as his whole history abundantly shows.

It is known that the Bishop never married. This state was not to him, however, one of choice, but necessity, and those who hear his reasons for not entering into the marriage relation will be satisfied of the propriety of his course. He says, "If I should die in celibacy, which I think quite probable, I give the following reasons for what can scarcely be called my choice. I was called in my fourteenth year. I began my public exercises between sixteen and seventeen; at twenty-one I traveled; at twenty-six I came to America. Thus far I had reasons enough for a single life. It had been my intention to return to Europe at thirty years of age; but the war continued, and it was ten years before we had settled, lasting peace. This was no time to marry or be given in marriage. At forty-nine I was ordained superintendent or bishop in America. Among the duties imposed upon me by my office was that of traveling extensively, and I could hardly expect to find a woman with grace enough to enable her to live but one week out of the fifty-two with her husband; besides, what right has any man to take advantage of the affections of a woman, make her his wife, and, by a voluntary absence, subvert the whole order and economy of the marriage state, by separating those whom neither God, nature, nor the requirements of civil society permit long to be *put asunder?* It is neither just nor generous. I may add to this, that I had little money, and with this little administered to the necessities of a beloved mother till I was fifty-seven. If I have done wrong, I hope God and the sex will forgive me. It is my duty now to bestow the pittance I may have to spare upon the widows, and fatherless girls, and poor married men."

Our limits will not allow us to extend much further this brief sketch, and we must, therefore, bring it to a close.

Coke and Whatcoat, the colleagues of Asbury in the episcopacy, had ceased from their labors and entered into rest. Wesley, too, the venerable founder of Methodism and father in God of the Church, had closed his long and laborious career upon earth, and entered upon the rest and blessedness of heaven. Asbury stood alone, like a venerable tree left by the woodman's ax to proclaim the ancient glory of the forest. Incessant traveling on horseback an average of five thousand miles a year, exposed to all the changes of climate and variations of temperature, together with the immense anxiety growing out of the care of all the Churches, in labors more abundant, if possible, than the tireless Wesley, preyed heavily upon his constitution.

After he had passed his "threescore and ten," he transferred to the gifted M'Kendree the principal burden of visiting the conferences. As it is interesting to trace the religious experience of this venerable man, in his journal we find the following: "My soul is blessed with continual consolation and peace in all my great weakness of body, labor, and crowds of company. I am a debtor to the whole continent, but more especially to the north-east and south-west. It is there I usually gain health, and generally lose in the south and center. I have visited the south thirty times in thirty-one years. I wish to visit Mississippi, but am resigned. My eyes fail. I will resign the stations to Bishop M'Kendree. It is the fifty-fifth year of my ministry and forty-fifth year of labor in America. I die daily; but my consolations are great. I live in God from moment to moment." This was his last entry in his journal. How like the sun at its setting did his mind expand with holy emotions and benevolent sympathies! The mellow light of his experience and example shone out clearly and calmly over the goodly tents of Jacob as he was gently sinking into rest.

In the sunny south, on the 21st of March, 1816, on a bright and beautiful Sabbath, the dying patriarch was seen to raise his hands when speech had failed, as a token of victory through the blood of the Lamb, and then, reclining his head upon the faithful Bond, his traveling companion, without a struggle he breathed his last—

"As fades the summer cloud away—
As sinks the gale when storms are o'er."

The personal appearance of Bishop Asbury presented nothing remarkable. His form was slight, but erect, and hence dignified and graceful. He had a vigorous constitution, and hence an elastic step. His eye was stern and bright. His countenance was strongly marked, with features expressive of decision, energy, sagacity, and benignity, shaded, at times, by an expression of deep anxiety, if not depression. And, to conclude in the language of one in regard to his character, "His parallel for practical sense and practical energy can scarcely be found. As a ruler of state or a commander of armies he would have ranked among the greatest men of history; and if ever an impartial ecclesiastical history of this nation is written, Francis Asbury, as well for his personal character as for being the chief founder of its largest religious organization, will occupy a position in it above the competition of any other name whatsoever."

CHAPTER XXIV.

SKETCH OF BISHOP M'KENDREE.

I HAVE already alluded to the camp meeting which I attended in the summer of 1809, on the farm of the Rev. John Collins, on the east fork of the Little Miami. To this meeting the tribes of Methodism from all parts of the country repaired. It was the annual celebration of the feast of tabernacles, under the Christian dispensation. I had passed the Red Sea of repentance, and the wilderness of doubt and uncertainty, and now I was prepared to take my family and tabernacle on Mount Zion with the people of God. The distance we had to travel was about thirty miles, mostly through an unbroken forest. It cost something then to enjoy the means of grace; not too much, however, for their value. When obtained, they were appreciated in proportion to their cost, and richly enjoyed. In good season we arrived. Just before reaching the consecrated spot, our attention was arrested by the clear and melodious strains of the children of Zion, singing that memorable camp meeting song,

"Stop, poor sinner, stop and think,
Before you further go;
Will you sport upon the brink
Of everlasting woe?"

A large number of people had collected already upon the ground, and had pitched their neat, white canvas tents. The preachers' stand was filled with ministers, the most of whose faces were familiar to me. There was one, however, who was a stranger. He had a noble, dignified appearance, and seemed to be somewhat above the common stature. He was evidently in his prime, though beyond the middle age of life. His voice had a sweetness and compass that were remarkable. There was great symmetry in his features. His forehead was expansive; eyes dark, but beaming with the fire of intelligence. Luxuriant rolls of dark hair covered his head, and his general appearance would at once impress a stranger with the idea of his being an extraordinary man.

When he rose to give out the hymn, every eye was turned toward and riveted upon him. Indeed, I felt as if some supernatural being was going to address us. The hymn being sung we kneeled down for prayer; and such an address to the throne of the heavenly grace I never heard before. There was a simplicity and earnestness about it truly surprising. It seemed as though he was talking face to face with God, as a child with its father. Every heart was interested in that prayer, and it seemed as if heaven had come down to earth.

When he arose he announced for his text John iv, 24: "God is a Spirit, and they that worship him must worship him in spirit and in truth." Every word that fell from the lips of the sainted M'Kendree was devoured by the eager multitude. There was but one mind and one heart. That one mind received all the truths that were uttered, and that one heart beat responsive to those truths. I can not possibly describe my own feelings on the occasion. I had taken a position in front of the speaker, so that I might have a full and uninterrupted view of his person. Never was I so entertained. I could see nothing but the speaker; I could hear nothing but his voice. While I listened I was unconsciously drawn, as if by some magic spell, toward the preacher; and when he closed, to my astonishment I found myself within a few feet of him. All around me was the most intense excitement—loud shouts of glory and cries for mercy—yet I knew it not, I heard it not, till the preacher ceased, and the charm was broken. O, it was a heavenly time! and it seemed to me that I was quite on the suburbs of glory, drinking full draughts from that "river the streams whereof make glad the city of God."

That afternoon brother Axley came to me and said, "Bishop M'Kendree desires to see you at his tent." "But," said I, "I have no acquaintance with him." "Then I will introduce you," said Axley. So I went to the tent and was introduced. I felt greatly embarrassed on approaching the Bishop; but the ease and cordiality with which he received me at once banished all my fears, and inspired me with confidence. After brother Axley retired, he commenced conversing with me with as much familiarity as if he had known me all my life. He asked me in regard to my family, and many other things, and how long I had been a professor of religion. He also asked me if I had not been exercised in regard to preaching the Gospel. Though a stranger, he gained at once my fullest confidence, and I opened to him all my heart, spoke of my experience, conflicts, trials, and frankly informed him that I could not think myself qualified for the work of the ministry. He then conversed with me as man never did before, and as man never can again. There was an overpowering sweetness in his manner and words, that filled me with love and reverence for the man that lasted all through his life. I wept like a child, and telling him I was ignorant, and lived in the wilderness where there was no one to guide me, he laid his hand gently on my head and said, "My son, be of good cheer; God will supply you with fathers and mothers in the Gospel." Such a manifestation of regard for me completely overcame me, and from that moment I felt that this venerable man would treat me as a son in the Gospel; and from that day on till the day of his death, no man lived, except my father, who had so strong a hold upon my heart, and in whom I could so implicitly confide, or one whom I felt myself so implicitly bound to obey, as this amiable minister of Jesus. I never saw any thing during his life which would lead me to suppose that he did not feel for me as a son in the Gospel. Throughout the meeting he frequently called me to his tent, and conversed with me in the most free and unrestrained manner.

An incident occurred at this camp meeting of a deeply-thrilling character, and one which produced an entire change in my views in regard to the qualifications necessary to partake of the holy communion. I supposed that only such as were converted, and were the children of God by faith in Christ Jesus, were entitled to a place at the Lord's table. There accompanied us to the camp meeting a young lady. To the graces of her person, for she was charmingly beautiful, were added a brilliant mind. She was an amiable and lovely girl, the pride of the neighborhood. Scarcely had we arrived on the ground ere she was convicted. During Saturday and Sunday she seemed to be in the most extreme agony of mind. Her prayers and tears excited the sympathy of all hearts.

On Monday morning the sacrament of the Lord's supper was to be administered. After singing,

"Glory to God on high!
Our peace is made with Heaven;
The Son of God came down to die,
That we might be forgiven,"

the ministers were all invited around the table to partake of the holy emblems. The venerable Bishop offered the consecratory prayer, and then distributed to the under shepherds the bread and wine. It was a deeply-solemn time.

A solemn stillness reigned around, only broken by a deep sigh or a half-suppressed sob, while one after another of that large congregation came to celebrate the scenes of Gethsemane and Calvary. Nearly in front of the Bishop, beyond the altar, stood the weeping penitent, reclining her head upon the shoulder of a converted sister, and sobbing as if her heart would break, while she gazed upon the scene. Her appearance and manner attracted the attention of the benevolent M'Kendree, and looking toward her he said, "My child, come here and kneel at the foot of the cross, and you shall find mercy."

"Do you think," said she, through her tears, "so vile a sinner as I may venture to approach the sacramental board, and take in my unholy hands the emblems of the Savior's dying love?"

"Yes, my child; it was just for such sinners as you the blessed Jesus died, and while writhing in his last agonies, he demonstrated his willingness and power to save by taking the penitent malefactor with him to heaven."

"Then I'll go to Jesus," said she; and hurrying to the table she fell upon her knees and cried aloud to God. With streaming eyes the Bishop administered the bread; and just as her lips tasted the wine of the sacramental cup, pardon was communicated, and heaven sprung up in her heart. Instantly she rose to her feet, and her face shining like that of an angel, while, with an eloquence that went to every heart, she told the simple story of the cross, and the wondrous power of Christ to save. All seemed to partake of the common joy of that renewed spirit.

The same fall I was admitted into the traveling connection, and every year, till his last visit to our conference, he called to see me, or I was with him. In 1811 he was at my camp meeting on Knox circuit, in company with his venerable companion, Bishop Asbury. From this camp meeting I accompanied him to Xenia. On this tour he preached in Granville, and the Calvinists sent him a note requesting him to preach his principles in full. This he did to their satisfaction; and, in addition thereto, as a work of supererogation, gave an exposition of Calvinism. After the discourse, three elders of the Presbyterian Church came to his lodgings, and attacked him with great zeal. In a short time, however, they were so completely confounded that they went away ashamed of the inconsistencies of their doctrines. The next evening he had an appointment at Franklinton, near Columbus, where he preached in the old log court-house. The ensuing day we started on our journey in the rain, and getting lost in the Darby Plains, we wandered about all day, and at night, finding a cabin, we took up lodgings.

No man, perhaps, ever made more rapid advancements in grace and gifts than did M'Kendree. After his conversion, which was in the thirtieth year of his age, he went on with giant strides from grace to grace. He was evidently designed by the great Head of the Church as a leader among the armies of Israel; and after becoming most thoroughly acquainted with practical itinerancy in the wilds of the west, he was prepared to enter upon episcopal duties and services with a heart touched with itinerant trials.

The circumstances connected with the election of M'Kendree to the episcopacy, were of a somewhat interesting character. When he visited the General conference as a delegate from the west, having been so long absent from the east, he was not generally known. On the Sabbath before the election for a bishop was to take place, he was appointed to preach in the Light-street Church, Baltimore.

"The house was crowded with strangers in every part, above and below, eager to hear the stranger; and among others, most of the members of the General conference were present, besides a number of colored people, who occupied a second gallery in the front end of the church Mr. M'Kendree entered the pulpit at the hour for commencing the services, clothed in very coarse and homely garments, which he had worn in the woods of the west, and after singing he kneeled in prayer. As was often the case with him when he commenced his prayer, he seemed to falter in his speech, clipping some of his words at the end, and occasionally hanging upon a syllable as if it were difficult for him to pronounce the word. I looked at him, not without some feelings of distrust, thinking to myself, 'I wonder what awkward backwoodsman they have put in the pulpit this morning, to disgrace us with his mawkish and uncouth phraseology.' This feeling of distrust did not forsake me till some minutes after he had announced his text, which contained the following words: 'For the hurt of the daughter of the people am I hurt; I am black; astonishment hath taken hold on me. Is there no balm in Gilead; is there no physician there? Why, then, is not the health of the daughter of my people recovered?' Jeremiah viii, 21, 22.

"His introduction appeared tame, his sentences broken and disjointed, and his elocution very defective. He at length introduced his main subject, which was to show the spiritual disease of the Jewish Church, and of the human family generally; and then he entered upon his second proposition, which was to analyze the feelings which such a state of things awakened in the souls of God's faithful embassadors: but when he came to speak of the blessed effects upon the heart of the balm which God had provided for the 'healing of the nations,' he seemed to enter fully into the element in which his soul delighted to move and have its being, and he soon carried the whole congregation away with him into the regions of experimental religion.

"Remarking upon the objections which some would

make to the expression of the feelings realized by a person fully restored to health by an application of the 'sovereign balm for every wound,' he referred to the shouts of applause so often heard upon our national jubilee, in commemoration of our emancipation from political thralldom, and then said, 'How much more cause has an immortal soul to rejoice and give glory to God for its spiritual deliverance from the bondage of sin!' This was spoken with a soul overflowing with the most hallowed and exalted feelings, and with such an emphasis, that it was like the sudden bursting of a cloud surcharged with water. The congregation was instantly overwhelmed with a shower of Divine grace from the upper world. At first, sudden shrieks, as of persons in distress, were heard in different parts of the house; then shouts of praise, and in every direction sobs and groans. The eyes of the people overflowed with tears, while many were prostrated upon the floor, or lay helpless on the seats. A very large, athletic-looking preacher, who was sitting by my side, suddenly fell upon his seat, as if pierced by a bullet, and I felt my heart melting under emotions which I could not well resist.

"After this sudden shower, the clouds were dispersed, and the Sun of righteousness shone out most serenely and delightfully, producing upon all a present consciousness of the Divine approbation; and when the preacher descended from the pulpit, all were filled with admiration of his talents, and were ready to 'magnify the grace of God in him,' as a chosen messenger of good tidings to the lost, saying in their hearts, 'This is the man whom God delights to honor.'"

This sermon, according to the prediction of Bishop Asbury, secured his election.

No man ever made more full proof of his ministry than did the laborious M'Kendree. For twelve years he filled the office of a presiding elder, and for nearly twenty-seven years he filled the more important and responsible office of bishop. In the midst of all the trying scenes through which he was called to pass, he manifested the greatest devotion to the Church. It may be said of him, as a presiding officer, that the utmost impartiality characterized all his official acts.

When it became evident that the work of this great and good man was finished, his character shone out more and more clear, and, like the sun at setting, the graces of M'Kendree were more fully developed as he was nearing the horizon of time; and, like that sun, which, on the eve of a calm, quiet summer day, goes gently down in a cloudless sky, so sweetly sank the dying saint. The last response of this faithful watchman on Zion's walls, to his companion-watchers, was, "*All is well, all is well!*"

CHAPTER XXV.

SKETCH OF REV. DAVID YOUNG.

The father and mother of the Rev. David Young were both of Scotch descent. The ancestors of his father belonged to the clan of the Campbells, and tradition says it was not for convenience but for safety that they went over to the north of Ireland; and some century and a half since some of them suffered extremely in the celebrated siege of Derry.

His grandfather came to North America, and landed at Newcastle, Delaware, in 1742, his father then being one year old, and moved westward into the neighborhood of Havre de Grace, perhaps on the place where Hughes's Iron Works were afterward erected, and which were burned by the British in the last war.

His father settled in Bedford county, Virginia, where young David was born, March 7, 1779, and the next year he removed to Washington county, in the same state, where David was raised, in a place and at a time where and when religious privileges and experience were very little known or prized. His father belonged to *High Kirk*, and his mother thought there was nothing like the Erskines and their secession. They both were firm believers in the Westminster Confession of Faith and Fisher's Catechism. The old gentleman had a good library for the times, where the son could at least examine one side of the question between Churchmen and Dissenters, and Calvinists and Arminians, and this he was careful to do, as the sequel will show.

He was taught the Lord's Prayer, and the Creed, and Catechisms, both "shorter" and "longer," and he could repeat them with great fluency when quite a small boy. This was thought too wonderful, and the way he was praised might inspire any thing but humility. He says in a communication to me, "Among the earliest recollections of my life the thoughts of invisible beings and agencies were the most common and important. The beings called God and devil, the places called heaven and hell, the things called death, judgment, and eternity, were the subjects of my childish meditations, thousands of times before I was five years old."

In the summer of 1786 he went to meeting with some of the family, and during the first prayer was so deeply convicted that he had sinned against God, his King and Savior, that his heart was melted, and he wept in bitterness of soul. But shame quenched his feelings and tears, and he relapsed into indifference. From this time till the fall of 1790 there was nothing very uncommon in the exercises of his mind. At that time, however, he was powerfully awakened by the Holy Spirit; and though there was nobody that he knew who prayed in secret, yet it was his constant practice for nearly a year. Those were dark times in religion. Possibly, if he had been blessed with the company of some one to have taken him by the hand and directed him in the right way, he might have been kept from falling away. Many a child no older have I seen happy in God's love, and there is nothing to prevent all young children from being truly pious. He broke through the restraints his parents imposed, particularly by desecrating the Sabbath day, and made continuous efforts to throw off the influences of the Holy Spirit. He did not, however, succeed in his rebellion. In February, 1796, being sent one evening, with some other boys, to fix the boiling apparatus for making maple sugar, they had a brand of fire with them, and, passing by an exceedingly large poplar-tree, whose roots projected far out above ground, one of them being hollow, they put the fire-brand to an aperture seven or eight feet from the trunk, and discovered a very strong draught of air ascending up the hollow tree. It suddenly caught fire, and in a few minutes blazed out sixty or seventy feet high, where one of the forks had fallen off and left free vent to the air. In a short space of time brother Young lay down on the ground to peep in the hole, and saw the lava running down in a stream as thick as his arm. The heat was so intense that the light partly blinded him. At that juncture the remaining fork of the tree, weakened by the fire, snapped off with a great noise. He sprung to his feet, and ran with all the speed that fear could inspire. By the time this great branch of the tree struck the ground he was sixty-three feet from the stump of the poplar, having providentially passed under this great half-tree beyond where its fork fell on the ground. Nothing struck him except the burning bark, which flew off and crushed him down to the earth amidst its fiery coals. If he had lain still at the root of the tree no evil would have befallen him. The other boys, however, came and pulled him up out of the fire. They found him by his groans, with his clothes some burnt, and his hat cut through in two or three places, and his head all in a gore of blood, together with his collar-bone broken. Unprepared for death, how narrowly did he escape!

His father was a farmer in easy circumstances, and attended to the education of his children; and so well had David improved his opportunities, that when time had legally made him his own master, he taught a grammar school two years in Hawkins and Sullivan counties, Tenn.

On the 27th of June, 1803, he left his father's, in Virginia, and went to what was then called the "far west," now Middle Tennessee. Sunday, August 14th, the Methodists had a quarterly meeting on Mill creek, near Green Hills, where were assembled a strange mixture of people. Among the rest were what have since been called the "Cumberland Presbyterians," who seemed to be as numerous and as busy as the others. It was impossible to tell who had the direction of the meeting; but they preached and prayed very well. David, however, left on Tuesday, and went to a dance.

Afterward, while riding all alone, thinking about the late quarterly meeting, he meditated on some of the awkward expressions in the prayers of the new converts. His pride said, or the devil told him, that he could pray better himself. So he made a form of prayer for them, and succeeded in putting his form into words. At that moment this query rushed into his mind, "What are you doing?" This inquiry turned a pleasant evening into gloomy horror, and, in lieu of making prayers for others, he began to pray for himself with all the faith and earnestness in his power, accompanied with a flood of tears. From this time he prayed morning and evening, with strange and indescribable feelings and opposition. A stranger in a strange land, he was afraid to pray near the people's houses, lest he should be seen; he dare not go far off, lest the snakes in the cane-brake would bite him; and when he went out into the lanes the devil made use of the horned cattle to drive him from his devotions. Previously the Lord had converted some of his relations who dwelt in Western Tennessee. When he got among them he was encouraged. Attending their meetings, when called on he prayed with and for them, though his own sins were not yet forgiven. His poor soul was in great distress, and his constant cry was, "What shall I do to be saved?" He strove about twenty-seven days to "enter in at the strait gate." His heart condemned him, and he knew that "God was greater than his heart," and would also condemn him With these views and feelings he went to another "big meeting," as they were then called, Friday, September 16th, and Sunday, 18th. There was a mighty shaking among the people, while he stood condemned, distressed, and in the agonies of indescribable anguish, not to say distraction. He could neither sleep nor eat, under an impression, right or wrong, that unless he obtained peace with God before the meeting closed, he must perish eternally. God, who pities the distressed, pitied him, and enabled him, by faith in Jesus Christ, to *trust in his blood.* He was astonished at the effects of simple faith, and was transported with the joys of believing.

On the 19th of September, 1803, between nine and ten o'clock, A. M., the Lord spoke peace to his soul. He walked out in the woods, and the trees reminded him of this injunction, "Clap your hands!" All nature seemed joyous, and, as grace had brought peace and harmony to his heart, so all visible objects seemed to partake of the blissful change. Christians need not expect, however, to be exactly alike in their experience. Luther and Bunyan in this respect differed widely from most of their followers who were real Christians.

Being desirous to see his parents, he returned to his father's in Virginia, on the last day of October, 1803, ripped off his ruffles, and cut off his long hair, and remained in that vicinity a few weeks, an astonishment and a by-word to all his former acquaintance. He returned to Tennessee, and resumed his occupation, April 1, 1804, and pursued the business of teaching till admitted into the traveling connection. But during this period his mental exercises were powerful, mostly with respect to his call to preach the Gospel. Many an anxious day and sleepless night did he pass through. These conflicts were mostly like other men's, perhaps, except that he was more unyielding than common; for it is certain he never would have been a Methodist preacher if he had not believed that his soul would be lost unless he became one. His understanding and conscience forbade him being any thing else. His mother, sister, and brother William were all happily converted to God during the summer of 1804, which served as an incentive to his piety. In this year that strange disorder "the jerks" overran all Western Tennessee. It attacked the righteous and the wicked—an involuntary muscular exercise, which drew the subjects affected backward and forward with a force and quickness perhaps previously unknown to the human family. Five hundred of these subjects might sometimes be seen in one congregation, all in various motion, from twitching the head up to bending the whole body—first backward, and then forward, the head nearly touching the ground forward and backward alternately. Some people thought it belonged to, if it did not make a part of, the Christian religion, others that it was the work of the devil; and brother Young thought that the devil had a hand therein, to bring religion into disrepute.

The wildness which seems to have been generated about Cane Ridge, Kentucky, spread down south in company with the jerks, having first made Newlights, as Stone and Purviance, and Shakers, as Dunlevy and M'Nemar. At the same time the Methodists and Presbyterians had a kind of union, based on the opinion, it would seem, that every body would suddenly be good, and Disciplines and Creeds would be needed no more. The Methodists revived their Discipline, and saved most of their people. The Newlights and Shakers made havoc with the Presbyterians, and what is now called the "Cumberland Presbyterians" made a great breach in the Church.

Rutherford county, where he resided, was a frontier set

tlement at that time; so he was graciously almost out of the noise and hearing of all religious tumults. Their misfortune was, to have almost no kind of religion in their neighborhood; so they tried to preach, exhort, and pray, James Rucker and himself. God owned their endeavors, and there were about one hundred and fifty who professed religion on Stone's river and Smith's Fork during the summer of 1805; but they were not in the Church; so they got one of the Nashville circuit preachers to come out and form them into classes, pledging himself to take them into the circuit next year. Being recommended by one of these classes, without quarterly meeting, circuit, or station, brother Young was admitted on trial in the traveling connection by the following document; namely:

"To David Young,—You think it your duty to call sinners to repentance. Make full proof hereof, and we shall rejoice to receive you as a fellow-laborer.

"Lewis Garret.

"*September* 7, 1805."

This may be a literary curiosity to some of the boys of the present day, who think the Methodist Episcopal Church can not make a traveling preacher unless they first localize him. The next Western conference sat in Scott county, Kentucky, October 2, 1805, at which he was appointed to Salt River and Shelby circuit. But Wayne circuit having but one preacher on it, brother Young was changed to Wayne circuit, in the south side of Kentucky. This was done by the concurrence of William Burke and William M'Kendree, as the case seemed absolutely to require it. On the last week in October, a sacramental meeting was held at the Beach meeting-house, near William M'Gee's, Western Tennessee, where he first saw that great and good man, William M'Kendree, whose equal in every respect has not yet adorned the Methodist

Episcopal Church; and yet, by some fatality, no man furnishes us with his memoirs. He gave him the plan of his circuit, and on the first Thursday in November, 1805, he met his first appointment, as a traveling preacher, at Manoah Lassley's, on Green river, Kentucky.

His colleague—William Ellington—was a very good-natured, easy kind of a man. Their circuit swarmed with Newlights and Freewill Baptists. Ellington let them all stay in class meeting, but brother Young turned them all out; and this made Ellington popular, and they ran to him with their complaints, and even carried them up to M'Kendree, their presiding elder. On examination of the circumstances, the presiding elder ordered brother Young to take charge of the circuit, despite of all remonstrance. Ellington was delighted, but brother Young was alarmed at having the charge of a circuit. There were a great number dropped and expelled on the circuit this year, but the Lord made up all their losses with a small increase of numbers. His health was not very good, but his appointments were all filled, averaging thirty each and every four weeks throughout the year.

During this appointment the following persons were licensed to exhort: Lewis Anderson, J. T. Williams, William Lewis, and Isaac M'Kowen, all of whom were afterward traveling preachers.

Isaac M'Kowen's mother was a widow, and her house a preaching-place, at which brother Young had an appointment on the day of the total eclipse, in 1806. When it began to grow dark, the ignorant Dutch and Irish inhabitants of the neighborhood ran to meeting, some for the first time, not waiting to change clothes, or put on their shoes; and before preaching closed, the house and the yard were filled with the worst-frightened congregation that ever was seen. The preacher exhorted them to be religious, and escape the "blackness of darkness forever."

He visited his parents in Virginia, and returned to the annual conference, which assembled at Ebenezer Nolichucky's, East Tennessee, September 15, 1806.

It was at this conference the celebrated propositions and services of Dr. Coke, as bishop of the Methodist Episcopal Church, were rejected.

His next appointment was to Levingston circuit, Kentucky, extending from Hopkinsville to Tennessee river, and from the Ohio river south to Clarksburg, Tennessee, a district too large for a modern presiding elder, and a distance to reach it of seven degrees of longitude—at least five hundred miles. Crazy Kate said, "The Lord tempers the wind to the shorn lamb;" it must be so, for where are the men and horses now that would perform such journeys?

Before getting once round his circuit, he was taken with severe chills every day, alternated with violent fevers. The chills ceased, and the fever increased for two weeks, when he fell into a kind of stupor, partly senseless, unless roused up; and then he lay four weeks longer, neither doctor nor friends expecting him to live. For nine weeks he never saw the sun. When he began to mend the blood had ceased to circulate in his feet and ankles; and when it again began to circulate, such twinging, prickling, and excessive pain he says he never felt before or since.

This was the first time he ever had the ague, but he had it more or less every one of the next nine years.

It was a kind providence toward him that he fell sick at old brother Meanly's. It was a very kind family of pious people. They took care of him as though he had been one of themselves, for which may God reward them in time and eternity! The old gentleman's son John was afterward a traveling preacher. While he lay at Meanly's, M'Kendree, his presiding elder, came to see him. He asked him to write his will. Having told him what dis position was to be made of his farms and personal property, he began talking wild, and told him what he wished done with a boat-load of ingots of silver, which he imagined was coming from South America by way of New Orleans. At the mention of this last subject M'Kendree threw down the pen and burst into tears, which roused him up. The good man was not only sorry because he was sick, but he was exceedingly grieved at his being delirious.

Near Meanly's, and in the vicinity of the town of Dover, only across the Cumberland river, on the highest eastern bluff, there was a curious Indian burying-ground, with only six graves in it. Each of these graves was lined with four stones—a head and foot, and two long side-stones, measuring from seven and a half to eight feet for each grave. The edges of these gravestones seemed as if they had been placed even with the surface, and subsequent winds had blown away six inches of the upper-soil. Each stone was cut at right angles, and was well dressed with some kind of tools. There were no rocks of the same quality known to be in all that region of country. Here brother Young would wander to meditate.

He was in tolerable health through the summer, and had some prosperity in his own soul, and some increase on his circuit. In that place lived the father of Peter Cartwright, and the mother of E. Wilcox, his half-brother.

In one of the most populous settlements on this circuit, there were two classes, and, of course, two leaders. The classes were not very religious, except when they were at meeting; then they were exceedingly noisy. The leaders were both drunken; so when S. got drunk, he posted away to M'C.'s, confessed, and got forgiven; and when M'C. got drunk, he hastened to S., and he forgave him. They quoted Scripture for all—claimed rights seventy times seven. He could not begin to administer discipline without removing these leaders; and it was like leaders, like members; so they did not want new leaders, and would not turn out the old ones for getting drunk; but referring their cases to quarterly meeting conference, they got rid of the principal inebriates, and the few good members rejoiced and increased greatly, not only in that society, but generally on the circuit. They excluded over one hundred, yet they had a net increase of more than fifty.

This fall, conference was appointed at Chilicothe, Ohio, September 14, 1807. On his way thither he fell sick in Lexington. The preachers left him, and in a few days he rode out to brother H——'s, twelve miles, where his fever increased, till he believed the family thought he must die. They were afraid, as it got spread through the neighborhood that his disease was contagious; and had it not been for a good old sister G., who came to see him, he might have died; but she went home and got her husband to bring a two-horse hack, with a bed in it, and take him home with him, where he was very kindly nursed a whole month, till able to ride.

Thus far my old friend and brother has furnished me with a sketch of his past history. His subsequent history is the history of the Church in the west; for he has been identified with all her movements. His mature judgment and well-cultivated mind enabled him to render good service to the Church in all her ecclesiastical councils.

Brother Young is still living, although much advanced, and quite feeble, being in his seventy-fifth year. The personal appearance of brother Young is somewhat peculiar, and would strike a stranger with a little surprise as he would gaze upon his tall, slender, and perfectly-erect form, his sharp and expressive features, a keen and piercing eye, rather deeply seated in his forehead, and the luxuriant folds of hair of snowy whiteness, which fall down over his shoulders. As a minister he always ranked far above mediocrity. When in his prime few had greater power in the pulpit. His mind possessed great vigor and reach of thought; and had he devoted himself to writing, his productions would have exhibited great terseness and power. For many years he filled the office of presiding elder, always attending his appointments with the precision of clock-work. He has for a long time been one of the trustees of the Ohio University, at Athens, and his wise counsels in that board have always been appreciated by his cotemporaries. As it regards his habits, it may be said, no minister ever had better, and none ever observed them more closely. But few of the old pioneer fathers remain. One by one they are falling around us; and here and there we find them standing in our midst, like the few ancient trees of the forest, to tell what was its ancient glory.

CHAPTER XXVI.

SKETCH OF REV. JOHN P. FINLEY.

The Rev. John Patterson Finley, my brother, was born on the 13th of June, 1783, in the state of North Carolina. In September, 1810, he received license to preach in the Methodist Episcopal Church. Having received a classical education, he was early called to take charge of literary institutions; and from that time till 1822 he labored in that department with great success in different parts of the state of Ohio. During this time, however, he labored much in the pulpit, and strove hard to show himself approved of God, "a workman that needeth not to be ashamed."

In 1822 he was appointed Professor of Languages in Augusta College, Kentucky, the oldest Methodist College in the west, now a heap of smoldering ruins. This institution, the first-born child of the Church, cost much care and anxiety, and, alas! regrets. I have letters to show the part I took in the establishment of the institution; ay, in the earliest incipient movements connected with it, and, hence, the reader will indulge me in what remarks I may deem it proper to make.

Augusta College, like Cokesbury, seems to have been a child of destiny, to have been born under some malignant star. Patronized by the two largest conferences in the west, having a faculty, from time to time, composed of the brightest stars that shone in the galaxy of western literature, such as Durbin, Tomlinson, Bascom, Fielding, and others, and having for her *alumni* a host of talented men in every profession, scattered all over the country, still, like an ill-guided, but richly-freighted vessel in a stormy sea, she foundered and went down, and the waters closed over her unhappy fate forever.

During the connection of my brother John with Augusta College, he was received into the traveling connection, and, as far as his professional duties would allow, he preached the word, "instant in season and out of season." His connection with this college lasted till May, 1825, when it was terminated by death.

Professor Bascom, the great pulpit orator of the west, one of his colleagues in the faculty, and who has himself since passed away to the world of rest, paid the following tribute to his memory:

"I have thought I could not spend an hour more profitably, this evening, than in sketching a few imperfect notices of the late Rev. John P. Finley, of the Methodist Episcopal Church. I became acquainted with the amiable and worthy subject of these recollections in 1815. From that time to the period of his death, I possessed his confidence, and enjoyed his friendship; and, perhaps, no one of his numerous friends knew his mind and heart more intimately than I, during a term of nearly ten years. He has frequently assured me that even his own family knew less of him than I did, and that I had understood his whole heart. I may, therefore, be permitted to say a few things to preserve from oblivion the name and services of an able minister of the New Testament, and devoted friend of mankind. John P. Finley was certainly no ordinary man, whether we consider his natural parts, his literary pretensions, or his gracious attainments. Nature had done much for him, various learning had largely contributed to improve him, and Christianity had perfected him into a model worthy of imitation. By nature he possessed a strong, manly, and ingenuous mind; his education was good, and well directed through life; his Christian character was of the first order; and all conspired to render him strikingly interesting, both in and out of the pulpit. But as my remarks will be almost entirely confined to recollection, I can only furnish an imperfect outline of the character of my deceased friend. It has long been my impression, that men of *distinguished* worth in our Church, who have been removed from their 'labor of love' on earth, have not received those distinctive marks of respect, in the official obituary notices of the Church, to which they have been obviously entitled, from the elevation of their character, and the nature and value of their services; and I would wish, that in all such notices, instead of a general and indiscriminate commendation of piety and usefulness, our numerous readers might be able to form some accurate idea of the peculiar and distinguishing attributes of character in each individual, becoming the subject of biographical report. If men, and especially ministers, are to be 'esteemed in love for their works' sake,' they ought certainly to be esteemed and held up to imitation, in proportion to the nature and extent of their relative usefulness, as well as aggregate worth of character. I mean to say, simply, without indulging in any thing censorious, that it is the duty of the living among us, to report faithfully, and with some particularity, the various usefulness and diversified excellence of the dead. In looking over, recently, some scores of notices of the death and character of our deceased ministers, I have observed a generality of description, a sameness of report, which, I fear, is calculated to make an impression, unfriendly to the well-known fact, that we have had in our Church a great variety of talent and usefulness: and certainly it belongs to the history of the Church, the biography of her distinguished individuals, to point out, and clearly develop, the diversity of talent, character, and labor, of which we are now speaking. . . . But to return to our subject.

"John P. Finley was born in North Carolina, June 13, 1783. From childhood he was marked as possessing no common share of intellect. He was early placed at school, and while in his abecedarian course, he evinced an aptitude to learn, that induced his father, a distinguished Presbyterian clergyman, who is now, at the age of seventy, a Methodist traveling preacher, to give him a classical education. Owing to his habits of industry and perseverance, he soon acquired a competent knowledge of the sciences, and a reputable acquaintance with the learned languages. Of the English language he was a perfect master, and taught its proper use with almost unrivaled success. From the age of twelve or fourteen years, he was often deeply affected with a sense of sin, and the importance of repentance and faith; but his mind was so much perplexed with the doctrines of absolute personal predestination, of which his father was then a strenuous and able asserter, that he came to no decision on the subject of religious opinions, till he reached the years of manhood. About the age of twenty-one he married, and soon after was brought to the knowledge of salvation by the remission of his sins. Early after his conversion, he was convinced that a 'dispensation of the Gospel' had been committed to him. He weighed well the impressions and convictions of his mind and heart, in relation to the fearful and responsible business of a Christian minister; but when finally and fully convinced of his duty, he did not hesitate. There were indeed many reasons why he should confer with flesh and blood; but, with his characteristic firmness, he rejected them all, and took the pulpit, I think, in 1811. At the time of his conversion he resided in Highland county, Ohio. His ministerial career was commenced during a residence in Union, Greene county, Ohio, whither he had been called to take charge of a seminary. At the head of this institution he continued about six years, living and preaching the religion of Christ in its native simplicity and power.

"From Union he removed to Dayton, distant only about thirty miles, and conducted an academy in this place for two years. It was here our acquaintance and intimacy commenced, which ended only with his useful life. He left Dayton, beloved and regretted of all, and accepted a call to superintend a respectable seminary in Steubenville, Ohio. In this place he continued not quite two years. In his ministerial exertions he was 'instant in season and out of season,' and labored with more than ordinary success. His next remove was to Piqua, Ohio, where he continued as principal of an academy for four years. In all these places his pulpit efforts were highly acceptable; his social intercourse seasoned with dignity and piety, and his residence a blessing to all about him. From this place he made his last remove to Augusta, Kentucky. Here he taught a classical school for some time, and was afterward appointed principal of Augusta College, in which relation he continued till the time of his death. In these several places his labors in the pulpit were considerable, and extensively useful. All who knew him esteemed him as a man of talents and irreproachable Christian character. He was, indeed, all in all, one of the most amiable, guileless men I ever knew: never did I know a man more perfectly under the influence of moral and religious principle. His uniform course was one of high and unbending rectitude.

"One error, as reported in the 'Minutes,' respecting his conversion, I must beg leave to correct. I do it upon his own authority, when living, and that of his brother, the Rev. James B. Finley, superintendent of the Wyandott mission. There is something rather remarkable in the manner in which these worthy ministers were first brought to reflect with more than ordinary concern upon their latter end. John and James were amusing themselves in the forest with their guns; and as John was sitting carelessly upon his horse, James's gun accidentally went off, and the contents came very near entering John's head. The brothers were mutually alarmed, humbled, and thankful; they were more than ever struck with the melancholy truth, that 'in the midst of life we are in death.' They reflected upon their unpreparedness to meet death, and appear in judgment. Each promised the other he would reform; and the result was, they were both led to seek religion, as the only preparation for eternity. Both the brothers agree in stating that this circumstance was the means, in the hand of God, of their awakening and conversion, as neither of them was in the habit of attending the preaching of the Gospel before the inquietude and alarm created by this occasion. I have been thus minute in detailing the immediate means of his conversion, at the request of a surviving brother, in whose estimation the apparent incompetency of the means magnifies the grace of God, in this singular dispensation of blended mercy and providence.

"John P. Finley was in the ministry about fifteen years. He was ordained deacon by Bishop Asbury, on the 17th of September, 1815. He received ordination as elder at the hands of Bishop Roberts, July 2, 1820. At the time of his death he was a member of the Kentucky annual conference, actively dividing his time and energies between the business of collegiate instruction and the labor of the pulpit.

"As a *man*, the subject of these recollections was engagingly amiable, ingenuous, and agreeable. Equally removed from affectation and reserve, the circle in which he moved felt the presence of a friend, and the influence of a Christian and minister.

"As a *teacher*, his excellence was acknowledged by all

who were competent to decide upon his claims; and though he gloried more in being found a pupil in the school of Christ, yet he was no stranger to the academy and lyceum.

"As a *husband*, there is one living whose tears have been his eulogy, and to whom, with his orphan children, friendship inscribes these lines.

"As a *father*, he was worthy of his children; and in pointing them to another and better world, he was always careful to lead the way himself.

"As a *friend*, he was warm, ardent, and confiding, and not less generous than constant. His intimate friends, however, were few and well selected.

"As a *minister*, in the pulpit, he was able, impressive, and overwhelming. The cross of his redemption was his theme; and in life and death it became to him the 'emphasis of every joy.' In all these relations I knew him well, and can, therefore, speak from the confidence of personal knowledge and accredited information.

"The last time I saw him, I preached a sermon, at his request, on the 'Inspiration of the Scriptures.' When I had retired to my room, he called on me, in company with a friend, and, in his usual frank manner, embraced me, and observed, 'H——, I thank you for that sermon, and I expect to repeat my gratitude in heaven.' Little did I think at this interview that I was gazing on my friend for the last time, and that in eighteen months his ripened virtues were to receive the rewards of the heavenly world! But so it was; and I, less fit to die, am spared another and another year.

"He died on the 8th of May, 1825, in the forty-second year of his age, and sixteenth of his ministry; and at the same time that this bereaved family wept upon his grave, the sadness of the Church told that she had lost one of her brightest ornaments. Just before his triumphant spirit rose to sink and sigh no more, he was asked how he felt, and what were his prospects upon entering the dark valley and shadow of death. He replied, in language worthy of immortality, 'Not the shadow of a doubt; I have Christ within, the hope of glory. That comprehends all!' and then, with the protomartyr, he 'fell asleep.'

"Such is a very imperfect sketch of the life, character, and death of John P. Finley. God grant, reader, that you and I may share the glory that gilded the last hours of his toil!"

I will close this sketch by inserting the Rev. Jonathan Stamper's dream. He was intimately acquainted with my brother, and the remarkable dream which he had was in relation to him. It was communicated to me as follows:

"I was much attached to brother Finley and he to me. We lived in habits of the closest intimacy and Christian confidence. He was taken ill when I was at a distance, and the news of his sickness and death came together to me. I felt that I had lost one of my best friends, and mourned for him as a dear brother departed, and probably that gave rise to the dream. In my slumbers I thought I went to his house, where I used often to go with pleasure in his lifetime. He welcomed me at the door with his usual urbanity. I was glad to see him, and he expressed great joy to see me, though I knew he was dead. We sat down side and side by the fire. I was at once filled with curiosity to learn something from him respecting the world of spirits. He looked at me earnestly, and said,

"'Brother, you are filled with curiosity?'

"I replied, 'Yes, my mind has taken a very curious turn.'

"'Well,' said he, 'ask me any question you see proper, and I will satisfy you so far as I can consistently with the laws of the country where I live.'

"I then proceeded, and asked, 'Brother, are you happy?'

"'Yes,' said he, 'I am happy as heaven can make me.

"I then asked, 'When you died did you enter immediately into heaven?'

"'No,' said he; 'but I immediately started for it, and I was the space of three days arriving there, though I flew with more than the velocity of a sunbeam. I passed beyond the boundaries of this system, and lost sight of the most distant star that twinkles in these skies, and entered into thick and uninterrupted darkness.' Then pausing, he looked at me most expressively, and said, 'O, hell is a solemn reality! After this,' said he, 'I all at once burst into the glories of heaven.'

"Said I, 'The Scriptures represent heaven as a glorious city, such a one as was never seen on earth, and by other splendid and beautiful imagery. Is this entirely figurative, or is it a literal description?'

"'It is,' said he, 'partly figurative and partly real. Heaven is a local residence, gloriously fitted up for the abode of saints and angels, where the glory of God is revealed to an extent that is not known in any other part of his dominion, where the glorified humanity of Jesus is ever seen and admired by the whole company of heaven. There is nothing material there, but all spiritual, immaterial, and imperishable. All the beautiful imagery of the Scriptures are there seen, though of a spiritual character, such as the trees ever green, the golden streets, etc.'

"I then inquired if the saints in heaven knew each other.

"'More perfectly,' said he, 'than they did here. I knew at sight all the patriarchs, prophets, and apostles.'

"I then desired to know if the saints in heaven were acquainted with the affairs of earth.

"'Only,' said he, 'as they are permitted to visit the

earth, as I am at this time. This they often do, and are sometimes sent as ministering angels.'

"After this he said, 'I desire to know how you are getting on in the work of God.'

"I replied, 'About as we were when you used to be with us.'

"He then asked, 'Do the Methodists pay their preachers no better than formerly?'

"I said, 'No.'

"'O,' said he, 'what a pity—what a pity! The itinerant plan is the plan of God. He designs it to take the world, and nothing will prevent it but a want of liberality in our people. But,' said he, 'you must never locate. God has called you to this work. He will support you. You will live to be a very old man, and may be very useful.' He then repeated, with a very heavy emphasis, 'You must never locate. If I had my life to live again, I would travel if I begged my bread from door to door. You know I often told you I believed it was my duty to travel, and had I obeyed I should have shone much brighter in heaven than I now do.' He then added, with a most affectionate tone and look, 'O, brother, don't locate; God will support you.' He then reached up to the chimney-piece, and took down a considerable roll of bank-notes of the most singular and beautiful appearance I had ever seen, and, handing them to me, he said, 'Here, these are for you.'

"I said, 'Brother, I would rather you would give that money to your wife. You know your family are dependent.'

"He answered, 'No; it is for you. There is a bank in heaven for the support of itinerant preachers, and this is for you.' I then took it. He then said, 'It is almost time for me to go; but we must worship together before we part.' He sang loud and animated, and while I was praying he shouted aloud, as he used often to do when we were together at meeting. My soul became filled. I never was more happy; and even after I awoke my very heart sung praises to God. He then bade me an affectionate adieu, we parted, and I awoke."

CHAPTER XXVII.

SKETCH OF THE REV. WILLIAM B. CHRISTIE.

I HAVE already alluded to this beloved brother, and propose furnishing my readers with a short sketch of his useful life.

Brother Christie was born in Williamsburg, Clermont county, Ohio, on the 2d of September, 1803. In early life he embraced religion and joined the Methodist Episcopal Church. In the year 1825 he was admitted into the traveling connection and appointed to Union circuit. He was called to fill some of the most important appointments in the gift of the Church. In the several important fields of labor he sustained himself well as a minister, and by his zeal and fidelity he proved, under God, a great blessing to the Church. "That his labors were those of an accredited embassador of Christ is attested by thousands who were blessed with his ministrations. Numerous witnesses of the power of Christ to save were raised up through his instrumentality. That he possessed the affection and confidence of his brethren and companions in toil is evident from the fact that, by their suffrages, he was thrice honored with a seat in the General conference."

The personal appearance of brother Christie was pre possessing in an eminent degree. He was somewhat above the medium hight. His hair was black as a raven, his eyes dark and piercingly brilliant, and, when lighted up fully with the inspiration of his theme, they shot unearthly fires. About his countenance there was a bland

and sometimes almost seraphic sweetness, especially when, with soft and measured cadences, he would labor to win his rapt and listening audiences to the cross, or bear them away on imagination's wing to heaven. His equal in the pulpit for fervid oratory we never saw before; his like in rapid, impassioned eloquence we never expect to look upon again. His ambition—and who that excels has it not?—was of that towering kind which sought to rise above all others, but never stooped in envious flight to pluck another's honors.

I will refer to the admirably-written memoir contained in the Minutes of the Ohio conference for 1843:

"As a man, brother Christie was ingenuous, guileless, magnanimous, and ardent in affection. Dignified in deportment and courteous in his manners, he won the affections of all with whom he had intercourse. His mental endowments were of a high order, and having in youth enjoyed the advantages of a college life at Augusta, under the presidency of the Rev. John P. Finley, he received that training and acquired those elements and principles which qualified him for the attainment of those stores of knowledge which, in after life, were so richly developed during his ministerial career. Hence, as a divine, it has been justly remarked, that he had few equals, if any superiors. Profoundly versed in the science of theology and ecclesiastical polity, in the pulpit and on the conference floor, he handled his subjects with a power and skill that rarely failed of success. But the pulpit, pre-eminently, was the theater of his greatness, and the sufferings of Christ the glory of his theme. Calm and collected in his introduction, cautious in the statement of his positions, cogent in his reasonings, apposite in his illustrations, and appropriate in his Scriptural quotations, he carried conviction to the understandings of his audience, and then, rising with the inspiration of his subject, with the fervor and pathos of his appeals, under the glowings of the Spirit of God, he forced the citadel of the hearts of his hearers, and made them feel the power of the Gospel of Christ. Through him the violated law of God announced its threatened penalty, the claims of Divine justice were vindicated, till the sinner, self-condemned, was carried to the cross of Jesus, and offered and pressed for his acceptance, by faith in the blood of atonement, a present, free, and full salvation. And, doubtless, many through his instrumentality were saved, and will shine as stars in his crown of rejoicing forever and ever. But this bright luminary in the moral heavens was destined to be quenched ere it had traveled the whole length of the ordinary path of human life.

"In the early part of brother Christie's ministerial life his health failed him, owing to his abundant labors and his untiring assiduity in the pursuit of useful knowledge. Hence, for many years he suffered much affliction and almost continual pain, but did not intermit his labors till he was absolutely compelled to desist from his work and repair to the bosom of his friends to close his earthly career. For this purpose he left his station at Urbana, and went to the city of Cincinnati. But when he reached Dr. Wright's, in Cincinnati, on Tuesday evening, he was much prostrated, took his bed, and declined more rapidly than before. The next morning after he arrived, two ministerial brethren called to see him. His face was flushed with fever, and his system wasted almost to a shadow. He was much affected at the interview, and said his nerves were shattered, but his confidence in God was unshaken. He knew in whom he had believed. He had not preached an unknown or unfelt Savior, and the Gospel which he had long preached to others was then his consolation. The calls of his numerous friends so taxed his sympathy and his strength that his physicians found it requisite to lay some restriction on them, or suffer him to be much hastened in his departure; and, with all the care that could be taken by physicians and friends, he did not last long.

"Among the numerous incidents indicating the state of his mind during the last hours of his earthly existence, only a few will be recited.

"Saturday morning, a little after midnight, he requested a brother, who was sitting near him, to call Dr. Wright, who came in and found him rapidly sinking. He asked brother C. if he felt worse. His reply was, that he had great difficulty of breathing. After some means of temporary relief had been administered, he asked the Doctor, 'What does this mean?' In reply, the Doctor inquired if he would like to see some of his friends. Brother C. then said, 'Why do you ask the question? Do you think I am pretty near home?' On being informed that he was undoubtedly worse, he looked round upon his wife and friends, calm and collected, and said, 'I am not alarmed. I am not afraid to die.' Extending and looking at his hands, he remarked, 'Jesus, with his bleeding hands, will not thrust me away.' Next, he took his two little sons, embraced, and commended them to God. Soon after this, brother Sehon, having been sent for, entered his room, to whom he extended his hand, and, with a countenance bright with hope, said, 'Brother Sehon, I am almost home.' After exchanging a few words, he requested brother S. to pray, and during the prayer he appeared to be perfectly happy. This over, he beckoned brother S. to his bed, and by him sent the following message: 'Tell my brethren at the conference, if they think my name worthy of being mentioned, that I have not preached an unknown and an unfelt Christ. Tell them, that though unworthy and unfaithful, that Gospel which I have preached to others now sustains me.

Tell the preachers to preach Christ and him crucified. Tell them my only hope, my only foundation, is in the blood of sprinkling. Precious blood! O, the fullness, the sweetness, the richness of that fountain!' After praising God for some time, he turned his eyes on his weeping companion, and made some reference to his temporalities, but instantly observed, they were small matters, little things, assuring her that God would provide for her and his little children. About two o'clock Bishop Morris arrived, and found him bolstered up in his bed, covered with the sweat of death, and much exhausted by the efforts he had made to speak, as above described. He, however, reached out his hand, and said distinctly, 'I am almost home. I feel that God is good to me, and that Jesus Christ is my salvation.' No question was asked him, and, being exhausted, he desisted from speaking for a while, and then, looking at his distressed wife, we understood him to say, 'Jesus is precious.' When unable to articulate, he often lifted his cold hand in token of victory; and again, as though anxious to make us understand his meaning, he raised his hand high above his head, and waved it in triumph. After some time, he raised both hands at once, and extended them before him as if just rising on 'the wings of love and arms of faith;' and then, in an animating manner, brought his hands together, triumphing over death, his last enemy. At that time we supposed he would speak no more; for when his companion desired to hear his voice once more on earth, he could only look at her and point his finger to heaven. However, not long before his exit he raised his hands high, and brother S. asked him if he wanted any thing. He shook his head. Brother S. then asked him if it was power and glory. His countenance brightened up, while he nodded his head affirmatively, and his strength returning to him, he shouted aloud, clapping his hands and giving glory to God. The same peculiarity of manner, form of expression, and even gesture, which marked his pulpit and altar performances, were strikingly exhibited in his closing scene. To the last he seemed to be conscious and triumphant. About seven o'clock, Saturday morning, March 26, 1842, without a sigh or groan, his deathless spirit passed in peace and triumph from earth, to appear before the presence of God with exceeding joy. The overwhelming crowd of all classes of people that thronged to his funeral at Wesley Chapel, and attended his remains to their last resting-place on earth, afforded abundant evidence of the estimate they placed upon his character.

CHAPTER XXVIII.

INDIAN BIOGRAPHY.

MONONCUE.

This renowned chief of the Wyandott nation was about medium in stature, and remarkably symmetrical in form. He was one of the most active men I ever knew, quick in his motions as thought, and fleet as the roe in the chase.

As a speaker, he possessed a native eloquence which was truly wonderful. Few could stand before the overwhelming torrent of his eloquence. He was a son of Thunder. When inspired with his theme, he could move a large assembly with as much ease, and rouse them to as high a state of excitement, as any speaker I ever heard.

There is a peculiarity in Indian eloquence which it is difficult to describe. To form a correct idea of its character, you must be in the hearing and sight of the son of the forest; the tones of his voice and the flash of his eye must fall upon you, and you must see the significant movements of his body. As an orator, Mononcue was not surpassed by any chieftain.

I will give a specimen or two of the eloquence of this gifted son of nature. Imagine yourself, gentle reader, in the depths of the forest, surrounded by hundreds of chiefs and warriors, all sunk in the degradation and darkness of Paganism. They have been visited by the missionary, and several converted Indian chiefs. One after another the chiefs rise and address the assembly, but with no effect. The dark scowl of infidelity settles on their brows, and the frequent mutterings of the excited auditors indicate that their speeches are not acceptable, and their doctrines not believed.

At length Mononcue rises amidst confusion and disturbance, and ordering silence with a commanding voice, he addresses them as follows:

"When you meet to worship God, and to hear from his word, shut up your mouths, and open your ears to hear what is said. You have been here several days and nights worshiping your Indian god, who has no existence, only in your dark and beclouded minds. You have been burning your dogs and venison for him to smell. What kind of a God or Spirit is he, that can be delighted with the smell of a burnt dog? Do you suppose the great God that spread out the heavens, that hung up the sun and moon, and all the stars, to make light, and spread out this vast world of land and water, and filled it with men and beasts, and every thing that swims or flies, is pleased with the smell of your burnt dogs? I tell you to-day, that his great eye is on your hearts, and not on your fires, to see and smell what you are burning. Has your worshiping here these few days made you any better? Do you feel that you have gotten the victory over one evil? No! You have not taken the first step to do better, which is to keep this day holy. This day was appointed by God himself a day of rest for all men, and a day on which men are to worship him with pure hearts, and to come before him, that he may examine their hearts, and cast out all their evil. This day is appointed for his ministers to preach to us Jesus, and to teach our dark and cloudy minds, and to bring them to light." He here spoke of the Savior, and his dying to redeem the world; that now life and salvation are freely offered to all that will forsake sin and turn to God. He adverted to the judgment day, and the awful consequences of being found in sin, and strangers to God. On this subject he was tremendously awful. He burst into tears: he caught the handkerchief from his head, and wiped them from his eyes. Many in the house sat as if they were petrified, while others wept in silence. Many of the females drew their blankets over their faces and wept. "Awful, awful day to the wicked!" said this thundering minister. "Your faces will look much blacker with your shame and guilt, than they do now with your paint." I have no doubt but God was with Mononcue on this occasion, and that many were convicted of sin and a judgment to come.

On the first of January, at our mission in Upper Sandusky, while I had charge of the same, I was called to bury one of our little flock, an aged woman, the mother of Jaco, and aunt to Mononcue. She lived at the Big Spring reservation, fifteen miles from the mission house. On the Sabbath before her death, I conversed with her about her future hopes. She rejoiced, and praised God that he had ever sent his ministers to preach Jesus to her and her people. "I have been trying," said she, "to serve God for years; but it was all in the dark, till the ministers brought the light to my mind, and then I prayed, and found my God precious to my poor soul. Now I am going soon to see him in his house above; and I want all my children, and grandchildren, and friends, to meet me in that good world." She died a few days after, in great peace. I was sent for, to go and bury her. Brother Riley and myself rode there in the night, and early in the morning commenced making the coffin. It was late before we could finish it, and, consequently, late before the funeral was over. But I think I shall never forget the scene. It was between sundown and dark when we left with the corpse The lowering clouds hung heavily over us, and the virgin snow was falling. We entered a deep and lonely wood, four men carrying the bier, and the rest all following in Indian file. When we came to the burying-ground, the

Indians stood wrapped up in their blankets, leaning against the forest trees, in breathless silence; and all bore the aspect of death. Not one word was said while the grave was filling up; but from the daughter, and some of the grandchildren, now and then a broken sigh escaped. At last Mononcue broke out in the following strains: "Farewell, my old and precious aunt! You have suffered much in this world of sin and sorrow. You set us all a good example, and we have often heard you speak of Jesus in the sweetest strains, while the falling tears have witnessed the sincerity of your heart. Farewell, my aunt! We shall no more hear your tender voice, that used to lull all our sorrows, and drive our fears from us. Farewell, my aunt! That hand that fed us will feed us no more. Farewell to your sorrows: all is over. There your body must lie till the voice of the Son of God shall call you up. We weep not with sorrow, but with joy, that your soul is in heaven." Then he said, "Who of you all will meet her in heaven?" This was a feeling and happy time, and we parted, I think, fully determined to die the death of the righteous. We rode home that night, fifteen miles, and felt greatly comforted in talking of the goodness of God and the power of his grace. "Blessed are the dead that die in the Lord from henceforth."

Mononcue was of great service to the mission as a local preacher, and was always prompt in the discharge of every duty. He was

> "Bold to take up, firm to sustain
> The consecrated cross."

Ready for every good word and work, he engaged with the utmost cheerfulness in every thing his brethren desired him to do, that would advance the cause of his Master. I was most deeply attached to him, and lived on terms of the most warm and confiding friendship during his life. But Mononcue, my faithful Indian friend and brother, is gone. "He has fought the good fight, he has finished his course, he has kept the faith," and now he dwells with the Savior above.

BETWEEN-THE-LOGS.

The distinguished chief whose likeness the reader will find accompanying this biography, was born near Lower Sandusky, about the year 1780. His father was a Seneca, and his mother a Wyandott, belonging to the Bear tribe. When he was about eight or nine years old, his father and mother parted—a thing very common among the heathen Indians. After this, he lived with his father till the old man's death, by which time he had nearly arrived at manhood. After the death of his father, he lived with his mother, among the Wyandotts. Of the particulars of his life, previous to this time, there is but little known. Not long after his return to his mother, he joined Indian warriors, and with them suffered a defeat by the army under Gen. Wayne, in the decisive battle at the Rapids of Maumee. He then lived at Lower Sandusky. His good sense, persevering and enterprising disposition, with his prompt obedience to the commands of the chiefs, and faithful discharge of whatever duty was assigned him, began to call him into public notice in the nation, and laid the foundation for his being promoted to the office of a chief; and because of his retentive memory, and ability in discussion, he was constituted chief-speaker of the nation. He soon became the intimate friend and counselor of the head chief. When he was about twenty-five years old, he was sent to fathom the doctrines and pretensions of a celebrated Seneca Prophet, whose fallacy he soon detected. About two years afterward he was sent on a like errand to a noted Shawnee Prophet—Tecumseh's brother—with whom he staid nearly a year, and then returned, convinced, and convincing others, that the Prophet's pretensions were all delusive, and destitute of truth.

Shortly after his return from this Prophet, the late wai commenced. On the part of the Wyandotts, he and the head chief attended a great Indian council of the northern nations, at Brownstown, in which he firmly rejected all overtures to join in the war against the Americans, although surrounded by warriors attached to the opposite interest. They left the council, and, on their return to Sandusky, immediately joined the American cause. When Gen. Harrison invaded Canada, Between-the-logs, in company with a party of Wyandott chiefs and warriors, attended him. But the principal object of the chief, at this time, was to detach that part of the Wyandotts from the British interest, who, by the surrounding Indians, had, in a measure, been forced to join the English. This was effected.

After the war, he became permanently settled in the neighborhood of Upper Sandusky. He now sometimes indulged in intemperance to excess, on which occasions unbridled passion got the better of his natural good sense. In one of these drunken fits he killed his wife. As well as I now recollect, Between-the-logs was excited to this deed by a wretch who owed her some ill-will, and took the opportunity of his drunkenness, and insisted that she was a bad woman, a witch, etc., and that he ought to kill her. For some time he maintained that she was a good woman, and refused; but was, at last, overcome, and stabbed her. When he became sober, the horror of this deed made so deep an impression on his mind, that from that day forth he measurably abandoned all use of ardent spirits. Being deeply impressed with a sense of the necessity of a preparation for another world, and having a strong regard for his countrymen, he frequently besought them to forsake drunkenness, and pursue a righteous life.

In 1817 a new field opened for the exercise of his

wisdom and courage. The United States having made arrangements to extinguish the Indian title to the lands claimed by them in Ohio, commissioners were sent to treat with them. The Wyandotts refused to sell their land; but the Chippewas, Potawatomies, and Ottowas, without any right, laid claim to a great part of their land. Gabriel Godfroy and Whitmore Knaggs, Indian agents for these nations, proposed in open council, in behalf of the Chippewas, etc., to sell said land. The commissioners then declared, that if the Wyandotts would not sell their lands, they would buy them of the others. Between-the-logs firmly opposed all these measures; but however just his cause, or manly his arguments, they were lost upon men determined on their course. The Wyandotts, finding themselves so circumstanced, and not being able to help themselves, were thus forced to sell on the terms proposed by the commissioners. They did the best they could, and signed the treaty; but only from a strong hope that, by representing to the President and the government the true state of things, before the treaty was ratified, they should obtain some redress from government. In resorting to this course, Between-the-logs acted a principal part. Accordingly he, with the Wyandott chiefs, and a delegation from the Delawares and Senecas, immediately proceeded to Washington, without consulting the Indian agents, or any other officer of government. When they were introduced to the Secretary of War, he remarked to them that he was surprised that he had received no information of their coming by any of the agents. Between-the-logs answered with the spirit of a free man, "*We got up, and came of ourselves. We believed the great road was free for us.*" He so pleaded their cause before the President, Secretary of War, and Congress, that they obtained an enlargement of their reservations, and an increase of annuities.

About a year afterward the Gospel was introduced among the Wyandotts, by a colored man, named John Stewart. Between-the-logs was decidedly in its favor, and maintained its cause in the national council; and when, some time afterward, I formed a Church among them, he was the first man who joined society, the first who turned his back on their old, heathen traditions.

After he embraced religion, and his understanding became enlightened, he earnestly pressed upon his people the necessity of faith in Christ, and a life of righteousness. Soon after this, he was regularly appointed an exhorter in the Church, in which station he remained till his death, a devoted friend and advocate of the cause of God. He also watched with unremitting diligence over the temporal interests of the nation; enduring the fatigues of business, and of the longest journeys, for the welfare of his people, without complaint. He was uniformly an attendant upon the Ohio annual conference, at which he made some of the most rational and eloquent speeches ever delivered by an Indian before that body. He felt, and always manifested a deep interest in the welfare of the mission and school.

The following address was delivered by Between-the-logs, at the anniversary of the Missionary Society, in the city of New York, in the spring of 1826. After giving a history of the introduction of the Roman Catholic religion into his nation, and the influence it had on his people, he says: "It is true, we went to Church on the Sabbath day, and then the minister preached; but we did not understand one word he said. We saw he kneeled down, and stood up, and went through motions with his great dress on; and when Church was out we all went to a place where they sold rum and whisky, got drunk, and went home drunk. He would tell us we must not get drunk; but he would drink himself, and frolic and dance on the

Sabbath. We counted our beads, and kept our crosses about our necks, or under our pillows, and would sometimes pray to the Virgin Mary. But we were all as we were before. It made no change on us, and I began to think it was not as good as the religion of our fathers; for they taught us to be good men and women, to worship the Great Spirit, and to abstain from all evil. Soon after, the Seneca Prophet came to our nation, and he told us that he had found the right way; that he had a revelation and had seen and talked with an angel, and was directed to teach all the Indians; that they must quit drinking, and must take up their old Indian religion, and offer their constant sacrifices, as their fathers had done, which had been neglected too much; and, on account of this, the Great Spirit had forsaken them. But if they would come back and follow him, that he would yet drive the white man back to his native home. We all followed him till we saw he went crooked, and did not do himself what he taught us to do. Then we followed him no more, but returned to our old course. Some time afterward came the Shawnee Prophet, the brother of Tecumseh, and he told us that a great many years ago there lived a prophet that had foretold the present state of the Indians, that they would be scattered and driven from their homes; but that the Great Spirit had said that he would make them stand on their feet again, and would drive the white man back over the waters, and give them their own country; that he had seen an angel, and he told him that all the Indians must quit drinking, and all turn to their old ways that their grandfathers had followed, and unite and aid to drive the whites from our country. Many believed and followed him. But I had got tired, and thought it was the best for me to keep on in the old way, and so we continued. Then the war came on, and we all went to drinking and fighting. When the war was over, we were a nation of drunkards, and so wicked that the chiefs thought we must try and get up our old religion of feasting and dancing. We did our best to get our people to quit drinking. But while we were trying to reform, God sent a colored man named Stewart to us with the good Book. He began to talk, and sing, and pray; but we thought it was all nothing, and many made fun of him because he was a black man. The white traders told us we ought to drive him away; for the white people would not let a black man preach for them. We, however, watched his walk, and found that he walked straight, and did as he said. At last the word took hold, and many began to listen, and believed it was right, and soon we began to pray, and we found that it was of God. Then others came, and they told us the same things. The work broke out, and God has done great things for us. I was among the first that took hold, and I found it was the religion of the heart, and from God. It made my soul happy, and does yet. The school is doing well. Our children are learning to read the good Book, and promise fair to make good and useful men. We thank you, our friends, for all the kindness and help you have shown us, and hope you will continue to help us till we can stand alone and walk. We will do our best to spread this religion at home, and send it to all nations. When at home I am accustomed to hear my brothers talk; but since I came here I can not understand what is said. I wonder if the people understand one another; for I see but little effect from what is said;" meaning that the Gospel preached had but little visible effect.

I then followed, and gave some account of the mission, the work of God among the Indians, the school, farm, and our prospects generally.

Rev. James Gilruth, who visited Between-the-logs in his last illness, which was pulmonary consumption, says: "On my first visit I strove to be faithful. I asked him of his hope. He said it was 'the mercy of God in Christ.' I asked him of his evidence. He said it was 'the comfort of the Spirit.' I asked him if he was afraid to die. He said, 'I am not.' I inquired if he felt resigned to go. He said, 'I have felt some desires of the world, but they are all gone. I now feel willing to die or live, as the Lord sees best.' Some days afterward I visited him again. I found his mind still staid on God; but he was evidently approaching his dissolution. I informed him that there were some evidences that his son—Richard Reese, his only child—had experienced religion. He rejoiced, and said, 'I wish you to keep him at the mission. It is the best place for him. Keep him at school; keep him out of bad company.' A few days after this he closed his life, in peace with God and man, on the 1st of January, 1827, about the forty-sixth year of his age, and was buried in the graveyard by the meeting-house."

I preached his funeral sermon to a large, attentive, and weeping company of his people, the mission family, etc.

Between-the-logs was rather above the common stature, broad, and thin built, but otherwise well-proportioned, with an open and manly countenance.

Through his life he had to contend with strong passions, which, through grace, he happily overcame in the end. His memory was so tenacious that he retained every matter of importance, and related it, when necessary, with a minute correctness that was truly astonishing. And such were his natural abilities otherwise, that, had he received a suitable education, few would have exceeded him, either as a minister of the Gospel or as a statesman or politician.

Many interesting incidents might be given of this chieftain; but the space allotted will not admit of a more extended account. Few men of any nation or tongue, considering the circumstances under which they were placed possessed greater natural gifts than many of these sons of the forest; and had their descendants, as well as the other tribes of Indians, received that attention from the Church and the government to which they were justly entitled as the original inheritors of the soil, they might have remained strong and powerful to this day. But, alas! the doom of the entire race appears to be sealed, and in a few years the tide of Anglo-Saxon population will sweep them away, and nothing will be left to tell of their existence but the page of history.

BIG-TREE.

This remarkable Indian was a chief of the Bear tribe. He was in almost every respect an extraordinary man. Above six feet in hight, symmetrical in proportions, and graceful in his movements, he at once impressed the eye of the beholder with an idea that he was in the presence of one of nature's greatest sons. He had a Grecian cast of countenance, broad, expansive forehead, aquiline nose, and remarkably-regular features.

When I became acquainted with him he was about eighty years of age. He presented a somewhat singular appearance. The rims of his ears were cut, and the inner portion of them perforated, in which were hung many silver ornaments, such as the Indians have, from time immemorial, decorated themselves with. The cartilage of his nose also was perforated, from which depended a curiously-wrought silver jewel. His hair was cut off close to his head, with the exception of a small portion on his crown, which was long and plaited, inclosed in a silver tube. In other respects, he was dressed in the usual Indian costume.

Singular as was the appearance of this chieftain, no one could look upon his commanding person without feeling a respect for him. Age had not bent his erect, dignified form, or dimmed the fire of his dark, expressive eye, and his frank, manly, affable manners at once gained your confidence.

He resided on the banks of the Sandusky, near the mission house. The small field, which he brought under a high state of cultivation, yielded him corn, beans, squashes, and other vegetables sufficient to supply his wants. In the center of this field stood his wigwam. It was of singular construction. The materials out of which it was constructed were chiefly corn-stalks placed up on end like a shock, but much larger. In the middle of this he constructed his chimney, made of bark pealed from the trees. The chimney was set on poles, supported by four forks set so as to incline inward, and thus prove a brace to each other. The bark was then wound around each of these, and extended from one to the other so as to keep them in their place. The blades on the inside of the corn-stalks, forming the interior of the Indian dwelling, were all carefully pealed off, while those on the outside were all turned down. So regularly and exactly had all this been done that the whole dwelling was impervious to water and perfectly warm in the coldest weather. The only avenue through which light or air could be admitted was the door, which was small, and closed with bark. His bed was ten inches from the ground, and was constructed as follows: Three logs of wood three feet long were laid crosswise, at proper distances, parallel to each other. On these logs were placed pieces of pealed bark, lengthwise, and over these were placed his skins and blankets. His pillow consisted of a small bundle of clothes and his tobacco-pouch. The furniture of this rude dwelling was a brass kettle, some bark kettles, a wooden tray, and bark spoon. He had also a gun, tomahawk, and butcher-knife. Several horses, which got their living in the woods, belonged to him.

Thus lived this venerable old man. He passed, during his threescore years and ten, through many vicissitudes of fortune. When but a boy he was in Braddock's defeat, and took a part in the scenes of war and carnage. He was also in the war with the southern Indians, where he was taken captive by the Cherokees, from whom he narrowly escaped with his life, and, after traveling more than three moons, finally succeeded in reaching his home. He was in all the battles fought by the nation with the whites, and was frequently wounded. He related to me several thrilling accounts of hair-breadth escapes. From the testimony of others his daring and bravery were unequaled in the annals of savage warfare.

But what gives to the character of this intrepid chief the greatest interest to the Christian is that he was the very first of his nation to embrace the religion of Christ. He was converted alone in the woods, and the history of that conversion I will leave him to tell in his own simple, native manner: "I felt so great a weight on my heart I thought it would crush me to death. I fell on my knees, and cried out, 'O Father, have pity on your child that you have kept till his legs and arms are stiff with pains, and his whole body is worn out. This load will throw me down, and I shall never rise again. The trees to me will never again blossom; the corn will never again rustle in my ears, and I shall no more behold the harvest. O, take this load from my heart, so that I can walk forth again, and see the beauty of the Great Spirit in the stars that, like watch-fires, hold their places on the borders of the hunting-grounds beyond the great river!' While I was talking to the Great Spirit, my load was gone, and I felt young again. My heart was emptied of its load, and I felt light and happy, and could run like a deer in the chase." This son of the forest was a devoted servant of God. In the winter of 1824 he was called to leave his earthly tabernacle, and from his rude hut, on the banks of the Sandusky river, his freed spirit went up to that bright world where the saints of all ages and nations shall meet and live forever.

THE MYSTERIOUS INDIAN CHIEFTAIN AND HIS BRIDE.

On a certain day there came to the mission station, accompanied by his bride, a chief from some unknown tribe. His appearance and manners were such as to create quite a stir among the Indians of the village. The question in every mouth was, "Have you seen the strangers?" and many were the conjectures about their nativity, and the place of their residence. They were affable and communicative, at least as much so as any civilized Indians, but to all the queries put to them by chiefs and others in regard to these points, they observed an unyielding silence. They were evidently in cultivation and refinement far above the ordinary standard of Indian character in general.

They were invited not only to all the hospitalities of the village, but to the festivities where young chiefs and dark-eyed maidens vied with each other in imitating their dress and manners.

The arrival of a Kossuth and a Jenny Lind among the whites in one of our cities did not produce a greater stir among the inhabitants in proportion to their numbers, than did the appearance of these mysterious strangers in our quiet and peaceful Indian village. To all the entreaties which were made to get them to partake of the festive cup, they offered a respectful but firm declinature. Indeed, in this respect, they presented an anomaly in the Indian character rarely to be found, especially where they are associated with the whites. This, so far from lessening, only increased the interest which they had created in the minds of all. They were looked up to as superior beings, and such, in fact, they were in more respects than one.

The chief was a perfect model of manly beauty, and decidedly the handsomest man I ever saw of any race or nation. His form was erect, tall, and slender, but well-proportioned. So graceful was his walk and so dignified his mien, that the Indians called him "the proud chief." His features, though of the Indian cast, were remarkably regular and expressive. His eyes were not large, but dark and penetrating, and when a smile would play over his countenance he was perfectly fascinating.

He was dressed in Indian costume, and the style of it indicated taste. The Indians usually dress fantastically, and hang about their person a profusion of ornaments. Not to have some of them would be to renounce the Indian style, and be, so to speak, entirely out of the fashion. The dress of the stranger chief would, therefore, from the necessity of the case, not be devoid of ornament. His outer garments were made of the finest broadcloth. His cloak, or mantle, was ornamented with thirty silver crescents, half of which hung on his breast, and the remainder ornamented the back part of his dress. His head-band, which was richly and curiously wrought, was hung all round with beautiful silver pendants or drops. His belt was of the richest wampum, interwoven with beads and porcupine quills. His leggins were decorated with horse-hair dyed red, most beautifully fringed, and filled with silver pendants. His rifle-barrel and stock were inlaid with silver, wrought into many curious devices. The blade, handle, and pipe of his tomahawk were also inlaid with silver. The very trappings of their horses, which were high-spirited, noble animals, were also in keeping with their costume. In fact, all their equipage, saddles, bridles, buffalo robes, and blankets were highly and elaborately ornamented.

Notwithstanding all this exterior ornament, a close observer could discover in the thoughtful countenance of the chief that his mind was not engrossed by his dress and ornaments. He was evidently above them as he was above his red brethren in cultivation and refinement; and could all the facts be known in regard to his mysterious history, it would, doubtless, be seen that he was under the influence of a purer spirit than that which pervaded the nation in general. His total abstinence from the inebriating cup, and his unwillingness to engage in the wild and boisterous sports and festivities of the Indians, together with his studied silence in regard to every thing belonging to his kindred and locality—all these, while they excited a world of curiosity and conjecture, also would lead one to the conclusion that he had become a Christian. This, however, is reserved for that great day when all mysteries shall be revealed, when what is now unknown and deeply buried in the human heart beyond the penetrating ken of mortals, or what the waters of oblivion have washed away from the records of the world and the memory of man, shall be revealed and restored.

The young and beautiful bride of "the proud" chieftain was perhaps, if possible, still more an object of attraction and wonder. She was courted and caressed by the village maidens, and many a young chief culled wild-flowers from the banks of the Sandusky, with which he made garlands to decorate her hair. As her chief was a model of manly beauty, so was she no less a specimen of beauty to the fairer sex.

Her skin was not dark like the Indian; but she was, perhaps, what might be called a brunette. No; this does not describe her color, if, indeed, it can be described. It was clear and transparent, though tinged with brown. Her hair was dark and glossy as the raven, and, when not incased in her silver band, fell in rich and massy ringlets over her beautifully-rounded shoulders. Her eyes were soft and blue, with dark arches and lids, which gave her great beauty of expression. Her teeth were white and regular, and there was a bewitching sweetness about her looks that caused all the maidens to love her. Her person was tall, a little above medium hight, and perfectly symmetrical. She wore a dress richly embroidered and decorated with jewels, which gave her a magnificent appearance. Her morning dress, or *dishabille*, consisted of a robe of red silk, profusely ornamented with silver, and inclosed at the neck with a large silver clasp, while the waist was encircled with a zone of the same material. Few ladies in the most refined circles of society, in our large cities, could be found who dressed more richly, or, perhaps, with better taste, than did the chieftain's bride. In her person she was a model of neatness, and there was an air of freshness and buoyancy about her that ladies pent up within the walls, and dust, and smoke of the city could scarcely hope to acquire.

This mysterious couple did not pitch their tent with the other Indians, but selected a spot a short distance from the village. Their tent was composed of the finest materials, and furnished in a style perfectly in keeping with every thing else that belonged to them. None knew where they came from or to what nation they belonged, though it was generally believed that the tribe to which they belonged had become extinct, and that they were the last of a nation which had been numbered with the forgotten dead. Rumor, also, with her attentive ear and ready tongue, said that the proud chieftain's wife was a daughter of General Butler, that she had been reared in affluence, and enjoyed all the advantages of a polite education and the refinements of a fashionable life; but that, like a caged bird, when opportunity presented itself, she flew to her beloved wildwood, and, uniting herself with her early love, they sought together a home among the peaceful and semi-Christian Wyandotts.

In matters connected with the interests of our mission they both took a lively interest, though they never united with the Church. There may have been reasons for this course, which to a highly-cultivated Indian, who, nevertheless, retained his Indian prejudices, were quite satisfactory. Certain it is that they were governed in all their deportment and intercourse with the villagers by the strictest integrity and kindness.

The same mystery which hung so impenetrable a vail over their history, as deeply and darkly shrouded their fate. Whither they went, none knew—what became of them, none could tell. Many were the Indian surmises regarding them. Some of the more superstitious thought they were spirits sent back from the great spirit-land, and that their dress and equipage, their horses and dogs were such as the Great Spirit would bestow upon the good Indian when he died.

Another conjecture, however, was, perhaps, the more plausible. I have before remarked that they did not associate but little with their Indian neighbors, and many were heard to say of the chief, "He too proud to be with Indian." The conjecture to which I allude was, that a party of them, filled with envy, as were the brethren of Joseph in olden time, conceived the horrid idea of putting them to death. If this supposition be correct, so skillfully did they plan and carry into execution the deed of darkness, that no one knows to this day the place of their graves. The Indians were as careful to conceal the graves of those they hated in life as they were solicitous of their death. There is among them a tradition that messenger-birds can be sent with the blessings of friends to the spirit-land. Their mode was to take unfledged birds and cage them till they were able to fly; and then taking them to the grave, after kissing, caressing, and loading them with blessings, they set them at liberty, that they might fly away with their messages to the spirit-land. Knowing that the young chief and his blue-eyed, beautiful companion were beloved by many of the nation, and that their graves would be dear to them, they, perhaps, resolved that some deep glen or water-filled cavern in the dark river should forever seclude them from human vision.

NOTE.

I HAVE many reminiscences concerning the Indians which have never yet been published, and which can not be inserted in this volume. At some future day, should Providence spare my life, I may be able to give them to the public. Till then I bid my readers an affectionate adieu.

THE END.

www.ingramcontent.com/pod-product-compliance
Lightning Source LLC
LaVergne TN
LVHW021130110826
845150LV00005B/985

* 9 7 8 1 4 2 5 5 5 0 5 0 9 *